# Jeb and Dash

# *Jeb and Dash*

## A Diary of Gay Life, 1918–1945

### EDITED BY INA RUSSELL

Faber and Faber

BOSTON • LONDON

**Library of Congress Cataloging-in-Publication Data**

Alexander, Jeb, d. 1965.
    Jeb and Dash : a diary of gay life, 1918–1945 / edited by Ina Russell.
      p.  cm.
    ISBN 0-571-19817-1
    1. Alexander, Jeb, d. 1965—Diaries.  2. Gay men—Washington (D.C.)—
Biography.  3. Dasham, C. C.  4. Washington (D.C.)—History—20th cen-
tury.  5. Washington (D.C.)—Social life and customs.  I. Russell, Ina  II.
Title.
HQ75.8.A74A3   1994
305.38'9664'092—dc20                          93-10883
                                                 CIP

Jacket design by Catherine Hopkins

Jacket photo from the collection of Ina Russell

Printed in the United States of America

# CONTENTS

*Jeb and Dash*

# INTRODUCTION

"JEB ALEXANDER" is a pseudonym for a homosexual man who was born in Atlanta, Georgia, on October 17, 1899. Because of his father's connection to the grocery business, the family moved when Jeb was a child from Atlanta to Washington, D.C. Thereafter, except during attendance at college and on vacation trips, Jeb lived in his beloved Washington for the rest of his life. His diaries begin in January of 1912, when Jeb was twelve years old, and end about a year before Jeb died in 1965 after having been incapacitated following a cerebral thrombosis.

In this published version of Jeb's diaries, every effort was made to be faithful to Jeb's historical window into homosexual life as it was experienced by a man in Washington, D.C., during the first half of the twentieth century. Nonetheless, a great deal of material needed to be left out. Jeb's fifty volumes of diaries were highly detailed. He documented in most entries where he ate each meal, what he ate, whether he walked or took the street car, the condition-of-bloom of the flowers he saw, his mood swings, aspects of his finances, and a great deal of introspection. Space considerations required that I cut most of those references, as well as many wistful mentions of "bonny boys" of college days; hundreds of entries about unsuccessful cruising; brief infatuations, no matter how intensely felt at the moment; thousands of ruminations about Dash, uncountable dinners with Dash, years of breakfasts with Dash, jealousies over Dash, quarrels with Dash, thoughts about Dash.

The original diaries also contain many well-wrought descriptions of old Washington and its streets and architecture; an ongoing, irritated, thirty-year complaint about life as a Government worker; details of "Cheers"-like convolutions among friends and enemies at the Crescent in the fifties and sixties; Jeb's comments about his books, stamps, mugs, wine labels, theatre programs, and other collections; much commentary on politics; and innumerable descriptions, evocative of the era, of movies, plays, and performers—much of which appears here, more of which had to be left out. Jeb's dreams, which as he pointed out were relevant from a psychological point of view, have been omitted for the most part.

Jeb vacationed in Europe nearly every summer. One of his two trips to Europe with Dash is included in abbreviated form, as well as one other solitary trip. I cut most vacations to New York, Norfolk, and elsewhere, and left out most visits "to the house," that is, to Jeb's family home. I omitted a number of descriptions of family life that I considered too private for publication.

I cut all of 1912 to 1917. Some early entries had charm, but domestic history of the time is well known and nothing new seemed to emerge. The years 1946 through 1964 are also omitted here. During the McCarthy era, an important time in gay history, sometimes I'd think I had "a good one," as when Dash was fired from the State Department. Then it turned out that the cause was Dash's stubbornness and his own fault. (The fifties and early sixties were not entirely unpunctuated. News stories in the *Washington Post* pierced Jeb with fear; he was terrified that the hideous spotlight would freeze on him.)

Any lifetime, even of a shy person like Jeb, includes acquaintance with many people. For the sake of coherence, casual acquaintances were cut altogether and a few of the characters were given the task of bearing events belonging to more than one person. For example, in the published work Jeb has one brother. In real life, he was one of six children (three sons from his father's first marriage, and a daughter and two sons from his father's second marriage to Jeb's stepmother, Mama). If I had kept all these siblings, I think the reader would have found it tiresome to keep track of them. Over the years they wandered in and out of Jeb's narrative, and apparently their personality traits were so implicit to him that he seldom described them in interesting detail. I gave the occasional interesting descriptions concerning the brothers whom Jeb considered to be materialistic to Henry, and I gave Jeb's high-strung, literary brother's interesting appearances to Lansing Tower, who, like that brother, lived far away, sent exotic postcards, and even in his first appearance at college reminded me of that brother. As a family member, I believe these appropriately represent Jeb's relationships to his brothers. A few other characters are treated similarly and, I think, appropriately.

Originally Jeb's sister was included in the manuscript. She was my mother, and as a girl she played a bit of a Phoebe to his Holden Caulfield. The hard fact was that she added nothing to Jeb's window on gay life or to the poignant self-descriptions of a man who succumbed to writer's block, so I regretfully left her out. Their sister-in-law, Eunice, was given some of her lines.

Variations in spellings and grammatical items that have changed since Jeb's day have generally been updated to conform to contemporary conventions. The use of capital letters to begin such words as "Government" is retained because that was Government Printing Office style, and Jeb, an editor in a Government office, conformed to that style after he got home at night.

Certain other changes seemed essential. The sheer size of Jeb's diaries demanded fusing details: a vase of flowers set upon a table one night, the high-jinks of Junior Whorley several evenings later, Dash's wearing of white trousers on the following evening—all woven into a single summer night's vignette of *that* July, *that* stage of Jeb's relationship with Dash, to bring order to Jeb's long story.

Jeb was a circumspect person. Descriptions of Isador's practice of cross-dressing, as one example, were found on scraps of paper but not in the diary itself. When the end of the day arrived, Jeb apparently couldn't make himself document such facts as that Max had called Isador "a fine-looking woman." From a historical point of view, the many notes Jeb didn't throw away comprised an invaluable part of this project and several have been included in the text.

I used pseudonyms for most private individuals because some people from Jeb's diaries may still be living, and certainly most of them have living relatives. It was not my desire to bring anyone out of the closet without his knowledge or permission.

There will be readers who will object to the "political incorrectness" of Jeb's story being handled by a person who is not gay. A series of diary entries shed light on Jeb's own feelings about this. It happened that an attorney was a frequent companion at the Crescent, Jeb's favorite bar in later years. In April of 1962, Jeb wrote after visiting the Crescent that he and the attorney had discussed the writing of his will. Some days later, Jeb wrote: "At last I wrote my letter to Ina . . . about the diaries, asking her advice, and urged her please to answer soon." On May 14 he received my reply. He wrote: "Ina's looked-for letter at last came and it made me quite happy. It was exactly what I had hoped for, the answer I had wanted to receive from her. She was not sure that I had it in mind to leave her the diary, so she begged me to do so. It was an awfully nice letter. I took it away with me when I left here . . . hoping that I might see [the attorney] at the Crescent tonight." The attorney did not appear that evening, but clearly Jeb had been waiting to resolve this one problem remaining in his will, that of the disposition of his beloved diaries, for the next day he went to the law offices and without fur-ther comment signed his will.

Perhaps he left his diaries to me as an act of faith between lovers of literature. I was assisted, additionally, by having a cultural memory of old Washington that comprehends the lyrical love song Jeb wrote to his "beautiful, imperial city." In D.C. I learned at an early age, as Jeb did, to immerse myself in the joyous world of the Library of Congress. Like Jeb, I know what it was like before most people had air-conditioning to be in love on a sweltering, humid Washington summer night. You'd get so sweaty that you floated on one another's bodies like butter in a frying pan. Some of the happiest moments of my life took place on pre-air-conditioned Washington summer nights. Jeb likewise.

Additionally, much of Jeb's Washington lore was psychologically appended a generation later to my own life. For example, my Washington grandmother and my Washington mother told me, more than once, the story of the collapse of the roof of the Knickerbocker Theatre. I was born years after that roof buckled devastatingly under the weight of heavy snow, killing and maiming theatre-goers, but like any *real* Washingtonian, I know deep down in the fearful bones that you *never trust a building with a flat roof.* Jeb's mentions of the Knickerbocker tragedy gave me delicious, culturally-resonant *frissons*, as I suspect they gave him, too.

Jeb's story as presented here ends in the mid-1940s. At one juncture while I worked on this material, I decided for a variety of reasons to skip ahead and read the diaries of the fifties and sixties. I found myself sharing the life of a man who quietly reported "the nothingness of the last eighteen years..." It wasn't exactly a surprise. He was my uncle; I already sort of knew how the story ended. Still, on late afternoons during this part of the project I'd start having weary fantasies in which I would comfort Jeb or cheer him up; help him file his newspaper clippings from the *Post;* dust off his collections of cats, mugs, endless objects. Fantasy. He had been dead for years and lived only in my head.

While I was working on the diaries Jeb was reincarnated for me. Never mind that his life ended unhappily. Every life is precious. Soon after I completed this project I shopped for a gift in a men's store, and while my purchase was being wrapped I wandered around, browsing, and found myself wondering, *Which sweater would I like best if I were a gay man?* The realization that I could never know pierced me with something like homesickness.

If we lived in Kafka country, everyone who aspires to lead a creative life and does not would be required to read the whole of Jeb's diaries, and then would have to appear in a silent courtroom before a faceless judge who would ask: *Do you understand? Do you know what will happen if you do not use your talent?* And none would escape by saying, *But was it not enough that in my life I fell tragically in love?*

I have no connection to the world Jeb described beyond the pages of his diary. I have only the most meager information about what happened to his acquaintances. If Dash is still alive, he's in his early nineties. Max died from complications connected to diabetes. Mrs. Green developed acute alcoholism and wound up in a mental institution. Isador moved away from Washington, but faithfully visited the city from time to time. Junior was younger than the others; thus, of them all, he (somewhat curiously for me) is the one likeliest to read this book. If that occurs—dear Junior, please enjoy the memories.

Thank you, Jeb, Dashie, Randall, Max, Bolling, Hans, Bill, Junior, Isador, Nicky, Erich, Tony, Bennet, Tommy, Malcolm, and all the rest of you, for being a part of my life. You were an enrichment.

Boulder, Colorado
August 1993

*It occurred to me today with something of a shock how horrible it would be for this diary of mine to be pawed over and read unsympathetically after I am dead, by those incapable of understanding, who would be filled with disgust and astonishment and think of me as a poor demented wretch, a neurotic or a madman who was better off dead. And then the thought of the one thing even more dreadful and terrible than that—for my diary never to be read by the one person who would or could understand.*

*For I do want it to be read—there is no use concealing the fact—by somebody who is like me, who would understand. Yet Havelock Ellis is about the only person known to me, that is, known by name, to whom I could confidently entrust my life, my inmost soul at times.*

*—Saturday, 14 April 1923*

*PART ONE*

# ARMISTICE

# 1918

*Monday, 5 August 1918*

The day started in a downpour of rain. Mama told me to take an umbrella but I didn't because they are such nuisances. I had to run to the trolley line. The car soon filled up and at each stop a crowd of waiting persons rushed to the steps and was turned away. I got off at Fifteenth and F Streets and ran through the torrent, arriving at the bank fifteen minutes late. This was the busiest day we have had. Money came piling in so thick that we had to pour it into a wastebasket because the drawers were full.

I feel more content and worry less since settling down to work at the bank. But I cannot harbor the thought of remaining there permanently, of toiling on year after year, and growing gray-haired following the narrow way of the bank. Yet what would I do? If I expect to write it is time that I began.

*Thursday, 22 August 1918*

Mama and Dad have gone off to Atlantic City. I am living absolutely alone and independent, and yet I am not happy. I yearn for friends. At the Library of Congress today I read James Joyce's *A Portrait of the Artist as a Young Man.* I am going to write a novel some day based on my own life from earliest youth in the manner of *A Portrait.* It was an inspiration—the expression of a soul. Had I only with me James Joyce in 1900 and Robert Louis Stevenson in 1868, the two of them also eighteen years old, what kindred fellows should we be!

I left in an exalted spirit and descended the marble steps from the reading-room balcony like one in a dream, touching the beautiful mosaic with my fingertips as I passed. A coarse bellow from the guard, "Don't touch it!" jarred my soul. I hurried out and shrank against the base of a column, feeling wounded and unwanted. Slowly I started off toward the Union Station. A cool breeze stirred the darkness. The Capitol, with its stately dome, its arches and columns and flowing steps, showed silver through the interlacing trees. At the station I lingered, watching the departing wanderers. I am here, never satisfied, and if I were somewhere else I should long for Washington again.

*Friday, 23 August 1918*

In the evening I went into town to attend Keith's. Policemen were handling the people at the front of the theatre so I knew that Mr. Wilson was arriving. At quarter past eight his sumptuous car, with a motorcycle on each side, rolled up to the entrance. The President helped Mrs. Wilson out while the crowding spectators commenced clapping. I felt thrills coursing through me, as I always do whenever I see Woodrow Wilson; I don't know why—probably because I adore him.

After I got home I walked to the reservoir and practiced harmonica selections leaning over the dark waters. I felt hopeless of ever achieving obedience to that motto of Louisa Alcott's, *Rule Yourself.* My faults rose in my mind to torment me. I returned through the shadowy woods to conquer my timidity. My imagination is the cause of foolish fears so I make it weaker by forcing myself to realize that nothing new and terrible lurks in the blackness, there being merely an absence of light. A silver half-moon shone down upon the road and made everything, trees and fence and bushes, appear dim and ghostly.

> **Keith's** *theatres were prime bookings for vaudeville performers on the eastern circuit. The Orpheum topped the western circuit, and the ultimate booking was the Palace Theatre in New York City.*

*Saturday, 24 August 1918*

In the afternoon who should come sauntering into the bank with Dad but Henry, wearing his aviator's uniform. He strode up to my cage and broke into laughter at seeing me sitting there. He looked so strong and handsome that my heart swelled with pride to think he was my brother. Karnes and Mariani pressed up to the wire to look through at Henry. Karnes exclaimed, "Gee! That's a fine-looking fellow." They plied me with questions about when Henry expected to be sent overseas, and how he got to be an aviator. They wanted to know his age and his experience. They didn't know at first that he was my brother.

At night when I was home, Henry strolled up the walk with Eunice Martin. They sat on the porch with Dad and Mama. Eunice is the most beautiful girl I ever saw. She was a dream in filmy blue, dressed like a girl, not like an old society woman of thirty or forty with back bare to the waist.

> **Henry's aviator uniform.** *Henry was (according to family reports) too young to meet U. S. Air Force standards and was going off to fight in World War I for the Canadians.*

*Sunday, 15 September 1918*

At dinner there was trouble once again with Mama, starting with her impolite protest against my taking more than one spoonful of squash. Then unhappily the subject of my going to college was introduced and I answered *no* to her question whether I had written, according to her directions, to Uncle Jeb about being enrolled at Clemson under the plan of free tuition and military training by the Government. Mama began to call names, at which Dad remonstrated, and we had a full-grown quarrel.

Among Mama's wild words to me was a torrent, "You are a pawn on a checker-board! You won't do anything for yourself, you act like eight rather than eighteen, and I think you will never grow up." She turned to Dad and said, "All right, then! Jeb can remain a sissy all his life, since you jump on me whenever I try to do something for him." Dad sat quietly, then began talking to Mama, never raising his voice. Mama tried to ignore him and carry on a silly conversation, clutching at anything to say that came into her head. As soon as I possibly could I excused myself from the table, feeling heartsick. Mama went up to her room, crying. In a little while I heard her briskly go down the steps and start up the Victrola with "The Little White Church in the Valley," a thing which she has not done for months to my knowledge. I don't know whether she was doing it in defiance or in remorse.

I felt like going somewhere and racked my brains, finally hitting upon Alexandria. I took the electric car. The quaint old houses and their gardens were enjoyable, but toward six o'clock I was already homesick for Washington and took the next horse car for home. It shows how much I love this dear old beautiful city if nostalgia attacks me after two hours in another town.

When I got home I slipped quietly into the house, but Dad apprehended me and brought up the idea of trying to get me into a university. I almost dread that it should happen; it will be such an upheaval in my quiet life; such a sudden breaking off of my present existence.

*Monday, 23 September 1918*

At breakfast we tried to discuss the problem of what college to go to. Mama seemed incapable of viewing the situation as it is, continually harping on its cause with such nonsense as, "Less moving pictures and more application."

In the afternoon, Henry came into the bank with his friends Leroy and Ford. All three were clad in golf sweaters, white linen knickers, golf stockings and tan brogues, and traveled bareheaded. Henry told me they had been talking to Eunice Martin about me. He said that Eunice said that I was "the funniest boy" (*i.e.*, most peculiar, queerest) she had ever known. When I got home I headed over to the woods. There I amused myself by making the pods of jewel-flowers pop, and uncovering the sapphire seeds. I sat on a boulder carving a box out of an acorn to contain the "sapphires." Later a cricket was chirping in the kitchen, and Dad said it was a sign of good luck. Yet tonight I feel so wrought up that I can hardly bring myself to mention such trivialities as the incidents of daily life. A turmoil of remorse, self-abasement and despair rage within me.

> **Queer.** *The reader may find pleasure in observing in Jeb's diaries how the word "queer" changes its meaning from "odd" to "homosexual." Jeb's first use of the word occurs above, when he gravely provides the reader with a parenthetical translation intended to clarify the fact that Eunice wasn't talking about his wit when she said he was funny. In a later diary entry in the early twenties, Jeb's acquaintance Hugh speaks of his "rather queer books," but the word with its meaning of "odd" also appears several times. Then in 1928 Jeb takes a homophobic jab at his acquaintances by using the word to denigrate homoerotic gossip and affairs: "All that queer stuff. It makes me sick to think of it." The word by then was firmly in place as a synonym for "homosexual," and retained that meaning through the remainder of the diaries. After Jeb's time "queer" fell into disfavor, but the word seems to have a vitality of its own and in our era has emerged again.*

*Friday, 27 September 1918*

Dad telephoned to the bank and informed me I have been accepted by Washington and Lee University. I must report at Lexington on Monday. When I gave notice, Mr. Eades seemed more interested in my replacement than in my departure. I decided to walk the entire way home. As I ascended Meridian Hill, where the park is in process of construction, the rain that had been threatening all day came dashing into my face. I ran up the last slope and stood upon the summit. Beyond, the city dissolved into mist under the lowering sky. It was all I could do to keep tears from my eyes, thinking of leaving Washington and everything that is dear to me. I suppose I shall find happiness at the university, yet I have no idea how even to begin.

> **Lexington** *is situated in the western, mountainous part of Virginia, approximately 250 miles from Washington (which is the nearest large city). To travel between D.C. and Lexington, Jeb went by train, spending the night en route in Harrisburg. Two well-known colleges are located in Lexington. Jeb attended Washington and Lee University, established as "Augusta Academy" in 1749 and an all-men's liberal arts institution at the time of Jeb's attendance. The other school is Virginia Military Institute, established in 1839. During his college years Jeb made numerous observations about sightings of V.M.I. cadets, who as part of their military training were required to stay extremely physically fit.*

> **Meridian Hill Park**, *with its lovely descending levels of fountains, is located at Sixteenth and W Streets, N.W. A nineteenth-century survey that determined the prime meridian of Washington gave Meridian Hill its name.*

*Monday, 28 October 1918 (Lexington, Virginia)*

There is a chill smack of winter in the air. In the morning the bugle blows at the unearthly hour of six, and twelve minutes later we are expected to form outside beneath the starlit sky. When I got out there the detail was just leaving, so I had to run. I caught up as they started double time, so I was kept running all the way and was the last one in line.

After classes we drilled down on the athletic field. The sun was a blood-red ball showing through the fog. When we broke ranks, Poole wrestled in the ghostly fog with a pale-eyed freshman from Company C. The boy looked like a god, thrillingly beautiful. He got a good hold on Poole and wrestled him to the ground. Poole cried out, laughing, "All right, Dasham—all right!" The boy straddled him, and seemed about to whisper in Poole's ear, but Poole didn't like that and they stood up.

Tonight I asked Poole who the boy was. He looked displeased. "Oh, that one! I don't like his sort." I said, "But you were laughing—" He said, "At first I was." I asked again. Poole stared at me, then told me, "If you have your *reason* you want to know, his name is C. C. Dasham, he hails from Mississippi, he spends holidays with a married brother near Strasburg Junction, he doesn't do well in his studies, and I hope, Alexander, that he isn't your kind." Poole provided this information at top speed, but I am pretty sure I remember everything.

*Wednesday, 13 November 1918 (Lexington, Virginia)*

At the library I saw Poole and McCabe whispering. Poole came over and laid down five jingling pennies in front of me, saying, "This is the jit I owe you, Alexander," and walked away. McCabe stood snickering before he joined Poole. I feel it was done deliberately as a sort of insult. The incident aroused in me a bitter spirit, changing into dejection. It seems that my acquaintances—I can hardly call them friends, for I have no friends and I suppose that I shall never have any—are dropping away, or they regard me with amused tolerance. I have come to the conclusion that I shall never have normal companionship with other fellows.

> **Jit.** Short for "jitney," a turn-of-the-century slang word for a five-cent coin. A "jitney bus," for example, was a bus that carried a passenger for a nickel.

*Wednesday, 18 December 1918*

Again to roam Washington's dear familiar streets! I wandered about downtown, then met Dad at the new Peking Tea Garden. I had fried rabbit, a good meal, but I dreaded the moment when Dad would begin one of our little one-sided conversations about myself. And soon he said, "Do you mean to use your

education? What practical good will a literary or general cultural course do you?"
I found it impossible to talk frankly about my literary ambitions. He said, "I
expect you to 'mix' with other fellows, as part of the benefit of college." He will
be disappointed in that. I was feeling blue and thinking, "I shall have no path of
roses at W&L," when the music, a mechanical piano affair, struck up the "Old
Gray Mare." It took me right back to W&L and I felt homesick for the life there.

> We were only white birds, my beloved,
> White birds, on the foam of the sea.

If only, only, *only* we were.

### Tuesday, 24 December 1918

To town in the dripping grayness and cold. I wandered about looking at the
bustle of Christmas Eve. Went to Lowes' new Palace Theatre and saw D. W.
Griffith's *The Greatest Thing in Life*. One scene was so poignant that I cried—the
scene where the dying negro soldier thinks he takes a last leave of his mammy.
The photoplay was on a higher intellectual plane than the usual feature and I
enjoyed the subtleness of the love story it contained. The theatre is the most
beautiful I have seen, being more artistically decorated than Keith's.

Afterward I walked up to the public library. Finding it closed, I waited in the
shelter of the entrance. It was pouring down rain. I had no idea what I might do.
A young man with a mustache and a green hat, who looked different and intelligent, approached with a book. He turned away when he saw the closed door. I
imagined that he was a poet without money and I took a notion to follow him.
Once or twice I nearly lost him, and several times I passed him looking into windows. Then he turned up a side street. As I went by he was standing in the
entrance of a house. Perhaps he was waiting to see if I had been following.

### Tuesday, 31 December 1918

At night I went out to celebrate New Year's Eve, stopping first at Child's for
a midnight supper. It was the first time I had ever been to Child's. A drunken
lout in a fur coat made idiotic noises with his mouth and acted like a clown.
Leroy and Ford came in and started talking to me. They wanted to know about
Henry. They also spoke to the fool who made the clownish noises. When they
left they invited me to walk out with them. We stood stupidly by a cigar store
window, they talking about cigarettes while 1918, that glorious year, sped rapidly away and 1919 commenced in a drizzle of rain.

I was in a bad humor, from Leroy and Ford and the rain and most of all,
myself. Whistles screeched and people blew horns and beat pans and honked

automobiles. A girl knocked Leroy's cap off with her horn and he started after her and tried to kiss her in front of the old Commercial Bank location. Ford left "to dance the evening away," he said, and Leroy followed the girl and I followed after Leroy.

# 1919

*Thursday, 2 January 1919*

I left with only Mama to part from. I was almost sick with nervous anticipation. She told me, "Try to make friends at school. Begin over. Don't get the reputation of being quiet." Well meant, but when the stars sing to the moon, then shall I be talkative and likable.

My two suitcases, heavy and clumsy, were a hindrance. On Fourteenth Street hill, from the streetcar window, I saw Henry's friends Leroy and Ford. They turned into a tobacco store. Then to the station, and into the train and a pair of seats, red-plush covered. The train pulled out of the station and I told Washington good-bye. We flew on through Virginia. I looked through the misty windowpanes at the sodden country in winter. Night closed in. Beyond the pale glow from the train lights, a void of rain and darkness. At Strasburg Junction, C. C. Dasham got on.

He looked about the car, then sat with me. He has the palest green eyes I ever saw. He admired my tie and in his Mississippi drawl asked about my copy of *Dubliners*. He said, "It looks like a fine book." In a while he asked me what my goals were; my goals for life. After some hesitation I told him, "Authorship." He remarked, "I have no such specific dream for myself. I'm still in the 'having-fun' stage of my youth." The rain changed to snow and the flying flakes brushed against the window with a faint scratching sound. We reached Harrisburg and walked out into the storm. Dasham carried one of my valises for me, as he had only a satchel.

We climbed into the cavern of a hack and were driven to the Hotel Kavanaugh. The snow sailed horizontally into our faces. Dasham helped me bring my suitcases into the lobby. His cheeks were mottled red from the cold. We came upon two other fellows from school, and arranged to share two rooms, four beds, leaving instructions to call us at six in the morning. Dasham was in the other room.

*Friday, 3 January 1919 (Lexington, Virginia)*

Dasham sat across the aisle, reading. I looked out the window at brown fields, bare trees and frozen, sinister streams. Lexington looked strange and deserted. At the station, Harry Agneau, shivering, smiling, was waiting for Dasham. Agneau's father is a judge, and the family lives outside Lexington. He is refined, suggesting the far South, dark about the eyes with a sort of pleasant squint or narrowness of the eyes, finely freckled, dark hair pomaded in comely fashion. The two of them helped me with my suitcases till they turned toward Lee's. I struggled off across the campus toward East Dorm.

*Sunday, 5 January 1919 (Lexington, Virginia)*

Penetrating cold. I lay deep under the covers, miserably and ecstatically returning in imagination to the racketing train, *Dasham-Dasham-Dasham-Dasham.* I feel my life has changed forever.

Lexington on Sunday is the deadest town imaginable. I read some of Dante's *Inferno* and the book suddenly seemed cruel. The sexual intercourse (I hesitate to write the words, but there is no reason why I should feel prudish) seems to occur too often. Finally I took a walk. On Main Street I met Bennet, with a polite greeting and a pressure of his soft, plump hand.

*Friday, 17 January 1919 (Lexington, Virginia)*

Lansing Tower strolled in and sat on the arm of a chair beside me. He is only a freshman, but looks down on the world, or seems to. He has small eyes, close-set on either side of a patrician hooked nose, the eyes appraising, amused and secretive. "Alexander, do you want to join the Literary Society?" "No-o. What do they do?" "They have a weekly program, have debates." "I'm not much on debating." Tower said, "You can't learn any sooner," and left me.

After supper I saw that he, Poole, Garrison, Meek, were all going to the Literary Society meeting. I began to think that I might join after all, for it would allow me to get into the intellectual class of the students. But Tower didn't invite me again, and like a fool I didn't go. I walked off to the post office, feeling furious with myself. At the post office there was another letter from Dad sadly urging me to write oftener. A far cold moon was in the sky and the bare branches moved across it. Bennet approached me. "Come along," he said. "I'm off to the V.M.I.-St. Johns' game." But I refused.

Back in the dorm I was on the front porch for a while with others. The fellow they call "Kentucky" was sitting on the railing, when there came the sound of a metal object falling and rattling on the sidewalk under him. He looked over the railing and exclaimed, "Oh, my golly! I've dropped a box of cundrums." There they lay, the box open with people walking right by it. Amid shouts of laughter of those on the porch, he rushed down and recovered his embarrassing property.

**Cundrums.** *According to the* New World Dictionary of the American Language *(second ed., 1979), a condom used to be called a "cundum." It isn't clear in the diary whether "cundrums" was the word used by Kentucky , or whether Jeb, who had no personal experience with condoms, misheard the word.*

### Monday, 20 January 1919 (Lexington, Virginia)

For assembly Dr. Smith and the faculty wore black robes and square-topped hats, and looked peculiar. I indulged in a harmless vanity (I am trying to prevent my diary from being "a melancholy school of posturing and dreary self-deception," as Stevenson found his to be, by being frank with myself) and enjoyed a sense of being well-dressed. I wore my new suit, my silk collar, iridescent rose and gold tie, white shirt with shiny silk markings, spar-rock cuff links, polished tan shoes. The idea of describing my clothes like a girl!

I waited outside the assembly until Dasham approached with Agneau. Stepping forward, I said to Dasham, "Happy birthday." He seemed surprised and amused. "Well, Alexander, did I tell you my birth date on the train?" I said yes. He said, "My birth date is the thirtieth of January, not the twentieth. Still, that was kind of you, Alexander." As they went into assembly Agneau began to tease, and Dasham laughed, and they shoved one another good-naturedly through the door. I walked home in darkest mortification. Later I gave myself a talking-to. I told myself that I must not allow obsessions to dominate my life; I must live life to the fullest and let no person or thing stand in the way. I am going to be a great author.

### Saturday, 1 February 1919 (Lexington, Virginia)

Everybody turned out for the football game with Roanoke College. In the crowd I saw Dasham and Agneau sitting with Agneau's parents, the father dressed in black, the mother only slightly less somber. The students made a tremendous noise, cheering, yelling, whistling without cessation. The game went as fast as lightning, and we won, 39–18. When I was walking from the field Bennet approached me. He said, "That was a game 'worth a dollar,' was it not?" I replied, "It was a fine game, and gave me more school spirit than I have had yet." He smiled. "You should drop by my room for a 'bull session,' Alexander."

I am both attracted to Bennet and repelled by him. O, it is so hard to pour out my heart in this book. How I wish I could be a child again, sitting in the swing beside the cedar tree on a glorious June morning, when the pinks were in bloom and the lilacs filled the air with sweetness.

*Sunday, 16 March 1919 (Lexington, Virginia)*

Lansing Tower, sauntering along with his thin hair floating in the air, led us up a rocky hill. The cave we planned to explore was a dark hole between the rocks. We gathered about the opening so that Lansing could take pictures. I stood for the photograph beside Dasham, with Agneau on his other side.

Lansing led with a lantern. Agneau elected himself to be the one to lay down the string we would use to find our way back out. I found myself in line next to Dasham and Agneau. The way was pretty near perpendicular and the ground slippery with mud. Dasham was startled by a bat clinging to the clammy rocks about an inch above his head. I heard it hissing, and striking at it with a stick, knocked the bat down. Dasham said, "Are you all right?" I said, "I'm afraid I might step on it." He reached out his hand, and I clasped it for an instant, then plunged past the bat that shot up behind me.

Agneau's drawling voice echoed, "This isn't *my* idea of what a cave would be." Dasham replied, "Nor mine. My ideas about caves came from *Tom Sawyer.*" The two of them had foolishly thought—as I had—that the floor would be flat and the passages like hallways in houses. But the place was a honeycomb of fantastic rock formations and holes which, when investigated, were apparently bottomless. Voices echoed strangely. The ground was greasy and treacherous. At places were names carved with the aid of candles. I found one faint inscription of a W&L student, "D. H. Smith, September 12, 1819," made a hundred years ago.

A light appeared in the darkness, followed by two V.M.I. cadets. The pair had unwisely come in with no string laid to lead them back. If they had not met us, they would probably have got lost. Dasham said, "They say that several years ago, a man who brought in only one candle was lost in here, and nevermore seen." I said, "Perhaps he fell into one of those horrible pits." Dasham turned toward me. In the candlelight his eyes looked like reflecting silver. He said, "Well, Alexander, perhaps the man did fall into a pit. But that's supposing the outlandish story to be true. Do you realize that until this moment, you haven't spoken a word since you knocked down the bat? I had almost forgotten you were *here*, Alexander."

We finally clambered back, clinging to the surface until we glimpsed daylight. Hastening up the steep incline, Dasham slid, causing Agneau to lose his footing, and they disappeared frighteningly backward in the darkness. Lansing Tower called out. Up they climbed, laughing. Then out into the light. All of us were smeared with red mud. More pictures were taken and we raced down the

hill to home and supper. Dasham and Agneau trailed the rest, laughing and lark-
ing about.

### Sunday, 23 March 1919 (Lexington, Virginia)

As I returned from the cemetery with daffodils I had picked there, I passed
Dasham and Agneau. "Hey, Alexander," said Dasham, "those are lovely." I gave
some daffodils to him. On my desk as I write, the rest are radiant with beauty. O,
I know I am shy and weak, but I believe that with Dasham I would be godlike,
and he would be godlike with me. I declare, he is the most beautiful thing I ever
saw—so wholesome and healthy, so full of youth. I imagine us on the high seas;
I imagine us shipwrecked and cast adrift to lost islands. Every day I live a joyous
life with him, if only in my imagination.

### Sunday, 1 June 1919

D.C. sizzles under a blazing hot spell. I walked down to the National Art
Gallery, and it was like walking over an oven. Still, I was glad I went. I like Corot
better than any other artist. I should love to paint beautiful landscapes. It ought
to be a happy life.

At dinner tonight a general argument, in which I took my part, about the
South, Mama saying she was sick of talk about the Southern Gentleman and so
on—but tonight, especially, I hate to write about Mama; she is contemptible and
small. I pity her. Today is the anniversary of the death of my real mother. Who
knows how much richer my life might have been had Mother lived. I was so
young when she died. Henry was a sturdy lad of eight, but I was a frightened
four-year old. The lilacs and the pinks were in full bloom. The nurse came on to
the porch and stood looking about in her cat-and-mouse way. When she saw
Henry and me, she approached us where we sat in the green swing under the
cedar tree, and told us that Mother had "gone away to heaven." It hurt so much,
to think my mother would leave me. And then, there came a day when Henry
asked the little nurse, "Why are you going to live with us?" She told him, "He
needs someone to take care of his boys." After that she and Dad were married,
and she was Mama. What a starved, repressed childhood I had.

### Wednesday, 2 July 1919

I gazed into the sunset, dreaming of departing for the Golden Gate. I long to
set out across the thousands of miles of forest and farm and prairie and river and
mountains to the golden West. Tomorrow I start work again in that horrible
bank, tedious hours in heated rooms among flirting girls and senseless boys. No

one can imagine how much I wish I had a glorious companion and freedom, to wander the wide world.

Around midnight the doorbell rang. Putting on my bathrobe, I went down and to my amazement found Henry. He landed three days ago at Montreal. "You look good, Jeb," he said, patting me amiably on the back. "First thing I did after I put on my cits was take the train to New York . . . went to see Edith Conte. She's an actress. I've been corresponding with her for months. She accompanied me on the boat down to Baltimore . . . " He is going to surprise the family in the morning. He has a narrow moustache, his hair is parted in the middle, his voice deeper—such are Henry's physical changes. And how glad I am to get him back, safe and sound.

**Cits:** *Civilian clothes, "civvies." Though the war was over on Armistice Day, November 11, 1918, Jeb does not explain why it took Henry six months to don "cits" and get home.*

### Sunday, 20 July 1919

This afternoon we went for a ride in the Reo: Dad, Mama, Henry, Eunice Martin, and I. According to the desire of Eunice and me, we drove into Virginia. I took pleasure in the old houses in shady groves, the huge trees by the roadside, and the whitewashed cottages. Eunice taught me the words of that beautiful song, "Till We Meet Again":

> Smile the while you kiss me sad adieu . . .
>     When the clouds roll by
>       I'll come to you.
> Then the skies will seem more blue . . .
>     Down in Lovers' Lane, my dearie
> Wedding Bells shall ring so merrily . . .
> Every tear will be a memory
>     So watch and pray each night for me
>       Till we meet again . . .

We sang the words over and over, until Mama and Henry insisted we find a different song.

### Friday, 25 July 1919

A sweltering, roasting Washington day. White House, gleaming in the sunlight, beautiful through green foliage . . . Tonight, Keith's, a splendid bill, including Vinie Daly singing "Till We Meet Again," with its haunting lyrics creating a cloud of dreams . . . Outside afterward, to the long street car ride home . . . I dreamed of a cabin on a mountain spur above pines and rocks and white flecked rapids, together with my love in the wild beauty of Night . . . fragrant spruce bed . . . murmur of evergreens . . . stars . . . deep blue sky . . .

*Tuesday, 12 August 1919*

We were allowed time off to see the parade of the "Devil Dogs," the marines who fought at Château Thierry. Last night on the porch Eunice Martin heard me speaking of the parade to Henry, and arranged to meet me today in Lafayette Square. Through the teeming streets she strode, light of foot, wearing a blue linen dress, cleverly locating me in the crowds. She complimented me, saying, "You found us a place so close to the reviewing stand, Jeb. This will be the best look at the President I have ever had." I didn't tell her it was almost luck. In fact I had been thinking that it was Eunice who had managed to bring us so close to Mr. Wilson's reviewing stand. And perhaps it was Eunice.

The marines were in battle array, with steel helmets and fixed bayonets, a formidable body of men. General Neville rode at the head of the column. The last company passed and the President and Mrs. Wilson crossed the Avenue. Amid the surging mob of people pouring into the street, Eunice clung to my arm. The President and Mrs. Wilson shook hands with the wounded soldiers, sailors and marines. We were close enough so that we could hear their cheery greeting to each maimed or crippled man. Eunice told me that she "could not have found the parade half so much an interesting experience" had she not been with me. When I started back to work she called, "Tell your big brother to look his most handsome this evening—" Of course I had no expectation of seeing Henry before he went out tonight.

Later at home, after midnight, I recognized the voices of Henry and Eunice, the latter whispering so loudly that I was afraid she would be heard by Dad and Mama. When they got up to the third story Eunice staggered into my room, fell against the wall and full-length on the floor. She was drunk, drunk as a fool. I was alternately shaken with nervous mirth, and filled with fright and disgust. She got the drink in Baltimore with Henry. She fell down the stairs in going to the bathroom. My opinion of Eunice, formerly so idealistic, is considerably lowered. Henry finally got her into his bedroom and shut the door.

**Château Thierry:** *During World War I, American marines helped block the German advance on Paris by preventing German troops from crossing the Marne River at Château Thierry. According to tradition, the Germans gave the name* teufelhunde, *or "devil dogs," to the marines who fought there. Cynical writer H. L. Mencken claimed the term was a propaganda phrase conceived by a U. S. war correspondent, but the U. S. Office of Naval Intelligence asserted that captured German prisoners did use the term.*

**Wendell Cushing Neville** *(1870–1930). General Neville was at that time the Commander of the U.S. Marine Corps.*

### Wednesday, 13 August 1919

As I was walking out Fourteenth Street, Henry and Eunice stepped out of Sari's, both of them savoring ice cream cones. With a few flirting but unequivocal words Eunice made it appear that I was the one who should be chided for having seen her drunk and going into Henry's room last night, rather than herself. Henry said, "Live and let live." I said, "You are right, and 'Live and let live' is my own motto." "Good," said Eunice, smiling. They proceeded toward Sullivan's to pick up Dad's car. It is impossible not to like her. She is less an ideal, though. I continued homeward in the sizzling heat. It suddenly came over me how silly it was to keep on my coat instead of taking it off and being comfortable. I immediately handed off my coat and walked the rest of the way home with coat and cap across my arm, feeling cooler and more independent of ephemeral worldly customs.

### Tuesday, 19 August 1919

Around midnight Henry came home, bringing Leroy with him. He directed Leroy to Mama's room, instead of the bathroom. We heard Mama's sharp voice. Leroy came hastily out saying, "Aw, this is a bedroom." A fine way to treat his guest but Henry and I laughed a great deal over it.

### Monday, 1 September 1919

Out to Glen Echo with Henry and Eunice, at their insistence. Maryland fare increased, now six cents. Eunice in a blithe frame of mind. Futile attempts by Henry and me to win a box of candy on the Wheel of Chance. I took a stroll down to the canal in the gathering darkness and wandered along beside the rowboats and canoes. When I returned I watched Henry and Eunice dancing. The music included that favorite of mine, "Till We Meet Again" . . . "When the clouds roll by . . . I'll come to you . . . "

We took a number of rides on "Derby"—exhilarating, through the crisp night air with the half-moon shining above the old stone tower. Another young fellow alone, seated in front of me, handsome, dreaming, repeated the ride over and over also.

Coming back, the open streetcar was filled and ready to leave, when a mannish-looking athletic woman jumped on. Shouting to her companion, a shrinking black hired girl, "There's only five in here, there's plenty of room," she sat down on top of me, and I was forced to make room for her. Henry roared with laughter. The woman loudly urged the hired girl to sit on her knee, pulling her by the arm. The girl refused and the woman insisted and pleaded, until people all over the car were laughing and loafers outside were calling out facetious remarks. Eunice pressed her face against Henry's shoulder, tears of laughter running down her cheeks. The strong-minded female was not disturbed. The girl presently sat on her knee. The woman swung off the car at Dupont Circle before it even stopped, and the unhappy hired girl hurried after her.

**Glen Echo.** *An amusement park not far from the District line in Maryland.*

*Friday, 5 September 1919*

At breakfast Henry told me he planned to go to New York. The idea made me wildly eager to take a trip to the great metropolis. I asked him what he expected to spend. "Fifty or sixty dollars, but the trip could be done for forty. Are you going to New York?"

Why ask. Forty dollars is far too much for me to spend out of my summer savings. Henry remarked that it was almost time for me to go back to school, or as he phrased it, "return to winter rest camp." He asked what I planned to do after college, a mystery to me. He said, "Dad said that if you don't have good marks by Christmas, he is going to take you out of school." It is dreadful to think of leaving W&L in such a manner. But I could only sit there thinking that it seems hopeless for me to get good marks.

Tonight Henry began indulging in his old custom of mean nagging. He quarreled at me for being up so late, for keeping a diary, and for reading, calling me *silly fool, poor little sissy,* all sorts of damned stuff to make me mad.

**Sissy.** *The conventional child-rearing wisdom of the day was that a boy who was a "sissy" might yet grow up to be "manly," provided that his sissified behavior was corrected. In the entry for September 15, 1918, when Mama calls Jeb a sissy, his perception is that she is a difficult woman whose criticism makes his life miserable, but from Mama's point of view, she is embarked on a frustrating attempt to help Jeb overcome a defect—and in fact, his shyness and failure of nerve did diminish his ability to lead a happy and productive adult life. Whether either Henry or Mama made a connection between homosexuality and "sissiness" is hard to say. Mama was intelligent and widely-read, but she grew up in the Victorian era and throughout her life took a stance of denial in matters involving sexuality. Henry's perceptions are discussed by Jeb in the entry dated February 6, 1924.*

*Wednesday, 10 September 1919*

I could hear Mama and Dad down on the porch—and listened, eaves-dropped if you want to call it that. Oh, they discussed me in and out. Dad said *he* didn't know what to do. "I can't get anything out of him. He won't speak, he won't answer a question."

Mama said, "Every time he has an opportunity to make something of his life, he runs off to the moving pictures." Henry got home and they kept on talking about me. It made me wretched. "What about his schooling? He doesn't apply himself, so what's the good of it?" "What does he want out of life?" I felt utterly alone—perched in the chilly air on a great peak while the brightness of the world passed by far below—miles and miles away. Oh, why can't they stop talking about me, and let me live my life as I will?

*Saturday, 13 September 1919*

I rambled about among the Saturday afternoon crowd. At Parker Bridget's corner, Ninth and the Avenue, I joined a number of people looking in the show window at a realistic wax model, which was said to be a live man posing there made up as a dummy. I stood at the window a long time, alternately believing the model was alive and that it was not, finally concluding the latter.

While I was standing in the crowd, there came the beginnings of an experi-ence which I hesitate to describe, the cause of which was a stoutish young man about thirty. I was aware that he was looking at me. Almost against my will, I glanced round. He murmured, "With your dark eyes, you look like a lost child . . ." He moved close behind me, continuing to talk, and I experienced that extraordinary phenomenon, so stupefying on the public street that it was far from a pleasure and indeed, was agonizing.

When I got home and attempted to hurry upstairs, Dad called me into the sitting room. He was lying on the couch. "Come in here, Jeb. I want to have a talk with you about yourself." His usual remarks. He believed a general academ-ic course would fit me only to be a generally educated man and a specialized course would prepare me for my life work. When he asked if I had decided on my life work, I was silent. "Well, *try* to decide." I told him I *was* trying, then hurried up to my room.

*Monday, 22 September 1919 (Lexington, Virginia)*

For the first day of classes Harry Agneau was wearing a bow tie—very "colle-giate"—and had his hair parted in the middle, just as I wear mine. When he mentioned that Dasham wasn't arriving until tomorrow, his amused condescen-sion was infuriating. To hell with Harry Agneau! I don't want people thinking

I'm a fool. Hereafter when I see Dasham and Agneau I'll greet them as if they meant nothing to me whatever.

*Friday, 26 September 1919 (Lexington, Virginia)*

Lansing Tower told me that he is writing a novel; has been for almost a year. We had a long talk on the topic. Later at night I saw him at the post office and suggested going up to the cemetery. On the way up we discussed long hair and independence of ordinary conventions. Lansing spoke affectionately of "cranks," and I told him, "I should like to be considered a 'crank,' by being independent." He said, "You are pretty sure to be thought a 'crank' by at least a few."

The cemetery was quiet at that hour, though the stones gleamed uncannily. Except for one start of nervousness on coming round a tomb I felt at ease. But I didn't mind confessing to Lansing that I shouldn't like to go there alone, not that I am afraid of ghosts, but just from nervousness at being in such a place at that time.

*Friday, 17 October 1919 (Lexington, Virginia)*

Wore my new suit and when I came down to breakfast everyone gave a W&L yell-yell for "Puny Alexander's suit." They didn't know today was my twentieth birthday. Later we had a rally at Wilson Field, with yells and singing. Agneau and Dasham sat in the bleachers. Dusham waved to me, his eyes pale green and beautiful, his face full of life. He, a young god on his throne—and I in dumb adoration and abasement, dreaming dreams of ourselves . . . and as much as I long for him, I am fearful of the slightest response, fearful that it will pull him from his pedestal, afraid that a touch of earth will destroy the celestial vision. Dear boy, would that I knew what he thinks of me, how much of that beautiful smile of his is contempt, or whether it is serene wonderment and nothing more.

*Saturday, 8 November 1919 (Lexington, Virginia)*

Football! We beat Georgia Tech, unbeaten by a Southern team for six years! The score was W&L—3, Georgia Tech—0. It took W&L to blow up the "Golden Tornado," to take the sting out of the Yellow Jackets! The Lyric had a wire to Atlanta, so it was almost like seeing the game, with each play described and a diagram on a blackboard showing the location of the ball. By the time I got up there, a surging mob of students was struggling to get in. Dasham and Agneau beckoned over the crowd, and behind them I squeezed through the door. We were in a fever pitch of excitement. The W&L orchestra played jazz, stopping short when every few minutes a telegram came. Jimmie Mattox was taken out injured in the first quarter, Silverstein with a wrenched shoulder at the half, and

Paget with a broken arm. In spite of it all we triumphed. *O, what joy* when Mattox kicked a field goal!

Afterward, as we spilled outdoors among the excited crowd, Dasham and Agneau told me that they were going into town. They didn't invite me. Oh, well! I walked back alone, joyously reliving every play our team had made. Beautiful night, the air bracing, stars glittering frostily in the sky. Up to my room and found Lansing Tower had made a fire, was sitting in my chair, reading my *New Republic*, with his feet propped on my table and *attired in my bathrobe*, all of which I could forgive except the last. He said there was too much noise outside his own room. The arrogant idiot still refuses to join in the excitement about football.

> **New Republic.** *Jeb was an ardent reader of magazines that offered a strong blend of social criticism and literature, including the* Freeman *(1920–1924),* The Nation, *and the* New Republic.

# 1920

*Thursday, 18 March 1920 (Lexington, Virginia)*

Instead of studying, tonight like a fool I went to the show, just as I have gone every night this week. The show was Mildred Harris in another splendidly true to life picture of Lois Weber's, *Home*. Like *Borrowed Clothes*, the photoplay follows the Griffith school of realism that I used to glory in at the Strand and Garden. Bennet sat beside me. Several rows ahead I saw Dasham and Agneau. Bennet and I walked home together, he with his arm in mine. Above us in the night sky there came a thunder storm. I was glad, because thunder is a sure sign of spring. Bennet talked of himself and of how much he likes me, and said I won't talk, but he never took any interest when I did try to say something. Repeatedly he has invited me to his room; again tonight I refused.

> **Lois Weber** *(1883–1939) started out as an actress; by 1920 she had become, at Universal Studios, Hollywood's first important woman producer.* Borrowed Clothes *was produced by Weber in 1918 and, like* Home, *starred Mildred Harris.*

*Monday, 20 April 1920 (Lexington, Virginia)*

As I went down the steps I saw Dasham in front of the "bulletin board." It made me feel refreshed just to see his beautiful face. He was tanned, as he had been playing tennis. He turned about, and with a sweet, friendly smile, greeted me. It was the first warmth he has shown me in such a long time that I thrilled all over. We might have spoken more but just then Lansing passed by and asked if I were going to the library. I walked off with him before I could think of a reason not to, and immediately was filled with the bitterest grief. I glanced back and Dasham was still standing there—my beloved lad! I hardly listened to Lansing's chatter but was plunged into melancholy imagining what I might have done or said.

Walked later along the river bank. The bloodroots were getting into their prime. The hepaticas were just past it. I picked a bunch of each. I longed for my real mother, to be kneeling at her lap saying my prayers, a trusting child. Thought of a wife, which I have not done in a long time. She was different from the woman I usually imagine. Instead of a passionate brunette creature of powerful intellect and artistic tendencies, she was a homebody, a tender, motherly woman who would coddle me and take care of me. Longed for comfort and love.

*Monday, 19 July 1920*

At the Municipal Beach the sun shone across the water into my eyes. I waded into the cool ticklish water and plunged forward, delighting to strongly bear my body through the water. Then my enthusiasm vanished. Nobody paid attention to me; all were shouting and frolicking. I sat on the sea-wall, picking up pebbles and sifting and catching them. Later I checked my bathing suit and wandered about. At that time of evening the streets are crowded, then all of a sudden people disappear and there are only aimless strollers. In all the great city I have not one friend. Those who might be my friends, who are capable of giving me companionship, are hidden away from me, buried in the crowds.

**Municipal Beach.** *People used to swim in the Potomac River, in this case at the beach which is now the reconstructed Tidal Basin.*

*Friday, 23 July 1920*

Henry has been indulging in his old pastime of scolding me for writing in my diary. I cannot imagine why he objects so idiotically to it. Tonight he tried to persuade me to go with him to the Krazy Kat, a "Bohemian" joint in an old stable up near Thomas Circle. He told me about the conversation in there, of artists, musicians, atheists, professors. I wanted to see something of the place, but was afraid I'd make a fool of myself by my backwardness. In a crowd Henry's ready tongue would give him mastery of me.

I left for town instead. Drops of rain began falling from a gloomy sky.

Listened to the Salvation Army band, to "Brother Hammond," "the Ensign," "the Cadet," and "Mother," who was known in the Bowery Corps as "Sunshine." They had an organ and a trombone to aid in the work of washing sins away. The Ensign, a stout red-haired girl, sang unaffectedly, as though she were really speaking to us.

> A robe of white, a cross of gold,
> A harp, a home, a mansion fair,
> A victor's palm, and joy untold,
> Are mine when I get there . . .

I don't know why I should take such pleasure in these exhibitions. The crude music attracts me, I guess, making more significant the surroundings I am looking on, as music does for me. I wandered on. I thought of writing and determined to get a theme this very night. If I can't make myself write now, how can I *ever* expect to do so? Roamed past dismal houses, steep steps and no yards, across from the Pension Building. A girl on a dim step with dreamy eyes stared into the darkness. From another house, the wistful tones of a piano in a gloomy parlor.

*Saturday, 21 August 1920*

The Salvation Army service was the farewell service of the Ensign and the Cadet. They will leave for Pennsylvania on Tuesday. I am sorry to see them go. It was their beautiful singing, and a personal interest in the Cadet, that has been the chief attraction for me. They sang tonight and each one gave a moving talk. Yes, the Cadet's talk moved me, because I felt sadness at the earnestness with which he spoke.

Later on I went into Lafayette Square and near the Von Steuben statue watched two fellows furtively engaged in mutual masturbation under cover of the dimness. They were frequently interrupted by the passersby. When I left, I walked close by to see their faces. Both were handsome, clean-looking chaps, refined and cultured.

Wandered down to the Union Station. The dreamy girl I used to watch in Child's is now in the Union Station soda fountain. Hair bobbed. Gazes melancholily over the great waiting rooms. Russian-looking. With a resolution to get a story written, I thought of an idea about the girl, and worked over it as I wandered about on *the* three streets whereon life concentrates, Pennsylvania Avenue, Ninth Street and F Street.

**Lafayette Square** *was the place in Washington to cruise for homosexual encounters. The park is directly across from the White House.*

*Wednesday, 25 August 1920*

I have at last found a friend, a lovable, handsome fellow, a realization of the friend I have dreamed of during all those lonely nights while I walked alone through the streets. Above all, our friendship is mutual. It has burst into full blossom like a glowing, beautiful flower. It happened like this: I went to Lafayette Square and found a seat in the deep shade of the big beech. It is the best bench in the park. A youth sat down beside me, a youth in a green suit with a blue dotted tie. He has beautiful eyes and sensuous lips. He wants to become a diplomat, but is devoted to music. Earlier tonight he had been singing at the Episcopalian Church, and is taking vocal lessons. His name is Randall Hare.

We strolled down to the Ellipse, where we sat affectionately together on a dim bench. Later we came to rest in the moon-misted lawns near the Monument. With an excess of nervous caution I gazed about, watching for some prowling figure. "We are safe," Randall whispered. And he was right. Nothing disturbed us and we lay in each other's arms, my love and I, while the moon beamed from a spacious sky and the cool night breezes rustled our hair. The black trees stood like sentinels against the silvery grass. Afterward, we lay close together and gazed at the stars above, becoming fast friends, exchanging confidences. Ah, happiness! As Wilde said, "Youth! Youth! There is absolutely nothing in the world but youth!"

> **Oscar Wilde** *(1854-1900). Wilde's relationship with "Bosie" (Lord Alfred Douglas, the son of the marquess of Queensberry) resulted in his being found "guilty of homosexual practices," for which he spent two years in prison. Wilde's writing, such as the plays* The Importance of Being Earnest *and* Lady Windermere's Fan, *assure him a permanent place in English letters, but Jeb was more interested in Wilde as a victim of Victorian hypocrisy.*

*Sunday, 5 September 1920*

Randall and his mother live with Randall's uncle in one of the oldest houses in Georgetown, a rambling stone mansion on Prospect Avenue. Several apartments occupy the house. We entered from a court. The walls are mostly of large bricks and the living room has an enormous fireplace and ceilings with heavy rafters. Randall told me that the rafters are said to have been taken from Thomas Jefferson's house in Georgetown. I was delighted. "This is most unusual, charming, quaint, artistic, ancient—" Randall smiled, "—and other adjectives. Now look at my room." He has fixed up his room in jade green, like a sunlit green bower. The whole apartment is filled with interesting objects—bric a brac, unusual furniture, paintings, and old musical instruments.

The uncle came in while we were there. He is a painter named Mr. Dieterlie. He wore yellow walking shoes, an old checkered suit and a green tie with a green-striped shirt. They showed me the painting that "Uncle Dieterlie" is working on right now. It shows a round moon rising, and fairies dancing in its light. On the right is a Lombardy poplar silvered by moonlight, and on the left is a shrub. Mr. Dieterlie showed me other paintings, various Japanese prints, and ornaments. Randall burned incense in a bronze brazier. We were late in leaving Randall's house and the streetcar trip to Brookland was a long one, but I sat back comfortably, savoring the pleasure of companionship with Randall. Out in Brookland we entered the Catholic monastery and went into a great cross-shaped hall. The service was profoundly beautiful. The monks chanted in Latin high up in the gallery. At little altars in the wings were clusters of colored candles, blazing like jewels, a wonderful sight.

During the ride back Randall had his hand lying on mine, and a girl across the aisle made an audible remark about it to her companions. But Randall in his melodious voice said, "We should worry," and kept his hand on mine. He said, "Be glad she noticed, so she won't be shocked the next time she sees it." He said there was no reason boys should not be demonstrative toward one another, as girls and Frenchmen were.

**Monastery.** *The Franciscan monastery, catacombs, and gardens are located at Fourteenth and Quincy Streets, N.E., in the Brookland section of Washington.*

*Sunday, 12 September 1920*

On this day I realized complete disillusionment. My "friendship" with Randall Hare was a fabrication! Friendship indeed! We went to Washington Cathedral. As we left the beautiful open air service and strolled together across the lawns, we had an unpleasant exchange with some rudeness on his part. I became somewhat stammering. Randall said scornfully, "What *have* you been believing? Did you think that when I wasn't with you I was *singing?*" I replied, "I did think that, and I feel deceived." He leaned back looking disgusted. "If I wanted a clinging vine I'd find—a woman." End of my friendship with him! I shall never find real friendship, never!

# 1921

*Wednesday, 12 January 1921 (Lexington, Virginia)*

In English class I told Lansing I had changed my mind concerning what he spoke about last night. He said, "This afternoon." Before supper I went to his room. There I found Howard, the light-colored negro youth who works in the kitchen. Howard had the pint of corn whiskey but said he hadn't been able to find "the $4.25 man" and had to go to another place. He wanted another dollar, and a quarter for himself. Lansing loaned me the additional money.

It is the first time I have ever drunk whiskey, except when I was a child and took it for medicine. I opened up my Keats and sipped the fiery liquid while I read the "Ode to a Nightingale"—that sensuous poetry that many a time has made me long for wine. But the poetry was more beautiful than the taste—at least of this wine of the Land of the Fire!

*Friday, 11 February 1921 (Lexington, Virginia)*

Scurrying clouds; flakes of snow. In the library I was reading "Modern Love" in George Meredith's poems when Dasham in his quick way strode in and seated himself to study. I gazed at that dear head bent over a publication. My fingers longed to stroke that lovely brown hair.

I want love and affection. Damn it! All that Stevenson said about journals is true. This diary of mine is a tissue of posturing. My real thoughts on such matters as sex are not admitted even to myself. I *will* be frank. I am madly in love with C. C. Dasham. "Sexual inversion," Havelock Ellis calls it. I always had some "hero" whom I adored and observed at every opportunity. It is not only Dasham with whom I've had visionary adventures, shipwrecks, desert isles, and the like. For years I have loved and worshipped other boys and youths. Before college there was Henry's schoolmate Bunny Alcott (think of it!). Then Hennessey, a god-like fellow, never seen or heard of since; and Morphew, a boy now gone to Tulane. The only one I even *spoke* to was Dasham. I have had a big-brotherly interest in some, an artistic sympathy for others. With Randall Hare the attraction was purely physical.

I left the library, not knowing where to go or what to do. Walked to the river bank, coat collar upturned, in the teeth of the chilling cold wind.

> **Havelock Ellis** (1859–1939) was an English psychologist and specialist in human sexuality. Jeb somehow acquired Ellis's book in Lexington in 1921. No doubt as a result of having read Ellis's work, Jeb in his youth sometimes labels a male homosexual an "invert," and a female homosexual a "female invert."

*Friday, 8 April 1921 (Lexington, Virginia)*

The only thing worth mentioning today is the baseball game with Roanoke, a tight little game, a well-played game. Light rain fell, almost unheeded by the drifting, shifting spectators. Observed the graceful elegance in the present styles . . . their careless simplicity, the long trousers falling loosely over the shoe tops.

Bennet and I were standing together next to the fence when Roanoke made a couple of hits, tying the score. I went angrily to the bleachers and took a seat. "There is no need to worry," Bennet said, following me. "Our best hitters are coming up next." He was right. We made the winning run. Bennet invited me to his room. I had a good talk with him and we came to an understanding. I told him I liked him a whole lot but he didn't appeal to me in a certain way. He walked with me to my room, so I could loan him Havelock Ellis's *Sexual Inversion,* which he had not read.

Now it is after midnight. I hear my dear friend the screech owl, complaining outside at the chilly night. I have come to listen for the owl every night in the trees outside.

*Saturday, 9 April 1921 (Lexington, Virginia)*

Loitered on the porch. Idly listened to the darkies in the store across the street. One played on a banjo, and others sang with him. Earl Podboy and Lansing Tower taught me to dance. Earl evaluated the process, his head to one side. "One more time," he said. Lansing and I went spiritedly round and round to the tune of "Li'l Liza Jane." Earl declared, "You know it now, Puny. You need only to practice."

*Monday, 11 April 1921 (Lexington, Virginia)*

My heart is pounding and my hand is almost too moist to hold the pen. Dasham and Agneau have been expelled from school. What is to become of me? It seems like a terrible dream. Only hours ago I stood on the upper porch watching the fellows throw and catch. Others were lying in the grass. Lansing was digging worms in the outhouse yard. I came in and lay on my bed to study Spanish, but, realizing I could never pass the exam, I set off for the river. Now all that seems so long ago. Returning, I passed some fellows from Lee's. "Hey, Alexander! You might want to know—" "Oh, *he'd* want to know!" I stood mute as a stone. Even under the calmest circumstances, I never can talk and think at the same time. "It's Dasham and Agneau. They weren't proper gents—or maybe you know that already. Those two are gone." And Poole, with a hideous grin, fluttered about with his arms in the air. I managed to come to my room where I barricaded my door with a chair. Finally realizing that I was pacing back and forth like a caged felon, I came to my desk. What is to become of me?

*Thursday, 28 April 1921 (Lexington, Virginia)*

Poor Agneau—living just beyond the outskirts of Lexington. More than once I've hiked out there, walking past the fences, in the hope that I might see him and talk with him. Perhaps they were sent from school with an insignificant story of poor scholastic performance. I know nothing, only that it appears almost impossible that I shall ever see Dasham again. Perhaps he was for me only a dream, a part of an obsession that threatens to ruin my life. But how could such a passion rule a human soul if there were no meaning to it, if this were the end? What, now?

*Thursday, 6 May 1921 (Lexington, Virginia)*

Anything, just to see the sun shine again. People are wearing overcoats. The sky is a gray mass hanging low over our heads. A letter from Dad announced that Henry and Eunice are to be married. Then a discussion of my grades, asking if it were not too late to improve my performance. I am horribly depressed, with the miserable loss of Dasham and Agneau, the dismal weather, my studies, the spying meddlesomeness of people—all of it, and the gray vista of years stretching ahead.

*Saturday, 8 May 1921 (Lexington, Virginia)*

Walked alone, going without coat or hat and with sleeves rolled up. "I want to be unhappy," as Stevenson said. Went up the millstream where the swift waters were reflected with shadows and leaf tracery. Returning, I saw Bennet and golden-haired little Walton, both on horseback, crossing the narrow, unsafe bridge over the mill trace.

Just before supper somebody shot a screech owl near the chapel. I asked why the owl was shot. The response, carelessly, was, "Oh, just for the pleasure of it." The sky blazed in the yellow sunset while the owl lay dead, gone from the beautiful world.

*Saturday, 29 May 1921 (Lexington, Virginia)*

The kitchen door swung open. Howard stood before us. "Been a boy drowned in the river." An even greater shock when Howard told us, "*Who?* That poor dead boy be Judge Agneau's son."

I started off for the river with the other fellows. It was inconceivable to think that Harry Agneau had drowned himself. We were picked up by a Ford on the road and carried to the hill above Whistle Creek. From there we ran down through an interminable yellow wheat field that rolled down to the trees on the water's edge. Underneath the steep cliff I saw Harry's father, hatless and mud-spattered. Dr. Smith directed the work. There was a crowd of townspeople and students, a silent, solemn crowd. Naked fellows worked over the water, diving or dragging grappling irons. It hurt to think of such an end for Harry Agneau. It was pitiful. Bad as this unjust world is, it is better than black nothingness. I started helping students build a fire to warm the swimmers. Nearly the whole student body was there, and I could see them still winding over the dark hill through the wheat field. Wet bodies glowed in the dusk on the dark lines, with silent onlookers on the banks, and the lurid glare of the flames over it all.

Later, when they still hadn't brought in Harry's body, Earl Podboy and I walked uptown on the dark roads. Earl mused, "Harry Agneau was a student in my Romantic Movement class. Perhaps it was the reading of melancholy poetry that brought this about." To my astonishment, dear, stupid Earl gravely recited from "Ode to a Nightingale": "Now more than ever seems it right to die . . . To close upon the midnight with no pain . . . " We walked on uptown. There some townspeople told us that Harry's body had been recovered.

*Tuesday, 14 June 1921 (Lexington, Virginia)*

Commencement Day. Wiedemeyer's Orchestra played outside the chapel. Dr. Flannery gave his usual speech on the Old South. I sat in the bleachers with my coat off. The sight of the golden wheat fields bordered in green trees was so beautiful that for the first time since Harry Agneau's death I had a sense of joy. I realized what heavy burdens I bring on myself. I worked on my overdue thesis later. Around two in the morning, with a great sigh of relief, I finished it. Then I dismantled everything in the room, taking down my pennants and ruining completely the little quarters that have sheltered me and my innermost thoughts.

Just before dawn, I was free to go over and watch the dance. In the east a pink, dewy glow appeared along the horizon. At that hour there was a spirit of recklessness at the ball. Confetti and streamers were strewn everywhere and the dancers whirled in joyous abandon. A party of chaperones stayed gamely at their post, utterly resigned to their fate. Unobserved, I went up to the balcony. Bennet was up there, with his feet propped on the rail. He greeted me with an amiable wave of his hand. "Some of the girls have left," he said, "but those who remain are the liveliest." I pulled a chair near him, and we watched the joyous scene below. I watched Lansing Tower considerably. He was with a girl who had wild yellow hair, bobbed and flying about. She wore a crimson dress to her knees with a train that she had draped over her arm. Her little black heels clicked in lively fashion.

Bennet remarked, "Your friend Tower doesn't appear to be indifferent to his garb." In fact Lansing bore a self-conscious happy look, as though he were trying to act the part expected of one wearing a dress suit. Bennet said, "See the girl with Earl Podboy? She's from Charleston, West Virginia. I've been told she's been put off of several public dance-hall floors for improper dancing." It must have been delightful to dance with her. Other boys besides Earl seemed to enjoy her.

The great windows began to whiten. The light of dawn peeped through. The orchestra marched about the ballroom and boys fell in behind, swaying with the music and singing. Bennet rose from his chair, smiling slightly. "Time to put myself to bed. Now that I have graduated, I don't expect that you and I will meet again. *Au revoir*, Jeb Alexander." We shook hands. He sauntered quietly down the steps.

I also had to tear myself away to get some sleep. Outside birds were singing and the eastern sky was aflame with rosy clouds. I felt giddy and gay and danced madly across the lawns and fox-trotted past old Graham's grave. Then into my still, gray room. The blank summer was staring me in the face.

*Wednesday, 29 June 1921*

Fiendishly hot weather. Washington has a tropical climate. I read Dante's *Inferno* to match my mood of exile. I have no idea what I shall do for a job. The condition is getting uncomfortable, with Mama's hints that I ought to be working instead of living off of Dad.

I walked the shimmering streets downtown, not caring to spend what little money I have on car fare. Went to the Senate. There Coolidge sat on the throne with the sourest, nastiest expression on his face that one can imagine. He looked like a typical grocery clerk, so cheap and common that I half expected to see him put on a long white apron to look more natural. His voice was the worst nasal Yankee twang I ever heard, as bad as the stage caricatures of it, and he spoke in an ill-natured tone. He seemed most of the time to be sunk in the gloomiest of reveries.

*Friday, 1 July 1921*

I can't believe it is any hotter on the equator. Much talk at breakfast of Henry and Eunice's approaching wedding. Mama forced me out to look for a job. I went to the Public Library. Near me sat a youth with dark hair and a gentle look about his eyes. I smelt a deliciously enchanting perfume and was puzzled to know its source, but then seeing him pick up and put to his face a silk handkerchief, and smell it rapturously, I knew that that was the source of the odor, and liked him all the better. When he got up I left also, and walked with him. He is eighteen years old, and his name is Archie Bushnell.

*Sunday, 3 July 1921*

Mama told me someone from the Riggs Apartment called while I was out, and gave me the telephone number, Main 6341. When I called a man's voice answered. "I have a guest by the name of Mr. Archie Bushnell. Would you like to visit us and see him?" I asked to speak to Archie. I could hear their voices murmuring, as if Archie were unwilling to answer. Then I heard Archie in a weak voice say, "Hello." We made a few casual remarks and I asked, "Do you want me to come down there tonight?" After a moment's pause he said, "Yes, around eight."

When I got there I found that my host was a dark-haired, big-chested man of about thirty. He introduced himself simply as "Hugh." Behind him I saw Archie, radiant and rosy and handsome. Archie was dressed in elegant simplicity, ease and carelessness, in a fashionable loose tweed suit, soft white shirt, and dark narrow tie hanging untidily. I think Dorian Gray in his prime of youth must have looked like Archie.

Hugh's apartment was delightfully furnished. He has models of statues, reproductions of paintings, knick-knacks of iron and bronze, quaint lamp shades, and an altar for Buddha. On his table were copies of *Pagan* and *Playboy* magazines, booklets of souvenir cards from France, photo album and scrapbook, and Wilde's *Lady Windermere's Fan*. There was a book by Mrs. Mary Baker Eddy, so he is probably a Christian Scientist.

In addition to Archie there was another boy, John Boydston, eighteen years old and good-looking. Boydston talked in an easy flowing strain. "I patiently wormed out of Archie all the facts about you, including that you think the parks are not any place to go. So you see, that is why we invited you." I remarked on the way everything in the apartment made for ease and comfort. Boydston said, "The flower of Washington frequents this apartment." Hugh smilingly nodded, "Ten or twelve of us make up my charmed circle." He asked me, "Which do you prefer—jazz, or good music?" I said, "Either," but he insisted on a choice so I selected operatic selections with Caruso. I sat leaning back in my wicker chair, smoking cigarettes. Hugh told me, "I have several thousand dollars' worth of erotic or rather 'queer' books." Soon after he said, "Though it appears I have money, I exist on nothing at all." "That is what I have been trying to do," I said, "for several weeks." Hugh asked if I had been successful and I answered, "After a fashion."

They mentioned an old man named "Skinny." Boyd winked at me and said,

"Archie is fond of Skinny." Archie answered in his delightful, naive way, "Yes, I'm right much infatuated with Skinny." While Hugh or Boyd did most of the talking I did all right, but then Hugh said I should talk about myself. I talked about Washington and told them how much I loved the dear old city. Hugh nodded. "No city is tiresome, nor even is the smallest hamlet, if you have the right circle of friends." But there's the rub. How is one to find the right circle? I think I have found some of them tonight, if I could only make myself one of them.

Hugh sent Archie out to get refreshments. When he returned we enjoyed a quart of vanilla ice cream. Boyd and I left around midnight. He waited with me until my trolley came. As innocent and boyish as he looks, he said that once he lay with one girl eleven times in a single week. Hugh had jocularly said of Boyd, "Boyd must either give up the girls or give up the fellows. We can't have competitions . . . " I like all three of them. I delight in Archie, but most of his conversation consisted of boyish banter with Boyd. It seems that it must have been Hugh who had me down there, that he got the facts out of Archie and then offered to have me there, to which Archie acquiesced as he does to anybody's request. When I left, Hugh told me, "The next time you feel bored, promise me you'll call."

**The Pagan** *(1916–1922). Subtitled "A Magazine for Endaemonists," The Pagan more or less defined the culture of the Greenwich aesthete.*

**The Playboy** *(1914–1924) was a portfolio of art and satire.*

*Monday, 4 July 1921*

Hot as a jungle. I strolled up and down in front of the Riggs Apartment. Saw people wander out to Hugh's porch, sit down, get up, move about. When I got home my bedroom was stifling. I slept with the sleeves and trousers of my pajamas rolled up, but was totally uncomfortable. I should like to sleep naked. Heard a tremendous outcry from a cat below, then a dog barking, and Mama going downstairs and opening the front door.

*Saturday, 9 July 1921*

The sun was drowned in a haze of humidity, a yellow circle moving across the sky. I sprinkled lime under the back porch where the poor cat was found, with neck broken by the boards falling on her. After supper Mama and Dad went to ride, seeking coolness in the night air. Henry and Eunice played the Victrola. Clearing away the rugs in the den, Eunice persuaded me to dance. "In two more days I'll be your sister-in-law," she said. "You aren't permitted to be shy any longer." She wanted to dance her way and I wanted to dance mine and we got tangled and didn't know what we were doing. Yet we never had an argument about our methods of dancing.

*Monday, 11 July 1921*

Mama sent me to Foster's downtown for her gloves. When I got back I had to dress for the wedding ceremony in a great hurry. The Martins' house was full of white and pink roses in jardinieres. Eunice came down in a simple blue dress. She looked radiant and beautiful, with her chiseled delicate features.

At the church the organist softly played "Oh Promise Me" during the ceremony. The use of such phrases as "forever" and "till death do us part" affected me more than I had expected to feel. Henry made his replies with a faint smile. Eunice seemed at ease. Then we returned to the Martins' house for a luncheon on tables in the back yard. I saw Dad whisper to Eunice. She walked in her confident stride over to me saying, "Jeb, you are the only one who hasn't kissed the bride." She gave me a full kiss. It was a pleasant sensation, the first time I was ever kissed by a girl. Then we saw them off, heading away for their little row house in Baltimore. Eunice leaned from the car window, waving and smiling.

Mama and Dad set out for home. I went downtown. There came suddenly a torrent of rain. I sat in Lafayette Square on the Wishing Bench under the big beech and had perfect protection, as the foliage was thick enough to serve as a roof. I imagined the rain pattering down in Baltimore where Henry and Eunice were beginning married life. Took a streetcar home. Called up the Riggs Apartment. "May I please speak to Archie Bushnell?" Hugh recognized my voice. "Jeb! Archie isn't here—running errands—preparing for company— join us. Be here when Archie arrives!"

I went through the downpour around nine o'clock. Hugh let me in and took my umbrella. Through the open porch door, at the end of the hall I heard rain spattering in the dark on the awning. We should have been cozy and happy in Hugh's apartment. We weren't. Hugh became sinister and seemed not able to be aroused until looking through his "rather queer" books with others. Present were two men even older than Hugh, though younger than Archie's Skinny, who pranced in acting as if he were the belle of the ball. Also present was a rosy-skinned Jewish youth who seemed mentally glazed-over and in a kind of hypnotic state. Archie—the reason I was there—behaved like a servile puppy, doing everything he was told to do.

When I came away the rain had stopped. I took a trolley through deserted streets. When I got off at the Union Station, a few people were resting or sleeping on benches. All looked impoverished, forlorn and pathetic.

### Wednesday, 20 July 1921

Dad finally persuaded Mr. Mariani to put me to work. Today unfortunately resulted in a difference of $550 which was traced to two mistakes of mine. I had labeled a thousand-dollar packet of twenties with a five-hundred-dollar strap and I had counted a four-hundred-and-fifty-dollar tray of quarters as a four hundred tray, which they usually are. The teller next to me called my attention to the Woodrow Wilson account, and we looked over the checks together. All were signed by Edith Bolling Wilson. The balance was about $1,100, quite small for the Wilsons.

At night I sat on a bench in Dupont Circle, and who should come strolling along the dirt walk but Randall Hare. He appeared well-dressed, with a good-looking tweed suit, red striped tie, and a panama hat. He looked at me, but I was sitting in the shadow, though with my hat off, and I really don't know whether he recognized me or not. He sat on a bench farther on. I debated with myself whether to speak to him, decided not, and walked up the dark forest way of New Hampshire Avenue.

### Sunday, 31 July 1921

On a dim bench in Lafayette Square I saw a well-dressed youth with chestnut-colored hair. Along came another young fellow. He plopped himself down beside my lad, and soon they walked off toward the White House. I felt thwarted and disappointed.

Randall Hare roamed through the park, dressed in white ducks and a tan shirt, as if he had been playing tennis. He sat down beside me and spoke—but I didn't answer. A queer look came over his face. He looked at his watch and left. A well-dressed elderly man sat down but I ignored him. He said pathetically, "I don't know what you're looking for, but I know it's not me."

### Wednesday, 17 August 1921

Tonight I forgot myself in the voluptuous beauty of Pola Negri as Carmen in a movie show dramatization of the opera, called *Gypsy Blood*. She is the type of alluring beauty I like, black hair and eyes. Then to Lafayette and the big beech. Randall strolled by, looking like a rube. He had a stiff collar showing an inch or two above his coat. His trousers were short enough to show several inches of socks, and the socks were *white* with a dark suit.

On the way home a woman got on the car and sat beside me. She was a bewitching creature with jet-black hair. When she sat down she calmly began singing to herself, a peculiar thing for a woman to do on the streetcar. She looked at me, but I said nothing to her. Always my shyness dooms me to an outcast existence.

**Pola Negri** *(1899–1987). An exotic star of the silent film era, Negri was born the same year as Jeb; she would have been his age (twenty-one) when she starred in the film he saw.*

### Friday, 19 August 1921

I sat on the bench I call "Nighthawk." Two youths passed in front of me. The dark-haired one was sportily dressed in college style, with a suit of extreme cut, a felt hat molded with the correct degree of carelessness, brogue shoes, and a striped tie. The other, a slim blond, was not so conspicuously dressed. As they passed me the blond one sang the simple title line, "All by myself," of the popular song, and I looked at him and smiled. He walked over and sat down, breezily asking, "Know of any place where we can find some excitement—or anyway, something doing?"

He spoke in such a laughing, intimate manner that I was put at my ease, and laughed and chatted with them. They had heard of the Krazy Kat and I gave them instructions how to find it. "Blond" said good-naturedly, "You shouldn't be sitting in the park. I've heard about Lafayette Square all the way down in the Virgin Islands." Later he said, "Some old grandmother in an automobile tried to pick me up, but I said—*nothing doing.*" He added facetiously, "I'm just a pure, innocent young girl." The dark lad dryly said, "A bit wise, that's all." They set off to find the Krazy Kat. I felt cheered up after they had gone.

### Thursday, 25 August 1921

The anniversary of my first experience of love and its consummation with Randall Hare. To observe the anniversary I went to Lafayette Square. Sat on the self-same bench, the Wishing Bench under the beech tree. How well I recall the ecstasy of that dewy moonlit night, the knowledge (as I thought then) that I had at last found the friend I had so long looked for. Later I sat near "Nighthawk's" bench. He was there, attired in a dark suit. A pleasant-faced man about thirty, in a well-fitting Palm Beach suit, sat down across from me and gazed at me steadily. I had thrown my cigarette stub on some newspapers lying by my bench and they were fanned into a blaze by the breeze. It was like having a spotlight thrown upon me. The man across the walk came over, asking if I objected to his talking to me. He urged me to have dinner with him but I refused. Finally, failing to prevail upon me, he got up and left, after some remarks intended to mislead me.

Whenever I glanced at "Nighthawk" he looked in the other direction. When he looked at me I turned my head away, and that seemed to make him look at me oftener. On my way home I saw a fellow I had an adventure with last month. He looked slim and fluffy-haired, strolling along beside a short dark companion. I pretended not to notice him, though I should have spoken had he been alone. What a hell of a life to lead!

*Saturday, 27 August 1921*

A good-looking youth sat down on the next bench. He made a beckoning motion with his foot. I repeated the motion. He got up and walked slowly away, glancing back. I followed. He sat down near the bed of flowers behind the Wishing Bench. I asked for a match, just to open the conversation. We sat talking, then strolled down past the White House offices, around the Ellipse and across the Monument lot. It was a lovely night. Behind the Bureau of Engraving we passed the greenhouses and slipped through a hedge. There seemed to be few people or cars. We lay in the shadow of the hedge, facing the moon-silvered lawn, fretted with trees casting dark shadows. The experience was exquisite, but later as we walked down the street, the dear lad was remorseful and conscience-stricken. When we parted I walked up to the Avenue with a feeling of detachment and exhilaration. The artist's life is the only life.

*Thursday, 15 September 1921 (Lexington, Virginia)*

Back to school. Lansing Tower followed me to my room to use my whisk broom, shoe brush, hair-brush, and mirror. He is changed—dressed up in a gray-checkered suit of fashionable style, with the mental outlook of a man of society. His conversation was of girls, dancing, and cars. The damn fool makes me positively sick with his affectations. He insisted I study physics with him, on *his schedule he has set up.* He and I bought a pint of corn liquor, dividing it. It cost $3.50 and a quarter to Howard for getting it.

*Wednesday, 5 October 1921 (Lexington, Virginia)*

At the post office I found the following letter which pleased and surprised me:

> Dear Mr. Alexander:
>
> You have been elected and are hereby invited to become a member of The Sesame, of Sigma Upsilon Fraternity. Please notify us of your acceptance by speaking to the local secretary or writing him about the matter. The initiation will be held in Dr. Shannon's office Friday night, the 14th of October, at 7 p.m.

Sigma Upsilon is an honor literary fraternity limited to twelve active members. I showed the letter to Lansing. He already belongs. It means something to me to belong.

*Wednesday, 12 October 1921 (Lexington, Virginia)*

Earl Podboy, with his grammarless language, was discoursing about some trivial matter. What a hell of a place this is, with these yokels and their tawdry talk. I wanted gentlemen, culture, elegance. Brushing through the bunch, I started off for the library. "Where ya going?" "Who is she?" One of the Brisbane twins joined me as I returned from the library. I can't tell which twin is which. One, presumably Tommy, but possibly Malcolm, smiles at me in physics class. This one walked with me to my room and sat on the bed talking. A nice-looking boy with pink skin, dimples in clear-complected cheeks, and dark hair combed straight back.

*Friday, 18 November 1921 (Lexington, Virginia)*

With the Brisbane twins on a walk. Near the bridge, a company of gray-clad cadets on horseback. Mountains ahead of us, hazy in the sunshine. Bare trees. A man ploughing. By the river in a thicket we took off our clothing, though not shirts and vests, and in the chilly air one twin and I engaged in lovemaking, with the other watching, though not dispassionately. Then the other twin had his turn. A little man with a red-headed wife passed nearby, both with fishing gear. On the other side of the river a yellow dog was caught on the cliff, unable to go up or go down. He whined and moaned piteously. Two hunters whistled and called the dog.

Afterward, the twins and I sat on a rock, gazing at the river. A flock of noisy crows flew over our heads. I got up reluctantly when the twins suggested going home. We rode back to school with a black man driving a motortruck full of sand. At the covered bridge, four fresh-faced cadets with surveying apparatus scrambled over the rocks.

*Tuesday, 6 December 1921 (Lexington, Virginia)*

Dr. Stevens talked of the physics exam, "the day of judgment." Oh it drives me frantic to think of missing my degree. The thought is sickening. Dad bitterly disappointed, Mama taunting Dad forever—my life wrecked. Oh, I can't bear it.

*Sunday, 25 December 1921*

Christmas day. I was beset by Dad in the parlor and forced into one of his fruitless discussions of my future. I didn't tell him what my ambition is, even when he taunted me with having no ambition. He would think I am an impractical fool, with a romantic idea of becoming a great author. I'll be damned if I'll tell Dad again.

*Wednesday, 11 January 1922 (Lexington, Virginia)*

I deliberately neglected my studies to write my story for the literary society. Literary development is the thing I came to college for, and that takes precedence over physics and other such dreary forced work. I paced my floor, digging into my inner consciousness for something in my experience to serve as a basis for a story. Finally I evolved a mental outline of a realistic sketch: *A bank teller suddenly realizes what a terrible rut he has gotten into, how much of the romance of life he is missing, how many foreign lands he has yet to see, and resolves to break away and leave for Europe the next day. He is filled with exaltation and makes preparations. Then the next morning, in the gray light of a rainy dawn, his enthusiasm has vanished. He realizes what a fool he was to think of leaving a good job. He goes back to the drudgery and routine of the teller's cage.*

I wrote till three in the morning. I tried to write in the style of *Three Soldiers,* firm, solid, and colorful.

> **Three Soldiers.** *Highly acclaimed after its publication in 1921,* Three Soldiers *was written by American novelist John Dos Passos (1896–1970). The work was based on Dos Passos's experiences in the Ambulance Corps during World War I.*

*Friday, 13 January 1922 (Lexington, Virginia)*

I drew Number One and was the first to read my work. Dr. Shannon said the story was "an excellent psychological study." Taking his advice, I named the story "In a Rut." Lansing said if we had a serious magazine in college then the story would be published. He had written a story with a metaphysical idea, and said he was trying it out on us and that he would have to rework it. But his story was excellently told, with a swift style something like O. Henry. Tonight's meeting was an evening that I heartily enjoyed.

*Wednesday, 18 January 1922 (Lexington, Virginia)*

Out walking with the Brisbane twins on muddy roads. They both had on a pair of those sporty white-and-tan shoes. We went down to the boat house and gamboled somewhat. Returning home, skylarking on the road, we popped green-jointed pliant reeds so the water squirted from the stalks into one another's faces, and made and threw snowballs, and tossed walnuts, and performed exercises remembered from physical education classes. We laughed a great deal. I have begun to tell those cavorting cherubs apart. The first says: "Malcolm?" The other: "Yes, Malcolm?" Then, "Draw the curtains, Malcolm, will you?" "Certainly, Malcolm." "Thanks, Tom." "You're welcome, Tommy." Malcolm is the handsomer one. I still can't identify them in what could be called personal circumstances. My sense of lacking a real relationship is accentuated when the curtains are drawn, the room darkened, by not having the most basic information—the identity of the boy in my arms. "It doesn't matter," they say, and they seem to mean it.

> **Sporty white-and-tan shoes.** *Almost the only drawing found in fifty years' worth of diaries accompanies this entry. Jeb's tiny, charming cartoon shows a saddle shoe.*

### Sunday, 29 January 1922 (Lexington, Virginia)

Horrifying news passed through the campus that a theatre in Washington had collapsed under the weight of 36 inches of snow, killing nearly 100 people and injuring others. It was terrible to think of it happening in Washington, my Washington. I had nothing to go by, not even knowing what theatre it was. My fancy pictured Dad and Mama dead in the rubble. But still I knew that they were safe, that 100 people is only a few in 400,000.

The suspense of waiting for a paper was torture. All day my mind filled with depressingly vivid pictures of the occurrence, and morbid wishes that I could have been there. At last I got the Richmond paper, the *Post* not having come because of tied-up Washington trains. The theatre was the Knickerbocker at Eighteenth and Columbia Road. The only time I ever went there was to see *Birth of a Nation*, with a little Confederate flag in my buttonhole. Headlines said many were still imprisoned under the debris. The steel roof was perfectly flat. I came up to my room imagining the snow-laden surface buckling, collapsing with a sound like thunder, the screams of trapped people, the news spreading like wildfire over Washington, and thousands swarming about at Eighteenth and Columbia Road, held back by soldiers.

I actually began to feel homesick and full of tenderness toward my people. Later I got out my diaries and began reading on and on, from the humiliation when I failed to graduate from Central High School—to my discovery of Joyce's *Portrait of the Artist*—and then in my freshman year my fascination for that beautiful boy C. C. Dasham. Because of what I felt about him, I confessed in my diaries that I loved boys. Sweet boys! I love them all. Could we but dance together, vine-crowned, intoxicated, and joyously on the windy hills over the green grass beneath a cloud-tufted sky.

*Friday, 10 February 1922 (Lexington, Virginia)*

I learned from the Registrar that I must make an appointment to see the Dean. Unsettling intelligence. For months I have felt that I was walking toward an academic precipice over which I should fall in June, but it seems that I am to be dashed over the precipice now. The thought that I shall not graduate fills me with despair. If only I had studied! I am a heedless dreamer—or as Dad said of me in a heated moment, a drifter, oblivious of the gathering clouds of tomorrow. I live like a butterfly in these fleeting days of summer, but winter is ahead of me.

*Friday, 31 March 1922 (Lexington, Virginia)*

The first ball game of the season. It had begun raining, but not hard. I sat with Tommy and Malcolm in the grandstand. Love is a curious thing. I genuinely love the twins, yet if I never saw them again I wouldn't think a thing of it. Baine Howard came over and made a few remarks, though we had never spoken before. I watched students streaming up through the gate, and saw the one I call "Jean Christophe," bareheaded with his hair smoothed down by the rain. His raincoat was slung carelessly about his shoulders, giving him an air of graceful insouciance. Little Walton sat alone with no protection from the rain. I might as well be in love with the stars as all these bonny lads.

*Sunday, 21 May 1922 (Lexington, Virginia)*

Baine Howard came up to my room. He was lying on the bed and I sat beside him, he very affectionate . . . Later I went with Tommy and Malcolm to go swimming. It was hot walking down with the sun on our backs. A lad about fifteen joined us on the road and accompanied us to the boat-house. He was coarsely dressed, but had gentle ways and a curious sleepy expression about the eyes. I fell in love with him. He undressed and put on his bathing suit but didn't go in because of the complaints Tommy made of the coldness of the water.

I hesitated long and then jumped in. I hadn't realized that the current was so swift. Before I knew it I was some distance from the landing, and struggled, and then decided to drift with the current and land farther down on the bank. Malcolm too was having a hard time getting back. Tommy dived from the rock but didn't go far out. I looked at my little "Absalom" (I have given him that name, in accordance with my custom), sitting on the step, then dressed with the others. Dreams of Absalom on the walk back—living with him as my little comrade, loving him, teaching him, and fathering him.

Those childish roughnecks, the fraternity boys, had torn up and wrecked Tommy and Malcolm's room in our absence. The twins were furious. I helped them clean it up.

*Saturday, 10 June 1922 (Lexington, Virginia)*

Hot. More coatless men appearing. It is a good idea and ought to be carried actively into the cities. The pockets are convenient—the only use for a coat. Everywhere there are girls in town for the dance. Some are quite pretty. Lansing and I went up into the hills and I found a colony of purple trillium, the first I ever saw. Lansing told me he will be elected to Phi Beta Kappa. I am glad he came out so fortunately even though it makes me feel worse about not getting my degree.

At night I took a nip from my bottle and went over to the dance. "Endymion," angelic lad, was sitting on the other side of the balcony and I gazed at him filled with longing. It made me angrily jealous to see bald-headed MacMillan, his fraternity-brother, put his arms playfully about my angel and sit close beside him. I saw many fellows I knew. Earl Podboy never looks well in dress clothes. Slowly home under the full moon.

I wish I were graduating. I got a letter from Dad, saying he wants to put me to work in one of his grocery stores as soon as I get to Washington. He reminded me that he and Henry began as grocery clerks and went forward in the business. He spoke enthusiastically about the possibilities of advancement. Never! I shall *not* get into the clutches of the grocery business.

*PART TWO*

# THE ROARING TWENTIES

*Thursday, 22 June 1922*

Mr. Mariani said there is no job for me at the bank. I tried the National Personnel Service Bureau. The woman had the same old words, "Sorry, the job's been filled." I have to do something—Dad's grocery store plan is too dreadful to think of—to go to work *an hour before the Government clerks do* and to work *two and a half hours after they get out.*

In the middle of the day I took a break from job hunting. At the Tidal Basin, the wind was whipping the water into choppy waves. I passed a dark-haired man and a good-looking youth, both in summer suits. The older man looked at me with an expression of amused interest. I passed on, recognizing him as my old friend Hugh of the Riggs Apartment. Went down to the Ellipse and read the employment ads, glancing at the sword blade of the Monument thrust against tufted cumulus clouds. Decided to ascend the Monument, but the South Dakota people started unveiling a memorial and no one else could go up. Finally we were allowed to ascend. Pleasing lads up there, looking out the windows. Doll houses and tiny toy automobiles below.

I am sick of this job-hunting business. It's the most discouraging thing imaginable. My feet have blisters from walking in new shoes.

> **Memorial and Monument.** *Washington is full of memorials and monuments, but in Jeb's diaries references to "the Memorial" are to the Lincoln Memorial, dedicated in 1922 and located at the west end of the Mall facing the Reflecting Pool. References to "the Monument" refer to the Washington National Monument, a 555-foot-high white marble and granite obelisk.*

*Friday, 23 June 1922*

Lafayette Square. On the Magnolia Bench, a pleasant-faced boy in cap and brown knickerbockers sat down beside me. He was poorly dressed, but not rough-looking. I still don't know how much to believe of what he said. He told me, "I sleep on park benches—unless the cops drive me away." I asked, "But when it gets cold?" He said, "Oh—I spend my winters in California and don't come east until April. With all my heart I long for a stable existence. Right now I'm trying to get a job as a taxicab driver." A regular young hobo, in fact, and I was interested to hear him talk. But if he had not been attractive I would not have suggested taking a walk toward the Monument, which I did.

At the shady lawn south of the pool the boy whispered, "Watch out—"
There the cop was, lurking in the shadow against the wall. "You get used to
cops," the boy said. We saw the cop sneaking across the grass, so we turned
toward the Tidal Basin and strode purposefully along the seawall. We passed a
man and woman looking disarranged, sitting close together by the water.
Looking back we could see the outline of the man and the woman against the
water, the man engaged in an up-and-down motion. Suddenly they got up and
walked hurriedly away. "Look," said my hobo. I saw the black figure of a cop. We
crossed the speedway again.

There we lay on the terrace talking, without doing anything else, hardly. He
is the most accomplished liar in Christendom. He passionately swore that he had
never done certain things. "Why, tonight was the first time I ever set foot in
Lafayette Square." With my hand playing with his hair, stroking his face, I said,
"I saw you there last Thursday." But he denied it. He told me what a hard lot it
was not to know where the next meal was coming from, to have no bed but a
park bench, to sleep in winter in a cold box-car. He talked me into giving him the
money I had with me, except a few cents in change.

As for what I intensely wanted from him, the boy stuck to his attitude of
innocence. I could only accept the situation philosophically. Finally we walked
toward town. I told him, "You must think me an easy mark. Was that the easiest
money you ever earned?" He replied earnestly, "It was a loan. I swear, I'll pay you
back after I get that taxicab job."

Lafayette Square was now almost deserted. I felt profoundly dissatisfied and
yet there was nothing I could do. While I waited for my car he called across the
street, "See you again." I replied with a meaning, "I hope so." I rode home feeling
I had been made a fool of, keenly regretting the money. But in spite of the way
the lad fleeced me I felt affection for him—dear, unscrupulous, handsome hobo.
Home after two. Mama let me in with a shocked comment about the lateness of
the hour.

*Monday, 26 June 1922*
Boldly strode toward Riggs Bank, that cruel-looking stone building. At the
steps my heart failed me. I only glanced in the door, and walked away. Then to
Washington Loan and Trust, but got only to the vestibule. How can such a timid
creature as I get along in the world of business?

At Dikeman's orange juice booth I got two drinks, served by a lovely lad
with whom I fell in love—a boy with warm dark eyes and gently-bred appearance. Our hands touched when I paid him five pennies for my second drink. So
many beautiful boys. I am filled with love for all of them, a passionate tenderness,

a spiritual and physical hunger, a desire to protect and care for them. Another slim, brown-haired lad on the streetcar. Our eyes met and he too was gone from my life.

### Tuesday, 27 June 1922

Up at ten after Mama's irritating call up the stairs, "You oughtn't be lying around!—it's lazy. Estelle wants to clean the third story." Thank heaven I don't have to spend the summer with her. She and Dad will be up at Cape Cod until November. When I went downstairs, Mama told me that while they are in Cape Cod the house is to be rented to Italians attached to the Embassy. I asked, "But if you rent the house to the Italians, what will happen to *me?*" She said, "You'll take a room at the Y.M.C.A." I sat down at the table. "*Really?*"

> **Y.M.C.A.** *The Y.M.C.A. buildings, such as the one Jeb was going to stay in, then at 1736 G Street, N.W., made rooms available for single young men. Activities included gymnasiums, reading rooms, libraries, and devotional meetings. As Jeb makes clear, the Y.M.C.A. could be a comfortable haven where homosexual young men could meet one another.*

### Tuesday, 4 July 1922

Mama rushed through her preparations and was ready by quarter to eleven, instead of quarter to twelve, by mistake. She sat inside the door resting, then suddenly discovered at eleven-forty that the train left at noon, instead of twelve-twenty. Henry and Eunice rushed Dad and Mama into the car and they sped away while I waved good-bye. The boat left Baltimore for Boston at five, daylight savings time. I wandered around the silent third story and was looking out a window when the Italians drove up to take over the house. They had children and a maidservant, hatboxes and breakable objects. The wife upset me with her interested perusal of the house. Disturbing was the information that the maidservant will occupy my room on the third story.

Henry and Eunice returned in time to straighten things out with the Italians. Then they gave me a ride downtown to the Y.M.C.A., where I signed up for my room. It's a dark place with one window opening on a brick wall. By craning our necks at the window, Henry and I could see the sky. Bending our heads in the opposite direction we discovered an alley below. Henry said, "This is pathetic." It was a hideous outlook. It's going to be like walking into a box and shutting the lid to enter this room.

After Henry and Eunice set off for Baltimore, I went to the Tidal Basin. There was a line of several hundred waiting, coatless and perspiring, to get into the locker room. A soldier treated me to a Coca-Cola from a negro who was rushing about in the blazing sun selling cold drinks to the waiting line. I saw the soldier later in the water, his hair plastered in a brown fringe across his forehead. The water was glorious, cool and buoyant. I swam back and forth, resting only long enough to be able to start off again.

*Friday, 14 July 1922*

With no job in sight, I had to write Dad and accept work in one of his grocery stores. The job is hellish, a combination of the duties of a servant, a delivery boy, a negro porter, a chambermaid, and a salesman. How could Dad wish it for me? To think of going on like this is appalling. Ten hours a day—and thirteen hours on Saturdays. I can't keep my self-respect going out with a white coat and apron to deliver groceries to petty housewives.

*Saturday, 29 July 1922*

After thirteen hideous hours of imprisonment I hurried off with my paltry $15 salary, out at last into the cool night air. I gazed at the dome of the Capitol in a daze of delight. It stood out against the night like a palace of dreams, thrillingly beautiful. Day by day I realize how much I love Washington, my beautiful, imperial city. I am going to do anything to get out of this damnable grocery slavery.

*Saturday, 26 August 1922*

My future falls down in mire and ashes. Dad said *no* in response to the letter I wrote him about my idea of sending me back to college. I opened his letter in my room and was overcome with the shock of grief and disappointment.

> I can't feel justified in sending you to W&L again. It would be of no benefit
> to you if you went another year and got your degree, for you would end up
> exactly where you are now.

And then a lot of disgusting cant about hard work not hurting me, that Henry started in the grocery business at the bottom and was rapidly climbing, that I must develop a new attitude toward work and advancement. Dad's stony heart and commercialized mind cannot comprehend that I have no interest in advancement in this damned slave work. And Dad says not to think him unkind!

I lay on my bed in a paroxysm of despair, weeping and tearing the bedclothes in a hopeless frenzy. With this hellish grocery store job, life is not worth living.

*Saturday, 9 September 1922*

Say it is Saturday and nothing more is necessary. My youth is being wasted in slavery and desperation. At night, tired and wretched, I smoked a Fatima in the chilly, almost deserted realms of Lafayette Square, a farewell to the season. Along came a person with crudely high collar and curly hair and it was Randall Hare. He went over to a boy in bi-colored sport shoes. Across the street in the White House, Mrs. Harding was lying near death, but here in the square, life went on oblivious of her. Poor simple woman—the world will wag on and never miss her. Gradually Sport-Shoe-Boy seemed to thaw. He and Randall were getting along nicely, so I came away. Everything is black and hopeless.

*Sunday, 8 October 1922*

Henry unkindly showed me a letter he received from Dad.

> I have tried to prepare my sons for making their way in the world and becoming successful men, and you are exhibiting commendable ambitions . . .

Pointedly I am left out. My ambitions are not to be taken seriously—mere literature. I said angrily, "He considers me a shiftless fool with only idle desires to be an author. All this in spite of my assertion that the only ambition I have is success in literature." Henry shrugged. "It's hard to conceive of *success* as anything but financial or social success." Henry acts sometimes as if he does not care a straw about me. It is his jealousy, hardly blamable, because Dad sent me to college and didn't send him. But it is not my fault.

*Tuesday, 31 October 1922*

I carried out ninety-one crates of bottles, egg crates, peanut butter pails, and bags full of bags, from the cellar to the sidewalk to be carried back to the warehouse. Wretched and hellish existence.

Halloween at night—the most uproarious Halloween I ever saw in Washington. I sallied forth into the humming lamplit night, into the carnival throngs amidst flying confetti, streamers, blowing of horns, and shouts and laughter of merrymakers. A great number of young people were dressed in clothes of the other sex, both boys and girls. I laughed out loud at some of the antics. One couple, I think they were male, were attired as a rube couple from the country, being panic-stricken by automobiles in the street—screaming and darting this way and that. Shiveringly homeward under the gleaming moon.

*Tuesday, 14 November 1922*

With thoughts of Whitman and Nietzsche I forced myself to seek a job at the bank. But it was no use. Going back outdoors I shivered from the wind that whipped my flimsy raincoat about my legs. Later, unpacking lemons—they were marked "Palermo, Italy"—as I unwrapped the tissues I scratched the yellow skins with my fingernail and savored the sun-sweet scent of the peel. *Ah, Italia!*

Dad strolled into the grocery store and told the old Walrus and his wife that they had to let me off next Thursday to go to the dentist, an event I dread almost as much as I dread each day of work. It seems that I am stuck fast to hell, imprisoned like a fly on fly-paper.

A strange mood tonight, probably as a result of reading Yeats, a mood of tragic exaltation, a feeling that I am stepping into eternity, that I shall be a failure, but it cannot be helped. I shall have to make the best of it. Somebody whistles down the hall and slams a door. What does it amount to?

> **Walt Whitman** *(1818–1892). Jeb's diaries, especially in the younger years, are peppered with mentions of the American poet Walt Whitman. Whitman was tremendously important to him. The poems in the "Calamus" selection of Whitman's well-known* Leaves of Grass *celebrate in large part "the manly love of comrades."*

### Saturday, 18 November 1922

The hideous thirteen hours ended. Utterly depressed, I went down to the *Post* to see the score of the W&L-V.P.I. game. The score was such a grievous shock that I became overwhelmed with wretchedness. V.P.I. beat us 41 to 6. In blackest hopelessness, I dragged myself toward my room. On the Avenue the Salvationists were singing "If Only I Could Blot Out the Past." Could I blot it out, I would graduate from W&L and would care for my teeth—my chief regrets. Then I could endure my sordid, slaving life.

### Friday, 24 November 1922

At work I straightened up the cellar— the stink of rotten onions and rotten potatoes; thick dust—disgust and hatred of it all. It is as if a malignant fate had destined me to this job. Imprisoned, poverty-stricken, wildly unhappy, I set off for the dentist. A bleak wind penetrated my layers of clothing. He had to take out one of the seven fillings he put in last week and do it over. I suppose I must pay for his mistake. He had cages in his reception rooms, with about fifty canaries and cardinals. A female cardinal was allowed to fly free. She perched on the window ledge, whistling to a male cardinal in the bare trees outside. She made a diversion while I sat with my mouth trussed up in rubbers and braces. A nightmare with *boing, boing, boing, boing* endlessly on my lower front teeth. When the bird flitted out of sight I tried to divert my mind by thinking of my first erotic adventure, that summer night on the dim grass with Randall Hare. In the pounding misery of the dentist's chair I was sorry I had remembered it.

The freight, 213 cases, the largest we ever received, was waiting at the store. And just before a thirteen-hour Saturday, too.

*Monday, 25 December 1922*

Christmas Day. The tiresome ride out to the house bored me. I realized that I could never return to living out there. The trolley ride takes so much time from one's free hours. But of course the real reason is Mama. She makes me feel watched, as though an inhibiting presence were making itself felt through the air.

I found a blazing fire in the parlor and a Christmas tree twinkling. Eunice, wearing a white wool dress with a white fur collar, was dancing with Henry. We had a delicious roast beef dinner. Afterward Dad, Henry, and I sat in the den, smoking black cigars while Henry and Dad heatedly discussed the emergence of the extremist movement in Germany. I sat beside Dad, smoking, saying little. I had no idea Henry knew so much about the crisis with the German currency.

Just before I left, I told Dad and Henry that I was going to take the Civil Service Exam and try and get a Government job. We had an unpleasant discussion about the grocery business. I went out of the house into a penetrating wind and hurried down the dark street to the car barn. Then the long ride home—for this room at the Y.M.C.A. is *home*, now. Settled under my snug covers and read in Frank Harris's *Contemporary Portraits*—a study of the violet-scented, violin-haunted, moon-mad nineties.

> **Frank Harris** *(1856–1931) was an arrogant, lively Scottish-English journalist, best known for his embellished autobiography,* My Life and Loves *(1923–27). The work, banned in England and the U.S.A. when it was first published, paints a libertine portrait of the Edwardian era.*

# 1923

*Monday, 8 January 1923*

Fog and mist resting on the trees. Into the Government examination rooms. A sharp-tongued woman demanded, "Do you know where you are going? What are you going in *there* for? Editorial Clerk isn't in there. The third room down." I went to the third room and got a seat. My examiner was a dreary woman with a wooden smile that she shifted meaninglessly off and on to her face as an aid to her speech. I was appalled to find that the Civil Service exam was to take *seven consecutive hours.*

*Friday, 26 January 1923*

Henry has been in Washington from Baltimore, is staying with Dad and Mama, is looking over his new grocery store in Anacostia, and is in an ebullient mood at the prospect of moving back to Washington. I have come to realize that Henry loves this beautiful, dull, gray town as much as I do.

At night he went with me to the Ram's Head Players for Wilde's *The Importance of Being Earnest.* The playhouse is a part of the residence of Alexander Graham Bell on Connecticut Avenue—reached by a sort of alley and then up a stairway. Henry had never been there. It is just a small room, tastefully done in cream and green; a narrow stage at one end, and a sculptured ram's head over the proscenium. A gentle-looking lad of about sixteen was taking the tickets.

After the play Henry and I walked downtown. Ahead of us I beheld Randall Hare, loitering in front of a dark store window, apparently having nothing better to do. As Henry and I passed, Randall started on. He recognized me and gazed appreciatively at the man at my side. Henry, conversing and striding comfortably beside me, had the unmistakable manner of an intimate companion.

*Thursday, 8 March 1923*

The Jeritza concert was just over. A crowd, chiefly women, was gathered at the stage door to see the prima donna come out. Henry and I each lit a cigarette and waited. And there she came—a bewitchingly beautiful young creature with a mass of astonishing pale gold hair all bare in the chill wind. In the midst of the drab-colored crowd, she seemed an exotic blossom from a strange climate. She wore a luxurious snow-white fur cloak with a collar that she pulled half over her face. The people waved their hands, tipped their hats, and called good-bye. She in adorable shyness made sweetly awkward gestures of farewell. She was whisked away in a taxicab with two men. "Damn," said Henry, and we walked on.

*Maria Jeritza (1887–1982) was a Viennese-born operatic soprano whose statuesque height, emotional fire, and superb voice made her a personality of the twenties.*

*Friday, 9 March 1923*

A possible vacancy at the Y.M.C.A. on the sixth floor. I hesitated, thinking of the trouble of moving my belongings. But Henry said, "You would be an *idiot* to stay in 205 if those people rent rooms that allow daylight. If you're worried about getting those piles of trash of yours into a new room, I'll help you move."

After thinking about it I decided he was right. We made trip after trip, carrying boxes, books, my collections, clothes, junk. It is appalling to think I endured gloomy 205 for eight months and got accustomed to it, even attached to it. Here, I have a rocker as well as a straight chair. Out the window Henry and I could gaze on the Mall. Scattered lights twinkled in the misty darkness.

### Sunday, 11 March 1923

Eunice is pretty, a spirited woman, but a child. She has no interest in anything beyond movies, clothes, town gossip, domestic matters. It seems a shame to talk about her like this, but *c'est la verité*. We had a drive around town, principally to look at Henry's store in Anacostia. Eunice sat in the back seat between Mama and me. What could we talk about? Mama gazed at the passing scene in her meditative and not unpleasant trance, as she does sometimes. I did try to talk to Eunice about plays, literature, art, and music, but nothing would keep her amused. Toward the end of the ride she appeared to have become sullen. Henry sat with her riding home.

### Monday, 19 March 1923

After rainstorms heard in dreams through the night, a gray morning broke into vivid sunlight as I started toward my first day as a Government Editorial Clerk. Good-bye to the grocery business, with its stench of rotten potatoes! Up to the new offices. From my window I have a view to the Potomac, blue and misty, winding past the War College among the hazy hills. Mr. Brown, all alone at a far desk, greeted me by name. He is a tall, diffident man about thirty-five, with the gentleness and shy loveableness of an invert. Behind me are the "artists," two older women and a girl painting lantern slides. To my left is a Miss Contadeluci, whose sturdy figure suggests the once firm, dark beauty of girlhood. Mrs. Utott, our mosquito-like "boss," has her own cubicle.

Mrs. Utott put me to work editing extracts. Ye gods! What fantastic sentence structure! I could have written a dozen sentences of my own while I was twisting into decent form the words of some hazy-headed officer. After work I walked out joyously into the polar air. Around the Ellipse, past the Monument, around the gray and tortured waters of the Basin, past the dismal shuttered bath house and the beach, and across the bridge in the teeth of the bitter wind. I was warm and refreshed when I returned to my room. At night, wanting a celebration, I drifted into the Strand. I no longer ignore the fact that one of the theatre's attractions is the same that Lafayette Square has in summer, that is, the opportunity for amorous intrigue with other males. Next to me sat one who in the darkness was not bad-looking. When we left the theatre together, I found he was a puffy cheeked, greasy-looking fellow in pointed black shoes and gray spats. He asked me to go home with him. Back to my room disgusted, and still somehow not regretting the experience. At least it was experience and not mere passive existence. And while it lasted, the illusion was beautiful.

*Tuesday, 27 March 1923*

When I got away from work, the sky was streaked with pink. Slowly to Keith's. Next to me was a dear lad about sixteen. I was filled with a fury of longing to take him in my arms. With him was a plain, unattractive boy who put his arm around my lad, jealous of his attention toward me.

Mollie Fuller, an old star making a "comeback," recited a verse about Broadway. She mentioned "your pale faced men with eyes too bright" who never appeared in the day but only "slink out at night"—whom she would like to put in the country where they could rest and be cured or some such folderol. The allusion was in a more kindly vein than any I have ever heard but still it is horrible to be thought of in such a way. I was bitter and filled with the old misery. Why must they be talking of us, making fun of us, persecuting us? Everywhere I go I feel that a hundred fingers are pointing at me, a hundred tongues whispering about me. Fight as I will, I cannot overcome it. It is like a demon gnawing at the roots of my heart.

*Sunday, 1 April 1923*

How I wish that glorious spring would arrive so my dingy overcoat could be laid aside. The garment has a depressing effect on me. I feel an inferiority complex when I wear it, so different from the assured feeling that comes from being well-dressed.

At night I went to the Columbia where I saw *Where the Pavement Ends,* unusual in having a tragic instead of happy ending. As the romantic young chief, Ramon Navarro was a beautiful figure with his clustered hair and shapely manly body almost nude. Much better than the average movie. Afterward a brisk walk, watching the orange sun set behind the hills of Virginia.

*Sunday, 29 April 1923*

To the house. Trees turning green, even the oaks budding. Daffodils were glowing yellow beside the fish pond, nodding and being admired by Henry and Eunice. The two made a handsome couple, with heads companionably bent over the golden flowers.

Though entirely a businessman in his way of thinking, Henry has his soft side, as shown by his love of flowers. He will never understand me, but I think I may understand him. In Henry's pursuit of business success, Washington is for him exactly what it is for me—the Isle of Golden Dreams. Unlike me, Henry is handicapped by essential stupidity, by the smallness of his soul, but there is a strong analogy between having those handicaps and having the curse that is ruining me.

When I got home I read in *Sons and Lovers*, and felt flesh and blood persons in the places of the characters, as though I were choosing a cast to act the parts before my mind's eye. Paul, the protagonist, became my latest male love, a youth here on the sixth floor whom I usually see in the lavatory every morning. He is superbly formed, physically, with full breast and shapely limbs. Eyes dark blue, even features, healthy tanned face, and waves of crisp curly hair. Yesterday morning I watched him in the great mirror the length of the washroom and he seemed calmly, tolerantly, kindly aware of it. Then tonight, picturing him as Paul Morel in *Sons and Lovers*, I feel as if I have been with him all evening, and have become acquainted with him. And I love him all the more. But the book made me feel more drawn to women than I have in a long time, and I sat in my chair clenching my fists full of rage at Fate, wishing that she were a tangible being before me so that I might strangle and choke her. Oh, why, *why*, why must I suffer under such a curse? Why can't I escape it, overcome it? As well ask why the canary doesn't calmly fly away from the cage.

*Tuesday, 29 May 1923*

Perspiring in my felt hat, I hastened after work to Meyer's to buy a new one. I got a snappy straw one with a fancy braid, yellow straw and a brown band—soft, comfortable, good-looking. Then I went to the Oriental Bazaar and bought a Japanese incense burner, with incense—wisteria, lily, and lotus. At home the perfume of wisteria incense put me in a mood of dreamy imaginings. I sat in my rocker, reading John Addington Symonds' *In the Key of Blue*, the beautiful book of life and love that brought Swinburne's brutal sneer about Symonds' describing "his blue-breeched gondolier to his fellow Catamites." I am one of Symonds' fellow Catamites and I am proud of it.

**John Addington Symonds** *(1840–1893) was an English scholar, poet, essayist, advocate of homosexual emancipation, and correspondent with Walt Whitman.*

*Wednesday, 6 June 1923*

To Lafayette Square. Sat listening to radio concerts from in front of the White House. A spectacled idiot of forty-five flopped down on my bench and tried to make conversation but I got rid of him. Three bitches sat opposite and seemed interested. They got on my nerves. They sat and sat. I moved over to the Wishing Bench. That damn plain-clothes man, the one I call "the Sneak," strutted up and down staring at everybody until I got disgusted and left. The idiot might as well wear a uniform if he is going to act like that.

*Saturday, 9 June 1923*

One scorching, sizzling day. After dark I sat on the Wishing Bench. A curly-haired figure veered from his nightly prowl and joined me. "Good evening," said Randall Hare. I looked the other way, ignoring him. He chuckled. "I am almost always successful in this business," he said, "and you, almost never. Don't pretend you don't know me. Can't you admit you might learn a few things? Haven't I seen you watching me?"

I was determined to squeeze an adventure out of the old Square tonight, and as it had only just gotten dark, I decided there would be no harm in wasting a few minutes with Randall. He settled in. "I've been observing your methods. You sit waiting for someone to start something. Well, you can sit *a while*. Then if nothing happens, make a tour of the park. Find one that appeals to you. Then *you* sit down with *him*." He stood up. "Keep moving," he intoned, "or you won't find one." I did stand up after he left. On my first tour I located a young boy who appealed to me, but I couldn't get up courage. Presently the boy left. I followed. We passed by Randall, sitting beside a good-looking marine. Outside the Square my lad stopped to look in the window at Child's. I went on to the Willard, and thus lost him. Back to the Square. Randall and the marine were gone, so Randall must have got his.

I finally came to an understanding with a well-dressed chap about thirty. It was too bad I had to be disappointed. We went to his rooms, a small house with two doctors' plates on the front. I think he was one of the two. I stayed about an hour. A one-sided affair entirely. It was in several ways a new experience for me. I learned a new phase of the general subject.

*Sunday, 10 June 1923*

To the Corcoran Gallery. *Mercury in Repose* was exquisite. I longed for him to be transformed into flesh and blood. I strolled on down to the Tidal Basin feeling disillusioned—the effects of Saturday night. There I saw a youth whom I picked up without results at the Freer Gallery a few weeks ago. He was with a girl and looked at me curiously. There was a sailor with blue eyes who stood around waiting for me to approach him. My shyness prevented it, though. When I had dinner at the U.C.S. I learned that my Monument Lad has told the other boys there of our meetings. Now they chatter and comment. Damnable irritating and upsetting, but after all, leading the necessarily double life that I do, I must expect unpleasant incidents. I had thought better of the boy, though. I had thought him a decent, gently-bred youth. And I still think so, except for that action. I love him yet.

Later I made a night of it in the Square. I got nothing. As usual I let such lads as I found attractive slip through my fingers. Randall Hare was sitting between *two* soldiers. He never fails to get something. He sees what he wants, and takes it. If I only had Randall's easy assurance and powerful abilities!

*Wednesday, 13 June 1923*

I sat in last summer's favorite bench, just above the Wishing Bench. A sailor approached me. "Got a cigarette, Jack? I'm all out." And then with a laugh, "And a match?" He had a friendly hearty voice and was a clean-cut chap, not a roughish type of sailor. I gave him both cigarette and light but he sauntered on before I could say anything. In a few minutes he returned along the north walk and sat down facing me. I longed to go to him but I could never manage a sailor. I shouldn't know what to say, do, or expect, and if I walked down the street with him I should feel as if I had a brass band at my heels. When he strolled away I swore in impotent fury. But never mind, maybe some summer evening I can have an adventure with a sailor friend, some evening when I am feeling free and independent.

*Monday, 2 July 1923*

At work it was a trying day, I in one of my worst Monday moods of resentful brooding. I became rebelliously angry at Miss Contadeluci because of the insulting way she called me "Old Lady."

At night as always. Randall and I passed each other with a smiling, "Hello." Sat on the Magnolia Bench in the middle of the Square. The Sneak—the broad-beamed Lafayette plain-clothes cop—passed by and stared at me. I strolled up to Farragut, a sort of exclusive suburb of the Square. There I became friendly with a bare-headed, boyish fellow of the athletic normal type, with no suggestion in manner or looks of the homosexual. He said his home was in Atlantic City. "But I've been in Washington all winter . . . I'm supposedly attending college, but actually, I'm just having a good time . . . " We crossed over to Connecticut Avenue, turned up an alley, and stopped in a dark triangular-shaped open space beside a fence. He seemed to return my affection but later when we were back in the park he appeared listless. "Last night, and the night before that, I had similar experiences. I'm beginning to feel 'all in . . . '" He was indifferent when I left him. I did not like, in fact I abhorred, his childish and narrow-minded attitude toward persons who passed by. One fellow, a nice-looking man about thirty who appeared to be a gentlemen, passed by us. The boy said, "Oh, him! He's passed by here before," and belched to him as long as he was in sight. A strange streak in an otherwise decent boy, due probably to Atlantic City manners and to ignorance of the subject.

> **Homosexual.** *According to David Halpern (in* Hidden from History: Reclaiming the Gay & Lesbian Past, *1989), the word "homosexual" was invented by a Hungarian writer named Benkert, as a compound of the Greek* homo *(same) plus the Latin* sexus *(sex). A translator named Charles Gilbert Chaddock is credited by the* Oxford English Dictionary *with introducing, in 1892, the word "homosexuality" into the English language. It appears to be a word not much known outside the medical profession in the years when Jeb was growing up. Jeb may have had to do much reading to learn the word.*

### Tuesday, 3 July 1923

To Lafayette Square. That odious plain-clothes man, the Sneak, stopped just before he reached me, pretending to watch a speeding automobile. It was really to make me look up at him. And I did, not knowing it was he. To my horror, he *sat down beside me.* I felt dazed, so nerve-wracked that my eyes blurred with moisture. After he had strolled away down the walk, I sat fuming, thinking of that contemptible beast. Am I to be one of the ones picked out, made a scapegoat, watched and harassed? What have I done to deserve this? Why in God's name would human society want its morals to be watched over by a creature with a soiled hat and a cheap coat?

It took me an instant to realize that the youth striding blithely in my direction under dark trees was Randall Hare. I cried out, "Randall!" He said, "Well, it isn't all *that* good to see me, is it?" He sat down, attired in white flannels and a white sweater. The Sneak strolled back and forth in front of us. Several times I almost looked that fool in the face, but there would have been no benefit to it. Randall told me that since he saw me last he has become employed as an aide to a Foreign Service diplomat. He confided, "I spent today riding with the diplomat and *five* girls." No wonder he acted so self-assured! And imagine *me* in such circumstances! Impossible!

### Thursday, 5 July 1923

There came a bold knock at the door and it was Randall. He was nicely dressed, "collegiate" style—tweed topcoat, gray hat, blue-striped bow tie. But how shallow he is, how fond of pretensions! He suggested we go to a show, so we went out to see Charlie Chaplin in *The Pilgrim*. I laughed until my body ached, though in my silent way, when Charlie sat at the table trying to carve a sauce-covered derby hat that had been placed over the pudding by the kid. After, Randall and I decided to walk down to Potomac Park. He said he usually accompanies a girl home. I don't like his interest in girls. The "manly love of comrades" is nobler and sweeter and ought to be sufficient.

Hundreds of automobiles were on the speedway, their occupants seeking the nighttime coolness of the river breezes. Lights along Highway Bridge cast reflections like columns of gold across the dark water. Across the river, the brilliant lights of Arlington Beach extended along the shore, surmounted by whirling lights of the airplane merry-go-round, like the jeweled skirts of a dancer billowing out, then gradually gathering in and settling. Suddenly lightning flashed ominously. The river billowed up. Randall and I hastened under dark trees in the face of the dust-scented wind, not knowing where to go. Then came the happy thought of George Washington University. We reached the buildings as the rain poured down in torrents. Taking shelter in the vestibule between two doorways, we made ourselves quite contented.

I walked home rather happily and settled into my leather-seated rocker and read in "Calamus"—the heart of *Leaves of Grass*. What a noble, lovable man old Walt was! And he was a Government clerk too, like myself. Often, I yearn toward Walt as toward a father, look up at his picture, then close my eyes and feel him beside me, rugged and strong with his gentle hands caressing and comforting me.

*Wednesday, 18 July 1923*

Dad called me at the office and invited me out to lunch. When we met outside Child's, who should be loitering there but the Sneak of Lafayette Square. Oh, *he* knew me! His few words—his insinuating looks at Dad! What in God's name must Dad have thought when that hideous plain-clothes man insinuated himself between us? Dad drew back, a dignified gentleman. The creature said, "You keep an eye on this fine young man." Cheap checkered suit, ugly brown tie! Mean, insinuating smile!

*Saturday, 21 July 1923*

Morbid fear and imaginings since Dad and I saw the Sneak. After that horrible occurrence I have stayed home in black despair. Finally I crept out tonight, obsessively driven to the Square. Crouched on dark benches. Couldn't bear to stay.

*Thursday, 26 July 1923*

Filthy policemen! Why in hell can't the beasts leave us alone? It is such a

hideous feeling to be under the surveillance of the police, to be spied upon, followed, sneered at, by such filthy swine. The vulture that roosts over the corner at
the Avenue has set tongues wagging. I have stopped going to Reed's because of
the beast who manages it. I have stopped patronizing the imp of a newsboy from
whom I bought my *News* for months. And today the hitherto polite man in the
cigar store tossed my Fatimas on the counter and almost threw my change at me.
I am avoiding the corner as much as possible. To think that I—the innocent,
bashful, good child who once was, should now be regarded as a criminal by the
police, be spied upon and tormented.

*Sunday, 29 July 1923*

To the house. After supper a roaring storm broke. We sat peacefully in the
parlor while the rain raged outdoors. I like my family when we are not quar-
relling. I left about ten. I don't know why I did it, but I set out for the park. It
appears that I cannot be satisfied without going every night. But I am under this
horrible inner necessity of being cautious and hiding my face.

*Monday, 30 July 1923*

For the first time in two months I wore my felt hat. It helped me to feel
slightly disguised for "cruising" in the park. But I lay low. Then I ran into a swin-
ish policeman, and after that I never left the outer circle of walks. After hiding my
face at the approach of every passerby, I left early. I knew I shouldn't be in the
Square, but when I am not there I feel I am missing something. I am tired to
death of creeping and sneaking, of lurking in shadows and hiding my face. Why
can't they take the matter for granted and leave us alone? It goes on quite the
same anyway—except that we are made into miserable, furtive, persecuted
creatures.

*Wednesday, 8 August 1923*

Who could have imagined what this day would bring me? Harding's funeral
procession started predictably enough—rows of brown-clad soldiers afoot and on
horseback . . . then gleaming sailors, youthful and clean . . . lines of marines . . .
automobiles filled with politicians. Woodrow Wilson tottered forward with a
grave expression, looking terribly old. Union veterans trudged by, and one lone,
gray-clad Confederate veteran. Then, as the silent onlookers removed their hats
and the horse-drawn caisson bearing Harding's coffin came abreast, I heard,
"Alexander!" Someone waved to get my attention, not close by. I saw C. C.
Dasham. He smiled his dazzling smile. A group of fellows were with him, making a path through the bystanders away from the Avenue, apparently having seen

enough of Harding's funeral procession. Dasham pressed through the crowd behind them. He didn't look back. But he had seen me, felt like calling out my name.

After a moment of emotion-laden paralysis I decided to follow. A policeman on horseback clattered up to tell me to keep back, that I must not step into the Avenue. Foreign diplomats passed by in gaudy regalia, engaged in conversation with bursts of laughter. American Legion . . . Jewish Welfare Board . . . Boy Scouts . . . women. At the tail of the procession came black people's organizations, rows of solemn negroes. Then the crowd surged toward the Capitol to view the body. I hurried toward F Street, hoping—but not expecting—to see Dasham, and not seeing him.

*Monday, 13 August 1923*

At night I thought I saw Dasham turning into the south walk of Lafayette Square and rushed around that way so as to meet him. But there was no sign of him, and I knew I must have seen someone else; I must have been imagining that I had seen him. I hurried this way and that, toured the whole park and hastened downtown on the hope that I might chance upon him. It seemed almost too much to bear. I roamed or sat, eating out my heart with despair. The regal moon shed her silver light in vain—all wasted. I could have lain in my bed, holding my dearest in my arms. I wanted no one else; there was no one who could take his place.

*Monday, 10 September 1923*

For the first time in a month I went to the Square. I sat down by a well-dressed youth. But he was haggard, tubercular-looking in fact, and therefore unattractive. Still, we talked for some time, chiefly of New York, where he spent last winter. He asked if I had ever gone out Riverside Drive—the additional proof I needed that it was the Lafayette Park of New York. I was sleepy and, allowing myself to show it, I made a graceful departure to "go to bed early."

*Monday, 17 September 1923*

Today I received a postcard from my W&L classmate, Lansing Tower—from Rio de Janeiro. It took a while to decipher the hasty scrawl:

> Mark up another one, former companion mine. Took in a restaurant, a bottle of Madeira, the police station and a headache. Lansing

Word from faraway Brazil! My own horizon seemed broadened; I felt exhilarated.

*Sunday, 18 November 1923*

Stayed home in the evening, according to my fortunately-acquired habit. I finished the revision of my short story, *In a Rut*—typed it and prepared a cover letter. In the morning I shall mail the story into the contest being held by the *News*. To bed with wild ideas that they would publish my story.

*Wednesday, 21 November 1923*

It actually happened! I have won the $100 first prize in the *News'* short story contest. Like a happy dream my sensations were when Milton MacKaye, the short story editor, came to the office and stutteringly informed me, asking me to come to the office to approve changes in the wording of my story. We jumped into his taxi and went to the Y for me to get my photograph for publication. Then to the *News* office. I was in a state of dizzy delirium, though I think outwardly calm. We went to the big editorial room on the third floor where he introduced me to Leonard Hall (whose writing in the *News* has been the chief reason I read the paper), and to the editor, a keen-eyed man with a cigar screwed into the side of his big face. Most of the changes were deletions of adjectives, which I had used pretty freely. I agreed to most changes but refused to the cutting (I don't know why) of "and lit a cigarette."

*Friday, 23 November 1923*

I took the *News* up to my room and could hardly switch on the light before sitting on the edge of the bed to read "In a Rut" in print. I read the story over and over, savoring the almost unbelievable knowledge that people unknown to me whom I would never meet or know were following the plot that had come from the privacy of my inner mind, and enjoying the theme and the words and perhaps later thinking about what they had read. Indescribable elation!

*Thursday, 13 December 1923*

Surprised when Randall Hare called (talk about fair-weather friends). "I saw your story in the *News*. Enjoyed it!" I said, "Thank you, Randall. Did you read it?" "Of course I did. How *are* you?" And so on. Eventually, the melodious voice, "I want you to take one of the girls in the office to a dance Saturday night. We have fun—food and wine—important people—" I invented a previous engagement, but foolishly allowed him to believe that I might be available some night for an informal dance or party. He insisted that I write down his telephone number. "You know, if you want me for anything." Yes, I knew.

*Tuesday, 24 December 1923*

Christmas Eve. Agonizingly lonely tonight. I thought I would try to write something in here to get rid of the blackness that weighs me down. To go on thus in life, a wretched outcast, without a soul to companion mine along the ways of life; to love those who are incapable of returning my love; to long for companionship and yet realize that I should be awkward, a mere imitation of my real self; to be unable to express the noble, fantastic thoughts that are mine; to worship scores and not be worshipped by one; to have a flaming spirit that defies the universe—sun, moon, and stars, and a stammering, timid body and a hypersensitive self that is agitated by the slightest trifle; to have ambition that overtops the skies and a will so weak that it cannot make me do trifling tasks; to be regarded with amusement and contempt that are magnified by morbid imaginings into a conspiracy against my happiness; to be tied down to one spot on the globe when I yearn to sweep across oceans, to sail rivers, to seek love and the passionate thrills of life—to be such as I am, a gnat feebly stretching its wings in the awful waste of eternity—is it any wonder that I am miserable?

*Monday, 31 December 1923*

The tumult dies, as meaningless as when it began. First I saw the American premiere of Sutton Vane's *Outward Bound* at the Belasco. Then I became a wandering observer of the horn-blowing and confetti-throwing. The one night of all the year most dedicated to a good time, to conviviality, good fellowship! This double curse—why, oh why is it inflicted on me? Is it not bad enough that I must be what I am, without this shyness that isolates me? And what can I do? There is only hope—hope that some influence will turn my life in a direction less dark. A measureless ocean of love is dammed up within me and I have no way of letting it out.

Near Thirteenth and the Avenue I passed by Randall. Our eyes met but with no sign of recognition from either. Randall even drew his hand closer in as though to prevent his glove from touching mine as we passed. After midnight I crept through deserted Lafayette Square. There I saw Randall again. He was seated on the bench next the one where first we met. What must my loneliness have been, that I should impulsively sit down beside him? Of course I could expect no understanding there. Words, words, words! His only pauses were for remarks on my quietness. And a theatrical comment, "You're not on the surface. You're deep. You're fathomless." And then accounts of his experiences. The lucky fool! Why should he be able to pick up whatever he wants—while I—hell, I don't think Randall would have believed me if I had told him that I haven't had an experience in *four months*. ("Like ships that pass in the night," I remember the fellow expressed it, during the experience. A fine chap.) Several times I thought I would try to tell Randall some of the things that weighed on my mind. But I didn't—partly because that egotistical idiot could not understand (what, indeed, does he know of suffering, superficial fool!) and partly because he didn't give me a chance. We separated. And here's 1924. Hell, what's the use.


# 1924


*Wednesday, 2 January 1924*

Nasty, abominable day of rain, sleet, and wind. Slept deeply until the wind blew a shoe brush off the windowsill with a clatter. That woke me, so I got up and closed the windows. A long day at the office, settling rebelliously into the old routine. The day seemed a week long before it finally died. I walked in the rain up to the university, only to find the door locked, the windows dark, and to remember that classes were to start the 3d instead of the 2d. Sleek and well-groomed, I sloshed out into the rain for my rendezvous with Randall.

The Franklin Square Hotel—what memories! Friday nights with the hideous grocery store looming on the morrow, passing the dimmed lamps of Franklin Square and the bright windows of the hotel, wishing myself in a room there with a certain little blond god of long ago. The days of innocence.

And then the summer of 1921; a June night when I was followed from Lafayette by that impossibly tall, leathery-looking brute of a marine officer; going to the Royal Café, a cheap cabaret on Ninth Street; the spirit of adventure, of don't-give-a-damn, of seeking for experience, of raw life. Going with him to the Franklin Square Hotel for the night; he under a false name—I, likewise. All this swam in my mind as I approached the hotel. Randall said for me to "hurry right up." He follows his diplomat to France in two weeks, to live for three glorious years in Paris. What luck Randall has! He was in room 518. He received me in negligée, that is, pajamas and dressing gown, and apologized for it, though I knew what it meant.


*Saturday, 5 January 1924*

The wind shrieked around the building; the windows rattled as though they would break. I could even see white-caps on the Potomac. When I went outside, the wind seemed to have come from the North Pole. I chased around town, half-frozen, trying to find an *American Mercury*, but the newsstands were out. Then I came to Brentano's and found a window full of them.

I stayed in my cozy room tonight. First I copied out in typewriting Rupert Brooke's "He Wonders Whether to Praise or Blame Her," without a title, signature or anything except quotation marks, and sealed it and addressed it to Randall. "Dear fool, pity the fool who thought you clever . . . " I want him to know that *I* am dropping *him*—that he did not discard me. I won't have him thinking of me as a pathetic fool, pitying me. No! Then spent the rest of the evening reading in the *Mercury,* while outside the mercury dropped. The magazine is beautifully gotten up and printed, with a thick cover of a rich green. A clever article, "Aesthete: Model 1924," by Ernest Boyd, knocked pretty hard the half-baked *Dial* crew, Gilbert Seldes and his like—but why drag in Marcel Proust?

**American Mercury:** *Until 1933 the* American Mercury *was the vehicle for the sharp-tongued influence of H. L. Mencken (1880–1956) on American letters. In later years the magazine went on to have a curious history, being purchased by increasingly conservative publishers until finally, by the time it ceased publication in 1980 (under the name* Mercury), *it had become a white supremist rag.*

**Dial.** *The editors of this little magazine had an extraordinary grasp of new directions in twentieth-century letters and published work by T. S. Eliot, Ezra Pound, D. H. Lawrence, William Butler Yeats, e. e. cummings, Gertrude Stein, and most other major emerging writers of the time. Though Jeb calls the* Dial *crew "half-baked" here, he seems under ordinary circumstances to have respected the magazine. He collected each issue, and in November of 1922—the year when the appearance in* Dial *of "The Waste Land" made T. S. Eliot famous—Jeb submitted to* Dial, *without luck, a rare short story that he had composed for his writing class at George Washington University.*

### Saturday, 12 January 1924

A great commotion at the office. We learned that Bill Prentiss, the ruddy jolly chap whose room adjoins ours, is married and has been since September, 1922. It seems that several matters caused them to keep it a secret. He was a Catholic and she was not, and then too, they were not in a position to go to housekeeping. In addition, she was afraid of losing her job at the Veterans' Bureau if she announced that she was married. I suspect that Prentiss was satisfied, too, to postpone the "ragging" that the announcement would direct to him at the office. But he will get it now. The girls are planning to decorate his desk and have a gay time of it.

Miss Contadeluci said he told her as soon as it happened. He wished her not to speak of it, and often talked with her about their troubles. He is a fine fellow and I am sorry to see him settle down into the shackles and the inevitable disillusionment of married life. Simple chap, though, so I suppose it makes little difference.

> **Gay.** *The reader may note that "gay" is never used with its current meaning in Jeb's diaries. How did this word come to be a designation for homosexuality? There appears to be an ambiguous use of the term "gay" as early as 1889 by a London prostitute to refer to male homosexual and female prostitutes (see* Wicked Words *[1989], by Hugh Rawson), but the prostitute might have meant that this group of people led a freewheeling life. One contemporary researcher suggests that "gay" as a designation for homosexuality has its roots in the name of the goddess Gaia. However, if "gay" had ancient roots, one would have expected Jeb's contemporaries to know and use the word with this meaning.*
>
> *Jeb frequently used the word to mean "blithe, carefree, and merry." During the thirties, he increasingly also used "gay" as a term to describe a happy, uninhibited state acquired through drinking alcoholic beverages. Meanwhile, in the films and popular culture of Jeb's era, most allusions to homosexual men were to men such as two characters who appear later in the diaries, blithely "gay" Isador Pearson and boisterously "gay" Junior Whorley. It appears that during the middle years of the twentieth century, the presentation of them as "gay" in film and popular culture engendered among homosexual men a new and ironic appropriation of a word that pertained to the heterosexual world's clichéd perception of homosexuality.*

### Sunday, 13 January 1924

At night to Poli's—the American debut of Mistinguett of the Casino de Paris, in a musical play called *Innocent Eyes*. She was a luscious exotic creature, gorgeous and fascinating. She sang, acted, and danced, but most of the time she was merely lovely. The "million-dollar legs" were guarded from view except at rare times. There were some tableaus, quite the finest I have ever seen. Radiant maidens were nude from the waist up, revealing full round breasts with little nipples in the middle. Through my opera glasses I could see plainly and was rather surprised that the sight gave me such a pleasurable feeling. I am not, then, entirely one-sided.

> **Mistinguett of Paris** *(1873–1956). After many years in obscure French music halls, she made her Paris debut in 1907 and for years thereafter was considered a great European revue star. For a time Maurice Chevalier was her partner and lover.*

### Wednesday, 16 January 1924

Prentiss back, fresh cheeks, dark under eyes, gay as usual. He was showered with rice. His desk was loaded with rice, was decorated with streamers of bright paper. An enormous red Christmas ball hung overhead; signs on the wall:

HE WAS SUCH A NICE FELLOW, TOO
. . . and . . . JUST MARRIED—NO!

At night I went to the premiere of Elsie Ferguson's new play, *The Moon Flower*. The theatre was packed. Ferguson was a bewitching creature with a crown of red-gold hair. Sydney Blackmer played excellently the role of the law student. I could have enjoyed every minute of it had it not been for my neighbors—women. Between the acts they talked in loud, piercing tones—*gabble, gabble, gabble,* until I became nerve-wracked. I was not angry, merely filled with scorn and disgust. One of them behind me was laughing almost hysterically. I turned around and stared at her, and she ceased laughing. She was looking at me or I suppose it was another slimy beast's wit that amused her. The creature beside me said something like, "Looks too effeminate. He looks like a sick calf." I don't know whether she was discussing me or Sydney Blackmer, who also seemed to come under her displeasure.

Much of my enjoyment of the evening was marred. How I hate women! I was, mentally, utterly nauseated by that suffocating atmosphere of female nastiness. I almost stepped on the two rather harmless women between me and the aisle in my haste to escape. Then, out on the streets, the old trouble. I was seized with that hideous feeling that every person I passed was inwardly mocking me, saying, *There goes a fairy,* or something worse. It started from the tiniest of things—a look, a gesture—in fact I don't know how it started. I know that I walked this way and that, always trying to get away from those cruel faces and finding them everywhere. It was one of the worst of such experiences I have ever had. There seems to be no way to end it. This tyrannical self-consciousness seems inescapable, and then the real cause, that is of course congenital and entirely inescapable.

*Tuesday, 22 January 1924*

Suddenly made up my mind to go see *The Marionette Man*. A misprint in the program caused merriment in the audience. The third act, according to the program, took place, "The same night, some days later . . . " Enjoyed myself, but the eternal women—damn them. Beside me was a country-looking creature, chewing raisins and dashing the seeds on the floor, boldly scratching her groin, leaning on the arm rest the whole time, forcing me to the other side of the chair. How I detest vulgarity in a woman.

Walked home filled with vivid imaginings of companionship. I have created a friend, my dream boy, Vincent Eric Orville. He is my companion during solitary walks, evenings here in my room alone, inner imaginings—my beauteous, light-hearted love. He is *Mercury in Repose* with the addition of soft brown hair and wide, filmy green eyes. His life is as real—though it takes place entirely in my imagination—as that of any person I actually see from day to day.

### Monday, 4 February 1924

Saddened by the death of Woodrow Wilson, I wore a black tie. At the office I found that nearly everybody else wore black—the women black dresses and the men black ties. That they should all separately decide to wear black seemed to me a sign of sincere regard for the memory of Woodrow Wilson. Flags everywhere. Sand spread on the icy Avenue, in preparation for the parade.

### Wednesday, 6 February 1924

Tonight Henry provided me with a cruel reminder of the world's attitude toward us unfortunates who live in this half-world of thwarted desire and unreturned love, of jeers and whispered comments and meaning glances, of eternal seeking and never finding. He stopped by and, sitting on my bed chatting, he blurted out, "There was one fellow down in the lobby ought t'have been taken out and frailed hell out of—*a damn fairy!* Down in the lobby of the Y.M.C.A.!" I sat calm, though seething within, and desired to ask what the fellow had done. But I didn't dare. I was afraid that the remarkable self-control I have developed might desert me and my face tell tales. I wondered for a hellish moment if Henry knew that I was one of those he contemptuously speaks of as "fairies," and if he was saying that for my benefit. A moment later he rose to go and gave me an affectionate good-night. I don't believe he suspects. It shows how little Henry's knowledge comes from observation and understanding, and how much from hearsay and the derisive chatter of his companions. To bed in an agony of futile revolt.

> **Frailed.** *The word derives from the Middle English word* fraiel, *or "whip." Henry uses this regionalism, which was not uncommon in that era, to say that the fellow in the lobby should have been beaten.*

### Tuesday, 4 March 1924

Drawing class was in a hilarious mood, trying to establish Venus de Milo with proper lighting and position for drawing. One student, named Hayward, sat down beside me. Professor Bibb strolled over. He took me into the front room with the advanced drawing classes and set me to work on a bust of George Washington. Once before Hayward was sitting close to me. Professor Bibb prevailed on him to move—"I am sure if you put your chair thus, please, Mr.

Hayward, you will find a better view of the model . . . " A wise old bird, but wise for nothing in this case.

*Thursday, 6 March 1924*

Bibb spent much of the class praising the drawing being executed by that precocious, unsmiling boy, Max Stone. We had as our model a youth with sensuous lips, yellow hair in curly waves, and a nose as straight as a god's. The model was so lovely that it was an inspiration to draw him. I said as much to Max Stone. After class he invited me to walk home with him.

He is eighteen; has small keen eyes and a tough-looking nose; pale hair cut short, light eyebrows; not bad looking, although not my style. He lives with his aunt near Scott Circle. His basement room is entered by outdoor stairs descending behind the aunt's house. And what a sophisticated boy he is—he has decorated his room with pillows, a silken bed cover, an oriental atmosphere, drawing table, a vase of gorgeous pink roses, and drawings and books about art piled all about. He briefly attended Wisconsin Military Academy and showed me pictures of handsome lads in uniform that were very good to look upon.

My interest, aroused first tonight during class in drawing our curly-haired model, followed by the excitement aroused by conversations with Max Stone, both inclined me strongly to want to work seriously as an artist. When I got home I spent about two hours completing my picture begun in class. I used blues, lavenders, yellows, and golds. My painting pleases me, because it reminds me of my green-eyed Vincent Eric Orville, my dream boy.

*Wednesday, 4 July 1924*

Since 5 June I have worn a hat just twice, one day that was raining, and last Saturday night when I went adventuring in the parks. Going hatless is giving me a healthy tan, helping (I hope) my hair, and, by the fact that it renders me somewhat conspicuous, is developing that self-confidence that I have begun to acquire since I began trying to follow young Max Stone's advice—"You must be brazen." About two months ago I had a premonition that a new influence was coming into my life, and that influence was keen-eyed young Max Stone. He has taught me much, given me friendship (even love), introduced me to new acquaintances (and friends)—in fact, has helped me escape from the dark cell of my former loneliness. He has been a true friend indeed.

Strolled bareheaded through the balmy night to visit Max in his "sunken villa"—his basement room in his aunt's house. He was expecting another visitor. "I'm going to introduce you to a sweet thing from Boston . . . " There came a knock on Max's door, and Tommy Freskin entered, well dressed in bow tie and tweed suit. He said, "I'm Max's 'buddy,'" and shook my hand warmly.

The three of us went out into the delicious summer night for dinner at Café Louise, a quiet basement place. Infinitely pleasant, to dine with comrades! Tommy is devilishly clever. After the meal we took a walk up to Dupont Circle. Streets almost deserted—a remarkably dull Fourth, with few flags out. A delicious breeze was blowing, rustling the tree tops. It was a beauteous night, but Max and Tommy were boisterous and I felt uncomfortable. Tommy acted in a kiddish romping way that I did not like at all. All that sort of thing ought to be kept behind doors.

### Sunday, 24 August 1924

Tonight in Max's room, idling while he dashed about in his vivacious way straightening his room, putting up pictures and rearranging them, cleaning out the closet, and so on. Returning home I saw from the streetcar a lovely youth in Farragut Square. Not the first time I have been fooled by the old Square! I got off the car and walked back. He wasn't what he had seemed. Certain ways he had, indicative of lack of breeding, were distasteful to me. Then I saw a policeman gazing at me. I started toward the street and lo! there were three more of the swine who stared and discussed me. Tommy Freskin strolled by. He saw me, but I didn't speak because he was not alone. A moment later, along came Mr. and Mrs. Martin, the dull, upright parents of Eunice. They saw me there. The damned place is becoming accursed. But I walked on in slow and dignified way with head in the air, and was not really bothered more than a trifle. Different from last year, when I hid my face and slunk in the shadows. But now—to hell with them all! I do as I please and shall and will for the rest of my life!

### Sunday, 21 September 1924

Rain most of the day, but the Holy Name Society paraded nonetheless, 75,000 strong. I missed it, however, spending a quiet day out at the house. Mama behaved herself and was even rather sweet and lovable. A delicious dinner of boiled smoked tongue and kale. After dinner Henry and Eunice went off in Henry's high-powered Stutz to a tea dance. Dad drove me downtown. We stopped at the *Times* building to watch the baseball returns on the electric scoreboard. Washington is getting nearer and nearer to winning the pennant and bringing the World's Series here, and everybody is baseball-crazy. Dad and I stood in the crowd of hundreds in the drizzling rain for two or three hours.

*Tuesday, 23 September 1924*

In the elevator while Max and I were going down from my room, I over-heard a mean nasty remark from that brazen blond beast which used to work at the Civil Service Commission. It upset my mental equilibrium, throwing me down in the depths. I am sure Max heard too, for as we set out for dinner through the equinoctial rains he said, "Struggle, boy, against that morbid state of mind that you feel coming on." I struggled and fought it off to some extent. Max was in good form, raw, smart, ironic. Our favorite waitress, Catherine, served us a good meal. We went back to my room and had one of our long, intimate, com-radely conversations about love and friendship among homosexual and other people, about the joys of reading and owning books, and other subjects. Max is my cherished friend. Not that we are in love—I don't mean that at all. I mean that we have established a real friendship based on mutual interests and common qualities.

*Thursday, 6 November 1924*

Drawing class was cheerful. I dashed right into my drawing, got interested, and worked steadily. Maureen Eden and Kate Harrison and Donald Stein were there—three who arouse and interest me. Kate and Donald are very affectionate. I like the caressing way she pronounces his name, as though it were spelled "Doddled," with a touch of the "d" sound. Maureen sat by me and occasionally touched my arm with hers. She had on a new coat, reddish-brown, and was look-ing sweet and pretty, realizing it, too. She chatted and at the end of the hour gave me some chocolate. I told Max afterward, "I wouldn't walk off with her, even though I know she wants me to. Why should I pretend to an attitude that is not natural to me?"

# 1925

*Wednesday, 14 January 1925*

Meeting Max for dinner I found him with his tall, gangly German friend Hans Vermehren. Hans had papers spread over the tablecloth, and was drawing maps and spilling coffee and spreading cigarette ashes into the butter. He wanted to talk about the unpleasant goings on in Germany. He said that the future was going to be identical for Germany and Italy—that is, both countries would "lose their national character" under the present political developments. Later we got to discussing the recent onslaught on alleged intolerable indecency in the theatres, and the courageous attitude of Kenneth McGowan in refusing to withdraw O'Neill's *Desire Under the Elms*. Defiance thrills me with admiration—that is, usually. It depends on who, what, and why.

### Sunday, 18 January 1925

To Scott Circle and down the basement steps under the aunt's house. I found long-legged Hans Vermehren lying face down among Max's pillows. I said, "What's the matter?" Max looked solemn. "A dreadful thing has happened. Trotsky reigns supreme in the USSR." Hans rolled over. "No, no!" Max said, "All right, it must be Stalin." Hans said, "You can laugh." "I'm as concerned as you are, Hansie. I'm trying to help you endure your sufferings."

He persuaded Hans to put on his overcoat, and we left for dinner. Hans in his overwrought way didn't enjoy the evening. Max leaned back in his chair and lit a cigarette. He was wearing the worn black sweater of which he is so fond. His hands, emerging from the dark cuffs, were ivory-white, the knuckles alabaster and bony. He said, "I'd solve Europe's problems for you, Hansie, but the difficulty is, I'm too young."

> **Trotsky and Stalin.** *The reference here is to the fact that Leon Trotsky had been ousted from the Soviet War Council. Hans understands the implications of this event, and indeed, by 1929 Joseph Stalin had succeeded in banishing Trotsky from Russia. Trotsky was murdered in 1940 in Mexico City, probably by Stalinist agents.*

### Monday, 23 February 1925

At dinner Max said that Tommy Freskin took the train down from Boston Friday night and spent the weekend. I said, "And didn't even stop by my room!" Max said, "We came up twice to see you, but found you not in both times." I retorted, "I was in Friday night—as well as part of Saturday afternoon and all of Saturday evening, staying up until two o'clock."

I don't really mind. I have cooled toward Tommy. I sent him as a birthday present Carl Van Vechten's book, *The Blind Bow-Boy*. I liked it—for example the nobleman who has inscribed upon his crest, *A thing of beauty is a boy forever*. Oscarish. But Tommy wrote me back a note in which he thanked me in the briefest way. I told Max, "He signed himself, 'Respectfully, T. Freskin.' Not even 'sincerely,' or 'faithfully,' but 'respectfully'!" Max answered, "Tommy wrote me, asking how to reply to your gift. I wrote back and told him he had to be distant, to keep you from becoming attached." I said, "I wasn't interested in Tommy in that way." Max said, "That isn't what I meant." I felt bitter throughout the rest of the meal.

*Carl Van Vechten* (1880-1966). *American novelist; music and drama critic. In his satirical, comedic works Van Vechten usually wrote about the jazz-age world of New York City.*

### Wednesday, 25 February 1925

Hans Vermehren has found a room at the Y, and tonight we walked together to join Max for dinner. Max treated me as a child to be told stories and lectured to. "There is no place for you, Jeb, in this merciless world." He talked in a loud voice, so that Hans and everyone else in the room could know what a smart youth he was. He gets along with people best who permit him to dominate them. Max and Hans seemed to have little secret understandings, while I was the tolerated outsider. "What do you think, Hansie? Is not Jeb a sensitive plant, shrinking at the slightest breath, or a mere touch?" Max even made fun of my opinions, something we had never done with each other, always exercising a mutual tolerance. He made sarcastic references to drawing-room anarchism. But I have an individuality of my own—I am damned glad to say—and I am not going to let some young pup treat me as a pair of ears to drink in his outpourings. I said nothing much during the meal but was filled with rebellion inside; proud and scornful.

### Thursday, 26 February 1925

To charcoal class. I was in a bad humor and got into the sort of condition in which I cannot draw. I made savage marks, then sat and tapped with my charcoal on the paper. When I returned to the Y some animals in the lobby made comments about my color-box and painting board, and laughed stupidly. I came into my room, slammed the door, threw myself on the bed, wept. I have tried to make a place for myself in this alien world. The animals, vile beasts! Lying there, I felt that life was hardly worth living. After all, Max is the only friend I have, and if I lose him, what am I going to do? I beat against a stone wall with my fists but there is no way out. To right and left only the stone wall. And behind me there is no way to return to the land of childhood and contentment.

### Wednesday, 4 March 1925

Saw Hans standing outside the Y, wiping his nose with a blue handkerchief. I invited him to accompany me down to the Avenue for the inauguration of that scared rabbit, Calvin Coolidge.

Plenty of flags, but only thin strings of people standing along the curb. Coolidge looked solemn and sour; Mrs. Coolidge smiling and vivacious. Hans had never attended an inauguration, and here his first one was as unimpressive as the character of Coolidge himself. I found myself apologizing, trying to atone for the lack of excitement by describing the tumultuously enthusiastic inaugurals of Woodrow Wilson. When the ceremony finally started, every word of Coolidge's dull, pompous address came out clear and loud through the amplifiers. Then Hans and I hurried around to the Avenue with the crowd to see the parade pass by. We missed the first female governor, Mrs. Ross of Wyoming. Gifford Pinchot, a picturesque figure on horseback, smiling and waving his hat, aroused more applause and enthusiasm than anybody else. It was all over by mid-afternoon. We walked slowly through the swarms toward home. Men were struggling in long lines to get into the public toilet at Pulaski Park. Well, that is a trivial matter to mention in my diary.

> **Gifford Pinchot** (1865–1946). A tall, lithe, intense man of action, he was at one time governor of Pennsylvania, but is best known as a conservationist and an advocate of public management of forest lands.

### Sunday, 8 March 1925

I haven't seen Max in days. We seem to get along better when we see less of one another. He taunts me with having gotten into a rut, with no hope of the literary fulfillment that always seemed to lie ahead of me. Feeling lonely, missing Max, this afternoon I got out past diaries, especially 1920, and relived those days. Youth was in its full blush then—an eager joy in life! And yet that was the year when Randall Hare initiated me into the cursed business of homosexuality, that dark cloud that has brought me to my present state. Still, I was bound to come to it sooner or later.

I walked around the Tidal Basin and up the river in the cold sunshine. The sight of the bathing beach—soon to be destroyed by an imbecile Congress—roused melancholy regrets. Never again shall I swim joyously in the intoxicating open spaces of the Basin, never again return with delicious weariness across the culvert, and gaze at the Lincoln Memorial rising like a Greek temple above the trees.

If only I had my ideal comrade, my beautiful, affectionate, imaginary Vincent Eric Orville, my dream boy. Dreams, dreams—my dream boy is more real to me than dozens of actual persons I see every day. I know what he thinks, does, is; all his opinions, his life history, and scores of times have I lived, entirely in my imagination, through our meeting in Washington and the days following it.

### Saturday, 14 March 1925

I got off work early to take Hans to the Senate. He wanted to hear the speeches and watch the vote. Our time was wasted—we sat on the hard marble stairway for forty-five minutes, but the only people let up to the galleries were the people with "pull." At night, still intent on educating Hans, I escorted him through the blustery night to the Auditorium to hear the debate on capitol punishment between Clarence Darrow, the celebrated Loeb-Leopold lawyer, and ex-Senator Stanley of Kentucky. We were disappointed again. About 10,000 people were struggling in the lobby. We could not possibly get in. In the surging crowd Hans allowed the crowd to press him against me. People on all sides shoved us toward the entrance. At last we reached the doors, burst through, and hastened away, the wind yelling like a demon, the night getting colder.

> *Loeb-Leopold. Nathan Leopold and Richard Loeb, both nineteen years old, Jewish, intellectual, and gay, beat fourteen-year-old Bobby Franks to death in a famous "thrill killing" case of 1924. Their lawyer, Clarence Darrow, offered a defense unique at the time: emotional illness. He used their homosexuality as evidence of insanity. The two were sentenced to life imprisonment instead of being executed.*

### Monday, 16 March 1925

On our way to breakfast Hans and I saw forsythia in full bloom. Spring is on its way. We went into town and both bought new clothes. I bought a slip-on sport sweater of a checkered design in buff and sky-blue, and a pair of light tan shoes. Hans bought one of the new broad-brimmed straw hats with a blue and gray striped band, and also a black leather belt with a bright blue stripe running around the center of it. Men's clothes this spring have brighter colors than in many years. I told Hans, "Men have been dressing like moles and bats long enough." We wore our new things away. Feeling pretty good these days. Morbidity, "the Cloud," is not troubling me—I mean that torturing self-consciousness on the street.

### Wednesday, 22 April 1925

I got off work early to meet Hans so we could attend the opening of the baseball season. We sat in the bleachers facing the sun and kept our hats off to get sunburned. Coolidge and his wife, she in a bright brick-red coat, arrived and the crowd rose to its feet. I got up reluctantly, not desiring to show respect to that damned nincompoop. The game was too one-sided to be interesting, though Hans enjoyed it. We won 10–1. I enjoyed the contact with attractive youths in the crowds and on the car coming back.

*Sunday, 3 May 1925*

Max called and asked Hans and me to come over to see the flowers that he and Tommy Freskin got on their picnic at Great Falls. Tommy had been with him all weekend, having ridden down to Washington on the excursion. Max appeared happy and contented, and said that Tommy was "like a faun in the woods among the flowers" and enjoyed himself hugely.

Later in my room, Hans began winding the Victrola. Something snapped loudly inside. The disk gave a violent spin that threw the record several inches into the air; then it stopped and would not turn again. Hans fiddled with it unsuccessfully. "Only a Victrola belonging to you would do such a thing. Now we have no music." I read aloud to him from Norman Douglas' *Fountains in the Sand* while he dressed and got ready to leave for his acting class. When I went out later for a milkshake, in the store I saw Isador Pearson seated alone and looking very lonely, with his slick black hair, his Maude Adams eyes, and his wide hands. I have more than once caught myself pitying Isador because he was so alone and ineffectual. Then I have realized that I am just like him in that way (except I have so many interests), and have wondered if Max perhaps pities me and regards me as he does Isador.

Walking out of the store I saw a handsome boy and girl. Both were bare-headed and self-assured, swinging along the walk beneath the rain-laden trees. The girl looked at me calmly and impersonally, as she might have glanced at a lamp-post, and said audibly, "*That's* a fairy . . . " If I weren't so sensitive. But I struggled and didn't suffer from it as I might have done.

> **Maude Adams** *(1872–1953) was an American actress of the teens and twenties. She became famous in the leading role of* Peter Pan. *She had pale, wonderfully expressive eyes, and was adorable.*

*Wednesday, 13 May 1925*

About thirty of us from our section took the morning to act in a department motion picture called *Poor Mrs. Smith.* The scenes were taken at the Seventh Street Station showing Mrs. Smith hastening through a jostling crowd to greet her sister. The director told us to "bump" her and I bumped her so hard that I nearly knocked the poor woman down.

The morning was great fun—I entered into the spirit of jollity and became almost "one of the gang." My temperament prevents me from becoming reconciled to the monotony of work, and yet after all, I get a lot of amusement out of work. I watch as the Utott languishes out of the room swaying a glass in her upraised hand to "let on" that she is going for a glass of water. The witless Green rushes from room to room. The Sweetwater makes eyes at me as I approach her desk—pretty with or without her tortoiseshell eyeglasses. The witty Contadeluci chatters with melancholy Winegardner and indulges in delicious word bouts with the strutting Kraznovski, he giving tit-for-tat in facetious repartee. The Amazon from the lower regions arrives upstairs to chat with the King, a sallow, dissipated young brunette with a mass of wiry black hair. The Amazon is the only woman I have ever been able to identify as a female invert.

*Friday, 15 May 1925*

In the evening Hans and I walked up to Max's room. Dear Hans is attempting to dress in a more American way. Except for a silk shirt with purple stripes, and a green silk knit tie, he was nicely attired and might pass for a college student. He and Max spent a long time arranging bird's-foot violets in a yellow bowl. Candles were lighted and the room looked even more bright and beautiful than usual. At the doorway as we were leaving, Max leaned over and gave me a sudden kiss. Hans bid Max a very short good night.

*Tuesday, 9 June 1925*

My last day in old D.C. for a week, for tomorrow I am taking a tour of New England grocery stores with Dad and Henry. I darned socks and Hans helped me do a thousand things that ought to have been done before.

*Friday, 12 June 1925 (Hotel Draper, Northampton, Massachusetts)*

When Dad, Henry, and I drove into Northampton about eight in the evening, we found that Smith College commencement was going on and the hotels were full. At the Draper, Dad persuaded them to let us have the parlor. They put up beds for us, then we walked out to see the town. The streets were swarming with chic young girls and alumni, and yellow and white bunting draped the lamp posts and trees. Dad decided to go to the movies. Henry and I walked on through hundreds of girls. We went by the home of Calvin Coolidge, but it was too dark to tell which was the house. All were similar, simple and modest. Then we had to tour the business section, because Henry was interested in "our" grocery store and the chain store competitors.

Returning, we found the parlor dark, and a person asleep in one of the beds. Henry said, "Is that you, Dad?" We thought we heard a woman's voice say something like "This is a woman." Henry said, "Let Dad handle it when he gets back," and went to the writing room to write Eunice a letter. I crept into the parlor to get my diary. A squeaky voice from the bed squealed, "Will you please get out of here?" I hastened out and told Henry that they had actually put a woman in our

room. We laughed over it, but then it occurred to me that it might be Dad playing a joke on us. So I went back. I heard a heavy tiptoeing behind me and Dad
threw his covers around me. He burst out laughing. He lay on the bed and
laughed and laughed. And I'll have to admit that I was taken in for fair, at first,
anyhow.

*Tuesday, 6 July 1925*

Hans and I have been enthusiastically planning Max's birthday party festivi-
ties. We put everything, including a superb selection of food and two bottles of
bootlegger's liquor, on Hans' bureau surrounding his Buddha. We then sat
smoking and gazing at the shrine, thinking that we had time to get things ready.
But when we carried the glasses into my room to set the table there, and returned
to Hans' room for the other stuff, Hans put the wrong key in the lock and it got
caught. Nothing we could do would dislodge it. We both tried to climb through
the transom, but it was too small. Hans fumed up and down the hall and began
to curse in German. We didn't want to ask for help at the desk downstairs
because they would get wise to the party and perhaps the liquor.

Isador Pearson emerged from his room wrapped in a kimono. Hans and I
were amazed to see he was wearing women's makeup. He volunteered a nail file,
and we tried it, but it did no good. Isador trotted back to his room and reappeared with a coat hanger. He crouched before the lock, tinkered with the coat
hanger, and the mischievous key fell out and the door opened. "Glory be!" We
hugged each other in our joy, and invited Isador to the party.

The table looked very attractive when we finished it. Max arrived and
appeared pleased. The party was worth all the trouble and we had a glorious time.
My most vivid memory of the occasion is of Isador in a yellow gown mixing the
drinks—grinning broadly and pouring in orange juice and lemon juice and the
bootlegger's whisky and White Rock, and shaking it up in the cocktail shaker.
Max kissed him on his rosy cheek, saying, "He's a fine-looking woman!" Isador
shook the cocktail mixer first on one side and then the other and then over his
head. Sometimes the mixture would fizz up and run out on the floor amid cries
of amused dismay. After a few drinks I felt as if floating in air. I was absurdly
happy. Isador sat on the floor with the telephone, saying he wanted to call up a
girl he knew, but Max wouldn't let him. Everyone told story after story, all very
vile, and we laughed and laughed even between stories, and at nothing.

*Sunday, 2 August 1925*

Lansing Tower was in Washington on his way from Rio de Janeiro. He is
going to hitchhike to California. We arranged to meet at the Willard Hotel.

Maybe it was the hurry I was in—anyway I went off without my tie and just happened to notice on my way out of the lobby. I hurried back to my room feeling like a fool and wondering how many people had seen me.

Rushed into the hotel and saw my old school companion Lansing reclining in an armchair, reading the *Post*. He has changed undoubtedly—has acquired a narrow moustache under that sharp nose of his, his wispy hair is parted neatly on the side, and he wears eyeglasses to read. He looked suntanned and well. Over breakfast he talked so vividly of his days in Rio de Janeiro that I got a real "kick" out of the occurrences. His account of watching cargo to keep the thieving stevedores from robbing the cases was a fine piece of realistic narrative. Damn! I wish I could go on such a trip. But imagine me bossing around brutes like that!

But the wanderlust stirs again. Think of hiking to California! What a glorious adventure that would be, were I not handicapped by my nature, aside from my being tied down to a permanent good job. When I parted from Lansing, wishing him luck with a strong handshake, I walked home filled with dreams. Of course I was accompanied by Vincent Eric Orville, my beauteous blend of green-eyed C. C. Dasham and the statue of *Mercury in Repose* at the Corcoran Gallery.

At night while Hans studied his lines for his acting class I sat down and read, marveling and inspired, in the unpublished manuscript Lansing Tower left with me. It is sure to be published. How could a young man of Lansing's age write such a true and stirring book? Perhaps I shall overtake you yet, Lansing. I am not precocious like you, but I am slowly maturing and in a few years my novel will appear and will startle the world. Just wait!

*Sunday, 1 November 1925*

To the house. I saw for the first time Henry and Eunice's baby. Much is being made of little "Daisy," and quite properly so. At twilight I walked down to the drugstore to purchase cigarettes. When I got back Henry and Eunice were in the den subduedly playing the Victrola and dancing together to "The Vamp of Savannah." I sat on the front porch unobserved, observing them through the window, and I felt old, very old. A train sounded, lonely and faraway out in Maryland, arousing in me as always that wistful longing to travel to distant lands.

*Friday, 11 December 1925*

While Hans was dressing to go to the Bal Bohéme at the Willard, he gave me an account of Isador Pearson. "He's a natural child of an independent woman— shall I wear this odd hat? What do you think? I don't like this costume." I told him, "It's becoming. You make a handsome Pied Piper."

"Thank you. I like costume balls. I am not too serious for such things. So,

Isador's mother took up with an Irish woman—they are unusually fond—and, why not? Let them have their fun. The sad part is the visit of Isador to his father. First, after his mother fell in love with the Irish woman, Isador got it in his head to enter a monastery, but he was quickly expelled from there for obvious reasons. Then he decided to visit his father. The father lives with his English wife and children in London. Isador knocked on the door and introduced himself. The father stepped out of the house and asked Isador not to return. He said a visit from Isador was destructive." Hans shook his head somberly. "Poor boy, sailing for England with his head full of dreams . . . "


# 1926


*Saturday, 9 January 1926*

The old year 1925 had been too happy—something horrible had to happen. It had its origin the night of the 11th of December, the date of my last diary entry, written while I lay under my snug covers waiting for Hans to return from the Bal Bohéme. He arrived and joined me and did me such an enormous injury, though meaning no harm. Poor Hans was wretched and sorry, but not half so wretched and sorry as I. He accompanied me in the cab to the hospital. Dr. Belt is treating me. He says I'll get well. I'll not go into all that, though. My Christmas was spoiled. I have had to give up alcohol, coffee and tea, spicy foods, late hours, and all sexual excitement or indulgence. O the devil! Why discuss that abominable subject.

Isador Pearson had one of his parties tonight, with dancing and real liquor. Lounging on the bed when Hans and I arrived was Junior Whorley. He is an odd, tiny, delicate but charming young lad newly arrived from Corpus Christi, where he played the organ in a movie theatre. Junior's crisp russet-colored curly hair was piled at least six inches above his head, loose and free. I envy him such beautiful hair.

Max arrived with Tommy Freskin, who has recently moved down to Washington from Boston. Tommy has gotten a job as a journalist with the International News Service. Max told me, "I hope it'll inspire you, Jeb, to learn that Tommy has had a story published in *Harper's.*" He and Tommy lay on the bed affectionately close, until they departed "to write letters." The rest of us turned back the rugs and danced to the music of Isador's Victrola with my dance records. Tony Baretto furnished the drink. Of course, I could not have any. Tony is a butler at the Portuguese Embassy, but refined and intelligent. A delightful-looking chap, tall, poetic and dark, with artistic hands. He refers to Isador as the "Rose Lady," and the two are very affectionate. Another of Isador's friends came in for a little while. But he had just been to church and was so shocked at the dancing and liquor that he soon left.

We had a fine time, but I took the elevator back up to my room dissatisfied. If Tommy can have a story in *Harper's*, why can't I? I can write, but it takes somebody standing over me with a horsewhip. Tonight I decided to write something in the way of letters or themes, but have done nothing except read newspapers and mull over my clippings.

### Monday, 18 January 1926

Last night I dreamed that little russet-haired Junior Whorley was killed. Some kind of warfare was imminent and Junior was dueling with others at the edge of the city. By mistake they were fired on from our own fort, and Junior was killed. His mother came up from Corpus Christi. I can't imagine why I should dream such a thing—certainly no suppressed desire is involved.

Tonight I received one of Isador's excited telephone calls telling me to "hurry down quickly." I rushed down thinking something had befallen him, but found only Bolling Balfour. Bolling is an artist, or aspires to be. He is about thirty-five, blasé and sophisticated, quite prominent socially. He must have been utterly beautiful ten years ago. At our first meeting, Christmas Eve, he seemed to become infatuated with me. On New Year's Eve he sent me a copy of Carl Van Vechten's *Firecrackers,* inscribed, "To the Man of Silence. Perhaps you may smile at some of the sentences written herein." No name was appended so I didn't acknowledge it, although I guessed who was responsible. Then last week he sent me a gorgeous bunch of violets, huge ones an inch or more in diameter and so fragrant that they perfumed the room with their sweetness.

Tony Baretto arrived, having worked late at the Portuguese Embassy and having managed to ferret away a bottle of champagne from a party there. He put on "Yes We Have No Bananas" and pulled back the rug so that he and the "Rose Lady" could dance. Bolling Balfour leaned over me and made protestations of love which I did not return.

### Monday, 25 January 1926

Isador gave Hans and me two tickets to hear Schumann-Heink sing tonight before the Department of State Club. Isador originally had the tickets for himself and "Helen," a middle-aged widow who recently took a fancy to him. He has been staying with "Helen" for days now in the Chatterton. The tickets were for seats on the aisle about halfway down. Only two other men were in day-clothes;

everyone else was in evening dress, but I refused to allow myself to be made uncomfortable by this fact. Madame Schumann-Heink was an ugly mountain of a woman but her voice was beautifully rich and full and I enjoyed it. She gave several encores in response to wild applause and cheers.

Afterward Hans and I wanted to get her autograph on our programs. We could see Madame Schumann-Heink donning her cloak in an outer room, but a pompous State Department official barred our way with the curt announcement, "No passing through here, please," accompanied by blocking the door. As we turned away, several young couples in evening dress, waiting for the dancing to start, stared at us with curiosity and politely disguised amusement. I dragged Hans away, although he had an idiotic desire to stay to get something to eat.

> **Ernestine Schumann-Heink** (1861–1936) was an Austrian-American contralto, the last of the great singers whose career spanned both the nineteenth and twentieth centuries.

### Friday, 23 July 1926

Hans had a drinking party with Tommy's bottle of North Carolina moonshine. It was sickening, vile stuff but heady. Hans laughed immoderately and cut up. Tommy acted foolish. Max took Tommy to Isador's room and put him to bed. While I helped Hans undress, Isador unearthed the bottle in the closet and tried to down the remainder. I struggled with him for it and he almost knocked me down. I put it back. To bed reluctantly, feeling fit.

### Saturday, 7 August 1926

Max left for his painting trip in New Mexico without having told me goodbye at all. My last recollection of him was seeing him irritated, trying to get the fellows to hurry because the car was waiting. I won't see him the rest of the summer. It is astonishing to me to realize the influence he has had over my life, both directly and indirectly.

Isador got on the elevator as I was going down. We walked together to our art history class. He was in his usual hilarious condition and told me of events last night that occurred after I left Max's going-away party. Those remaining misbehaved, urinated on the wall in the basement, and were rowdy in Child's. Tony Baretto passed a flask of gin around, and was arrested for drunkenness and disorderly conduct as he emerged into the street.

### Monday, 11 October 1926

Isador told me that his blue-eyed friend, the one with the distressing Middle Western ideas and attitudes, carried off his typewriter, and most of his clothes. "I was hurt. I had trusted the boy perfectly." I replied, "Trust in human nature—bah!"

*Sunday, 19 December 1926*

C. C. Dasham, the idol of my college days, is domiciled in this building. And having seen him, I do not love him. It is almost like a death. Isador telephoned my room and said, "You must appear instantly." I thought he meant a Christmas gift, and placidly took the elevator down to the fourth floor. Isador's door was open and face to face with me stood Dasham. He has still that beautifully molded mouth and chin. He appraised me, smiling. "Well, Alexander, you look *wonderful.*" When we all sat down, Dasham crossed his legs in an attitude of easy composure and complacency. He still has an indescribable air of boyishness about him. Yet the moment I saw him I knew I did not love him.

The realization was an unwelcome sensation. Probably one cause is the fact that the appearance of Dasham will make dreaming of his shadow, my imaginary Vincent Eric Orville, so artificial that I suppose it will be well-nigh impossible. Years of yearning for that beauteous boy . . . he with white shirt open at the collar, a delightful fellow, slim with boyishly expressive face and ethereal eyes. He was a happy-go-lucky fellow, always getting "bawled out" for some act of carelessness, forgetfulness, or, even better still, of apparently deliberate defiance and disobedience. How I have loved him, and how long I have loved! Dasham is a sweet chap, though. We shall no doubt become friends. How peculiar it will be, though, to have him here.

# 1927

*Sunday, 7 January 1927*

A cloudless day. Patches of snow on the walks. Isador arrived in a cab to pick up his belongings that had been packed by those magnificent Christians of the Young Men's Christian Association. I watched the scene from inside the lobby door. The packages and bags had been placed outside. Thompson, the malignant desk clerk, stood on the sidewalk with his arms crossed. The cab pulled up and Isador emerged, wearing a brown suit with a tan handkerchief tucked in his pocket, and a tan felt hat. Thompson pursed his lips as Isador, attempting a futile, jocular conversation, began to load his possessions into the back seat of the cab. He got in front with the driver and as they pulled away, his eyes met mine through the glass of the door and he waved vigorously, calling, "Thank you, Jeb, dearest." Thompson turned round. My heart sank when I saw the expression on that reptilian beast's face.

Thompson wiped his feet on the mat. "I didn't realize that Mr. Pearson was a friend of yours." I replied, "He is a classmate in my art history class at George Washington University. We share school books." "Can't you share with someone less unnatural?" My voice shook, but I told that reprehensible beast, "I consider it a valid economy to be sharing books with Mr. Pearson."

Waiting for the elevator took an eternity. I found myself imagining that I was helping Isador put his packages in the cab, until the details became so vivid that it almost seemed that in fact I had helped him. And after all, there is no benefit in having two of us evicted from the Y. It is bad enough for something so humiliating to happen to one.

*Monday, 10 January 1927*

At night Isador invited me out to Georgetown to see his new room. It is a small room, on the third floor of an ancient house filled with Victorian furnishings. We went down to the parlor and Isador was playing the piano and singing when who should walk in to see his new lodgings but Randall Hare. His three years in Paris have given him a great deal of sophistication. He was dressed with perfect taste, his clothing graceful and expensive and seemingly part of him, and he has taken to smoking his cigarettes with a long silver cigarette holder. He told me to my amazement that he has a fiancée. I stammered, "Do you!" He seemed amused. "Yes, she's a lovely girl from Charlottesville. I met her on the Riviera." He said no more about her, and seemed rather attentive to me during the evening, offering to drive me back to the Y when I was ready to leave.

He came up to the room for a while. The conversation was a bit strained. I just couldn't make myself unbend and be easy and chatty with Randall as I so much wanted to. People don't realize how lucky they are. Randall can get along with anybody of any age and any station in life in a natural, friendly way appropriate to the person, while I struggle with this accursed self-consciousness, formality, and inability to think while I talk, and therefore inability to talk except in a strained and punctilious fashion. Hans arrived at my room unexpectedly— before Randall left.

*Friday, 4 February 1927*

This evening in my room Junior Whorley said rude, sarcastic things about my literary ambitions. He has grown much more effeminate since I last saw him. That is one thing I do not like in a man. Of course I am not narrow-minded about it in any way. I realize that effeminacy was born with him and sympathize with his handicap. I like gentleness, love it in a youth or man, but effeminacy repels me. Thank God I have been spared that. Homosexuality may be curse enough (though it has its wonderful compensations and noble joys) but it is a double curse when one has effeminate ways of walking, talking, or acting.

Junior's remarks made me resentful and self-conscious and angry. He tried to make it up later. I hadn't forgiven him and was still upset when he left. Hans, as is the case whenever anything distressing happens, became physically attentive. We didn't settle down until around two in the morning. Afterward I lay there telling myself that I should simply begin my career as a literary artist. I did get up and put on my bathrobe. But instead of starting something original in the way of letters, I have been puttering around and writing in my diary.

*Sunday, 6 February 1927*

To Georgetown with Randall Hare, to the charming old apartment where he lives with his mother and uncle, and where in June he intends to bring home his bride, the "lovely girl from Charlottesville." We looked at magazines, conversed, and played the Victrola. Most of the time we talked of Paris. He told me about Chez Maurice across from the Montmartre Cemetery, a resort for homosexual men, and about Chez Regina, a lesbian resort. Randall became affectionate late in the evening and told me a lot of rigmarole, which, because of what I know of him, I believe only half. He said he had been in love with me for a long time and since returning from France had schemed to separate Hans from me so that he would have a chance. He murmured, "I introduced Hans to various men for the purpose of freeing you. In fact I even pretended to be in love with Hans to draw him away from you." He didn't mention the $25,000 which Isador said he had recently inherited.

*Tuesday, 8 February 1927*

At night Randall took me to ride in his touring car out across Chain Bridge and into Virginia. I drank in the strong blast of mist-filled river air like fresh cold water and gazed with the keenest enjoyment, full of Wordsworth and his spirit, at the blue shadows on the rocks, with pearl and white and silver clouds above them, and the shadows on the river. It was fiercely exhilarating as we tore along the dark curving road with the cold wind whipping through the car and tugging at the robe that I had wrapped snugly about my body.

*Monday, 21 February 1927*

Tonight Dasham visited my room. Isador and Junior burst in later. Junior got into one of his high-spirited moods. Late in the evening Randall arrived, and seemed uninteresting and much too affectionate. He has had his play on hermaphrodism copyrighted and has sent it to a New York publisher in hopes of having it printed.

*Tuesday, 22 February 1927*

Hans to my room. He angered me extremely by his jealous unreasonableness and by saying that I was always telling him lies. I went to the window and looked out until he left.

*Thursday, 24 February 1927*

Returning to the Y, I saw Dasham and Tommy laughing and horsing around outside the front entrance. I watched Dasham stride up the messy walk making a last snowball to throw at Tommy's departing back. His face was rosy and wreathed in boyish smiles. He seemed so happy and young and wholesome, so full of health and beauty and vigor that I felt a sudden sweeping sense of how morbid and unhealthy I am compared to him, a disconcerting feeling almost of shame. A moment later he strode inside, followed by Junior and Hans. Junior irritating as of old with his rude sarcasm—especially to me. And Hans was in a petulant, disagreeable mood. Dasham looked round past the two of them and smiled at me.

*Monday, 7 March 1927*

"I have become intensely interested," I said to Hans and Dasham at dinner, "in collecting Whitman books, by and about old Walt, and am resolved to make as complete a collection as I can." Hans was in one of his childish, flippant moods. Sometimes he affects a European peasant demeanor that irritates me extremely. He waved his fork over his dinner plate. His mouth was full of string beans. He said, "You collect everything. You dream everything." I ignored him. Dasham said he thought my collection was a wonderful idea.

*Thursday, 10 March 1927*

At night Dasham and I got ice cream and brought it back to eat in his room. For the first time we spoke of the old days at W&L. He said he learned in a horrible way of Harry Agneau's death. "I received a mean letter from Judge Agneau, with a cruel implication that I should feel responsible." I could think of no reply, but Dasham can't stand silence for long, and soon launched into cheerful subjects. His whole being is one of jaunty ease, but not of the cocksure boldness that so many have and that I so heartily detest.

*Friday, 11 March 1927*

Cloudless weather. Saw two robins, my first of the year. Scuttled around among the bookshops and got Sawyer's *Walt Whitman* and Saunders' *Parodies on Walt Whitman.*

At night with Dasham out to Bolling Balfour's studio on Columbia Road. Max was already there, drinking bootlegger's gin and restlessly puttering around in Bolling's papers and collections. Bolling is the perfect aesthete. His studio is delightful, filled with quaint, beautiful and precious things. Isador and Junior arrived. Junior danced; became unruly. He made sarcastic remarks to me in his pretended-serious manner but I retorted each time and on the whole got the better of him. Late in the evening Dasham told us that he has received an offer of a position on a mule boat for a two months' voyage to Barcelona and back. We talked about it a great deal. The offer is so sudden that Dasham can't make up his mind.

*Wednesday, 16 March 1927*

To Woodward & Lothrop's to help Isador select a lamp. Then we had dinner with Hans and Junior at the Government Cafeteria, where Mrs. Noyes, the kind gray lady, was very cordial. After dinner Hans had to go to rehearsal. Junior pranced off beside him, nominally to see if he could arrange for work as a piano player. Junior and Hans have become very intimate.

Isador and I went to see J. M. Barrie's *The Legend of Leonora.* When we came out the moon was shining and a cool night breeze was stirring. We walked about and had ice cream in Farragut Square. Chattering on about our acquaintances, as he does, Isador said, "Did you know, Dasham has decided to sail on the British mule boat *Hydaspes.* He thinks conditions will be agreeable except for the food. The first port will be Oran, Algeria, to put off some of the mules, and then Barcelona, to deposit the rest, and then Genoa to unload a cargo of coal." I was much interested. It was exhilarating to imagine Dasham leaning on the railing to watch the sparkling waves, his eyes wide open in that steadfast, straightforward gaze full of the passionate purity of youth. Isador said softly, "You like him, don't you . . . " Startled, I replied, "Oh! He's a sweet-enough boy."

*Saturday, 26 March 1927*

How I envy the boy! As I write, well after midnight, Dasham is about twenty-four hours out from port. Think of it—sleeping in his snug bunk while the ship rocks on the waves and ploughs on toward Africa and the Mediterranean.

*Friday, 1 April 1927*

Randall and I had dinner at Danish Rose. Then to the National to see the all-star revival of *Trelawney of the Wells.* As we walked to the theatre, the drizzly mist flying in my face made me feel animated and light-headed, so that an automobile nearly ran me down. I said, "I should like to be a vagabond." Randall gallantly replied, "Nothing on earth would please me better than to be a vagabond with you." I didn't tell him that he was far from being my ideal companion on a vagabond journey.

Now it is one o'clock and I have about my shoulders my faithful gray wool scarf with the stenciled green and black design. The windowpane is bespattered with drops of rain. A train rumbles far away, awakening within me longings and wanderlust. I wonder whether Dasham and the mules have arrived yet at Oran.

*Tuesday, 12 April 1927*

Mrs. Green, a nervous little body, would like to be transferred from her clerking duties to the new editorial position in the office with Miss Contadeluci and me. I was given the job of interviewing her. This authority, and her subservience, had the curious psychological effect of making me assured and self-confident for the rest of the day.

I left early to go to the opening game of the baseball season. The usual spectacle: massed thousands, flags flapping, President Coolidge throwing out the first ball, the band playing, players marching across the field. I stood the whole time; all seats in the grandstands were taken. I chatted with a slender, well-dressed youth and was going to walk off with him but was surprised to find that an older and coarser looking man nearby, probably his father, was accompanying him.

Isador stopped by in the evening. He told me he had been to a party at which he met Richard Halliburton, who is to make an address at the "Author's Breakfast" to be given by the Presswomen's League next Saturday. Isador, who had been wearing a royal-purple tie, asked Halliburton, who was wearing a red tie, for his autograph. Halliburton remarked, "Our ties speak a language." In Isador's autograph album Halliburton wrote: "To Isador, a good boy, from Dick Halliburton, another one." Rather intimate from an acquaintance of a few minutes. Isador said he walked with Halliburton as far as the house where he was staying (with the Misses Finch near Dupont Circle).

**Richard Halliburton** *(1900–1939) wrote* The Royal Road to Romance *(1925),* The Glorious Adventure *(1927), and other books, and led an astonishing life, travelling around the world in his own aircraft, and tracing on foot Cortez's conquest of Mexico. He was lost at sea while sailing a Chinese junk from Hong Kong to San Francisco.*

*Wednesday, 13 April 1927*

Max's latest craze is aesthetic dancing. He said he would dance for me, and did so, with only the scarf that Bolling Balfour had painted. He was awkward and gawky, the air in his basement room was heavy, and the dance seemed silly and puerile. Restless and bored, I soon left, saddened that I should have been so embarrassed and irritated by Max and realizing that after all, friends can go only so far—I can depend only on myself.

> **Aesthetic dancing.** *Max's craze was probably influenced by Isadora Duncan (1878–1927). A pioneer in modern dance, Duncan led a passionate, tragic life and was an icon for the* avant garde. *Others who influenced "aesthetic" dance forms were Ruth St. Denis and Martha Graham.*

*Thursday, 21 April 1927*

Walked over to Georgetown to see Isador. The moon swam in a hazy sky. Georgetown at night seemed alluring, somehow unreal, stimulating. Isador served ice cream and chocolate bars. He showed me his scrapbook, or as he calls it, his "yearbook of 1926." He said he is worried about his mother, who decided to go alone down to the Eastern Shore. "She left her intimate friend Mary Riley, she left my grandmother, and she left me." I had no answers; all I could do was assure Isador that she'd return to her loved ones.

We took a streetcar to the Belasco to see Kalich in *The Riddle: Woman.* Years ago I saw it and had my emotions so much stirred that afterward I walked home working myself into a sort of internal frenzy. This time it had no such effect, although Kalich was, as always, full of passion, vigor, and strength. After Isador and I parted, I walked home in the rain looking at the lovely reflections in the wet pavement, wishing I could dream beautiful dreams as I used to do.

> **The Riddle: Woman** *(premiered in 1918). Starring Polish-born actress Bertha Kalich (1874–1939), the play was written by Charlotte E. Wells and Dorothy Donnelly, and concerned itself with Danish social life. The wife sinned; the husband forgave.*

*Tuesday, 3 May 1927*

Max and I went up on the roof of the Y to watch the workings of the new contrivance called the "aerograph," a thing which flashed pictures in the sky with a searchlight. Max told me, "Isador went backstage after *The Cradle Song* and arranged an informal supper party with Eva Le Gallienne." I was astonished. "That was damned presumptuous of Isador." Max said the guests were to be himself, Mrs. Muriel Phillipson, Junior, and of course Eva Le Gallienne. I was envious and disappointed that I hadn't been invited.

The aerograph device was almost pointless. The pictures were visible only when turned on the Monument.

**Eva Le Gallienne** *(1899–1991) has been called "the high priestess of American drama." A small woman with a mannered method of delivery on the stage, she formed the off-Broadway Civic Repertory Company in 1926 and starred with élan in such productions as* Liliom, The Rivals, *and* The Master Builder.

*Wednesday, 4 May 1927*

The Le Gallienne party was a failure. Junior told me that the rest of the party waited in the coffee shop of the Willard, while Isador went backstage to get Le Gallienne. "She would not see him. She sent word that she had been ill and would have to break the engagement." I said bluntly, "I don't blame her." "Nor I," Junior said, his eyes widening, "not after the way Isador acted on Monday night. Isador chattered incessantly and hardly gave me or Miss Le Gallienne a chance for a sentence." I was filled with a malicious glee as Junior told of it—probably because I had wanted to be there myself. At night I went to see Le Gallienne in Carlo Goldoni's *La locandiera,* a sprightly and amusing eighteenth-century comedy.

*Friday, 6 May 1927*

Isador visited me. He is having his tonsils out on Monday and has made his will and put his affairs in order. When he gave me my copy of *The Master Builder* that he had Eva Le Gallienne autograph for me last night, he said, "Eva is thawing." I told him, "She'll be long gone from Washington before she melts." Isador said, "I *know,* Jeb. But I adore her . . . "

*Tuesday, 17 May 1927*

Junior Whorley arrived through a tremendous downpour, appearing in my office, startling me (and unfortunately, wide-eyed Mrs. Green) by showing up at my place of work. But more startling was the news Junior brought—that Isador's mother committed suicide on Friday. Junior told me that Max, who was waiting outside in the cab, telephoned Isador today by chance and learned of the tragedy. The funeral services were to be at two o'clock. We had minutes to spare. The rainstorm was terrific and traffic was terrible.

When our cab splashed up in front of the church, Randall's automobile was just pulling in. He parked behind Mary Riley, the woman who lived with

Isador's mother. She was sitting motionless in her automobile. As Randall ran through the downpour, Max gestured toward Mary Riley's automobile and called out, "Shouldn't we help her into the church?" Randall glanced at the motionless figure, scarcely visible through raindrops streaming down the windows. "Don't—she's sure to be smoking a reefer. She'll come in when she's ready."

Inside the church, the air was heavy with the odor of funeral flowers. From outside, we heard deafening cracks of thunder. Hailstones clattered. Isador, astonishingly composed, asked us to view the body. When we gazed into the coffin, what we saw was a mask-like countenance surrounded by ringlets of black hair in disarray. When Mary Riley entered the church, I was much interested. I'd never have guessed that she was an invert. She could have been any attractive woman of medium height, with the coloring of the "black Irish"—fair skin, black hair, blue eyes. As we were leaving the church, Junior, the fool clown, told her, "The mass was *divine.*" She gave him the curt Irish reply, "That is the intent." Later, in the cab as Junior and Max and I rode downtown through the torrential storm, Max remarked somberly, "Isador's mother looked like Isador gone awry, got up and dressed the way he has always wanted to look." All told, a distressing business. The rain kept pouring down for hours.

*Saturday, 21 May 1927*

To the *Post* building to get the news of Lindbergh. Cheers! I wish that in Paris there was a young fellow trying to make up for lost sleep. Let's greet Lindbergh with such accolades that we'd wake the lucky fellow, all the way across the Atlantic!

> **Charles Lindbergh** *(1902–1974). In May of 1927 Lindbergh flew his monoplane, the* Spirit of St. Louis, *from New York to Paris in the first aviation solo non-stop Atlantic crossing. Lindy was boyishly handsome and idolized by thousands. Jeb's fantasy about the young man who needs sleep in Paris appears to be pure wishfulness; nothing in Lindbergh's history suggests he was gay.*

*Sunday, 22 May 1927*

Dasham is back from his mule-boat adventure. I saw him for a moment. He was hastening bare-headed down the hall and had time only to say, "Conditions were bad on the return trip. But ask me, when we have time, to tell you about the women in Algeria." He stepped into the elevator; the door closed upon him and he was gone. I had been on my way down, too. I had to push the button and wait for the elevator to ascend again.

*Thursday, 26 May 1927*

This morning when I was shaving in the bathroom, in padded C. C. Dasham in his pajamas and slippers with sleepy eyes and tousled hair. He smiled hello and playfully tickled me under the arm as he passed. An odd boy, at times cold and distant, and then again friendly and full of apparent liking for me.

*Friday, 27 May 1927*

To the university. Got invitations and tickets for my graduation exercises. At last I am graduating—lessening somewhat my regret about not graduating from W&L. The scatterbrained girl gave me only five tickets, but I went back and got the other five that were due me.

Isador and I went to the Little Theatre to see the movie *Chained.* A moving and tragic story of a great artist's love for a handsome youth: *No one can realize the bitter loneliness in my life. Let me try to find what happiness I can in my own way.* But we who are afflicted with this terrible and exquisite curse that uplifts us to the stars one moment and drops us in the mud the next, can find little lasting happiness in any way—our own or that of the unsympathetic world.

> **Chained** *(1926). The first American release of this film was titled* The Inverts. *The film was adapted from Hermann Bang's novel* Mikael, *said to be about the sculptor Rodin. The principal role in the film was played by Walter Slezak.*

*Saturday, 28 May 1927*

With Dasham, Isador, and Junior to see the one-act plays given by the students of Mrs. Reyerhorn's acting school—in two of which Hans appeared. When the performance was over we walked out P Street to the bridge and leaned over the rail, lighting cigarettes. I gazed down at the creek with its sand bars and wooded bends. "The usual amateur rot. I was bored sick." Junior quickly replied, "But Hans was the best of the lot." He was, but he was by no means remarkable.

At home I read the April *Vanity Fair* until I became bored and disgusted by the attitude of shallow sophistication. There was, in particular, an article about "What the Fashionable Man Will Wear." I cannot, do not, want to be the Fashionable Man.

*Wednesday, 1 June 1927*

In my box I found a congratulations card from Dasham in reply to the invitation and ticket to commencement I had given him. On the card he had written that he wanted to make me a present of his tapestry of *The Bay of Naples,* which he acquired on his trip. The card was signed, "Su Amigo, C. C. Dasham." I was much pleased.

Spent the evening in my room. Cut out clippings about Charles Lindbergh and photos of him in Europe, which have just reached this country. Lindbergh will land in Washington June 11. A glorious young hero!

### Wednesday, 8 June 1927

Graduated from George Washington University. Attending were Dad, Mama, Henry, Eunice. And across the hall—Max, Dasham, Hans, Isador, Randall, Junior.

### Saturday, 11 June 1927

Arrival of Lindbergh from France. Parade and monster celebration. Lindbergh a handsome and charming youth; I had several good views of him. Returning to my room, I saw Dasham's door open and Dasham inside, listing and bundling his laundry. He called out in his soft Mississippi drawl, "Come on in, Alexander, for a visit!" I did. We chatted for a while and decided we both needed a long, leisurely walk. We strolled down to the Pan American gardens, one of the loveliest spots in Washington. The air was fresh, rain-washed. We leaned talking on the white marble balustrade above the Aztec god of flowers that presides over the water lily pool. The moon shone on silvery wraiths that rose from the lawns. Then to the Potomac. Gazed at the lights of Arlington Beach, the bridge reflected in the water, and the whirling lights of the pleasure flying machine. There was serenity in the view: one bright star, three lights clustered on the dim Virginia shore, and the dark, silent river.

### Wednesday, 13 July 1927

Off at noon with Dash for a photographic jaunt. Rode to Cabin John and ambled back as far as Chain Bridge. We trailed a big blue heron, with Dash trying to snap him. The gorgeous bird started back the other way so Dash snapped wildly. We don't know whether we got him or not.

> **Cabin John** *was at this time a rural, wooded community along Cabin John Creek in Maryland, not far from the District Line. Long-standing tradition had it that "John," the eighteenth-century hermit for whom the creek was named, had left buried near his cabin the gold he acquired by working as a spy for the British. Jeb's diaries contain tantalizing clues, obtained from stories told to him by his co-worker Miss Contadeluci, as to the location of the gold.*

*Thursday, 14 July 1927*

Dinner at Cleves with Dash. He was in one of his most amiable moods. When he rose from the table he gave me his most dazzling smile. I smiled back, smiled at his wonderful eyes, soft clear healthy skin, light brown hair so lovely, his straight, well-formed limbs.

*Friday, 15 July 1927*

After office I went to the Eastman shop and bought the first good camera I have ever had: a $26 model (No. 1, Series 3), the latest, most improved style of Kodak. Went home and tried to straighten up the clutter on my table. Dasham arrived. We sat on the bed looking over my new camera and talking about it. Glorious moonlit, intoxicating, adventurous night, lying dormant behind his inscrutable eyes! I initiated the camera with a time exposure of him, and he took one of me. He stayed in my room all night.

*Saturday, 16 July 1927*

O, that look in his eyes as he pressed me hard, that look of wistful, yearning tenderness—I shall never forget. And the tone of his voice as he said good-bye— it lingers so sweetly in my ears. I love him to distraction. Couldn't go to the office. Loafed and rambled about town in the hot sun. Chanced upon Randall. Asked him how it felt to be a married man. He said, "The condition suits me." I declined his invitation to accompany him to a party at a radio announcer's apartment in MacDougall Alley, where he was to sing. Returned home tired and nervous. Dinner with Dash. His entrancing personality so enthralls me! So beautiful, so beautiful. I would do anything for him.

*Sunday, 17 July 1927*

Dash and I spent a delightful day picnicking on the cliffs below Great Falls. A cold spring of delicious water was nearby. Not far off were the ruins of the canal surveyed by George Washington. We had a bounteous lunch, topped off by excellent beer (real stuff). It was the first alcohol I had had in months (how I do bemoan prohibition) and made me feel gaily dizzy. We wandered the woods, observing the flowers and trees and climbing rocks. I am passionately in love with Dash. I believe that if I could have him with me I could be happy the rest of my life on a desert isle. Just the two of us alone. I feel that I should like to be father, mother, brother, wife, friend, and lover to him all at the same time. Returned to Washington after an idyllic day. Never a harsh word spoken or a moment's annoyance shown by either of us. Dash's is a lovable nature, eager, vivacious, and receptive to beauty.

When I got back to the Y, I had a message to call the house. Mama answered the phone. She told me that Uncle Jeb, whom I have not seen since I was a child, will be in Washington on July 28th. Mama said, "He wants to see you and meet your friends." I hung up the phone and lay back on my bed with my hands over my face. Eleven days until Uncle Jeb meets my friends.

*Sunday, 24 July 1927*

Off on a holiday with Dasham to Atlantic City. Our train departed from Union Station at midnight. Dash leaned back and prepared to nap. After a moment he said, "What's the matter?" "Uncle Jeb." He said, "Ask Isador to take your uncle on a fishing excursion." "How can I take my uncle fishing in the company of a man who gives imitations of Queen Victoria and Whistler's mother?" Dash said, "Oh, well, you think about it." He settled himself to sleep. I did think about it, gazing at the dark night beyond the train window. We came near Atlantic City under a streamered crimson-yellow sky. I looked at Dashie's face, his soft hair on his forehead, his eyelids closed. I thought he would wake from my gaze.

We arrived at 5:40 and watched the red sun rising. We waded into the water, and walked for hours on the sand. Dash said, "Your uncle will merely think that Isador is over-bred. And you haven't thought of anything else. Besides, it's beginning to sound like fun. I'll go with you." He plunged into the surf. I followed, deciding I would do as he suggested. The salty waves felt cool and refreshing. For the rest of the afternoon we amused ourselves by partaking of boardwalk diversions and watching the fish-haul at the Million-Dollar Pier. Just before sunset we waded into the darkening water and swam parallel to the beach for a long distance. We swam slowly in beneath a lavender sky, riding dark and groaning waves, ducking under the foam.

But returning on the train was wearisome. Both of us were cross, already suffering from a miserable sunburn. Imprisoning ourselves in our shirts was torture. It was almost unbearable to tie our ties around our necks. Putting on our coats was hellish. While we were looking for our seats on the train my arm accidentally collided with his, and we got into a foolish altercation and didn't speak for more than an hour.

*Thursday, 28 July 1927*

Uncle Jeb, Isador, Dash, and I began our climb up a deserted mountain road, lined by tangles of briars from which we picked and ate quantities of blackberries. Isador had dressed in work trousers, a checkered shirt, and a cloth hat. He wore rings on both hands. Uncle Jeb also wore work trousers, a checkered shirt, and a cloth hat, but he traveled without jewelry, and from his mouth jutted a blackish cigar. Dash murmured, "They're really almost identical, aren't they?"

On top of the mountain we came to a schoolhouse situated in a level clearing. The pupils, a bare-legged, wild-seeming set, stood stock still to stare at us, then all ran away across the yard. In the valley below we saw a cultivated farm with a cottage surrounded by apple trees. This was Hanby's, where we were to obtain bait. When we had descended and crossed the fields, we found Mrs. Hanby seated on the porch in the midst of chickens and children. We dug up worms along the fence, then Mrs. Hanby told us, "Now you can help yourselves to eating apples from the tree by the barn." One of the children objected, "You ought not send those men to that hell-snake tree." She snapped, "Hush." At the barn we warily gathered apples. No rattlesnakes appeared.

From Hanby's we tramped through a wild region of rocky paths and obstructing branches that slapped our faces. On a slope we came upon a deserted cabin with a zig-zag rail fence that held back the woods. Uncle Jeb, gazing at the shadowed cabin, mused, "This region must have been first settled by fugitives from justice." Isador shuddered, "Criminals!" Uncle Jeb nodded, "Murderers, counterfeiters, bootleggers." I said, "There is something ghostly about the place," and hurried on. Uncle Jeb told Isador, "A little of this living away from civilization would go a long way for Jeb," and they laughed heartily.

The mountain torrent in which we were to fish flowed through impenetrable forests. The stream was narrower than Rock Creek at home, but it was wild, wild with tangled twisted trunks of gnarled old rhododendrons and laurels. Isador and Uncle Jeb showed Dash and me how to cut fishing poles from the thin saplings along the bank. Then we started the grand adventure upon the stream. The passage up the mountain creek, pausing at likely pools and fishing as we went, was the most difficult, obnoxious thing that I have ever had to do in my life. Moisture and decay and unseen reptiles oppressed the atmosphere. Tangled fastnesses of rhododendron and laurel rolled down to the water, impending darkly over its surface. I had on my waterproof high shoes but they were useless. I was wading nearly up to my waist. The others found it easier than I did.

We clambered up huge boulders. We jumped from one slimy rock to another, I often slipping and falling. Sometimes I miscalculated my distance, and tottered in agonizing unsteadiness until I gained an uncertain foothold, or landed on the water with a great splash. We trod soaked, rotten logs and climbed over decaying trunks of ancient trees fallen years before across the stream. We struggled around thundering, foamy falls and I fell into deep, mysterious pools.

I caught no fish. I was too much occupied in trying to keep within sight of the others, and they obtained only about twenty-five fish altogether. When they ran out of bait, Isador gazed across the stream, pointing at a hornets' nest that swung from the foliage. "We can get the young for bait," he mused, and disturbed the nest by slapping it with his pole. An infuriated insect attacked the wrong fisherman, stinging me painfully above my eye. At last, late in the afternoon, we came to a high waterfall. I sat down on a flat rock beneath the fall, resolved that I would go no further. Dash struggled back and peered through the cascade. "Not having fun?" I didn't answer. I felt unutterably homesick for the delights of civilized Washington. They were gone a long time.

Finally I saw them clinging to the rocks beside me. Struggling down the creek bed was easier than going up had been, but the skies grew overcast and by the time we reached the long, uphill trail through the forest, night was approaching and it had begun to rain. Through the noisy raindrops spattering the leaves, I could half-hear Isador's chattering remarks. "That was my mother's style of life, Uncle Jeb. I was born a natural child . . . " To think that Isador would be so frank—to say nothing of the fact that he had addressed my uncle whom he had only met this morning as *Uncle Jeb!* I followed them through the dark woods in horrified suspense, dreading that Isador might somehow suggest to my uncle that his nephew, his namesake, was Dashie's Raging Flame. Finally we reached the clearing where Uncle Jeb's automobile waited to take us back to blessed civilization.

*Sunday, 31 July 1927*

We had a beautiful afternoon out at the City Farm. Vast clouds overhead, but a luminous clarity in the air, good for photographing the sights and the strolling visitors. Dashie was in a teasing but affectionate mood. As we walked afterward down to the Capitol Grounds, I told him about Oscar Wilde. Returning, I had a stomach-ache that became worse and worse. I was sick and faint when we finally reached the Y. I lay on my bed, and Dash sat by me stroking my head and hands until I was almost asleep.

*Monday, 1 August 1927*

Hans made his professional stage debut in *Smilin' Through*. Dash and I went to see him. Hans did well; National Theatre Players, summer stock. While Dash was applauding the first act I glanced over at him. He looked the picture of youthful beauty, with eyes sparkling, cheeks rosy and hair tousled, and an eager, smiling, but rather sly expression on his face. We were loving comrades there, sitting with knees and legs affectionately touching. An occasional pressure of arm or leg meant more than words. Tonight, ah, tonight sweet happiness enveloped me like a pale rosy mist of perfume. "To burn always with this hard gem-like flame, to maintain this ecstasy, is success in life."

*Tuesday, 2 August 1927*

Dashie and I spent a couple of hours watching the filming of scenes of Will Rogers' movie, *A Texas Steer*. One scene was taken in front of the White House, but most of the time we were watching them at the Sherman Statue. Dash got several pictures of Will Rogers in action. Douglas Fairbanks, Jr., a handsome and charming young man, was also in the cast. He was begged by numerous girls for an autograph. Two girls asked him to autograph their golf bags, and he smilingly did. He and another actor, seeing Dash's camera, asked him to photograph them with their box camera. A crowd gathered around—much to the amusement of Dashie. He had one shot left on his own camera, so he took a close-up of me standing shoulder-to-shoulder with Fairbanks, Jr. Afterward Dashie and I walked downtown in the brilliant sunshine. I felt totally exhilarated.

*Sunday, 28 August 1927*

To the house as usual on Sundays. Henry said, "A black tie? Has there been the death of a photoplay actor?" I told him I am wearing a black tie in honor of Nicola Sacco and Bartholomeo Vanzetti, innocent men who were accused of anarchy and murdered by the State of Massachusetts last Monday night. Their funeral was today. Henry shouted toward the den. "Dad—Jeb's wearing a black tie for Sacco and Vanzetti." Dad coughed. Mama in a low voice said, "Jeb wouldn't do those things if Henry didn't challenge him." She didn't know I heard her. I marched to the double French doors of the den and told Mama, "I have worn predominantly black since Tuesday, technically the day of the murder." Mama protested, "It was execution, not murder," and a general argument ensued. But what did I expect?

*Thursday, 1 September 1927*

Dash and I left Washington for Niagara Falls in a drizzling rain. We enjoyed the scenery with a pair of well-dressed fellows who got on at Bowie. They also were Raging Flames, and we found them agreeable companions. The region was new to the four of us—York, Harrisburg, Williamsport, Buffalo. The train pulled into Buffalo after dark, but still we could see the Canadian shore from the train, and the new Peace Bridge. We had intended going to the Canadian side, but because of the late hour we went to the Wilson House, a tawdry-looking place—each of us taking a room without a bath for $2.50. Afterward Dash and I went over into the falls reservation. It was a poor view of the falls but enough to make us realize what a marvelous natural wonder it is. Clouds of spray drifted up continually.

**Peace Bridge.** *The U. S. and Canada established diplomatic relations in January of 1927 and the Peace Bridge, a symbolic link between the two countries, was dedicated by the Prince of Wales and U.S. Vice President Dawes less than a month before Dash and Jeb's visit to Niagara Falls.*


*Friday, 2 September 1927*

A full day of gorging ourselves with natural beauties. Dash and I toured Goat Island and the other little islands and the foot of the falls. At Table Rock we each paid $1 to go down behind the falls itself. We were attired in rubber. It was thrilling to see the thundering torrent of the cataract pouring down, dashing its spray upon us. Then we went to a pavilion run by the Government, and drank some of the weak Canadian beer. At the whirlpool we rode in the suspended cable car across the gorge and back. Dash enjoyed it greatly.

At night we crossed to Canada to look at the illumination of the falls. The most striking and imagination-stirring sight was of Horseshoe Falls with red lights on it. Dash said, "It is marvelously lovely." He is responsive to beautiful things. The chaps from Bowie strolled up and talked with us. When the lights went off the falls we all four ambled back downstream to drink more weak Canadian beer. We got into a gleeful mood and laughed uncontrollably over trifles.


*Saturday, 3 September 1927*

Dash inconceivably went off without me, when I foolishly overslept and got up too late to take the trip to Toronto. I had to spend a rather aimless day at Niagara. At night I met a youth from Pittsburgh, with whom I watched the illumination of the falls. He then had to join his family. I wandered up Falls Street and off to the east with another youth, a boy who had a room in a dilapidated house. There was an ugly iron bed and his clothing and plates from many meals tumbled all over the floor. I lost interest in the poor child and left. It was after midnight when I got back to the hotel. Dasham's door was locked. He didn't reply to my tapping on his door with my fingernail, nor, later, to my insistent knocking.


*Sunday, 4 September 1927*

The trip back was hot and uncomfortable. As the train rolled down through the countryside the conversation went in every direction but the one I wanted.

Dashie grumbled, complaining about my oversleeping yesterday. He told me things about myself which I found excruciatingly painful. He said, "I *hate* your eternal dawdling and chronic oversleeping." The angrier he got, the more Mississippian became his accent. He thrust himself back in his seat, crossed his legs, plucked furiously at his trousers crease, and grumbled disgustedly, "You' *jus' shif less!*"

*Wednesday, 7 September 1927*

We accompanied Isador to Mt. Pleasant to see his poor old grandmother whom he visits every evening. He and the grandmother will move this week into an apartment in the McReynolds across from the Y. We went from Mt. Pleasant to Georgetown and brought back on the streetcar, amid much gaiety, a lot of things of Isador's to the new apartment—suitcases, boxes tied together with string, kimonos, straw hat with ribbons, coat hangers, bathrobe.

*Friday, 9 September 1927*

The desk clerk at the Y said there was a package for me. Brought the parcel up to my room and opened it, revealing a dark blue-jacketed book with silver lettering, a published copy of Lansing's novel. Lansing had written on the flyleaf, "To Jeb Alexander, who knows more about fiction than I do." I sat in my rocker by the window and read for a while. I am impressed by his accomplishment. He has written a compelling book with a subtle satire on family life and a serious basic idea—the emotional poverty of materialism. I thought how ineffectual and inarticulate my life is, wondering when I shall find myself and give utterance to the genius that I *know* is within me. The time will come—*Der Tag!* I will show them yet. I will be famous—I know it.

*Thursday, 15 September 1927*

Dinner with Dash and Isador. When we got back to the Y, Thompson objected to Isador's going up to my room to get his books. Isador went anyway.

*Wednesday, 21 September 1927*

With Dashie and Isador to see the film *Beau Geste*—an adventure story of the French Foreign Legion in the Sahara. Enjoyed it immensely. Later we got ice cream to take up to my room and the swine at the front desk created another scene. Isador lost his temper and told him it was none of his damn business. Ugly and upsetting incident.

*Friday, 30 September 1927*

I have found a third-floor, front room at 1607 I Street and tomorrow am moving from the Y.M.C.A. The new room has a delightful view—a front yard with branching trees, a picket fence, a walled garden across the street, and, as soon as it is finished, a view of the Hay-Adams House.

Spent the evening insanely trying to finish my packing. Stood at my window for a last view. The moon was full in a clear sky. Dancing stars. Lights in the Mall sharp and bright; lights on the hills of Anacostia blinking and flashing like fireflies. Hard to believe that I shall say good-bye to old 621. In this room I spent two and a half interesting years of my life.

*Friday, 18 November 1927*

Cold and windy after yesterday's tornado in the Southeast section. Homes were blown down and hundreds of persons injured. I have not had a chance to go to see the ruins. Went to the Y after dinner. Above Dash's door a dark transom greeted me, so I walked around a few blocks and returned. His room was still dark, so I went on home. In about a half hour I heard my name shouted below and opened the window to see Dashie clamoring to be let in. The bell was out of order. I daresay Wu, my obstreperous landlord, broke the bell purposely to keep from being disturbed by my visitors.

Dash sat at my table reading the *Mercury*. I studied Thomas Carlyle's essays. From time to time I looked over at Dashie, his hair silken-brown under the light. If only he understood me, if only he understood my love for him. When he left, I looked out the window to see him. He turned and waved, and I watched him out of sight. The room seemed empty, as a room without him always does.

*Friday, 9 December 1927*

Dashie and I went to see America's foremost woman poet—Edna St. Vincent Millay—read her poems. Miss Millay was dressed in a clinging gown with a short train, the whole brocade red with oval yellow figures. She was simple and unaffected, whimsical and charming, very feminine, fragile. She recited her poems in a clear, melodious voice. Dash murmured, "This is the most enjoyable evening I have spent in a long time." The poetry reading was also a great treat for me—I admire Miss Millay and her work extremely.

Isador and a handsome chap sat across the gallery from us. Dash and I had our opera glasses and enjoyed them a great deal, also. We could observe much. After, Isador found Miss Millay and had her autograph my copy of *The Harp-Weaver* for me.

*Edna St. Vincent Millay (1892–1950) won a Pulitzer Prize in 1923 for* The Harp Weaver and Other Poems. *The lyrical world of love and moral freedom that she celebrated in her poems probably appealed to Jeb and Dash in terms that resonated with their own sense of the potential and the post-war freshness of life in the twenties.*

### Sunday, 11 December 1927

To the house as usual. After dinner there was a great argument and I came in for a roasting, particularly from Mama, for being "lazy" and objecting to work and so on. Dad and I went for a drive, taking a skim along Haines Point in the keen, still cold. I invited him up to my room. He opened the box of Mother's letters I have been keeping for him, and read some of my mother's tenderly beautiful letters. I realize what a wonderful mother I lost. How much richer and happier would our lives have been had she lived! What a contrast between her and Mama!

### Wednesday, 14 December 1927

Dashie said he made an engagement to go with Tony Baretto, the artistic-looking butler at the Portuguese Embassy, to see Beatrice Lillie, the incomparable, at the National. I was very much disappointed. After dinner I walked with Dashie to the National. Such a gathering out front! Isador, Junior, Max, Bolling, and Isador, surrounded by friends. Tony Baretto strode toward us—dark-haired, handsome, smiling. Then little Mrs. Green, from my office, arrived in a taxicab with her wall-eyed small husband. I fled.

*Beatrice Lillie (1894-1989) was an uproarious, clowning, cavorting performer. Everyone was crazy about her. She was generally considered the greatest comedienne of her era.*

### Thursday, 15 December 1927

Mist enveloped inscrutable, moody, drizzly old Washington. One of my bad days at the office, when I am listless and wretched and unable to work. Filled with wild desires, rebellious rages, and half-formed fears about Dash and Tony Baretto. At night in Dash's room the wind whistled shrilly at the windows. Dash prepared his Christmas presents to send home. I sat watching him, loafing, relaxing, smoking. It had been a turbulent day, emotionally, for me. Thinking of my Dashie-boy, worrying over him. Tonight I gave him a poem I had written for him:

To _____

No orchids cherished in a heated room

Or languid lilies drowsy with perfume
Would ever do as gifts for you;
Such artificial blossoms would not be
Appropriate to your sweet simplicity.
But I will seek spring wheat stems of the sheen
Of sunny oceans, that will match the green
Of far horizons in your eyes;
And from the oak tree on the hill I'll tear
A wreath of brown leaves for your wind-blown hair.

He was touched by the thought. After all, as long as his affection for me remains unchanged and my deep love for him continues, nothing else matters very much.

### Monday, 19 December 1927

Miserable unhappiness. He arrived in the icy wind. For a change, my dishonest landlord Wu had provided an abundance of heat that sizzled from my radiator. Dash sat at my table reading Havelock Ellis' *Studies* while I read Christopher Marlowe's *Hero and Leander*. And then I persuaded him to tell me about Sunday night . . . I feel as if something beautiful has been spattered with mud . . . Yet it was not so bad as it might have been. I have been worrying myself sick and now that I have got to the bitter truth, I may be able to reach calm. But there is something lost that can never be replaced. *Your sweet simplicity!* Oh my darling, there seems to be more misery than happiness in a love such as mine. I still love you passionately, wildly. It is a kind of merciless tyranny. The wind moans outside and you, no doubt, dear, are lying asleep in your little cot, while I sit here wretched and longing for you.

### Tuesday, 20 December 1927

Bitterly unhappy. It seemed to me as if I had possessed something sweet and clean and beautiful and it had been stolen by Tony Baretto. I took "sick leave" from work. Spent the day like a walking corpse among crowded, hot, nerve-wracking stores full of Christmas shoppers. Bought Christmas wrapping, tags and the like, all blue and silver, just to be different.

I had to see Dash. He was surprised when I walked into his office at the State Department. He introduced me to his boss, Miss Paravan, a deaf lady, but interesting. Their cozy office is separated from the rest of a large room by a partition, and has a fireplace in it. I had been under such emotional stress that I had worked myself into a fit of nervousness. When we got to Allies Inn for dinner, I could eat only with difficulty. My stomach felt as if it were jumping up and down all the time. Afterward, in his room I lay on his bed, resting and looking at him. I became much more cheerful. After all, I haven't lost him—it's merely my ideal which has been shattered.

*Sunday, 25 December 1927*

To the house. We had an excellent Christmas dinner. I came away as soon as I possibly could. Missed the first streetcar, arriving late at Isador's apartment for my second Christmas dinner of the day. Dashie opened the door, saluting me with a glass filled with red wine, the real stuff (pilfered, no doubt, from the pantry of the Portuguese Embassy by that thieving devil-butler Tony Baretto—but I said nothing). Isador's apartment was filled with the aroma of cooking turkey, sweet potatoes, and spices. While Dash poured me a heady glass of wine, Isador bustled out from the kitchen waving a dish towel. "Oh, dearest Jeb! I was afraid for my turkey when you didn't arrive—but first, look at the tree—" In the corner he had set up a tiny spruce decked with tinsel and ornaments. "And Dashie poured you wine—aren't we lucky to have real wine?"

He seated us as soon as I arrived. Others present were Mary Riley, Isador's grandmother, and Isador's midshipman friend Harry. Harry is an attractive chap, with his curly blond hair and lazy, sleepy eyes. The grandmother reminds me of an organ grinder's monkey. Her fingers are long, and at Isador's parties if there is drink being served she holds out her glass with both hands to ask Isador for more. The women talked part of the time in Spanish. We had a nice meal, though not a sensible one, but the table was badly crowded. I was ill and unhappy from so much food in one day. Mary Riley gazed at Isador and said in her Irish brogue, "I love you, Isador. You bring happiness into the world." Isador replied, "I love you, too, Mary, more than almost anything." Leaning over the crowded table, they kissed one another on the lips, then lifted their glasses in a toast to the memory of Isador's mother.

It was a memorable evening, but as we were leaving Isador said Harry wanted to tell me something. I felt it must be about Tony Baretto. Both Dash and I were agitated, although hiding it. When it was over Dash and I walked to the Y against a freezing night wind. When we got to his room I stood by the window and didn't take off my coat. We talked about this disagreeable Baretto topic and got things in a worse mess. I became bitterly unhappy. When I pulled on my gloves, Dash supported my leaving.

*Friday, 30 December 1927*

We had a delightful evening in Dash's room, desultorily reading *The Nation* and the *Star*. He was nicer than he had been in a long time. And then when I was ready to go, he announced that he was going to have another policy, a New Year's resolution, a "Touch Me Not" policy. I was stunned. He put on his overcoat and walked with me through the bitter cold, almost to my house. We stood across from the unfinished Hay-Adams House, shiveringly discussing the matter. I bitterly protested such folly. I urged him and asked him, "Where did you get this insane notion that our love is 'unnatural'?" He shook his head and said, "Hereafter I am not going to do it." I took bitter leave of him. It is so unnecessary. Why should we deny love, destroy happiness, suppress all natural feelings and desire?

*Saturday, 31 December 1927*

An endless day at the office. At night the streets were bitterly cold and windy. Up to Isador's apartment for New Year's Eve. I was blue and scarcely spoke to anyone. When twelve came I left, merely saying, "Good-bye, everybody," without looking at any of them. I walked around downtown for many blocks. The wind blew like a fiend and roared wildly through the parks and bent the tree tops of the White House grounds.

# 1928

*Friday, 6 January 1928*

Dasham was washing the windows, of all things, as if it were worth the labor and the risk of standing outside six stories above the street. He had to shout from outside to be heard. "I must make a declaration of independence for my own sake—even if it kills you, Jeb. Henceforth we must be friends, and nothing more." I stood inside the window arguing helplessly. He shouted through the glass, "You make too much of this, just the way you made too much of the incident with Tony Baretto." I cried out hoarsely, "You call that an 'incident'?" "What else would I call it? I merely drank so much gin that I felt give-inney and stayed the night." I became so frenzied mentally that the back of my head felt as if it were going to burst. I tried to calm myself. "I can't help loving you. You have come to mean everything to me." He answered determinedly, "I cannot be bound in any such way any longer. I have previously relented, but this time is final. You will have to accept it or I'll give you up entirely."

I went home feeling a longing for a cozy open fire, a comfortable book-lined room and someone gentle and patient to lend charm and to see that all went smoothly. I lit the candles on the mantelpiece and set incense to smoking in front of my Buddha, and listened to music, and cried. The greatest love that I have ever known and I am asked to pretend that it doesn't exist and at the same time am assured that, at least in the form of deep feeling and friendship, it is returned. His decision would be unbearable, as I have told him.

### Wednesday, 11 January 1928

Had a terrible nightmare last night. I dreamed that Mama and I were in a tornado, she driving a small, eggshell-colored car that skidded here and there while trees and houses toppled all about us. We were both worried about Dad, and I about Dash. When we finally found Dad, he seemed to be half-witted and told me not to spend the night in the park.

I woke to a beautiful fog outside. When I walked to work the Monument was magically shrouded in white mist at its base. The peak rose gleaming in the sunshine like a great snow-clad mountain. Just before lunch time, Dad appeared at my desk. I went out to the car to say good-bye to him and Mama. It was suitable wintry weather to be setting out for a vacation in Cuba, and I envied them. My last sight of them was as I ran up the steps; Dad sounded the horn and waved when I turned around. Then Dad and Mama were off for Habana, and the palm trees and the Gulf breezes.

Today I began thinking that I am wasting my affection on Dash, giving my greatest love to one who claims such love is unnatural, and neglecting everything for the sake of that affection for him—my personal affairs, my reading, my friends, my work at the office, and to some extent my family. But tonight when we met at Allies Inn he was so friendly and charming over dinner that all my thoughts of today were dispelled.

### Saturday, 28 January 1928

A foot of snow on the ground; an icy wind bearing stinging particles of snow that filled the air with swirling clouds. It was dim and cozy at breakfast in the narrow court at Allies Inn. The glass over our heads was covered deep with snow that excluded the light. When I walked to the office, the Monument lawns were covered with white snow and the air was filled with a whirling mist that rendered all things dreamlike. Not much work done. I gazed down from my window through the silent, drifting snow. Few streetcars were running and few automobiles.

We were let out early. Walking downtown I discovered Max, bundled in black, a vague shape hardly recognizable in a mist of swirling snow. He was gazing into the window of Thos. Cook and Son's Agency. We stood together looking at the little illuminated scene of Central America, arranged in the window like a stage setting. I frequently stop to look at this diminutive scene, because I like to imagine Dasham and myself swinging along that pictured road on a glorious holiday, the blue Caribbean spread out below us and palm trees waving in the tropical sunshine.

"Max," I said, "We need to talk frankly. You must admit that you don't have such a high opinion of me as you used to." He said, "I admit it." The snow whirled and fell on ghostly automobiles hissing and creeping past in the white street. Max smiled, his arms across his chest. "You have got in a rut in the Government. You think too much of comfort. You're losing your youthful zest and virility. You're mired up to your neck in the stiffness of monotony." I was shaking with cold. Max was smiling that hard, amused expression that is so much a part of my association of him. "I've thought about you," he said, "thought that you should take to newspaper work. There, you'd be thrown into the thick of life. You'd have to develop energy and push."

When we separated, I walked rapidly to get warm, determined to be invigorated and full of life and courage. Walked home rapidly through freezing crystals of snow, thinking of what Max had said, realizing what a deadening influence the Government has had on me, how little energy and initiative I have left, and I felt ready to attempt to be a fighter rather than a coward—to be a doer and not a sloth. Got some black coffee at Pickwick and returned home determined to write something in the way of a short story. I have several plots more or less worked out in my mind. It seemed, after all, not such an impossible task. About forty-five minutes later I had to go out for more coffee. By two I was so sleepy that I stopped, but my drowsiness doesn't seem to have prevented me from writing in my diary copiously. Now to sleep. "Weaving a cave in endless night . . . " Don't know where that is from.

*Monday, 30 January 1928*

Dash's twenty-eighth birthday. The day seemed long and I thought miserably of my love most of the time instead of working. How I long to go away with him, far away in the wilds of the mountains. In the evening I presented him with his birthday present, a scarf in three shades of brown. He seemed pleased. Max had given him Richard Halliburton's *The Glorious Adventure.* Went home worrying about Max. Perhaps Max is taking my place in Dash's affections. He spent $5 on the gift of the Halliburton book for Dasham, and that, after all, is a good deal of money, as much as I spent. It would be too bad if I should become jealous of my most respected friend. Oh, what a madness this is, this obsession of love. If I kept up like this my mind would weaken.

*Wednesday, 1 February 1928*

Breakfast is one of the greatest pleasures of the day, my snug breakfast with Dash, my hot cereal or shredded wheat, buttered waffles, sausage (egg most of the time), applesauce, and coffee with a cigarette. Then we walk out together until he turns off at the State Department, and after that I have my brisk walk through the morning-bright park. But today the breakfast ceremony was spoiled when Dasham told me, "I stayed at Junior's last night until after midnight . . . " I got foolishly wrought up. I had so wanted to keep him away from that crowd that goes to Muriel Phillipson's, with their petty intrigues and affairs, their sexual obsessions and idle gossip. All that queer stuff—it makes me sick to think of it. I want to keep him sweet and wholesome, simple and unspoiled; it would make him happier and me, too.

He finished eating and rose from the table before I was through. "I won't see you tonight. I have an engagement. But," he added coolly, "it isn't Max, so you have no cause to spend your day at work chewing up a blotter and spitting it out all over your desk."

*Saturday, 4 February 1928*

Along came the dark-haired Tony Baretto—and sat down with us, spoiling our breakfast. I hate him, because of the unhappiness he has caused me. Dash was excessively agreeable toward him, handing him the salt, handing him the sugar, laughing at Tony's anecdotes of woes in the Portuguese Embassy kitchen. Tony left us when we reached the street. Dash and I had an argument over my lack of politeness. I said, "I couldn't be a hypocrite." Dash angrily retorted, "Some day I might find out that I don't feel so kindly toward you as I once did. I won't be a hypocrite then. I'll let you know in no uncertain terms." I was stunned and hurt. But I shall keep struggling to establish again the sweet and wholesome comradeship that existed until, as Dash jocularly expressed it not long ago, "the snake entered the Garden of Eden"—the damned snake of the Portuguese Embassy.

After work I came home and burned incense and played *L'Apres Midi d'un Faune,* and read Shakespeare's sonnet 87, "Farewell, thou wert too dear for my possessing." I wept, thinking of the difference between then and now. Dear boy! I am always thinking of him and reliving the times we spent together. O, how I yearn for my darling lad. Ever since the Tony Baretto incident he has grown further away from me. It makes me frantic.

*Sunday, 26 February 1928*

I put on my dark blue, crimson-striped tie which I wear when feeling defiant or hilarious. When I got to Dash's room he said, "You look almost militant." I replied, "That's the way I feel." A walk across the Bison Bridge into Georgetown, looking at the houses. We then started back, both of us cold and shivery. I pointed out the detestable site on Pennsylvania Avenue wherein I was enslaved during the horrible year of 1922 by Dad's grocery business. When we got back to the Y the warmth was comforting. He gave me a sort of chronological outline of his life in response to my questions, that is, where he was and what he was doing in the various years. As he talked, with that faint half-frown coming and going as he tried to remember things, he seemed to be the same dear Dashie-boy that used to love me last summer, and I felt contented just to gaze into his clear eyes and hear him talk about himself.

*Monday, 5 March 1928*

To the McReynolds to see Isador, whom I found putting the finishing touches on his "scrapbook of 1927." Randall was there and rather friendly. We talked about the theatre and shows. Then Isador and Randall drifted into gossip of their affairs. I left feeling disgusted, with a bad taste in my mouth. I had barely closed the door before I heard them shrieking with laughter—probably something concerning me—the nasty little two-faced cats.

*Wednesday, 7 March 1928*

This morning at breakfast Dash made the remark that he didn't particularly regret the incident with Tony Baretto. I accepted the remark in pained silence. I then said, "You appeared to regret it at the time, and it caused you to change your relations with me." He said nothing. I remarked, "Our relationship had the opposite effect on me. Instead of making me promiscuous, it had kept me away from others. I haven't had any relations of that kind with anyone else since that first night with you last summer." After a moment I went on, "I suppose you have spent the night with others since Tony Baretto." Still he didn't speak. I asked, "Have you?"

After a pause during which he scowled angrily, he remarked, "The answer is no, but it's none of your *damn* business." I said I was sorry. He was smiling again in a minute. As we left the restaurant he asked me, "Is that what you've been worrying about all this time? Well, I'm glad you've got it out of your system. Why didn't you ask me before?" "Because it was none of my *damn* business." I told him he made such a mystery of matters, and I knew that others wanted to have such relations with him. He answered, "They were unsuccessful." And we parted by the State Department fence.

*Thursday, 8 March 1928*

This morning at Allies Inn he smiled but once during the whole meal. I tried to be bright and vivacious. Oh, Lord, I suppose this sounds pathetic. I wonder how I shall feel in years hence reading these pages of bewailing my lost love. What is it I want? Just one true friend, the Will o' the wisp that I have chased for so long.

Again, no hot water in my bathroom. Dasham's most recent rule, that I cannot any longer use his hot shower at the Y, is a disagreeable aspect of the overall situation. Hans and Max take showers from Dasham's room. If Dash won't let me, why should he let Max and Hans? I'll force that matter to a showdown.

*Friday, 9 March 1928*

To Scott Circle to see Max, who was painting when I got there. We got into a tense situation over Dash. He told me some things about Randall. "You have confirmed my opinion," I said, "that Randall is a contemptible, sneaking, dishonorable cad, with no sense of decency—he is trying to turn Dasham against me, merely to establish a fickle sexual relationship." Max said he was tired of discussing it. Of course I have kept my promise and have not told anyone, not even Max, of my true relations with Dash. I've had to lie, have said I have given up all sexual relations since last summer. I long to tell Max, so he would understand better.

He intimated I was making too much over trivial things. Said, "I've refused to listen to Isador's talk about Dasham and you." I replied, "I suppose I ought to see myself as others see me, that is, as foolishly jealous. I resent this. Let them keep on talking, but I'll keep trying to prevent Dashie from being drawn into that whirlpool. He's too fine and clean for that gang at Muriel Phillipson's. I know him better than anybody else. Why—Isador! With his fickle associations! What does Isador know?"

I turned on Max's Victrola, much agitated, playing "The Song of Love" and other records, and smoking several cigarettes. We finally got down to a basis of stimulating give-and-take conversation. Max told me of an experience he had Sunday night. He had long desired to attempt it, just for the sake of the experience itself. I was rather shocked and regretful to learn that he had finally gone to that extent, but I hid my feelings and told him his own attitude toward it was the one to be considered. He said, "You are sentimental to the point of weakness." I denied it and defended myself.

*Tuesday, 13 March 1928*

Dash was not home. Don't know where he was. Occurred to me suddenly that he might have gone to Bolling Balfour's studio, which he has endlessly admired. I didn't know what to do and went to Isador. He had a card party going, consisting of Mary Riley, himself, his grandmother, and other old ladies. Isador excused himself from the game and took me into the kitchen. He served milk and caramel cake, and put out his kitchen light to watch the rooms across the street at the Y, calling it his "box-party." I was not much interested. I talked to him pretty frankly about my grievances against him. We discussed his notoriety and promiscuity, and I admitted to him that they were none of my business. I went home relieved to have discussed my problems, even though Isador does not even now know my true relations with Dasham.

*Wednesday, March 14 1928*

At breakfast Dasham ate in a leisurely manner and read his paper. I pitched in and vented my feelings about being left to wonder where he was last night. He got up saying, "Calm down and enjoy your breakfast." And walked off. Late in the afternoon he called and asked if he might borrow my camera to take to Randall's tonight. I felt that by telephoning me to ask a favor he had made amends.

As I arrived at the Y with the camera, he and Bolling Balfour were getting into the elevator. Dash wanted to take the camera right there, but I went with them up to Dash's room. Dash was outrageously rude. He insisted on Bolling sitting down, ignoring me and talking to Bolling effusively and laughingly. I started to show him how to use the camera. He exclaimed, "I changed my mind. I don't believe I'll use it." "But why have you changed your mind?" "I have a right to."

Bolling started to put on his coat and Dash said, "Wait, Bolling. We'll all three go together. No—go on. I want to wash my teeth." Merely to get rid of me, to keep from being alone with me. Bolling and I started out, but I asked him to wait at the elevator and went back to Dash's room. I said stiffly, "It is apparent Bolling has taken my place in your affections." Dash said, "Is it?" I said, "Has he?" Dash said, "Ask him. Anyway, I don't have to answer your questions. I'll cultivate whatever friends I choose. You always imagine the worst, anyway." At that moment Bolling poked his head inside. "I apologize for intruding. I only came back to tell you good-bye—I must go." Dash picked up his coat abruptly and strode rapidly past us out the door. I told Bolling what I had said about him to Dash. He listened quietly. "Let me make it plain," he said, "that I am not in love with your beloved, nor do I want to be. He has never spent the night with me—in fact, he hasn't even been out to see me since that time with you." He told me confidentially something about his love for Beverly Nichols, the English novelist, and of his being with him in New York and staying with him in Baltimore. He read aloud from one of Nichols's witty, clever articles. He said the situation with Dasham might work out, if I didn't see him too much. "He'll begin to miss you, Jeb, and realize the value of your friendship." I went home relieved to have discussed the whole thing with someone who understands. It mostly depends now on Dash, I suppose. I think of Dash now with no bitterness, but not as a trustful, impulsive, eager little boy.

**Beverly Nichols** *(1898–1983) was an English writer best known for his scandalous autobiography,* Father Figure *(1972).*

### Friday, 16 March 1928

Dash said that Isador came into his office and stayed so long that Dash had to tell him to leave. He refused, and told Dash, "If I become incensed, I can be very dangerous." He also told Dash about my visit to him on Tuesday evening. When I heard that I said, "Damn him! He is absolutely untrustworthy." The idea of Isador going to Dash's office—even threatening him. Dash remarked, "It's easy to see that Isador is your confidant." I said, "You are wrong. I merely told Isador to stop making sarcastic remarks to people concerning you and me." Dash said slowly, "I am going to tell him not to come into my office again except on official business. The telephone girls are talking about him, and I don't want to be connected with him." It suddenly occurred to me that maybe Dash thought I had told Isador about our physical relations and under that impression might give it all away. I thought of all the things Isador might tell him that he ought not to be told. Carefully I explained to Dash that I had kept my promise of last summer. "I even lied about it. If anybody ever hinted at such a thing, I would deny it indignantly. I said it would be out of the question with you, that you were very much opposed to any such thing. And I said I had no intention of ever trying to start such a relation." Dash made no reply. In spite of all I have done, and can do, I am afraid my darling boy is going to be drawn into that whirlpool.

### Saturday, 17 March 1928

As I was hurrying toward breakfast through the cold March wind, I met Dash hastening from the other direction. He said, "Allies Inn is closed. I don't know why. But I can't eat breakfast with you." He went on. I turned around and tried to catch up with him. He stopped at Connecticut Avenue. "Why are you following me? I can't have breakfast with you." So I ate alone at the coffee shop . . . all this drivel . . . such a trivial incident . . . yet it says so much . . .

*Monday, 19 March 1928*

Dinner with Isador, who said Junior Whorley was ill. I went with Isador to the McReynolds and got off at the third floor to see Junior. Heard yelling and noise from his room before I got halfway down the hall, so I knew Junior was not very sick. There was another person lying on the bed, an uninteresting rustic person. He is the new fellow from Corpus Christi—it seems to be no end to Texans swarming into Washington. Junior's room was more disorderly and messy than ever. When the others left I stayed on. Junior served me milk, fruitcake, and animal crackers. Somehow we never seem to be at ease with each other. He told me I am the hardest person to talk to he knows. I can almost say the same. It's odd, too, for we have many interests in common.

We talked about the shocking death of Nora Bayes, which I read about in the noon *News* today. It seemed incredible—that big, strapping woman, so full of vitality. I told Junior how on my fifteenth birthday I saw Nora Bayes for the first time at Keith's, and how thrilled I was when she swept on the stage and started to sing, "You're here and I'm here, so what do we care . . . " I felt as if I cared for nothing else in the world as long as she went on singing. But that loud deep voice of hers will never again boom out across the footlights.

For some reason I told Junior much of my family history—about Mama, my troubles with her, the fact that she was Mother's nurse, and other things. I wish I hadn't, but I suppose no harm can come of it. Spent the rest of the evening at home worrying about Dash and feeling abandoned. It appears to be over—my beautiful love relation. I keep on thinking of how badly I treated dear, gloomy Hans when he loved me and I put him aside. What irony; what poetic justice! I was cruel to Hans then. I didn't know how he felt. Now I am in Hans' place—I am the scared instead of the scarer.

**Nora Bayes** *(1880–1928) was a vaudeville and musical comedy singer. Born Dora Goldberg, she was billed as "The Greatest Single Woman Singing Comedienne in the World." Her theme song was "Shine On, Harvest Moon."*

*Saturday, 31 March 1928*

Carried my camera to Eastman's to see what I could get for it as part payment on a camera of a larger size. They offered $8. I decided it was not worth the cost, since I should have to pay $22 in addition to giving them the old camera. So I shall keep my little camera. I have associations of sentiment connected with it, anyway—silly as it may sound. It is not silly though—why should I apologize for my feelings to some imaginary future reader? After all, I bought the Kodak on 15 July, 1927. That night I spent with Dasham for the first time—the happiest night I ever spent with anybody. And the first two pictures ever taken with my camera were of him and of me in our pajamas, just before we went to bed. They were not good enough to print, but the negatives show something of us.

### Monday, 2 April 1928

The telephone rang as I was going downstairs. It was Dash to say he couldn't have dinner with me. I asked him, "Why not?" He said, "Because I'll be someplace else." I answered roughly, "All right!" and hung up the phone. It was too much. I strode angrily down to the Memorial Basin and stood looking into the gray sunset above the Memorial. Somewhat calmed, I went to Allies Inn and ate alone. Then to the theatre and to my seat. Max arrived first and took the furthest seat, but when Dash got there he insisted on Max's sitting in the middle, and they changed places. This fresh piece of rudeness upset me. I leaned across Max and asked Dasham, "Why did you not come to dinner?" Dash pushed himself behind Max and curtly replied, "None of your *damn business.*"

The play was *The Squall,* set in Spain—a play full of fierce weather scenes and passion, about a Gypsy girl who comes to a household in a violent storm, is kept as a servant, seduces the father, son, and servant, and destroys the happiness of the house. I was too upset to get much pleasure from it. I leaned across Max's lap and whispered, "It is my *damn business* when you break an engagement with me." "I have no standing engagement with you for dinner." "You made the engagement this morning." He leaned across Max, saying, "It was damned considerate of me to 'phone." "If so, it was the first considerate thing you ever did." "I merely found that it would be impossible for me to get there from where I was, on time."

I got no pleasure from the play, and its ending was faulty, a solution brought about by chance, not by the characters themselves. Her Gypsy man returns and carries her away with him. As we left the theatre Max was laughing to himself, as he does sometimes. I asked him, "What did you think of the play?" He replied, "The setting, the passion, the acting, and especially the storm effects, were of a high order . . . "

**The Squall** *(1926). Written by Jean Bart. When the Gypsy girl first enters the house she says, "Me Nubi. Nubi good girl. Nubi stay." Well-known critic Robert Benchley dismissed Bart's play in his column with the words, "Me Benchley. Benchley bad boy. Benchley go."*

### Friday, 6 April 1928

The night was fresh and cool and moonlit. I enjoyed the walk to Georgetown. Dasham said, "Meg Deveraux was the girl I was to marry. The town of Natchez was waiting for that." I said, "Has she moved to Washington to entrap you?" Dash scowled, but answered, "I hope not. She'd be disappointed, and I'd be sorry for that. I'm extremely fond of Meg."

Miss Deveraux has moved into the interesting old building on Prospect where Randall and his wife, mother, and uncle have an apartment. I waited outside while Dasham went upstairs to see if Miss Deveraux were there. The window of the Hare apartment was open, and I could hear the voices of old Mrs. Hare-Worth and Isador, both talking at once. Dash came down and beckoned to me. Miss Deveraux' apartment was in the garret, reached by many steps. She is a pretty girl, though she moves, as Dash has said, like a slow motion picture. She talks the same way, slowly, precisely, deliberately. She taught English in a girls' school in Munich, and is interested in things German.

We stayed only a short time. A missionary lady who is soon to sail to India was also there, and a bespectacled woman in her thirties. I was sorry to leave so soon, but Dasham murmured, "We should interrupt their little group if we stayed." Miss Deveraux walked us downstairs and stepped outside with us. We lingered and gazed at the shadowy trees and moonlit sky, until Dasham and I told her good-night.

Dash and I walked over Key Bridge and stood for a time looking at the moonlight on the Potomac, the dim bulk of Analostan Island, the lights of the city along the shore, and the occasional red flame that flared up gorgeously from the gasworks. I don't think there is anything to worry about from Miss Deveraux. Things are going pretty well with us now. Not the old relationship, but friends.

**Analostan Island:** *Now named Theodore Roosevelt Island, the island lies off George-town in the Potomac. Throughout his life, Jeb continued to use the name Analostan Island, apologizing each time in his diary for being sentimental about the old name. In the nineteenth century the island was also called Mason's, having been at one time the home of James Mason. During the Civil War, black soldiers were encamped on Mason's to protect them from white hostilities.*

*Sunday, 8 April 1928*

Sallied out with Dash and Miss Deveraux to view the flower-laden branches of the cherry trees. From a distance as a spectacle, the blossoms this year were pale and with gaps in the trees, but close up they were marvelously beautiful, graceful and fragrant. I didn't get a picture of Dasham against the cherry blossoms because he acted too cranky.

He wandered off and left Miss Deveraux with me. She linked her arm in mine, and I suppose people thought we were out strolling together. A fresh south wind was blowing. The Basin was full of waves that dashed over the seawall by the John Paul Jones statue. We listened to a string orchestra and watched girls in Japanese costumes dancing. When Dasham returned he absolutely refused to let me take his picture with the cherry blossoms. Then he allowed some strange girls to photograph him after he had taken pictures of them. Miss Deveraux said in her quiet voice, "Stop fooling around, C. C. . . ." Finally he allowed me to take a picture of him with Miss Deveraux and—the irony of it— I took a double exposure and spoiled the picture.

We went from there into the yards behind the Bureau of Engraving. Dash and I scrambled over the piles of lumber taken from the White House roof. I got a shard of wood and an old nail, as historical souvenirs of the roof that sheltered the presidents for 112 years. Dash began dragging away pieces of wood. "Whatever," asked Miss Deveraux, "are you doing?" He replied in his serious drawl, "I want to have them made into a chair, Meg. Such a chair would be historical." She glanced at me. We smiled at one another. I like her. The three of us continued away up the Avenue, Dash dragging the wood noisily behind.

*Wednesday, 11 April 1928*

It was a delightful evening in Miss Deveraux's cozy garret. However, one incident has seriously marred the recollection. Soon after we got there Miss Deveraux called my attention to an unframed watercolor by Susan B. Chase, showing Washington's headquarters on M Street. She told me, "I'm willing to sell this." Dashie remarked, "Probably at a high price." Speaking in German, Miss Deveraux told me that she had purchased the watercolor for $20 and would sell it for $8 or even $5. It seemed such a bargain that I said in my meager German, learned in college and also somewhat from Hans, that I would give her $5 for it. She immediately went for paper and began to wrap it up.

Dash spoke up at once. "What? Did you sell it to him, Meg?" "Yes, he bought it for five dollars." "You sold it over my head?" She told him that he hadn't even wanted it. He answered, "*Now* I don't." I told him, "You can have it, because I don't want it all that much." "You wanted it enough to buy it in German." I said that I didn't know he wanted it. He scowled and said, "I don't want it now." Miss Deveraux said, "Goodness, you came here to enjoy yourselves." She got out a sort of Turkish costume and insisted on Dash's dressing in it over his trousers, with a turban improvised with a Turkish towel. He protested, but wore it and seemed to get back into a good mood. She served us dandelion wine she had brought up from Mississippi, along with toasted crackers. The wine had a pleasing, pungent taste. She and I smoked, and I sipped my wine and felt content. She read our horoscopes from some sort of booklet, and interesting they were, because they often fitted very well.

When we left, the rain had stopped and the streets were glistening under the lights. I was amazed when Dash began to accuse me of being unsportsmanlike in buying the picture in German. I told him, "I didn't start the talk in German. She did." He answered, "But you *went on* in German." Distressed, I offered to sell the painting to him at what I bought it for, begging that he take it. He said stubbornly, "I hope you enjoy it, after the way you got it." I argued and cajoled, but he wouldn't take my offer. He shook his head slowly. "It isn't the same picture, now." Damn her! It was her fault.

> **Susan B. Chase** *(Mrs. V. O.) was a member of the American Watercolor Society and an instructor at Anne Abbott School of Fine and Commercial Art. The painting Jeb bought "in German" was of an old stone house on M Street, between Thirtieth and Thirty-first Streets, N.W. This was Washington's headquarters while he surveyed Washington in 1791.*

### Tuesday, 17 April 1928

Mrs. Green took "sick leave" and both Miss Contadeluci and Mrs. Utott were stormy about the matter. The atmosphere all morning was deeply oppressive. Finally Miss Contadeluci exposed the scandal. "She preferred to *keep her job*," she whispered, "rather than do the womanly thing." After a moment's incomprehension I realized Mrs. Green must be having an operation to remove an impregnation (if that's what it's called—I mean the fetus). It was startling to think of the air-headed Green in that context. When Mrs. Utott marched out of her cubicle, Miss Contadeluci gave a meaning look, indicating that I had been told. The Utott was only too happy to discuss the matter. "That little husband of hers deserved offspring . . . "

"But," I objected, "if having a child meant she would not be able to keep her job—" Both women set upon me as if they were killing snakes. "Do you know what my husband and I would have given," cried Mrs. Utott, "to have had a child, a baby, a baby—" And Miss Contadeluci's eyes filled with tears. "You cannot imagine how I have envied other women when I see them with their baby carriages." I was immensely sorry I had spoken.

Went at night with Dasham to hear an address by Hugo Wast, the Argentine novelist. To our surprise Wast spoke entirely in Spanish. It was a total loss as far as our understanding him was concerned. He was a small, lean, bald man with dark restless eyes, and a gesticulating manner of delivery. But because we could not understand a word he spoke, we grew tired of it long before he had finished.

*"**Operation to remove an impregnation.**" Abortion was illegal at the time, but sympathetic family doctors (and alley abortionists) performed the operation.*

*Tuesday, 1 May 1928*

At the office came a joyful surprise—Winegardner told me he had recommended me for promotion to grade 6, which under the Welch Act would become $2300—an increase of $440! Hurried to Dashie's room and told him the news. If only he, too, could get an increase.

We took a streetcar out to see *Simba* at Poli's. It was a motion picture of the Martin Johnson expedition to East Africa and showed thrilling views of elephants, lions, giraffes, and other beasts in their natural haunts. A profitable evening. Home again and did chores, mostly tidying up my table and desk. Read an article in *Harper's* called "Babes in the Bois," by Barrett Richmond. It was on the excessively sophisticated youth who flee to Paris and give in to the cult of futility—disciples of Hemingway's *The Sun Also Rises*. My association with Dashie-boy has brought me a long way back along the road I had traveled, back toward simplicity and wholesomeness and away from smart cynicism and bored decadence.

*Friday, 4 May 1928*

Dash had gone out to Georgetown to see Miss Deveraux, so I went with Max to see *The Enemy of the People*. We had arranged to meet Isador and Junior in front of the theatre. It upset me exceedingly to recognize not only Isador but also Junior hurrying toward us in "costume." Junior looked exactly like a girl. I looked meaningfully from him to Isador and said flatly, "One is more than enough." They carried on, all the way up to the gallery. When we found our seats I saw Miss Contadeluci sitting almost in front of us. It was stifling there, though a welcome breeze came through the window between acts.

When we left the theatre and started along the Avenue, I was determined to be uplifted and fortified by the play. I remarked, "The play was an inspiration— 'The strongest man in the world is he who stands most alone'— what an assertion of the supremacy of the individual!" Junior said, "You, Jeb! To speak about standing alone! You have a terror of public opinion." When I heatedly denied it, Isador murmured, "Jeb, you are shaking with fear." I objected, saying that I was wet with perspiration from the heat of the theatre, and was shivering from the strong breeze that was blowing, tossing and shaking the maples. "No, Jeb," Isador said, "you are shaking with fear because some day you may have to confess that the individuality you adore is nothing for you but a word." Max looked at me. "And what does our independent thinker reply to *that?*" I put a stop to the discussion by saying that it was too lovely a night for a quarrel. We went to a drug-store and had milkshakes and sodas. I was angry and dejected.

*Saturday, 5 May 1928*

Supper at Allies Inn. Dash was fairly pleasant, most of the time. I was glad to be in familiar surroundings, with the old stone walls and drooping green ferns, the candle wavering on the table and Dashie's eyes, those clear pools, to gaze into. But he got in one of his moods; refused to make any engagement for tomorrow; said, "Something else might turn up." Sometimes he acts like a disagreeable child, and can't be taken seriously. I asked if he might be going to Miss Deveraux' tomorrow. He said, "What makes you think that?" and started to eat his soup. I was cold and distant the rest of the meal. A mistake for me to start acting that way again but I can't help it. Lately I've been thinking much about Meg Deveraux. I've seen how she can wrap Dashie around her little finger. And he is so damned unreasonable! Why does he try to hide everything he does with her and make a mystery of it?

*Sunday, 6 May 1928*

A chill, damp evening, with gray-black skies lowering. He said he was visiting Miss Deveraux. I asked if I might go along. He replied, "If you want to. It makes no difference to me." We started up the Avenue. He was silent. I said, "Whatever I've done, I apologize." He wouldn't speak and we walked on in silence. I suddenly said, "Good-night, Dashie," and turned back. He strode on. I ran to catch up with him, imploring him, "Won't you even say good-night?" Still he wouldn't speak and I lost my temper, dashed my cigarette to my feet and cried, "Go to hell, then!"

Almost in a daze, I walked to the Little Theatre to get it all out of my mind. The film was a German one—*The Trial of Donald Westhof,* a superbly handled picture. But when I came out I was in the depths of unhappiness. I walked home with the rain falling on my bare head and my raincoat turned up around the collar. My yard was dark and mysterious, embowered in its dripping shrubs and vines. Now it is raining hard. The trees are thrashing in the wind. Oh, to sleep on and on in a spacious cool chamber on my Isle of Golden Dreams.

*Friday, 11 May 1928*

This was a day with a glorious ending. At Allies Inn Dash greeted me with a sweet smile and I felt better already. After dinner I asked him to walk up to my room and he said he would, "for a minute." He seemed glad to walk up with me.

He ensconced himself in the big leather chair and began looking at travel folders, while I lit wisteria incense, my favorite, and sat down, feeling the usual nervous contentment at having him here in my room. Around midnight he said he must go. I urged him to stay longer. He sat down on the arm of the big chair. I went over to him and he allowed me to kiss him.

I told him, "This is the first kiss since mid-December." He kissed me. I clasped him to me in an ecstasy of happiness. I stayed there holding him in my arms and kissing him and telling him how much I loved him. After all these months of suppressed affection I poured out my love for him. "I love you. You know that, don't you? Haven't I shown it by this time?" He said *yes*. I told him, "I've never loved anybody as I've loved you. Nobody could love anyone more than I love you." And he, sweetly smiling, returned my affectionate embraces. I said, "I've spent so many miserable hours here thinking of you and wishing for you. Remember that I love you. It may excuse many things." This I told him at the door. He wouldn't remain, but I was passionately happy as it was.

He looked back and waved as he went down the steps. I opened the window and watched for him on the sidewalk. As soon as he came in sight under the bay window he was looking up. When he saw me he held up his hand again in a farewell gesture and smiled his dazzling smile. I sat down feeling limp, feeling as if I had released something long penned up within me. Those delicious kisses I shall not soon forget. Months of starvation and then a joyous feast, although incomplete.

*Sunday, 13 May 1928*

A happy day with Dashie, cloudless skies, everything sunny and serene. This morning on my bed he made my feast complete. Later we lounged around in the yard at my house taking pictures. The irises and spiraea were in bloom; the trees rustled in the breeze. I felt very high, glorying in the loveliness of the May and the sweetness of life. Dash lolled on the long grass of the yard and changed the film in his camera. Then he climbed the high garden wall across the street for a picture of my house. I went up and stood on the balcony. My rascally landlord Wu, seeing from the window that a picture was to be taken, hastened outside and posed at the gate.

Dash and I walked up to Dupont Circle, where he photographed the fountain's wind-tossed streams of water. Across Q Street Bridge to Georgetown, and ascended the hill to the strange, round, empty reservoir on Wisconsin Avenue. From there we had a magnificent view of the Potomac and the unfinished Arlington Bridge. Then to supper. Can Dashie ever understand how much he means to me? I have been thinking of the possibility of paying his way to Europe with me this summer, employing him as a traveling companion. With my promotion, I can afford it. There are hundreds who would jump at the chance.

*Wednesday, 16 May 1928*

A stroll through the damp spring evening with Dash, Hans, and Junior to the Pan-American gardens. The air carried the scent of flowers; the gardens were soothing and peaceful; the Monument looked ghostly and weirdly beautiful in the gathering mists of twilight. We leaned on the marble parapet, talking. Hans told us that he has taken a summer job out at Mrs. Fowler's water lily farms in Kenilworth. Junior irritated me extremely. Tonight I hated him for his fawning, pseudo-affectionate attitude toward Dashie.

Later we took a streetcar to the Senate gallery where the Welch pay-raise bill was to come to a vote. There was a big crowd. We stood on the gallery steps for more than an hour and a half. When the bill came to a vote we could hear the "ayes" being called, and the bill passed by a vote of 48 to 0. Immediately the galleries began to empty their hoards of Government clerks, all with a happy look on their faces. It appears that I really may be able to afford a trip to Europe with Dash.

> **The Kenilworth Aquatic Gardens** *are located at Kenilworth Avenue and Douglas Street, N.E. In Jeb's day, the fourteen acres of lotus plants, water lilies, and native plants in swampy lands that are now part of the National Park system belonged to Mrs. Fowler.*

*Sunday, 20 May 1928*

The bus let us off on the dusty road and we were greeted by good old Dr. Holmes. His dog, a pure Airedale named Clerk, scampered about. Dr. Holmes led me into a thicket to show me a rare fern. We got lost and couldn't get to the path for a while. He seems feebler than he did on our last visit. When we found the house, Dash was sitting on the porch. Dr. Holmes filled a decanter with some of his 1927 vintage and I relaxed in the giddy warmth of the strong, homemade wine and gazed off at the oak woods and the picturesque tobacco barn, ruinous and half hidden by vines and trees.

Shortly before dusk we left, dark sweetly coming on, stars beginning to twinkle in the skies. I came to the point of asking Dashie if he would accompany me to Europe, for eight weeks at my expense, as my companion. He was surprised, and refused. "Accepting an offer of going abroad at somebody else's expense would be contrary to my whole make-up and attitude toward life." I urged him to accept. "Life is short! Imagine that we were sitting at a table on the Rue de L'Opera, watching the crowd . . ." "I'd always feel under an obligation." "Dozens would jump at the chance." I almost exhausted my persuasive powers. I told him, "Follow your Cavalier blood. Take your fling while you are young." "I have no clothes for such a trip." That remark was promising. It meant he was thinking about it. I finally brought him around to the point where I could see he was won over about the trip to Europe but didn't want to say so.

We had by then reached Jenkens' Corner. A bus drove by at high speed and wouldn't stop, despite Dash's running out into the road to get the driver's attention. The uncouth yokels in the store told us that a youth among them could drive us to the District Line. We had hardly gotten started in the boy's dilapidated Ford when our rough driver pulled out a Coca-Cola bottle full of corn whiskey, drank the liquor, and the bottle went whizzing out the window. I was glad when we got to the District Line and our lives out of the safekeeping of that carelessly drunken fool. Now, standing at my bureau in my pajamas, as is my custom when writing in my diary, I feel elated, thinking that it is too good to be true! If only Dashie doesn't change his mind, I can go about making plans for the happiest summer of my life.

**Dr. Holmes** *was a botanist who worked for the Department of Agriculture.*

### Wednesday, 23 May 1928

I hastened nervously to Dash's room. He told me the verdict, which made my heart sink. Miss Paravan will not approve his leave. She said that it would be "inconvenient" if he were not here. Not a thing to prevent my wonderful summer except Old Woman Paravan at the State Department. To think that this devilish obstacle has come between us! The disappointment is all the harder because he has been affectionate, considerate and the true pal he used to be before he began to fight his nature and suppress what he thought were unnatural feelings. I begged him to speak to her again. After much persuasion, he told me he would try once more.

### Monday, 28 May 1928

Damned Miss Paravan! Dash said that she told him, "You oughtn't have planned to go to Europe when there is so much work to be done unless you had an exceptional opportunity." He said he told her, "But I do have an exceptional opportunity." Miss Paravan said, "If it is Mr. Alexander, I couldn't approve. Mr. Alexander has an unsatisfactory attitude about his work, proven by the fact that he leaves from breakfast at Allies Inn after nine a.m. each morning."

The idea of that meddlesome bitch criticizing me—in another Department. Dash said he was furious over it. When we parted he told me, "You have been so

patient, but this is too much. I had better withdraw from the plans for the trip."
I replied emphatically, "If you can't go, I won't go without you."

*Friday, 1 June 1928*

Dash was already there when I reached Allies Inn and had turned up a chair
for me, the first breakfast he has done so in months. I read aloud to him from
Baedecker about Vesuvius, Pompeii, and Capri. After breakfast, walking through
the dewy morning as far as the Ellipse, he promised he was going to insist on
Miss Paravan's giving him a definite answer. All day I waited anxiously to find
out if he had been able to talk to her, but he never called me.

In the evening, I knew he was going to see Miss Deveraux, so I walked out to
Prospect Street in the hopes of meeting up with him. I was lingering in the courtyard, undecided as to what to do next, when Dash and Miss Deveraux stepped
down from the garret stairs into the sultry darkness beneath the trees. I strode out
from my place under the shadows. Dash stepped into the light. "Imagine—it's
Jeb." Miss Deveraux slowly moved forward. She greeted me cordially, then,
glancing at Dashie with a smile I did not like, told us good-night. I was nervously waiting to hear about Miss Paravan. We walked through Georgetown and he
said nothing. Finally I asked. He said, "She says I can go, but only for five weeks."
Wonderful news, but how much better would have been the original plan of
eight weeks! So much to see, in such a short time.

*Thursday, 14 June 1928*

To Meyer's, where I helped Dashie open a charge account. We purchased
suits. Dash's is gray. Mine is a Rogers Peet, predominately blue. We each got a
lightweight bathrobe for travel, and I got some underwear. On New York
Avenue we stopped in a sporting goods store and purchased sleeveless sweaters,
buff, both alike, for wear on board ship on cool nights.

On the way home, a few minutes to glance over the early *Post.* Hoover still
not nominated. But there was an article of much interest concerning Mrs.
Fowler's troubles about the water lily farm. The Government is practically going
to confiscate the farm for the Anacostia River park system.

*Sunday, 24 June 1928*

Water lilies by the hundreds in lovely bloom out at Kenilworth. We talked
with Mrs. Fowler about her troubles with the condemnation proceedings by the
Government, then strolled around, enjoying ourselves. Roses, day lilies, and fantastic pitcher plants in full blossoms. Vegetation green from the rains, mist hanging from green woods and hills, and blue spikes of pickerel weed amid the lily

pads. Unexpectedly Dash said, "Everything would be so much better if I could be sure—if only I knew for certain that I were going with you to Europe." I asked him sharply, "What do you mean by that?" He admitted that there was nothing that could keep him from going. "Let me have you to understand," I said, "that it would be unthinkable for you to back out now, especially since I have purchased the tickets." We walked on in silence. Maybe the problem has been that Dashie has believed I was uncertain about taking him. I told him I had no regrets about it and didn't expect to have.

*Thursday, 28 June 1928*

Dash passed by outside as I was dressing and whistled to me. He was on his way to be inoculated for typhoid. Perhaps it would be a good idea for me to be inoculated, too. I may do it.

Things upset at the office. Mrs. Green cried because the radio announcements she had worked on went wrong. I had telephone calls and other such upsetting matters. I hate to use a telephone, especially the one by the window, where the noise of trucks and streetcars sometimes makes it impossible to hear. The day passes more quickly that way, though, and after all, that is all I want— to collect my salary and to get through the day to freedom as quickly as possible.

Out at last into the evening. Dash and I went to see Miss Deveraux, who had borrowed a radio so we could listen to the Democratic convention. I was surprised to find Randall and his wife, mother, and uncle climbing the steep stairs from their apartment to join us in Miss Deveraux' garret. It was the first time I had met Randall's wife. She has fluffy hair and an aristocratic mouth, and was wearing trousers and a collarless sort of long wrap, very theatrical and attractive. She seemed quite intelligent.

Miss Deveraux was in a good humor and was at her best, though her little garret was very hot. At her orders Dash went to the store owned by the Syrians and got some "near-beer"—mild, but refreshing. He has an irritating habit of sticking his tongue out, slightly, between his lips, after each sip of beer. The Democratic platform was liberal, therefore acceptable to me, and Al Smith was nominated. A liberal and a wet—so I am for him. But the evening was far from perfect. Dash and Miss Deveraux teased one another; Randall and his wife encouraged them; I was ready to leave long before we departed.

We walked downtown and wandered over in the pale mist behind the White House, talking of the trip. When I got home I became melancholy. Wondered if I should regret taking Dash with me or should wish that I had taken Max instead. If only I could endow Dash with the mind of Max and with Max's firm artistic temperament, and yet keep intact Dash's physical self and his youthful personality and those dancing green eyes that so enthrall me. But away with such thoughts! Can I never be satisfied?

*Friday, 6 July 1928*

We had to get a cap for Dashie, and smoked glasses for both of us. At twilight we strolled over to Randall's apartment in the equinoctial evening heat. Stopping at the Syrians' store for "near-beer," we found Miss Deveraux. She went with us to Randall's apartment. Randall's family group were conversing languidly in the sitting room: Randall, his wife Catherine, his mother, and Randall's uncle Dieterlie, quietly witty and homosexual in a restrained way. We had a pleasant evening looking over maps and postcards, and I taking down information about hotels and suggestions from Randall about places where we plan to go. Randall is somewhat more decent and likable now. On the way home, Dash and I stopped at Isador's apartment. Isador was pressing a linen suit and the place was like an oven.

*Monday, 9 July 1928*

I had to feverishly pack. Isador arrived and was a great help. He gathered everything up from table, bookcase tops, mantelpiece, and desk, and wrapped them and packed them away in the closet. He loves to do things for people—a generous nature. I lent him two albums of Victrola records. He left with the albums under one arm and my dragon plant under the other. This is the last night in Washington. It is almost unbelievable that I am actually going to Europe tomorrow with Dashie.

*Tuesday, 10 July 1928*

Isador stopped by to pick up two more plants. I joined Dash for a quick breakfast at Allies Inn. Raced to Dad's bank. Cashed his check for an advance on my salary. Hastened to Casten's, because I was worried that my bag and suitcase were packed too tight, and bought a larger suitcase. Rushed in a taxi to E Street to have it initialized. Back to my room to repack. I was drenched with perspiration. Got to the office, and did very little work. Miss Contadeluci gave me $5 to "get something with" for her, preferably from Italy. Hastened away to Dash's room. We left in a taxi at 5:05 with nothing to spare. Randall was in the station unexpectedly. We had only about three minutes with him. Then to the train and off at last!

*Wednesday, 11 July 1928 (SS Majestic, en route New York to Cherbourg)*

There was a swarming crowd around the gangplank. Dash wandered off to explore the decks. I stayed behind, watching a group of Irish patriots who were seeing someone off. They sang, cheered, and waved Irish and American flags. A youngish man with a mop of black hair clambered onto the rail and made a vociferous speech, none of which I could understand because of the noises. His speech brought cheering and applause from his group. Women along the rail were crying. The whole thing was a trying ordeal, and I got emotionally upset, a sort of sympathetic reaction. There was I, leaving my native country, while all about me friends and relatives were waving tearful good-byes. I had to struggle to keep from blubbering out loud. And it was so long drawn out, too. For a solid half hour before the boat sailed those Irish people stood there almost twenty feet apart looking into each other's eyes and waving handkerchiefs and smiling bravely. Finally the last gangplank was pulled in and we moved off—bound to Europe on the bosom of old Ocean. Every time I looked back at that pierful of frenziedly waving arms and handkerchiefs I had to fight back tears.

*Thursday, 12 July 1928 (SS Majestic)*

Studied odd characters among the passengers, looked at the ocean, watched potato races. That covers the morning. In the afternoon we saw the rain coming—a gray veil over the sea moving toward to the ship until it caught us and rain poured on deck. I loafed around in the lounge reading in a windblown *Times* that Dash picked up.

Tonight was a "gala dinner." Dash and I were the first ones at table, but presently the Breton lady appeared, then the elderly Jewish furniture dealer from Chicago. We had a gay meal. We put on colored crêpe paper hats, blew up balloons and tossed them about, made noises with our assorted noisemakers. When people at other tables left, the stewards gave us their abandoned balloons. We pelted one another with them and had a childish good time. The furniture dealer blew up a beautiful pale green balloon, saying, "I'd like to keep this one forever," just as a fresh young blonde in a red dress exploded it with her cigarette as she passed our table.

Dash wandered out to join the dancing. I spent the evening standing on deck enjoying the night—high-rolling waves, driving spray, roaring wind. I had a hard time to tear myself away and go to the cabin. Dashie was in bed and had closed the cover of the porthole, so I could not look out at the ocean. But I could feel the rising and falling of the ship, and I could hear the rude crash of the waves.

*Friday, 13 July 1928 (SS Majestic)*

The ship rolled far to one side, then far to the other. The drunken orange moon slid down behind the life boats and climbed up again, over and over. The sea was ringed with clouds, indescribably lovely. Dash joined the dancing to the music of the Cornell Collegians. I went down to the lounge and drank beers. The Breton lady drank gaily with the old French couple. A group of young people stared over at me, and talked about me. What do I care?

*Saturday, 14 July 1928 (SS Majestic)*

What good beer this ship has! At night Dash and I went on deck feeling pleasantly grogged up and sat in deck chairs discussing the folks at home. We were eyed considerably by a fellow from the ship's purser's office. He was a queer young fellow with a front tooth missing, who wore a huge silver ring about an inch wide. He had pink tinted nails that he allowed to grow to extreme lengths, Chinese fashion. On one of our turns round the deck, he grinned at us foolishly. When Dash and I returned to the lounge we wrote souvenir cards together, but I got to laughing so hard I had to stop. Wandered about on deck and tried to stop my hiccoughs.

*Sunday, 15 July 1928 (SS Majestic)*

I dreamed I was seated on a deck chair when a fierce mastiff dog leapt at me. I kicked wildly upward with both feet straight toward his head. My feet struck the bottom of the berth overhead and woke up Dashie, who called down a facetious good morning and asked what was the matter. I apologized and explained. Found that my right toe was gashed by an exposed wire on the spring overhead and was bleeding.

I went on deck looking for Dash and found him in the lounge with a black-headed girl with a broad nose. They were joined by the pretty blonde who had burst the old furniture dealer's balloon during our gala evening. When the orchestra struck up Dash started dancing with the black-headed girl. I wandered out to the windswept deck. The dance music began to seem sad, and the dancers malicious puppets. How I wish my Dashie could understand the beauty of my love for him. The blonde girl approached and leaned against the rail beside me. Her name is Miss Edwards. We watched the sky, the flying spray, and discussed life and our dissatisfaction with it. An interesting girl, about my age. She teaches drawing; says she has tried writing, art, singing, and failed in all.

*Monday, 16 July 1928 (SS Majestic)*

I helped Dash with his costume for the masquerade party. He used the sugar candy bag I gave him for a mask, and put on a tail made of plaited napkins and was effectively attired. He won second prize for the funniest costume, but deserved first. I stayed in the lounge until he joined me, bringing with him the girls. The dark one with the wide nose is Miss Ingersol. Unfortunately, we seemed to pair off: Dashie with attractive blonde Miss Edwards and I with the broad-nosed, gushing Ingersol. We went on deck. Several times the Ingersol and I joined Dash and the Edwards girl, but the Ingersol always moved away so as to leave them alone. I had a feeling of patient desperation. I listened to her chatter, wondering how far that blonde-headed Edwards would try to go with little boy Dashie, who is so easily led. Finally after midnight, I went down and found Dash in his pajamas, preparing to get into his bunk. He said he had been down for some time.

*Wednesday, 18 July 1828 (SS Majestic)*

We stayed on deck watching the sheets of rain. At last we could see the dim shore of England through our glasses. Tomorrow we shall be in Paris for breakfast.

*Thursday, 19 July 1928 (Paris)*

Dash and I wandered along the Seine looking at the bookstalls. Took a cab for the Eiffel Tower, and then another to the Rodin Museum. Next we went to the Arc de Triomphe and ascended the wearisome stairway to the top. A superb view. Had an altercation but soon got over it. At night we took a cab to Montparnasse and visited the Dingo, famous for its part in Hemingway's *The Sun Also Rises*. Enjoyed a Spanish omelet and wine. At a table nearby was a bunch of Americans. A snub-nosed newspaperman talked a blue streak in a loud voice. There were three girls at the table, but the fellow told of the wonderful massage one can get in Shanghai, with four Chinese women working on one, bringing on a perfect orgasm. I disliked the man intensely.

*Saturday, 21 July 1928 (Paris)*

To the Dôme, where we studied Bohemian and artistic sets. Dash drank two beers and I drank six. I became giddy, brazen without a trace of self-consciousness. Dash became irritated, but I wish to God I could be always be like that. I was enormously entertained by an absurd creature, the "Trick Cigarette Man." He walks up and down smoking a cigarette and smilingly jerking it from his mouth by means of a wire attached to his ear and then inserting it in his mouth again. Apparently his chief pleasure in life is to amuse the Dôme-ites with this contrivance. A woman artist sat down at our table with watercolors to sell. She showed a painting of a nude person, I couldn't make out whether a man or a woman, sucking a woman on a bed. She agreed to take 30 fr. for the painting, but I didn't buy it. Home in a cab feeling gay and cozy. But when we got upstairs

Dash hadn't forgiven me for drinking so much, and it took a long time to settle him down.

### Sunday, 22 July 1928 (Paris)

Breakfast in the pastry shop in the Rue des Saint Péres. Then to the Louvre. We saw the *Mona Lisa* and *Venus de Milo,* our chief objectives. Spent hours in Montmartre. The people were out drinking and enjoying themselves. We allowed a Russian to draw pictures of us. They were not especially good, but Dash took the picture of me and I exchanged for it the picture of him, which I shall always keep as one of my souvenirs of Paris.

### Monday, 23 July 1928 (Marseilles)

Here we are in Marseilles, tired, dirty, and sleepy after a wearisome ride. We had seats by the windows, and could see beautiful scenery, but Dash began to tire of the long ride and spent his time reading *So You're Going to Rome.* I looked out the window. The country became strikingly characteristic of the Mediterranean and we saw olive trees for the first time.

### Wednesday, 25 July 1928 (Nice)

We hired a horse carriage for our tour of Nice. The Mediterranean was a blue just as one sees in colored paintings. The horse briskly klip-klopped back to the hotel just in time for us to take the bus to Monte Carlo. It was hot in the roofless bus in the brilliant mid-afternoon sun. Dash complained that the casino was not so impressive as he had expected, nor the gardens so big as he had anticipated.

### Thursday, 26 July 1928 (Genoa)

Up early in the terrifically hot morning to leave for Genoa. We ate hastily and managed to catch our train, but the hotel porter had failed to get our bags aboard. We rushed crazily here and there, trying to find the luggage, then got off at the first stop and took the first train back to Nice. This time we saw our luggage into our compartment. As we rode along the Riviera it seemed to get hotter and hotter. Palms, dust, glare, and such heat as I have never known. At night, after we had checked into our hotel, we drank wine in various cafés. Dash became impatient, out of sorts, not himself. Around midnight, singing "Show Me the Way to Go Home," I walked back to the hotel on his arm.

### Friday, 27 July 1928 (Rome)

After much trouble and 18 lira to the cheats, we settled in to the hotel in

Rome that had been suggested by Randall. Dashie wanted to go to the Forum and I wanted to go into the little corner where Keats died, so we arranged to meet at the American Express. From there we went out into the streets for supper. Then beers, getting back very late, struggling with the electricity. We became hilarious and laughed heartily over anything we could find to laugh at.

*Saturday, 28 July 1928 (Rome)*

This morning we visited the Forum of Trojan. Saw dozens of cats. It is the place where stray cats are placed. People dump food down for them. In the afternoon we wandered in narrow streets and found the home of Isador's elderly priest friend, through whose assistance we hoped to get an appointment with the Pope. The priest seemed delighted that we knew Isador but he said the Pope had been ill and could not accept audiences. So we shall miss one of the prime tourist features of Rome—an audience with the Pope.

We hastened to the American Express just in time to catch a sightseeing tour. The group was in several automobiles, we being in an automobile by ourselves. Dash enjoyed himself thoroughly. He loves Rome. Everything here pleases him. Among other sites of interest, we were taken by Mussolini's magnificent estate. The final stop was the great Colosseum, where the tour ended. With the aid of Baedecker, we started rambling homeward. We stopped for a glass of wine from time to time, but Dash drank his share, and stayed in a good mood.

*Wednesday, 1 August 1928 (Sorrento)*

Pompeii was interesting, including the house of prostitution, the forum, and innumerable other sites. It was hot, dusty, and glary but we enjoyed it. We saw statues that they don't have on general exhibition, and phallic and "obscene" pictures, and frescoes in which men and women were shown in various styles of sexual intercourse. Then up a winding road over the mountains along a road hewn in the solid cliff above the bay of Salerno. Around four we arrived at Sorrento and our hotel, perched on a cliff.

*Thursday, 2 August 1928 (Naples)*

Dash took a picture of me in front of an old stone wall, behind which stood groves of olive, lemon, and fig trees. I felt myself in touch with the soil of Italy. We hastened away to take a steamer to the Isle of Capri. A man on deck looked like the pictures of Clifton Webb. We began to think he might really be Clifton Webb. The water became a deep indigo blue. We went into the grotto in a rowboat from the steamer. The entrance to the Blue Grotto is so small that one must lie in the boat while entering, and I felt constrained because I was lying on my back next to someone who might be Clifton Webb. The water was like liquid blue light, a lovely dreamland, unreal and mystical. When we came out Dash had absolutely gotten it into his head that the man next to me had been Clifton Webb. When the steamer returned us to port, a jolly Italian sailor leaning over the rail waved to us, although we had never spoken a word to each other. "Whoopee-ta-ta!" he shouted.

*Sunday, 5 August 1928 (Venice)*

A gondola took us to the hotel. Dash is charmed by Venice. There is an enormous bed in our room. I have had a great deal of beer today and became sick and have vomited twice. Dashie offended. Oh, well. I am too shaky and hazy-headed to write, so good-night.

*Tuesday, 7 August 1928 (Venice)*

We were eaten up by mosquitoes and suffered also from the heat. I woke before dawn in misery to pull the mosquito netting down over the bed. After breakfast we made a round of shops and I got beads for Miss Contadeluci, who had given me $5 for getting "something" with. We accomplished nothing else. Returned to the hotel to lunch, but Dash wouldn't eat anything. Then to the station, where we took our train to Pisa. A lovely ride along the valley of the Arno. Up the world-famous Leaning Tower, which leaned more than either of us had expected. We had scarcely three minutes for the Baptistery, but the guard demonstrated the echo for us. On occasion it sounded like the music of an organ. We ran to catch a carriage back to the station. The return trip was wonderful— Italian farm houses, vineyards, blue mountains, Arno flowing between lanes of poplars, flat-topped pines and cypresses silhouetted against the evening sky.

*Thursday, 9 August 1928 (Paris)*

Back into France, and in the railroad yards of Troyes we had just finished dinner and were lingering over wine, when there came a terrific jar and the coach fell entirely on its side and several others were derailed. Men with lanterns dashed frantically about and women screamed hysterically, but no one was seriously hurt. With much difficulty we stumbled with our baggage, along with the other refugees, down to the station at Troyes. We arrived in Paris after midnight, took a cab to our hotel, and after much trouble, awakened the concierge. It seems months instead of weeks since we were here last.

*Friday, 10 August 1928 (Paris)*

Rambling about in Paris. At the Grand Magazin du Louvre we got a fan to take home to Hans. On the Rue de la Paix I bought for 175 fr. a unique snake-skin tie, something unusual, attractive and very durable. The most pleasing purchase I made was of a Rosenthal porcelain figure about a foot high, a figure of a nude youth, apparently modeled after Lindbergh. Dash liked it, too. We purchased a silk scarf with a floral pattern for Isador, then went back and got an identical one for Meg Deveraux.

### Saturday, 11 August 1928 (Paris)

Our last dinner in Paris. Dash stubbornly refused to join me in a Bene-dictine afterward. We walked home almost in silence—down to the Place de la Concorde and through the Tuileries and across the river. When I taunted him with being glad to leave Europe, he said, "Yes, I am glad." "Why?" "Because I'm going back." I moodily feasted on the beauty of Paris alone, the beauty that I didn't want to leave. When we got back to the hotel room I started my diary regardless of the hour. I put out the light so that Dash would not be disturbed, and am writing sitting in a chair in the bathroom, separated from the bedroom by a curtain. So it's good-bye, Europe. I have had a wonderful time and I hate to go home.

### Sunday, 19 August 1928

To the house. Henry fatter. Eunice didn't look too well. All of us dispirited by the sweltery weather. No one seemed to want to talk much about my trip. Dad and Henry discussed the grocery business while Eunice and Mama showed Daisy the postcards I had collected. Daisy is a big girl now, four years old and extraordinarily pretty.

Took a streetcar back downtown. An oppressively hot, moist darkness. In Dash's room I found Hans, not looking well, suffering from boils on his neck. He said his family is having a difficult time in Germany. His brother was injured in a worker's brawl. Hans did admit to a bit of good fortune, telling us he had gotten a job as an accompanist for a whistling woman who does an act at Keith's. He spent most of the time looking through opera glasses at a nude man in a room across the street. The man was reading and idly handling himself. Abruptly the man switched off the electric light. We dragged Hans away to the McReynolds, stopping to buy raspberry sherbet in the deli, and went up to Isador's apartment for a chat with Isador and his grandmother.

### Monday, 20 August 1928

To Dash's room. The dear child had got his Europe postcards mixed up so we had to go over again the work we did of sorting them. We frolicked, showered and dressed, then strolled out into the summer night. Dash took a car to Georgetown to give Miss Deveraux her scarf from Paris. I walked to Scott Circle. As I descended toward Max's basement entrance, his aunt came round the house, saying, "Max is away painting in Massachusetts." She invited me inside. She is smartly dressed, with hair swept up in a coil and held in place by wooden sticks. We talked about my trip, about Max, and about Government work. She told me she remembered reading my story, "In a Rut," when it was published in the *News*. She said, "I thought it very good." I left walking on air. Praise of any literary effort of mine intoxicates me, for it is the one object of my life, naturally.

*Thursday, 23 August 1928*

As I was leaving Eastman's I came upon Dasham with Meg Deveraux and her visiting parents. They are fashionable-looking, kindly, and Southern. People walking past glanced at the mother's beribboned gray hat, a splendid apparition, and she clung lightly to her husband's arm, and seemed not to notice their gazes or even to see anyone. Dash told me that over the weekend they all are taking the train down to Richmond. I can't help feeling jealousy because he and Miss Deveraux will be together for two days. Their friendship is a serious thing. I am wondering just how far it may go. Whether there has been any sex in the relationship I don't know and can't readily learn, but I don't believe so. It is faintly possible. I try to convince myself that I am being absurd but I feel it all the same—although I conceal my jealousy absolutely.

*Saturday, 25 August 1928*

To the station with Dasham, who was looking very lovable. The Deveraux group were waiting at the gate. They all shook hands with me and I watched them out of sight down the steps. Twice Dashie turned around to wave. I walked out in serene contentment feeling strong and sure of his affection. And yet anything might happen.

To Allies Inn for dinner alone. The nice Italian waitress asked, "Where's the rest of the family?" I said, "He's gone down to Richmond." She smiled. "Miss him?" It was startling. I told her that he had only been away from Washington for a few hours. Home and opened up Sherwood Anderson's *Smyth County News* and read his page in it. Then one after another I read Anderson's page in all the issues that I received while I was in Europe. A great writer! If I could only force myself to write. I know I have it in me. I have no doubts of myself. It is just that I am so damnably indolent. I complain that I haven't enough time, yet if all my time were free—*NO!* If my time were free, I could force myself to write and I could become a great writer. I will, too. There is plenty of time yet. I am still young.

I wonder if my dear lad down in Richmond is sound asleep now. He has brought me unhappiness and turmoil and also peace and joyous happiness.

### Sunday, 26 August 1928

Arranged postcards of the trip in my album. I was finishing Florence when I ran out of the kind of mounting corners I am using. I can't see Dash and consequently the old sex morbidness has come upon me. Well, let's go to bed.

### Tuesday, 28 August 1928

As I got off the elevator there was Dash ready to get on. "Well, Jeb, took you long enough to get here." "It's just six o'clock. What time did you expect me?" "I didn't expect you. I didn't have an engagement with you." "Why, Dashie, of course you didn't have an engagement with me. If you want to eat alone, go ahead. I'll eat by myself." But he merely invited me around to his room. We sat almost in silence. He wouldn't let me put my arm around his shoulder. I was disgusted but conciliatory and patient, realizing that it was a return to that silly attitude of last winter when he tried to suppress his natural desires. His behavior is a result of the expectations of the Deveraux family.

We dined at Cleves in the court. Conversation was rather forced. Dash told me that Meg Deveraux is planning to move up to Connecticut because she has found a better teaching position there. I asked him if her decision had anything to do with her unsatisfactory relations with him. He became angry and said, "Meg and I were always good friends and we remain good friends." When I pressed the matter he furiously told me, "She is none of your business."

After dinner we strolled down Eighteenth Street and sat on a bench on the Ellipse. I said, "You're quiet. Are you feeling blue?" He replied lightly, "No, I'm not feeling blue." I decided not to speak again until he did. I became morose and irritated. He hummed and tapped, as if to show unconcern. After about twenty minutes with nothing said by either of us, he stood and suggested going back. I agreed curtly. At least I don't take it seriously. There is nothing to make a fuss about anyway. It's a result of his trip with the Deveraux family to Richmond. He'll be all right.

### Wednesday, 29 August 1928

I went to Isador's to get my begonia, the last of my plants Isador kept for me while I was in Europe. Isador wasn't home but I stayed talking to Mrs. Pearson, his little grandmother. She asked for a cigarette and I gave her one, then tried to show her the trick match box that I got in Paris. It was wound and started rattling and throbbing. I meant it as a joke but she jumped and dropped it to the floor in a hurry. I laughed heartily. Mrs. Pearson told me, "You laugh all you want. My husband and I were attacked by bandits in the West Indies and by pirates in the China Seas. When something starts to rattle, I don't take any chances." I asked about the pirate attack. Mrs. Pearson said she and her husband were on a steamer on the Yangtze when pirates swarmed aboard in the dark. "We fought them off with swords, cutlasses, and guns." She said they drove some of the pirates off the ship, and captured twenty-three. She leaned back in her chair and said in a matter-of-fact way, "I saw those pirates executed. The men were laid in a row and the executioner walked along, picked up a pigtail and slashed off the head with his sword. We had to watch to see that they executed the right men. Those desperadoes often bribed the jailers to put others in their places."

While she was telling the story, Isador walked in, accompanied by his Annapolis friend Harry. Kissing his grandmother on the cheek, he asked her, "Did I hear you telling Jeb about the Yangtze pirates? Don't say a word about the Prussian whorehouse. You'll ruin the family reputation." Mrs. Pearson told me placidly, "He teases me."

*Wednesday, 12 September 1928*

Dashie is himself again, just as I thought he would be, therefore I have no introspections, emotions, and conjectures to record. Not much else, either. We strolled down to the Pan American gardens, dim and peaceful as always. We knew the guard must be lurking in the misty shadows, and sure enough, he emerged from the loggia of the Annex and slunk past, no doubt disappointed.

*Tuesday, 25 September 1928*

Dash, Randall, Junior, and I walked over to Nichols' for ice cream. Randall told us that Bolling Balfour has been dropped from the Social Register, his name not appearing in the edition for 1928 because of Hans Vermehren, of all people. Randall is really very intelligent and is a remarkable and interesting personality. Still, he has bad traits too—slyness, cunning, falsehood, trickiness, conceit. Junior carried on that loud, rowdy way of his. Randall and Dashie were amused at his antics. I was tired of Junior before we had gone a block. My own Dash, modest, manly, and straightforward, was all the dearer to me for the contrast.

*Thursday, 27 September 1928*

Miss Contadeluci asked me, "Mr. Alexander, do you know Bolling Balfour?" I was surprised, although I knew that she and Bolling both were originally from

Cambridge, Maryland. I said, "I know him slightly." "He was younger than I," she mused, "but I remember him in school, with his bobbed hair at the age of eight or nine. I've been told that Bolling has turned out to be 'a fine sister.'" To this I said nothing. She said, "Well—*does* he have sissified ways?" I was disgusted with her at such an attitude.

### Saturday, 29 September 1928

The last half-holiday of the year. That damned skinflint Coolidge has refused to extend the holidays. I don't like my new responsibilities at work. I don't like for my work at the office to obtrude itself upon my consciousness, so to speak.

A damp and overcast afternoon. Max wanted to look for a studio and I accompanied him, prowling in musky, drizzly alleys. At twilight we took a streetcar to his room. Gone are the oriental pillows; everything is white except for two gorgeous bougainvillea plants in bloom—stunning pink blossoms. He showed me the oil paintings he did during his summer trip to Rockport. Some were well executed; others seemed crude. We sat conversing in the deepening twilight, talking of painting, of writing, of homosexuality. It is good to have him back in Washington again. Dash means much to me, but I get intellectual companionship from Max that I don't get from Dash.

### Friday, 5 October 1928

Max to my house, after having spent the day painting Pompeian murals on the walls of old Dieterlie's apartment. Dieterlie has moved upstairs to Miss Deveraux's little garret. She has left Washington to take a teaching job in Connecticut. Dieterlie will pay Max $75 when the mural job is finished.

Sprawled in my easy chair, Max told me he has heard about a draughting job in the War Department that pays $1680. He was not pleased with the notion of being in the Government. He was in a sour mood and criticized my room. "Too much of a mixture. The oriental objects don't harmonize with white formality. Your walls and woodwork are too white for bright items." I told him I didn't care. He stared dissatisfied out the window. "Look out there. The leaves are beginning to fall. I probably wouldn't get the War Department job, anyway, because there's some complication about a preference for military men." He sighed, not a Maxish sound. "I need money."

We arranged to get some alcohol. We'll obtain it from April, Randall's bootlegger, at $11 a gallon and we shall mix things with it after we get a chemical analysis of it. How disgusting is prohibition!

*Thursday, 11 October 1928*

Randall's wife, Catherine, is a Democrat but is strong for Hoover, having the Southern attitude in favor of prohibition. She follows the campaign closely by radio and newspapers. Tonight she knew much more about it than the rest of us did. She and Mrs. Hare-Worth described satirically the Episcopal church-women who are here for the convention, and their zealous attention to the bishops in the lobby of the Willard Hotel. They were very funny. Randall rested his elbow on Dash's elbow. I began to feel jealous anger. I can't help it. When I got home I cut out newspaper clippings while in the back of my thoughts, Randall lowered menacingly. As if Dashie would ever—with him! Not a chance. Besides, there is nothing to worry about. I have Dash yet.

*Friday, 12 October 1928*

Hans is constantly upset over his relations with Bolling Balfour. I can well understand, after my own experience with jealousy and brooding and excessive sensitiveness to every slight from a loved one. And yet tonight while Hans was bemoaning every unhappy detail I couldn't help but recollect Max's impatience with me last winter. Sometimes it seems so trivial when it is someone else. All I could do was tell Hans not to worry, not to take things seriously.

*Monday, 15 October 1928*

I heard Miss Contadeluci say that the great airship, the *Graf Zeppelin*, was expected to pass over Washington. Soon after I left for lunch, and while I was eating I heard a sudden exclamation, and looking out saw the monster itself floating above. I dashed out into the street. Hundreds of other people appeared, on the street, on roofs, and at windows, in great excitement. The dirigible circled about the Monument and sailed directly over my head. I could read its name. The great airship had traveled across land and sea, battling fierce gales above the wide expanse of desolate ocean, and there she was over my head. It was the biggest thrill I have had in a long time.

**Graf Zeppelin.** *On the day that Jeb saw the* Graf Zeppelin, *the dirigible had covered the 6,630 miles from Germany in four and a half days, completing the first-ever commercial flight of an airship. The development of lighter-than-air, rigid-frame airships was much influenced by Count Ferdinand von Zeppelin, a German army officer. The Zeppelin production facilities in Germany were destroyed by Allied bombings in 1944.*

*Wednesday, 17 October 1928*

My twenty-ninth birthday. The balmy, breezy day and the smell of the dead leaves, and the sight of leaves falling and littering and drifting, made me wish to be free for my own day. Took leave. Just forty-five minutes. All I could think to do in celebration was to stroll down F Street. After work Dash and I walked down to the southern terrace of the State Department. We leaned against the cool balustrade, talking for a long time. He seems to pride himself on ignoring birthdays and said nothing about it, although he has been amiable all day, so perhaps he knew. I talked to him about homosexuality in life and in literature and the insolubility of the problem. We saw a brilliant meteor streak across the southern sky.

On the way home we stopped to see Isador. He had remembered my birthday and served cake and ice cream. I was touched and pleased. Mary Riley was there—with Zaza, a dark woman, a Louisiana Creole. Miss Riley introduced Zaza as her "very close friend . . . " (!) Before I left, Isador invited me to accompany him next Saturday to Junior's for tea in honor of Frances Newman, the Atlanta author. I shan't go. I should like to meet Frances Newman, but under my present way of living I don't care for the kind of tea that it probably will be with Junior and Isador and that crowd.

*Frances Newman (1883–1928) was an Atlanta-born novelist. Her story "Rachael and Her Children" appeared in Mencken's* American Mercury *in 1924 and won an O. Henry Award. Her novel* The Hard-Boiled Virgin *(published in 1926) was banned in Boston. Jeb's account of her death (in the entry for October 29, 1928) differs from that of many biographers, who attribute the cause to a brain hemorrhage resulting from a cerebral aneurysm.*

*Thursday, 25 October 1928*

Max told me surprising news concerning the death of Frances Newman. He says that Frances Newman, the one Junior and Isador knows, is not dead. Although claiming to be the Frances Newman who wrote *The Hard-Boiled Virgin* and *Dead Lovers Are Faithful Lovers,* she is seemingly an impostor. She was in Junior's apartment when Isador read in the newspaper of the death of "Frances Newman." She fainted in Junior's kitchen. But she refused to notify the newspapers of the mistake, and this to me is proof of her fraudulence. Max shrugged and said, "If she is a fake, she is a mighty clever one."

I hurried to Dash and told him the strange story. He said, "She seemed awfully accessible for a writer of prominence." He said he had noticed contradictions and puzzles in the facts concerning her. Later, we went to the Auditorium to hear Josef Hofmann's recital. To our surprise, we saw Junior seated in the audience beside the woman he has passed off as Frances Newman. She is a short, plump brunette with a brazen stare.

*Josef Hofmann (1876–1957) was a a Polish piano virtuoso.*

### Saturday, 27 October 1928

A long line to get tickets to see Ethel Barrymore in *The Kingdom of God.* Far behind me in line, Junior asked me to get his tickets for him. When we walked away together, I asked him about the mystery of Frances Newman. "I'm puzzled," Junior said, "but inclined to think her explanation of the matter is the real one." We stopped at Seventeenth and G to continue the discussion. Up came Isador, gesticulating and exclaiming in his shrill voice, "What has happened? I expected denials and I find corroborations," referring to the items in today's papers about Frances Newman being poisoned. Junior said, "Frances *still* says that she is the famous author. But Frances says *she* prefers to keep quiet."

Isador and I chatted for a while. He told me that in his class at G.W., for the first time he heard the word "homosexual" used in a classroom. Professor Croissant told the class he was not interested in the "charge," for example, "that Charles II was homosexual," except as it affected the background of the literature of the era, or words to that effect.

### Monday, 29 October 1928

The *News* had an article about Frances Newman. She took poison on October 20, the day named in a parody of her work in *Vanity Fair,* in which the woman novelist kills herself on October 20. The *News* account said she had great timidity and feared criticism. Poor woman. I got a copy of *Vanity Fair* and read the parody aloud to Dash. I told him, "I know that no criticism could make me kill myself, though it might make me want to kill somebody else." We went across the street to visit Isador. Randall there, and several from the Muriel Phillipson crowd. *They* could talk of nothing but Frances Newman.

### Wednesday, 31 October 1928

Dashie and I sallied forth to see the Halloween merry-makers. We ambled along looking at the amusing costumes. There was pushing and rowdiness. A great crowd of Georgetown students were giving Al Smith yells and singing "The Sidewalks of New York." While hundreds looked on, they tried to "crash the gates" into the Fox. Traffic on F Street was not allowed, so there was plenty of room for snake dances and wild rushes. I lost Dash but he reappeared from behind me. He has an irritating habit of walking ahead without looking back, so that if people block my way there is no way to catch him.

I wearied of the rowdy crowds and empty frivolity, and tried to get Dash to leave. He suggested we go to Child's. We stood outside the brightly lighted window debating whether to go in or not. Then along came Hans Vermehren, Isador Pearson, and Junior Whorley with whoops and gesticulations. Several others whom Isador knew joined them and stood around to converse. It seemed as if we were holding a reception there in one of the brightest spots on the Avenue, with the people inside Child's as spectators. Isador and Junior were laughing loudly. Isador's face was flushed and hysterical. Junior put his arms around Dash and Isador, jumping up and down. I was in no mood for such business, feeling nervous and irritable. I excused myself and started home. Crossed over to the Treasury, where the street was almost abandoned, and felt relieved to be leaving the confusion.

*Thursday, 1 November 1928*

Hans joined us at breakfast at Allies Inn. He asked me why I left so suddenly last night. I told him, "I didn't enjoy holding a reception in front of Child's." He replied soothingly, at which Dash said sharply, "Don't humor him." I said to Dash, "You mind your own business." Hans said, "We all piled into a cab and went for a ride." I said sneeringly, "I'm glad I wasn't along—with a bunch of screaming hoodlums." Dash said, "I'm glad you weren't, too—it was mutual." I left before they did.

*Sunday, 4 November 1928*

To the house. I shocked everybody when they saw me wearing my bronze Al Smith button in the face of the warning from the Civil Service Commission. I told them, "I wear it deliberately as a protest against the impudence of the commission. I haven't given up my rights as a citizen merely because I work for the Government." Mama was afraid I would lose my job. I told her that I wear the button only as far as the Monument, then pin it under my lapel out of sight before I go into the office. She felt better when they learned I didn't wear the button at work. And yet we in the District don't even have a vote. What a hell of a country this is.

Eunice and Daisy helped me collect a basket of apples from the bounteous trees in the back yard. We put the apples in the back of Dad's car and Dad drove me downtown, inviting me to eat supper with him, just the two of us. I wanted to see Dashie, so I told Dad I had an engagement. But Dash had gone out, I don't know where.

"*. . . we in the District don't even have a vote.*" *The District of Columbia was under the jurisdiction of Congress at this time. The ostensible logic for not giving Washingtonians the right to vote was that many residents of D.C. were government employees, and thus might vote with skewed self-interest at the polls. Few historians of our time would argue that the real reason Washingtonians lacked voting privileges was because the population was predominantly African-American. With the ratification of the Twenty-third Amendment in 1961, D. C. residents could vote in presidential elections. Washington won the right to govern itself in 1975.*

*Tuesday, 6 November 1928*

At dinner I told Dash and Max that I felt resentful and humiliated that I am deprived of my right to vote. The campaign has stirred me considerably, and I want to express myself. Dash became moody and rude. Max set off to his sculpture class at Corcoran. I was anxious to get downtown to hear the results of the election so I hurried away. I joined the crowd at the *Post* building and the same gloom settled upon me that I experienced in 1924 and 1920. Late at night, the extra papers came out. I am ashamed of the United States for the verdict its citizens have rendered. That blockhead Hoover is now our president-elect.

*Thursday, 8 November 1928*

Gray skies; a chill in the air. Max invited Dash and me to dinner. We made a dispirited group. Max served alcohol acquired from April, Randall Hare's bootlegger. When Dash refused to drink any, I called him a baby. There was a flare-up. Eventually he drank some. I read aloud from *The Hard-Boiled Virgin* to show them what Frances Newman's style was like. Max brought out the pictures he painted at Harper's Ferry. Dash told Max that he didn't "get" that kind of painting. Max told us wearily that he is still looking for a job. He may try commercial art. I told him not to sell his soul for a mess of pottage. We talked a while about the man in New Jersey who committed suicide because of Al Smith's defeat, and the New Yorker, rightly disgusted at his countrymen, who moved to Canada. One of Dash's remarks tonight was that he was tired of "this aimless life." I too am tired of it but inertia and commonsense hold me in my prison.

*Wednesday, 28 November 1928*

All the other Government departments were to be dismissed at one o'clock because of "Thanksgiving" tomorrow. In our office no announcement came and there was railing and wonderment. I was furious. At lunch I took almost an hour, telling Miss Contadeluci after I got back, "I stayed out overtime deliberately." She said after a moment, "You probably want to know about Miss Bechtel.

Yesterday morning from her window she counted twenty-eight persons coming in late, and she reported them. It certainly raised a hullabaloo with Dr. Kraznovski." I demanded, "What time does *she* get here?" Miss Contadeluci made a face. "At eight-thirty, every morning." I said angrily, "And then spies on others from her window!" It was then two minutes before one. I looked out my window and reported to Miss Contadeluci, "The Treasury Department is already getting out across the street." At that moment came the announcement that we were to be dismissed. I was so angry at the way they had acted about it and at Miss Big-Tail's spying from her window that I indulged in a display of temper, kicking over my wastebasket and swinging the light switch violently, to the amusement of Miss Contadeluci. The Utott and the Green already had gone on leave.

*Friday, 7 December 1928*

I had forgotten to go to the bank. Dashie had only six cents so I tried Isador and Junior, but neither one was home. I tried Max. Found him playing *Liebestraum* on the piano in the company of a starry-eyed blond youth, a model from one of Max's classes. I apologized for butting in for such a sordid purpose as money. Max smiled in the direction of the golden-haired boy, loaned me a dollar, and purred, "Nothing tonight could possibly diminish my pleasure."

When I joined Dash at Allies Inn, Randall Hare strolled in. He told us that he has been given a great promotion at the State Department. He joined us—damn him. Why can't he stay home with his wife and mother? Later, under a silvery-black sky in front of the White House, Dash and I passed Hans, bundled like an immigrant with a woolen cap pulled down over his ears. He told us he has gotten work at the Belasco at $35 a week. His first job will be as one of eight chorus men in *Little Jessie James*. So many people with good fortune, yet my own life is passing me by.

*Saturday, 8 December 1928*

Max and I walked to H Street where he was going to collect some money for Christmas cards he made. He told me that he and his aunt had a big row last night. "While I was working on an illustration for "The Ancient Mariner" she stormed at me over the nude figures in my drawing. This started a discussion of the fact that she knew I was keeping bootlegger liquor in my room. She said she found the bottles while she was cleaning and became so upset that she couldn't work." He said he remained cool, telling her, "All my friends drink." She retorted, "Then it's time you got other friends." She then denounced Max's sweet model friend from Corcoran. Max said to her, "I didn't know you disliked him."

She said, "I hate him." Max maintained his independent attitude, telling her, "If you put your foot down, I'll pack up and move."

I said I felt sorry for her. He said, "I don't." He can be hard and cold-blooded at times. I went with him and waited outside while he got my bottles, three of gin, and two of what we have been calling "Benedictine." A damp night of penetrating cold, but I was afraid his aunt might jump on me if she found me inside her house. He said she had not mentioned my name to him, however. Finally he emerged, bringing the bottles in his briefcase. He carried the briefcase all the way to my house. Max has a way of striding along with his head up and his eyes keen, no matter how cold the weather.

*Monday, 10 December 1928*

Isador and Junior had a wonderful trip to New York. They attended a brilliant midnight performance of *This Year of Grace*. Isador gave us imitations of Beatrice Lillie in her various parts, augmenting his performance with whoops and screams. Dash and I sat back and laughed and enjoyed it. Isador also gave details of the evening. "Al Smith sat in the fifth row, in the center of the orchestra—" Junior interrupted, "—but not with his wife." Isador said, "—and Jane Cowl lounged luxuriously in a box, and Jeanne Eagels wore an *extremely* low-cut dress and a flame-colored cape. Then afterward we found a restaurant called The Parisian where we could get cocktails and wines. Then in Harlem we found a cabaret—what was it called, Junie?"

"Small's," said Junior. Isador said, "At Small's the drinks were served openly. The behavior of the patrons was *extremely* indecorous." Junior urged him, "Tell them about Carl Van Vechten." Isador said, "Carl Van Vechten is just about gone. We saw him in a Harlem night club biting and kissing the ankles of a young boy." Isador and Junior settled down some, but not much, when we finally went to dinner.

> **Jane Cowl** (1883–1950) *was a stage actress and playwright. Among other plays, she starred in the phenomenally successful* Smilin' Through, *which she co-authored with her friend Jane Murfun. In 1928 she co-authored* The Jealous Moon *with Theodore Charles.*

> **Jeanne Eagels** (1894–1929) *was a stage and film actress. Her most famous role was that of Sadie Thompson in* Rain.

> **This Year of Grace.** *Noel Coward's revue had already been a London hit, and in 1928 ran for months at the Selwyn in New York, starring Coward, Beatrice Lillie, Florence Desmond, and Queenie Leonard.*

*Friday, 21 December 1928*

There are Yale locks on the doors now at the Y.M.C.A., so my key to Dash's room does no good. I knocked. Dash opened the door in his undershirt. He didn't smile. I asked him what was the matter. This precipitated an awful scene. "You're always insinuating regarding me and my friends. I have *some* friends with whom sexual intimacy would be out of the question. I can't see anybody, even a second time, without your being suspicious—" He worked himself into a rage. I won't go into the details of his bitter denunciation of me. I pleaded, apologized, argued. Nothing did any good.

*Saturday, 22 December 1928*

Wretched day at the office. The Christmas party was a dreadful affair for me. Everybody had a present, each having drawn the name of a person to whom to give a ten-cent gift. I received two gifts—both insinuating, and I lost all pleasure in the gathering. One, from Miss Big-tail, who had drawn my name, was a box of chocolate cigarettes with the following typewritten note inside:

> If as a smoker you enjoy a "good drag,"
> You'll find these a very particular "fag."
> But if Lady Nicotine you've failed to meet,
> These "smokes" will prove to be both mild and sweet.

The sly emphasis on the final words in the first two sentences is obvious. The other present was a stuffed doll in a red and white dress with an unsigned card marked, "For the Lonely Hours." It was an entirely gratuitous insult.

*Monday, 24 December 1928*

Windy and colder. Dashie was fairly amiable and we dined pleasantly at Allies Inn near the gorgeous Christmas tree by candlelight. Hans arrived. He had been to a wedding and incidental celebrations and was so full of cocktails that he was utterly silly, so silly and foolish that I was bored and disgusted. Bolling Balfour showed up, just back from New York. Hans said bitterly, "Who did you meet this time?" Bolling replied calmly, "I met Mrs. W. Somerset Maugham, and she asserted she 'was going to divorce Maugham because he was going with some man.'"

We walked briskly through the night wind to my place, stopping for cigarettes, chocolate bars and marshmallows. In my room I found an old lemon and put slices of it in the drinks. They were rather strong. I gave Dash his Christmas present, an etching of the Ile de la Cité in Paris, mounted on a wood panel and covered with Pyroglass. He was pleased with it. I was amazed when Hans put his arms around Dash or his hands on him or something similar. Bolling as usual was sedate and dignified except that he and Hans carried on lovemaking with a candor that surprised and puzzled me. I played soft music and we drank and smoked, mused and talked. The first record I played was "Always." Dash read the *Nation* and pretended not to notice. When the song reached the line, " . . . not for just an hour, not for just a day, but always . . ." he put up his hand so as to conceal his face.

Bolling had a lot to say about Isador. "Isador is acting as though nothing has occurred between us and has planned a party tonight in my honor. I am *not* going to attend." The problem seems to be about Isador's attempts on Bolling's acquaintances in New York. Bolling said, "Of all the brazen, inconsiderate and crafty actions—" He could talk of nothing but the difficulties one encountered by allowing Isador to entangle himself in one's affairs and friendships. To some extent I could sympathize with him. Isador's brass, nerve, gall, can be simply impossible.

Late in the evening Max knocked on my door. He had brought his sketch pad, which he handed to me. "Your Christmas gift—a drawing for your bookplate." The drawing showed two nude youths dreaming under a pine tree on a cliff overlooking a river winding to the sea on which rode a solitary sail. It was beautiful. Still, I had misgivings about the impression that would be given by the nude youths, and suggested some changes. "I thought you might feel like that," said Max, but he readily assented.

We had a pleasant time, I and Dash, Max, Hans, and Bolling. But I am hurt that Dashie gave me no present. He told me that he was giving no presents, but he gave Max one—that beautifully cut bronze lizard from Naples that Max admired.

*Monday, 31 December 1928*
Dash and Max and I celebrated New Year's Eve with drinks in my room. This last day of 1928 was hazily sunny, and the evening became autumnal, not wintry. Max appeared with a red balloon. He was feeling gay, already having had two cocktails. During the evening he and Dashie frolicked with the red balloon, as I did somewhat. The three of us danced, sang, played, and were utterly silly. We consumed about a quart of April's bootlegger gin mixed in ginger ale. Max lifted his glass and said, "I bemoan prohibition and long for real drinks we might have in a free country." He took off his sweater, then suggested we undress, and proceeded to lead the way. I made a fool of myself—fortunately there was no sober person to complain. At midnight came the sound of steam whistles being

blown outside. I jumped up utterly naked, got out the big dinner bell I have, and rang it wildly out the window.

The rest is vague. Max and I lay on the bed. Dash lay on the floor. My poor darling was terribly drunk but he managed to object to various things. Toward the end, when Dash opened the window I exclaimed, "Don't let in the vulgar fresh air—it will make us sober and dawn-minded." Max applauded my choice of words. Later I remember rushing to the bathroom but finding Max there, and rushing down to the second story to vomit. As Dash says, the disgusting thing about getting drunk is that everybody gets sick. But it is wonderful up until then.

# 1929

*Thursday, 10 January 1929*

Hans telephoned and asked if we were coming to the show tonight *(Hit the Deck,* with Kate Smith as the extra special star) and I said we were. He then had exciting news. Kate Smith wanted him to go to Chicago with her. I congratulated him. We enjoyed the show. Hans as usual had on too much makeup, but he has improved in stage appearance and ease of manner. Kate Smith was great in her jazz songs, especially in "Hallelujah," for which she received an ovation. She is enormously fat, but graceful and full of energy, being very young. After the show Hans joined us at Child's, where we ordered tea and milk toast. He hopes Kate Smith will want him as her accompanist on her vaudeville tour of the Middle West. The salary—ye gods!—$100 a week or possibly $125.

> **Kate Smith** *(1909–1986). Her strong voice on radio and the stage, especially her singing of Irving Berlin's "God Bless America," was integral to the ambiance of the thirties and forties.*

*Friday, 11 January 1929*

Over dinner on the pleasant balcony at Seventeenth, the proprietress bustled upstairs and, seeing soiled dishes on a table, clapped her hands to summon a busboy. "Applause from the gallery," Dash remarked. Getting witty. And this evening in his room, looking out the window he turned and said, "Millions of windows to look into." I asked him where he got it but he said it was his own. Not a great evening, though. Such nerve of Randall, making an appointment with Dash right under my nose.

*Sunday, 20 January 1929*

Dash told me, "Isador wants you to come by tomorrow evening after eight." I responded, "His imperious commands have no effect on me." But I shouldn't complain about Isador. He isn't himself since his grandmother's stroke. Poor Mrs. Pearson is feeble and has hardly any memory.

*Monday, 21 January 1929*

"I am beside myself," Isador said. "A nurse comes every day but she isn't enough." He has managed to find solutions, though—sad though they are. Mrs. Pearson is to move in with her nurse. Isador is moving down to the third floor of the McReynolds.

I sat with Mrs. Pearson in the front room, sad to see her in such a condition. She didn't know me, but she rambled on about her daughter, Isador's mother, and told me what I already well knew—that in October of 1927, Isador's mother committed suicide. Poor Mrs. Pearson monotonously lamented, "It was wrong of her. She left Isador, and Mary, and me. She left Isador, and Mary, and me."

When I left, Isador walked with me downstairs. It was a drizzly night, but we stood on the sidewalk talking. He said, "Grandmother talks endlessly about Mother's suicide. Also, although it seems a great deal less important now, I was deeply hurt because Bolling didn't attend the Christmas party I gave in his honor. The way things are going, I think of committing suicide." He added plaintively, "I am too cowardly to do it." I felt a deep pity for him, and tenderness, but I could offer nothing but platitudes. I told him it was self-pity, a foolish state of mind, a negative attitude and the like. I—who lie awake at night to think of the black horror of nothingness to which death takes. There is little chance of my ever killing myself. Poor Isador!

*Wednesday, 30 January 1929*

Dash's birthday. We walked over to see Isador, who was making preparations for moving down to the third floor of the McReynolds. In the midst of his packing boxes and disarray he had set up a card table with hot chocolate, Lorna Doones, and almonds, in honor of Dashie's birthday. Mrs. Pearson was sitting up in a chair, eating her dinner with her nurse beside her. Mrs. Pearson said, "I'm going to move to the nurse's home tomorrow, so I won't get any more black eyes." That was an allusion to Isador's striking her. It is best for both of them, I suppose, that they live apart and she be taken care of properly.

We sat at the table among the half-packed boxes and had a pleasant little supper. But when Isador gave Dash a ribbon-bedecked birthday present, and it turned out to be Radclyffe Hall's *The Well of Loneliness*, which has been suppressed (that is, theoretically) both in England and in the United States, and for which Isador paid $5, I was filled with jealous resentment. And Dash was so profuse in his thanks, too.

**The Well of Loneliness** *(1928). This pioneering novel by English writer Radclyffe Hall (1886–1943) presented a sympathetic view of lesbian love.*

### Saturday, 2 February 1929

Isador had a "guest" for the night—a shy lad from Indiana. Mrs. Pearson has gone to live with her nurse. I stayed all evening, helping Isador move items from the old apartment down to the new one on the third floor. The "guest" was helpful but said very little. Isador sold me a ticket for *Götterdämmerung*, and didn't tell me until I bought it that he was going to occupy the next seat. He knows I don't like going to the theatre with him. That was a sly, petty trick.

I was amazed when I got home to find inside my package of cigarettes a Sporting Life wrapper containing a condom. I thought it was some novel method of distributing samples, almost unbelievable. Later I remembered that I had left my coat in Dash's room when I went to the bathroom, and he must have put the thing in my cigarette case as a joke. I wonder why and where he got it, to what purpose if any he uses them. Perhaps Max gave the condoms to him. Max's frustrations about his blond model friend, Jimmie, seem to have increased his enthusiasm about matters sexual. He has been talking about wanting to get condoms and to try to lose his virginity with a woman.

### Tuesday, 12 February 1929

Max stopped by to visit me after teaching his drawing class. Conversations, child's play, music, discussion of my writing ambitions, Max's painting ambitions, Dash, and those condoms Dash bought. Dash got a dozen, Max says, and sold Max three of them, having bought them to save Max the embarrassment. Max says he still has not yet had a night of love with Jimmie Staunton. We drank a little of the synthetic Benedictine. After Max left I felt a great longing to have Dash beside me and to clasp him gently in my arms.

I settled into my chair and started *The Well of Loneliness*. A beautiful, true, and moving book. It filled me with a deep melancholy and yet a sense of pride and courage and resolve to see it through to the end. The realization of my love for Dashie and all it meant to me swept over me almost overwhelmingly. I was filled with a desire to take him with me far away to some beautiful island where we might live out our lives safe from the panting pursuit of the wolf pack.

*Tuesday, 19 February 1929*

Randall was in Dash's room. Dash had bought a new tie and was all spic and span. He seemed to be in high spirits and full of energy. When he went out of the room to the bathroom, Randall crossed his legs, lit a cigarette, and remarked, "Before you arrived, Dash and I were talking about going to a show, and Dash said he wanted to select the show. It's usually the other way around. I'm usually the one who selects the show." I had no idea they ever went to shows together. There was a time when such an incident would have made me miserable. Now I have become hardened by neglect. All the same, I can't help feeling fairly upset. *Damn* that slimy snake from Georgetown!

*Wednesday, 20 February 1929*

At breakfast Dash read the paper, ignoring me. I tried to find out what was the matter. "What have I done now?" "I've often wondered." "What do you mean by that?" "You'll never know." An unhappy day. At night we ate at Allies. He said, "You're persistent. You're determined not to let me escape you." I pressed him to tell me what was the matter. He said in a low voice, "Listen—I didn't come here to be cross-examined. I wanted to eat alone but you won't let me escape. How can anyone act natural with you around? You act like such a damn fool—do I make myself clear?" I felt pain, tears in my eyes, and didn't look up from my plate.

*Thursday, 21 February 1929*

Dash and I went to Isador's apartment to help him get ready for the all-night party given by the Art Promoters Club. Isador was uproariously funny in a female costume, intended to be an imitation of Beatrice Lillie in *This Year of Grace*.

Max arrived to change into a costume borrowed from a Mexican boy who attends his drawing class. It is a beautiful suit of hand-tooled leather. An enormous leather sombrero and a scarlet bow tie went with it. A perfect fit, and curiously becoming to Max with his whitish blond hair and blue eyes. Junior appeared. He was going as an Oriental dancing girl, and pranced around, up to his usual annoying foolishness. Called me "Grandpa" and said, "You act like an old man." I ignored him as best I could and played the Victrola, especially "Dance Little Lady" and "I've Got A Rainbow 'Round My Shoulder." Isador and Junior took eternally long to get ready.

Dash went back to the Y to get his camera to take flashlight photos, and when he returned there were others who had shown up, most of them wearing male costumes. The arrival of Dash's camera produced a lot of effeminate carrying on. Isador chattered and screamed, although I tried to discourage him. It pained me to see Dash so much amused. Around two in the morning we crowded into the elevator and saw them all pile hysterically into a taxicab finally.

*Sunday, 3 March 1929*

Flags fluttering everywhere for the Inauguration tomorrow; streets teeming with automobiles. Streams of pedestrians; a festive spirit. In front of the Rare Print Shop I saw Dash looking at prints. I stood behind him until he turned. We chatted aimlessly, I feeling constraint because of his recent indifferent behavior toward me. We resumed our separate ways. I wandered on home and, tired, fell asleep. Woke to a dark room. Hurried to Dash's through big, wet snowflakes. Over our meal I remarked, "Randall's interest in everything is sexual. His interest in you is entirely sexual." Dash retorted, "That isn't very complimentary to me, is it?" I was sorry I had said it. It is true, though, and makes me hate Randall and feel fiercely jealous.

We walked through the falling snowflakes to the Lincoln Memorial pools. Dash said he would not be free tomorrow. To my questions he replied in a frustrating, sing-song manner, "Not going to *tell* you—Not going to *tell* you—" Drops of snow fell silently into the pools and were extinguished. The Memorial's new lighting effect gave old Abe an expression almost mirthful.

*Monday, 4 March 1929*

I shall not dwell on the inauguration of Herbert Hoover. I walked amid the crowds and saw Coolidge, pale and with a strained expression, and Hoover, red-faced fathead with a sour mouth, drive by on their way to the Capitol. Rain gradually settled into a steady light downpour. I proceeded, stopping here and there to peer between umbrellas at the bright pageant passing by.

In the evening I set out for Scott Circle. Max was playing Beethoven on the piano, his golden-haired, starry-eyed little Jimmie Staunton beside him, the boy's back to the piano and his legs crossed, balancing himself with one hand on the bench. He moved his free hand away from Max's thigh when I entered. I apologized for invading their evening, but they seemed glad to see me. I stayed until after eleven. When I left I passed scores of automobiles on their way to the Inaugural Ball.

*Wednesday, 27 March 1929*

The cherry blossoms are almost perfect this year. After viewing them I walked home through town in the balmy air, looking for signs of spring. Men carried overcoats on their arms. Florists' windows were gay with tulips and spring blossoms. Sauntered down to the McReynolds and had a haircut. Junior was there, getting a shampoo, and in one of his clownish moods. I had no patience with him. He facetiously asked me, "How's your sex life?" I told him the question was impertinent and that it was none of his business.

To Dash's room but had no respone to my knock. He is seldom home these days.

### Monday, 15 April 1929

A girl who used to work at the office came back to talk to the Utott about getting in again. When she had gone I said, "I don't see why anybody would want to come back to this place after once escaping." Mrs. Utott replied, "Outside of the State Department, where your friend works, this Department is the most liberal to be in. The Government is too soft, too liberal. They ought to be more strict." I was startled. I have never mentioned Dash's name or the fact that he works in the State Department. Perhaps the Utott put two and two together and came to the conclusion herself. And Miss Contadeluci, seeing us in the theatre, probably has said something. Talk, talk, and endless gossip!

### Sunday, 28 April 1929

Dash, Hans, and I had settled down to reading in my room. Hans, feeling blue, was reading Goethe; I was browsing in Walt; Dash was reading in the *Nation* and waxing indignant over the wrongs of the Southern mill workers, when who should arrive but Max. He stood in the door smiling. "I am head over heels in love with Jimmie Staunton and it's mutual." It's the first time for young Staunton and seems like a beautiful affair. Max told all about it.

When the group was leaving I decided to walk part of the way home with Dash. We talked about Max's account of himself and Jimmie. I said, "He reminded me of the way we were, Dashie, before the troubles came." That started a discussion. The same old story—only this time Dash made it final that we could be merely friends hereafter. I told him, "My love cannot be killed so easily." Well, we had a long conversation and reached an understanding that left me filled with sadness. It all seems such a pity; real love comes so seldom, and then to have to suppress it and to be told that it is not any longer reciprocated, is tragically hard. When we separated I said, "I love you, boy. I'm not shallow and fickle like some people; I'll keep on loving you." But he replied, "I can't let you." I trudged back to my room and looked for a long time at the little picture on the wall—the wind-blown hair, the clear eyes, the half-smile on those sweetly remembered lips.

I can't do without him. I thought how easily I could fall back into the old habits of flirting on the street and other such sordid business if I should lose entirely his sweet love and companionship. Put the picture on the mantel, dethroning Buddha, lit incense and played the Victrola—"Drink to Me Only with Thine Eyes," "Believe Me If All Those Endearing Young Charms," "Song of Love," "Serenade," and after that orchestral and instrumental pieces. If he had never returned my affection I could bear it better. To possess and then to lose is much more cruel than never to possess at all.

*Tuesday, 30 April 1929*

Spent a rather wild evening at Junior's apartment. Max and Jimmie brought real Scotch. Isador provided ginger ale. The mix was good stuff. People played jazz on the piano and we played a lot of records—"An American in Paris," "Sing Hallelujah," and "Shreveport," among others. Junior danced in his usual semi-nude state, with only his vests and draperies, and was crude as usual in his behavior and speech. There was plenty of dancing. Around midnight, the manager of the building knocked on the door and politely asked us to keep the noise down. Guests began leaving. Soon the only ones left were Dash, me, and Hans. Junior offered to drive Hans to Kenilworth. When he had dressed we went outside to his car, and found Max and Jimmie intimately together in the back seat. We took them with us. Junior poured forth a stream of filth in a loud-voiced monologue, but when he started in with gossip about me, I flared up angrily, "You needn't start your gossip, because I don't like it." "All right," he said archly, "I heard it by word of mouth." "You needn't repeat other people's lies."

We let Hans off on the drive. Riding back I found myself engaged in verbal shafts of sarcasm at Junior and his filth. Finally he became apologetic and talked of other things. He dropped my off at my house with a warm handshake. "Visit me again, Jeb, and hear my records." I cordially said I would. I hate for sweet clean Dashie-boy to be in with that crowd.

*Sunday, 5 May 1929*

To the house as usual on Sundays. On the streetcar going out, I glimpsed from the window Max sauntering uptown with Jimmie Staunton. Max was resplendent in golf stockings and linen knickers, the first I have ever seen him wear.

After dinner Dad, Henry, and I took a ride in Henry's Packard. A warm day, clouds drifting over the sun. Near Dupont Circle I saw Dash strolling along and we stopped to get him. Introduced him to Dad and Henry. It seemed so strange to have Dashie there in the car along with my family—always before they have represented entirely separate phases of my life. Dad and Henry let us out in front of Allies Inn. Walking home alone afterward I met up with Isador. He was obviously cruising and didn't want to walk on with me.

Dawdled in my room. Streetcars rattling. Clocks ticking. Occasional automobiles in the street below. Tonight I got out my diary of 1918 and read of summer days at the bank, of evenings under the moon in Rock Creek Park. What an innocent boy I was, before this accursed obsession took hold of me and clouded my life. How strange and puzzling and futile this life is.

*Monday, 6 May 1929*

Miss Contadeluci was having her monthlies and even with the windows open, that acrid odor pervaded the room. Isador called up to tell me he is having a party Sunday night so that people can meet Helen Falconer, the middle-aged woman who is fond of young men. She is the one who several years ago kept Isador at the Chatterton. I hope she doesn't take a fancy to my Dashie.

When I got home I sat daydreaming about Vincent Eric Orville—my dream-mate, my ideal comrade. I imagined our meeting, our sympathy and companionship. It has been a long time since I have turned to Vincent for an object for my affection. I become morbid if I am long without companionship. But what I need most—is self-reliance and independence. I used to have them. But that was before my nature asserted itself.

A letter from Lansing Tower, who wants me to travel with him in Mexico. It would be splendid, except for the revolution.

*"... except for the revolution." The condition of Mexico's agrarian poor had led by 1910 to an inevitable rebellion against the landed aristocracy. The Mexican Revolution was still very much in the news during the time of Jeb's trip west.*

*Saturday, 11 May 1929*

I have been thinking considerably about Isador's scheme for Dash to meet Helen Falconer. She is a vampire fond of youths, with whom Isador had an affair—whose plaything Isador was, in fact. I can't help feeling forebodings. My sweet little Dash! If this adventuresome Helen takes a fancy to my boy—she had better watch out! After thinking endlessly about the situation, I decided to talk with Isador. Went to the McReynolds and found him working on his scrapbook of Eva Le Gallienne, but he stopped to serve me chocolate cookies and coffee. Bluntly I asked him, "Why do you want Dashie to meet Helen Falconer?" He gave an evasive, offhand reply. He surprised me by asking, "Jeb, why doesn't Randall like you?" I returned home thinking and worrying.

*Sunday, 12 May 1929*

Scores of people were wandering about, looking at Mrs. Fowler's sunlit acres of lily ponds. Dragonflies darted above the lily pads. The hills were hazy in the distance. Dashie and I had a good time talking and looking at the blossoms and the swamp trees. Hans, wearing a snappy straw hat with a striped brim, showed Italian students around. All day I tried to persuade Dash not to go to Isador's party for Helen Falconer, but he was determined to go. Therefore I went, too. Isador had invited so many guests that people milled around in the hall outside his open apartment door. Randall had his pretty wife on one arm and his mother, with her cane, leaning on the other. She recently had a bad fall down the stairs leading to "Uncle Dieterlie's" garret on Prospect Street. Junior appeared with his mother and sister, both visiting from Corpus Christi. The sister carried a white dog, which made her skirt hang down in back, and looked unattractive.

Helen Falconer is a refined woman of about forty. She was simple and natural, without affectation. She bantered affectionately with Isador. Under other circumstances I could like her and be entirely tolerant of her "loose" way of life. Such an unutterably miserable and uncomfortable evening for me. She devoted almost her entire attention to Dash, who became animated and at his best. As the evening wore on I relapsed into glowering silence and became nervous and tense, furious at Isador, and wildly jealous of that woman because she and Dash appeared to find each other so interesting. My behavior was rude and conspicuous but I felt that I didn't care.

When Dash left, I got up to go. Dash warmly told Helen Falconer good-bye. She said, "I want to see your albums, especially those from Europe." It stopped just short of a definite date. I took leave curtly and rushed out of the room with the feeling that I was about to burst. Downstairs I said, "Well, that damned whore took quite a fancy to you. I suppose you feel flattered." Then I broke down and sobbed almost hysterically. "I love you more than anything in the world. You mean everything to me. I have no outlet for my feeling toward you—I have to keep it bottled up inside and look on while others who care nothing for you try to take you away."

He put his arms around me. "Those people mean nothing to me. You are the only friend I care anything about in Washington . . . except perhaps Max." He put his cheek against mine. "I always feel miserable when I think I hurt you. I don't try to do it. I'm not going to fall in with Isador's schemes. I'll tell him I have no interest in his woman beyond casual companionship." I felt calmer, but said, "If that woman tries to get you, I'll kill her." Dash murmured, "Go home and get a good night's rest." What a thing for me to have said! I did come home. Perhaps my outburst was good for me, instead of keeping my misery dammed up inside. It gives me comfort, too, to know that my darling cares something for me still.

### Tuesday, 14 May 1929

At lunch time I hurried down to Allies Inn in hopes of finding Dash. Randall Hare surprisingly appeared. He said, "I can't imagine where Dashie is. We always lunch together on Tuesdays and Thursdays." I delayed going back to the office, and drifted over to the Lincoln Memorial Pool. There I flirted with someone, thinking remorsefully that I was being untrue to my love and at the same time thinking bitterly that he had abandoned me, so what did it matter. When I got home I composed a night letter to Lansing Tower, confirming our vacation together in Mexico. The die is cast.

### Wednesday, 15 May 1929

Dash and I went to see Ramon Navarro in *The Pagan*. Superior to the ordinary movie, although the story, had it been in a book, might have been trash. The villain was a Christian trader in the Pacific Islands and the hero was a pagan, half-caste youth. There was beauty in it—atolls in the sun, palm trees against drifting clouds. Best of all, the conclusion was not on the side of respectability and Americanism. The pagan youth remained in his island paradise. The final caption was, "The pagan's only god is nature, and the pagan's only law is love."

When we got back to Dash's room there were timetables on Dash's bed. I inquired in a casual tone, "Are you going up to New York?" He became angry. "I'm not under an obligation to tell you about my plans. I don't need a chaperone, and why should you expect to go everywhere with me?" I tried to calm him and he snapped, "I'm not bound or obligated to you!" I left soon after, struck with the desire to visit Isador to get my mind off my loneliness. Started up the Avenue and saw that a police raid was in progress across from the Interstate Commerce Commission. I watched, filled with disgust. Police came out herding nine or ten men. A plainclothesman carried bottles of white liquor as "evidence." The men clambered into the patrol wagon, some smiling with a forced gaiety as if trying to make the most of the situation. A free country—bah! Isador wasn't in. I walked through the halls of the McReynolds and heard sounds of piano-playing and merry laughter in Junior's apartment.

### Monday, 20 May 1929

Dull, gloomy rain all day. At work the Green was in one of her spells. Glad to get away from the office. Had just entered Allies Inn when Dash walked in and stood behind me without saying anything. I'm not going to write pages of morbid outpourings as I have done in the past. We ate dinner together and had an altercation. He said, "I want your friendship, but I don't want your affection." He referred to our beautiful love-relation of two years ago as an "unpleasant subject." "I wish," he said, "that you'd let bygones be bygones. Let me assure you, you need have no hope that such a relation will ever be resumed."

Hans strolled in while we were eating. He gazed at me, shook his head, and said, "You are looking down." I told him I was in low spirits. The subject of Randall came up and I spoke of Randall as "that snake from Georgetown." Dash leaned across the table and proclaimed in a stage whisper that Randall was his lover, that he was going to put Randall in the Social Register, and a lot of other sarcastic tommyrot. I felt unhappy but in a proud and scornful way. Outside it poured rain. Going out, Dash held his raincoat over his head and over me, saying, "Get under the raincoat between us, Hans." Hans frowned. "It isn't raining enough." But Dash insisted. I got out from under the coat and left them, feeling a panicky misery.

*Tuesday, 21 May 1929*

As I approached the Y with head down against the rain I glanced up and saw two men in glistening raincoats approaching. I recognized Randall Hare and spoke to him, and then with a shock saw that his companion was Dashie, wearing a dazzling smile. I stopped blankly and asked, "Where are you going?" "To parts unknown. I shall be unable to have dinner with you. I have an engagement." Randall tried to ask polite questions about my upcoming trip to Mexico but I was so confused that I answered shortly, barely looking at him. I hurried blindly on feeling as if the ground had been knocked from under me. Anybody but Randall! That damned popinjay! Damn Randall to hell!

## Thursday, May 10, 1928

A beautiful sparkling bright day, mild and balmy.... Pub was already there when I walked across to him and had turned up a chair for me, the first time in months that he has done so. He walked with me through the soft, dewy morning as far as the Ellipse.... Nothing of note today. Physically I feel poorly — sleepy, nervous and run-down. But spiritually I feel acutely high, realizing and glorying in the loveliness of the May and the sweetness of life. Walked down to the tidal basin after lunch and leaned on the railing, watching the cliff swallows that nest in the sea-wall...... Went to Pub's room at 6.30 but he was not there. Waited on the roof 15 minutes, went back again to his door, and then went out to Cleves. Ate alone in the courtyard, where it was cool and quiet and I could have candle light and could see the sky and the branches of a tree through the opening overhead.... Pub's windows were dark and silent so I didn't go up. Strolled a bit in the twilight, feasting on the beauty of the trees and fair buildings and the shadows creeping over the lawns, feeling languid and peaceful. Came home and made out catalogue cards for 22 books, finishing at 10.30.... Have been thinking today of the possibility — should I not go to Mexico — of paying Pub's passage to Europe this summer with me, employing him as a travelling companion. It would be worth it to me, I wonder if he would agree to it. There are hundreds who would jump at the chance. 11. I hope to get 8 hours sleep tonight — God knows I need it and then some. ...——

(from 133) smiling and returning my affection, all embraces." "I've spent so many miserable hours here thinking of you and writing for you. I love you. Just remember that." It may excuse many things." Then I told him at the door. He would not remain as I asked him to but was satisfied as it was, and was intensely happy. He looked back and would as he went down the steps. I opened the window and watched for him on the side walk below. As soon as he came in profile from under the bay window he was looking up and when he saw me he held up his hand in a farewell greeting and smiled again that happy tired smile. I sat down feeling limp and crushed a cigarette and missed Leppig, feeling as if I had unloosed something that long had been pinned up within me. Those delicious sweet kisses I shall not soon forget...... As I wrote my diary, which I began at 1.10 my mind wandered again and again to Pub and my love for him and my plans for the summer and the hope that we might go abroad together. Consequently it is now 2.55 and I am just finishing four and a half months of starvation and then a joyous feast, even though incomplete.

A typical diary entry, 10 May 1928.
From the collection of the author

Jeb's stepmother, Mama, as a young woman in
Atlanta, circa 1900.
Mama married Jeb's father in circa 1905.
Courtesy of Emily Campbell

Jeb's father, Dad, circa 1910.
From the collection of the author

Jeb's family home in the Brightwood section of Washington, D.C.
From the collection of the author

Jeb as a youth, circa 1912
(the year he began his diaries).
From the collection of the author

Jeb's brother Henry in his aviator's
uniform, Lake Ontario, May 1918.
From the collection of the author

"Arrival of Lindbergh from France.
Parade and monster celebration.
Lindbergh a handsome and charming
youth; I had several good views
of him."—11 June 1927
UPI/Bettman

Jeb shortly after his twenty-second
birthday, October 1921.
From the collection of the author

"Off on a holiday with Dasham to Atlantic City."—24 July 1927
From the collection of the author

"Bill Courtland liked my room and looked about with interest.
He liked especially my Egyptian tapestries."—8 July 1929
From the collection of the author

In Jeb's day, Lafayette Park, across the street from the White House,
was *the* place in Washington to cruise. This 1930s photograph
shows the statue of General Andrew Jackson in the park.
From *A Manual on the Origin and Development of Washington*

The White House fire, Christmas Eve 1929: "All around we heard a roar
of fire engines. The Executive Offices in the west wing were afire."
UPI/Bettman

"I pulled my niece Daisy around in a sled for a while, then went into the house to listen to the radio."
—19 January 1930
From the collection of the author

Jeb took this photograph of the family on a visit "to the house" on 30 August 1931. The photograph shows (from left) Mama, Daisy, Dad, Eunice, and Henry.
From the collection of the author

Roosevelt's return to Washington upon his reelection: "Junior caught up with me . . . we rushed through the White House gates and took part in a demonstration of loyalty such as I never have seen before."—6 November 1936
UPI/Bettman

"This is my nest—the cozy disorderly corner where I have so many things within reach."
—25 December 1939
From the collection of the author

Jeb just after his forty-first birthday, December 1940. Europe was at war; the United States would enter the conflict a year later. From the collection of the author

*PART THREE*

# THE GREAT DEPRESSION

*Saturday, 25 May 1929 (Southern Railway, Piedmont Limited)*

Rapidly packed for my long train journey to Mexico where I shall join up with my old college companion, Lansing Tower. Isador came by for my dragon plant and begonias. He played the Victrola and we feverishly packed and prepared my room to be left at the mercy of Wu. Isador struggled away down the stairs with his arms full of plants. I looked out the window and saw Dad arrive in the car to take me to the station. He held the gate open to allow Isador to exit with my plants. They nodded, neither of them knowing who the other was.

Down to the station and to the end of the concourse to the "Piedmont Limited." Dad helped me with my bags onto the train. I had on my new tropical suit, new panama hat, and had received compliments on them at the office. A yellow Pullman porter called out, "Car 65—bound for Macon!" and I realized with a thrill that I was on my way. Dad waved good-bye. Then we were moving. I watched Washington from the windows, watched the Capitol dome and the river and the willows, my heart shouting, "Good-bye! Good-bye!"

*Sunday, 26 May 1929 (Clemson College, South Carolina)*

Hot, sunbaked farmland. The train entered South Carolina and how strange it seemed to be in my mother's home state. Spartanburg, Greenville—finally Calhoun. Uncle Jeb, bald and in a white suit, was at the station to meet me. Grandmother sat in the back seat of the car, feeble of memory. After dinner, Uncle Jeb and I sat in the porch swing. Insects darted about and crickets made a constant outcry. Uncle Jeb reminisced about our 1927 mountain fishing expedition. Chewing on his cigar, he mused, "That Isador was an odd one . . . "

*Wednesday, 29 May 1929 (Somerset Limited, and New Orleans)*

A long ride in a Pullman with a comfortable pillow to lean on, but with dust and fine cinders coming steadily through the screened windows. The country became increasingly southern in complexion and the Gulf country began to assert itself with long-leaf pines, the seedlings looking like luxuriant tufts of long grass. Then the ultimate—tangled swamps and bayous, low palms, water hyacinth, live oaks festooned with Spanish moss, cypresses. Glimpses of the Gulf of Mexico; lakes and inlets. As we pulled into Pass Christian there came a terrific thunderclap and a flash of lightning, and I thought I saw a ball of fire fall among the pine trees. On through sweeping stretches of flat land and water. It became dark and it seemed as if we were going almost constantly over a causeway through the water. At last, New Orleans. Rows of old houses with grilled balconies. The streetcars aren't running because of a strike, but I walked as far as the levee and could see Old Man River rolling along.

*"**Old Man River**" is a reference to "Old Man River," the stevedore's song of resignation about working on the Mississippi, from Jerome Kern and Oscar Hammerstein's 1927 musical,* Show Boat.

*Friday, 31 May 1929 (Southern Pacific Lines, west of Columbus, Texas)*
Through bayous and swamps—live oaks and cane and rice fields and into the flat, dry country of West Louisiana. On the train there are a lot of crude, noisy, friendly people from the West who are returning to California. I think most of them came on the Southern Pacific S.S. *Dixie,* which landed in New Orleans this morning. I spent most of the day on the observation platform, writing a nine-page letter to Dash. One of the conductors sat down with us, talking with a traveling man. In the evening we rolled into Texas over green prairies grazed by horses and cattle.

*Saturday, 1 June 1929 (San Antonio)*
I spent an hour in the fascinating Alamo, wandering around the building and gardens. Walked on, looking for the Church of San Fernando, but a rainstorm came up and I hurried back through the torrents to the hotel. Changed from my tropical into my brown suit. At eleven I took a cab to the station, almost deserted. A great stillness; myriad insects circling the lights. Two Mexican gentlemen and myself boarded the train.

*Sunday, 2 June 1929 (National Railways of Mexico, south of Saltillo)*
Through a desert of cactus, brush, and stunted trees. Jagged blue mountains began to appear, at first far away and then closing in toward the track on each side. Clouds drifted overhead. I became exhilarated to be in such a new, lovely land. In the buffet car I ordered a bottle of beer and drank a toast to my dear Dashie, my beloved companion in the drinking of many a bottle of beer. The beer, made in Monterrey, was good. The mountains in the light of the setting sun were indescribably lovely.

At night in Saltillo I got out in the station. Behind my car they were attaching an armored car, full of soldiers and having holes for their guns to fire through.

It gave me an adventurous thrill to know that I was to be protected by armed soldiers. However, I spoke with a Mexican student who was returning after spending two years in the States. He said, "The car of soldiers will be the first thing blown up. It's an invitation to attack. I'd feel safer without it . . . but after all, I haven't heard about an attack on a train in the last four months . . . "

Now almost midnight and the train has stopped. There's almost complete silence except for the distant barking of a dog, and the letting off of steam of the engine, rather faint. I hope I shall wake up alive.

### Monday, 3 June 1929 (Mexico City)

As I walked into the station in Mexico City, there was Lansing Tower, beckoning for me to *come on*, as matter-of-fact as ever. We had lots to talk about. He wears round, metal-rimmed spectacles now, perpetually perched on his narrow hooked nose. We left my bags at the Imperial Hotel, then took a bus downtown and ate at Butch's. Butch is enormous—apparently negro and Mexican combined. Butch used to be a Pullman porter; now he runs an excellent restaurant. This is a big, bustling city.

### Sunday, 9 June 1929 (Mexico City)

To the bull fight. Lansing's friend Kate, a San Francisco student who attends the Summer School, sat between us. Exactly on the minute at four the first bull was brought out. It began raining and soon poured so hard that most of the people crowded up into the galleries. We held our rented cushions over our heads but still got wet. My new panama hat got soaked but a more serious accident had already befallen it at breakfast, when Kate's cigarette fell from the ashtray and lay on my hat brim, burning for a few minutes, leaving an ugly black spot. One bull was afraid and it took twenty minutes to get him out of the ring by use of some steers. The last bull was the wildest. It was barbarous treatment of the bulls and the horses. Lansing said, "Try not to be sentimental over the animals, and just avoid looking directly at the blood."

### Wednesday, 12 June 1929 (Cuernavaca, Mexico)

Steadily up the mountain road, enveloped by fog. We crossed and recrossed the old Camino Real of the Spanish, a narrow road of flat stones. We constantly passed crosses at the side of the road, placed in memory of the person killed at the spot. Then down and down. We could see Cuernavaca long before we got there.

I suggested to Lansing and Kate that we stop so I could take photos, and there occurred an incident that threatened to spoil not only the day's excursion but my whole trip West. So inexcusable, too. Lansing, in Spanish, finally asked the driver to stop, and I walked uphill and took two pictures. While I was taking the second one, Lansing called angrily for me to come back to the car and they sounded the horn. Lansing yelled, "We're going on without you." I could see Kate trying to calm him.

When I got back to the car I said, "I was only seven minutes. You are making a mountain out of a molehill." "That isn't the issue! The issue is your self-centered egoism and essential selfishness!" I told him, "You need to learn to practice self-control." I kept calm but finally told him to go to hell. I decided to ignore him. The subject had been abandoned by the time we entered the quaint, entrancing town of Cuernavaca, dozing in the summer sunshine amid blossoming bougainvillea. When we sat down in the hotel for lunch, a brass band in the adjacent plaza began a concert. I enjoyed the beautiful place and its charm. Lansing was civil, but I avoided addressing remarks to him as much as possible. Presently he asked Kate if the El Paso train didn't leave in the morning—apparently an announcement that he would go back to the States and abandon me. Kate said finally, "Yes, it does."

I began to feel lonely and aloof, bitterly resentful of Lansing's pettiness, the Western vulgarity of him. I longed passionately for my dear comrade Dashie. Lansing cannot know that I have had to become self-centered and egoistic for the sake of self-preservation in this juggernaut of a society—trampled on, persecuted, scorned. He can't be expected to comprehend that I have forced myself to be self-reliant, to develop a hard outer shell that no enemy could pierce, to build up within myself a sanctuary where I can be unwavering and true to myself, oblivious to attacks and torments. He has no way of knowing any of that.

Driving back, at the summit it became cold. Mists lifted from the valleys. In spite of my shivering body and numb hands, the views were the most sublime I ever saw. The clouds were piled high into the sunset sky and the light was unearthly. Then down into the city and to Butch's for supper. After we had eaten, we walked back to the hotel in the dripping rain, I several paces behind Kate and Lansing, feeling blue and wishing for Dashie. Now in the hotel lobby the cabaret music is playing. Let Lansing go to the devil. I can get along without him.

*Thursday, 13 June 1929 (Mexico City)*

I decided to avoid Lansing all day to give him a rest from me. Rambled about. When I stopped in a cantina for a bottle of beer, a voluptuous señorita came all the way from the rear to get a toothpick and apparently to give me a lingering look. Got back to the hotel, looked out my window, and saw, beyond the dark mass of mountains that encircled the enshadowed city, sunlight gleaming on a towering peak that was covered with snow. The peak seemed unbelievably high and far away and yet in the afterglow it was clear, while nearer mountains were silhouettes. Lansing knocked at my door. "Ready to go to Butch's?" Avoiding him today seemed successful, for when we had dinner at Butch's he was himself again.

*Saturday, 15 June 1929 (Southern Pacific of Mexico, en route to Nogales)*
Kate went with us on the same train, but only to Dumas. There she got off to take her trip into the hills, forty miles in a truck and about sixty miles back into Durango. Lansing leaned out the train window shouting after her, and she waved, with a pack on her shoulders, her luggage piled beside her boots. Slowly we pulled away from Dumas. For a while Lansing and I listened to a group of passengers, Americans who live in Mexico. Interesting characters—telling dirty jokes, talking about dangerous adventures. After dark at one stop we all got out together to stretch our legs. Now the train is creeping along, stopping at every tree.

*Tuesday, 18 June 1929 (Los Angeles)*
This is the famous California sunshine I have heard so much about. Lansing called up a local girl he knows and she took us on an enjoyable tour. We visited the Hollywood Bowl, explored Beverly Hills, saw the homes of Douglas Fairbanks and Mary Pickford, Charlie Chaplin, Pauline Frederick, Tom Mix, and other movie stars. The city is filled with architectural oddities, such as small buildings in shapes of icebergs, hats, windmills, and the like. Then up in the tower of the new City Hall. If the air had been clear the view would have been superb, but as it was we could not even see the mountains or the sea.

*Thursday, 20 June 1929 (San Francisco/Berkeley)*
Only about two hours of sleep last night. I have been fagged and half-dead all day. Lansing and I boarded the ferry and bore out into the harbor. Lighted boats plowed through the darkness, occasionally sounding melancholy, deep-toned whistles. The lights of Berkeley twinkled and danced, clustered like a flock of stars on the other side of the dark bay.

The house where Lansing rooms seems plain but comfortable. I have a room across the hall from his. I should prefer to be in a hotel in San Francisco instead of way over here, but I am afraid it would offend Lansing were I to suggest it. It is so cold that I have on my gabardine coat over my pajamas. Silence except for the ticking of my clock.

*Friday, 21 June 1929 (San Francisco/Berkeley)*
Breakfast with Lansing at a place called Mother's. Then across on the ferry to the city. We decided to take a sightseeing bus and did not regret it. It was a joy—the beautiful views from Twin Peaks, the ride through the Golden Gate Park, the views along the cliffs by the Golden Gate. We walked down the beach, watching and hearing the breakers, green and white, roaring in. We poked about in the drift, picking up shells, seeds, and other drift-bits, and walked below the Seal Rocks along the sand. I could hardly force myself to leave. Coming back the ferry was jammed with people, it being the afternoon rush hour. The low-hanging sun made a golden track over the waves. I gazed off at the Marin Hills, dark in the twilight, with a rosy glow outlining their summits. Goat Island loomed black in the foreground. The air was bracing and gave me more energy than I ever have in Washington. We strolled up to the University and went over the library pretty thoroughly. Lansing showed me the books he had added to the library's stock, his desk, and the Bancroft library. Now as I write it is so cold that I have my sweater over my pajamas but still am shivering. In a bookstore that we visited tonight, there was an open fire blazing and it looked wonderfully cozy. Beautiful, romantic San Francisco—I should like to live here for a while.

*Monday, 24 June 1929 (Southern Pacific Railroad, somewhere in Nevada)*
I boarded the train at the Sixteenth Street Station in Oakland. My last glimpse of Lansing was in his bright red sweater, hatless, and making a parting salute with his hand. In the afternoon I became chummy with a young man from Kansas, although we didn't introduce ourselves. We sat out on the observation platform in the deepening twilight, looking at narrow streams and the glow beyond the mountains. Everything was going beautifully until we tired of sitting down and allowed two girls to take our seats. Kansas started chatting with them and before long we were a party of four. I wearied of those silly girls, but stuck it out.

*Tuesday, 25 June 1929 (Denver and Rio Grande Railroad, somewhere in Utah)*
Through desolate desert, part of it as devoid of vegetation as a paved street. Later we began crossing the Great Salt Lake, a lovely bright blue, calm with gulls flying over it and following the train as if it were a ship. About a third of the distance across the lake we had to stop and wait for another passenger train to cross. Kansas and I got out together to walk around. I learned his name is Jim Forrest. We climbed over blocks of granite and rocks that protect the causeway and got to the water to taste it. It was extremely salty at the barest touch of the tongue.

When we got to Salt Lake City, we had to change trains. The ticket agent said, "Why don't you ride together in the same upper berth? It's wide enough for two, and you'd each save three dollars." I said I was willing, and Jim said he was. We boarded a long train and bore on past green valleys, distant hazy blue peaks, the shining waters of Utah Lake, and a red glow after the sun had set. We rumbled through a narrow valley where mountains rose sharply on each side. I started back for my diary and the trip took seven minutes of walking each way. Now I am sitting in the observation car. Jim is on the platform. I don't know how it will work out—two of us in one upper, or what will happen.

*Wednesday, 26 June 1929 (Rock Island Railroad, east of Denver)*

Our sharing of the upper berth was not successful. The berth was roomier than I had thought it would be, but Jim said he would walk around a while. Later I found that he reclined in the observation car the rest of the night—talking with the brakeman, and, when dawn came, looking at the scenery. I was sorry that my restlessness had contributed to keeping him awake. Spent most of the day with Jim. A mighty nice chap, although he was tired from being up most of the night. The train went for home along the turbulent, chocolate-colored Arkansas River with mountains on either side, gradually narrowing into the much-heralded Royal Gorge. In Denver at night we walked downtown to the steps of the State Capitol, then back to the station, where I saw Jim onto the local train. I shall probably never see him again.

*Thursday, 27 June 1929 (Rock Island Line, east of Kansas City)*

Kansas was a surprise—a green, fertile, rolling country of cornfields, meadows, and wooded hills, with the placid Kansas River appearing and reappearing alongside the track. Probably the western part, which I slept through, was more flat and monotonous. I watched for Manhattan, Kansas, because of Jim. As we rumbled through, his hometown seemed not a bad place. His train was to reach there ten minutes after mine, although it left Denver an hour earlier. I had a seven-hour wait at Kansas City, Missouri. Their Union Station is enormous. They claim it is the largest outside of New York. The city seemed prosaic and uninteresting, the people crude and ugly. I saw few faces that looked refined and intelligent. Went at night to the War Memorial across from the station. Steam issued from the top and, colored red with electric lights, resembled a blazing fire.

*Friday, 28 June 1929 (Baltimore and Ohio Railroad, somewhere in Ohio)*

Stood on the rear platform while we chugged past St. Louis and along the Mississippi, the bridges and buildings dim and mysterious in the smoky haze. I saw gaudy excursion boats on the river. Spent most of the day in the parlor car.

Some women with babies occupied my seat. This train is so damned dirty that it takes away some of the pleasure of travel. Dust and cinders. In the West the train burned oil and in Mexico charcoal. Riding them was much more pleasant. I missed Jim today. I haven't even thought much about Dash since San Francisco, for some reason. God, how I hate the thought of going back to slavery Monday!

*Saturday, 29 June 1929*

Wu greeted me cordially at the gate. My room looked strange when I entered. I changed my clothes and unpacked a few things. Max called up, and Hans soon arrived. I started downstairs to call up Dash, but Hans said, "Dashie isn't in Washington. He left this morning to take his vacation in Natchez." I asked when he was expected back. Hans cleared his throat. "You'd have to ask Randall." So I am home again.

*Sunday, 7 July 1929*

Walked through the sultry night to meet Isador at his apartment. Going down the hall I heard "Carolina Moon" being played, blending with the sound of Randall's laughter. I gave the knocker a violent knock. Isador, barefooted but otherwise fully dressed in his white suit, was looking up clippings for Randall. He padded into the kitchen to locate one of his scrapbooks, saying, "Randy, guess what? I've persuaded Jeb to go with me to Muriel Phillipson's salon." Randall said nothing, and I said nothing. From the kitchen Isador remarked, "Do you know, we are going to have Frigidaire." I didn't get the pun, if it was one, until hours later. Isador had already told me that the management is planning to install Frigidaire in his apartment building.

Muriel Phillipson has her studio in an old stable behind her house on Connecticut Avenue. She has the place fixed up in a bizarre and Bohemian fashion, dusty and cluttered with paintings, old furniture, drapes, and all sorts of things. She is a middle-aged woman, with hair frizzed down over her eyes, and a wreath of what looked in the dim light like artificial flowers. She wore a longsleeved olive-green gown that trailed a foot behind her on the floor. Her voice was effusive, but kindly.

Isador led me back to a refurbished area that had formerly been a horse stall with a curved railing, which now contained a narrow brass bed. Over the bed was a dim light in the form of a new moon, very realistic. Isador christened it "the jealous moon," after Jane Cowl's play. We took a steep staircase to the loft, its doors wide and open to the night. Up there the gathering included several middle-aged ladies and a few girls, including one fat brunette whom Isador spoke of as "Mary the Great." The rest were young men, up to thirty-five years old. The youngest was a boy named Bill Courtland. He is a vivacious, dark youngster with unusual features, suggesting the Chinese at a distance and the Spanish when closer. I liked him. He said to me, "Let's go down and sit on the 'dirty-story bench.'" Down the narrow staircase we went, to a tree-shadowed, secluded bench behind the enormous Phillipson mansion. Beyond, we glimpsed the street, hidden by foliage. Passing automobile lights shone through the leaves and made lovely transparent shades of green and masses of shadows. Bill said, "I find you very easy to talk to . . . " We made an engagement for tomorrow. After all, I can't keep forever dedicating myself to Dash, especially when he has made so clear that that part of our friendship is over.

*Monday, 8 July 1929*

Bill Courtland liked my room and looked about with interest. He liked especially my Egyptian tapestries. He is not so much on looks, but is a fine boy, intelligent, well-informed, and well-bred. I played my new records, especially "Carolina Moon" and the "Pagan Love Song." Outside, a torrent of rain thundered down, making a roar on my tin balcony. I told Bill, "'Carolina Moon' haunts me." He said, "'Pagan Love Song' gets into my blood." I sat in the big leather chair and he sat on the arm of it. We discussed the pictures in my Isadora Duncan books, as he is especially interested in the dance. Bill said, "I like you. Play the 'Pagan Love Song' once more . . . "

Well, it happened again. After Bill had gone I lay on my bed in my rayon dressing gown in the half-light, listening the roar of the storm mingle with "Carolina Moon," feeling dreamy and romantic and well satisfied. I could smell the wet summer leaves of the trees outside my window. Strangely, I felt closer to my dear Dashie-boy than ever. I didn't have the guilty feeling or regret that I expected. I imagined that Bill was Dash.

*Sunday, 4 August 1929*

Downtown I chanced upon Randall. He invited me to go with him to Isador's "pajama party" in honor of Muriel Phillipson's birthday, and said Junior and Isador would be "in costume," and many others that I know. Hardly very alluring. I told Randall I already had declined Isador's offer quite firmly. I didn't ask Randall when Dash was due back. Every day I've been expecting a letter.

Strolled away aimlessly, looking into store windows. Hans emerged from a drug store. "Want to go to Isador's pajama party?" I told him I didn't want to go, but agreed to walk up to Junior's with him. When we got there Hans played show tunes on the piano while Junior dressed. Junior did female impersonations, which usually disgust and annoy me intensely. However, Hans was enjoying the performance so much that I didn't want to be a killjoy, and mellowed. I finally decided to go to the party, but set off ahead of them, before Junior was ready, because I didn't want to accompany Junior when he was attired like that.

Found Isador polishing silver candlesticks and making last minute preparations for the party. He chattered continuously and handed me a dish towel and asked me to dry the candlesticks. He finished his dressing, very elaborate, and was giving imitations of Queen Victoria when Randall arrived, accompanied by a handsome, silent boy who seated himself on the windowsill and began reading *Hamlet*. Randall lounged in a chair by the boy. Another guest followed soon after, a heavy-set fellow named Bob Estelwater. Estelwater announced that he had just returned from spending his holidays sunbathing naked at an obscure spot on the Eastern Branch. Randall said amiably, "A peculiar activity."

After a moment Randall gazed at me with a faint smile and remarked, "Dashie sent me a card, saying he would return from his vacation around the 12th." Isador said, "Yes, that's what Dashie wrote on *my* card." He bustled off to the kitchen to get the card. Muriel Phillipson and other guests arrived. Amid much conversation and laughter about the "pajamas," Isador returned from the kitchen and let me read the card Dash had sent him. I sat there outwardly calm and smiling but seething within, hardly hearing anything the others were saying. I excused myself and rushed home to write a bitter letter to Dash asking him why he had not written to me, since apparently he had written to everybody else we know. Now I wish I hadn't mailed it.

*Monday, 2 September 1929*

Thousands of people, mostly from out of town, were watching the Firemen's Parade. Sweating crowds were pushing everywhere. I got caught in the crush along the White House fence. Wearing of trying to watch the parade in the heat, I rode the bus over to Arlington Beach. Saw Junior and Isador just leaving the beach, squirting water at one another and acting so foolish that I didn't talk with them long. There was a sizable crowd, almost all men and boys. I swam almost constantly. Left the water and dressed slowly. Got a hot dog and a Nehi Grape at Jerry's and took the bus downtown. Glimpsed Max strolling out of the Y with a young fellow from the fourth floor, queer.

Sex has been on my mind today—the crowds, the new faces, the leisure of a holiday all contribute toward it. I have thought of Dash and wished for him, longed for the delicate charm of his personality, wistful and yet gay; his beauty, his soft voice, his quiet reserve.

*Tuesday, 24 September 1929*

Why in hell should it be necessary for Isador to introduce Dash to every friend that Isador has or makes? Tonight Dash announced that he is going out to have dinner Wednesday evening at Bob Estelwater's house in the woods in Cabin John. Randall immediately began to ask questions, showing that he was as suspicious as I was. I felt perturbed over Dash's announcement and warned him bitterly as to why Bob had invited him and what, having met him through Isador, Bob would expect. Oh hell, I can't keep on being upset all the time over real or imagined designs on him by others. After all, he is no baby and fairly capable of taking care of himself.

Six years ago today I started to work in the Government, and I am still there. Six years of my youth have passed away into eternity. Next month I shall be thirty years old and the best years of my life will be gone.

*Wednesday, 25 September 1929*

When I walked into Allies Inn I was overjoyed to see on the shelf the brown hat with the striped band that showed Dashie was there. I carried my tray over and sat with him, and he, eating his shredded wheat, toast, and figs, was in his most amiable mood. We walked out together. I told him, "Take care of yourself in Cabin John with Bob tonight." He sweetly said, "I will." As I hurried away through the park I looked back and waved my newspaper to him as he ascended the stairs of the State Department. He waved back and I went on feeling full of tenderness toward my dear comrade.

*Thursday, 24 October 1929*

The news that there was a panic in the stock market was telephoned to both Dr. Kraznovski and Mrs. Utott. I begin to be worried, not so much for my own apparently safe investments, even though I lose much money theoretically, but for Dad and Henry, who are inclined to speculate. Yet I have not bought a late paper, even though tonight's *Post* bore a great headline, *STOCKS CRASH IN HISTORY'S GREATEST PANIC.* I refuse to be worried over anything so sordid as financial matters until I am forced to be.

After work I stepped outdoors into a bitter north wind. Found Henry waiting for me at the curb in his Packard. He drove me home and had a late birthday present for me, a metal ashtray with a seated Indian on it. I have at least twenty ashtrays already. He was concerned about his investments, but not about his income, because the grocery business would see him and Dad through. "After all," he said, "Everybody has to eat." As for my situation, he said, "Nobody who

works for the Government has to worry about financial security." I was offended
by his attitude.

**Stock market panic.** *The diary entry for October 24, 1929, announces the events of*
*"Black Thursday," when the stock market crashed. Soon after, "Black Tuesday," October*
*29, 1929, became the most disastrous day in the history of Wall Street. Billions of dollars*
*were lost and countless investors were ruined.*

*Sunday, 17 November 1929*

To the house. Read the newspapers after dinner. Dad, Mama, and I went for
a ride in Maryland. The countryside, mute and wintry, lay low and misty under
a steady rain. I sat in the back seat looking at the gray roads and brown fields and
enjoying all the beauty I could find. We returned along the Baltimore pike
between hideous gaudy billboards and past scores of Bar-B-Que signs and gaso-
line filling stations. Ugliness and more ugliness. They let me off downtown. I
hurried to Dash's, but he told me he had an engagement, so I dined alone at
Child's. The "Large Child," the dull, pie-faced girl behind the dessert counter,
glared at me. I was filled with fury. I demanded, "What's the matter?" and she,
"Beg pardon?" Silly to get so upset but I couldn't help it.

At night the rain poured down, drumming on the tin roof of my balcony. I
settled into my chair in comfortable mules, wearing two sweaters and a woolen
scarf, with my cap on to warm my head. Max shouted up at my window from the
yard. Wu, the reprehensible creature, still hasn't fixed the broken bell. Max was
in a happy mood, being again in love, and having had his loved one with him all
night for the first time. I was bundled up with many garments to keep warm, but
he, with only a coat and no vest, seemed warm and comfortable. After he left I
felt frustrated about my life. If I had any guts I would give up my job and go live
in Europe. I could live on my small private income in Paris. But I am too much
of a coward to get myself out of this dreary rut.

*Thursday, 21 November 1929*

Idly listened, standing at Dash's window, to Hans translating a letter from
his sister in Germany. She wishes she could take her children to see *Steamboat*
*Willie,* starring Mickey Mouse. Far below, fog covered Washington's streets and
walks. Automobile lights shone and faded away. The airship *Los Angeles* appeared
in the sky. We went out on the roof to watch it—a great gray fish gliding through
dark water. Junior Whorley began expressing his usual pigsty attitude, then started picking on me. He screamed and carried on in a disgusting way. I made sarcastic remarks. He got mad and said, "If I start on you, you won't be left with *a*

*leg to stand on.*" I defied him to do it. He asked Dash and Hans, "Why do you always *kow-tow* to Jeb?" Before he left he tried to be sugary toward me and "make up" but I had become too angry in a cold aloof way and replied with sarcasm.

Tonight when I got into bed I had another of those attacks I have been getting lately—my chest and head felt strange and I was gasping for breath. I am afraid it must be my heart.

### Friday, 22 November 1929

Twirling his umbrella, Isador disappeared ahead of me into the elevator at the Y. I lingered at the fountain till the elevator had gone up. When I reached the sixth floor, there was Isador. Saying he had knocked at Dash's door without reply, he added, "But the light is on . . . " and leered in a disgusting way. I hope he doesn't get the habit of going to see Dash. It is seldom he ever does, knowing he's not wanted in the Y. I found Dash in the shower, where Isador had not looked. Dash shouted through the hot steam and downpour, "I have an engagement." As I walked home the thought of my dreamy Vincent Eric Orville came to me—he who has been almost forgotten. Once more, the well of loneliness.

### Monday, 25 November 1929

Dash, Randall, and I went to Junior's apartment to get Hans, who was going with us to the Belasco. Going to Junior's was embarrassing to me, because we are not speaking to each other (amusing, isn't it). Junior loitered in the bathroom. He didn't speak to me except to say, "Excuse me," when he finally emerged and I was standing in front of the bathroom door.

The play was Ernest Pascal's *The Amorous Antic,* an "ultra" sophisticated satire on the "ultra" modern artists. Immensely witty and diverting, but there was overdone satire on the cheap types of homosexual men that was displeasing and entirely extraneous.

### Monday, 9 December 1929

Skies were dark and icy rain poured on gray pavements ouside the window. All was dreary and depressing. The voices of the Green and the Contadeluci and the sounds of the typewriter wracked my nerves.

When the long, long afternoon ended I set off into the fairyland of ice-encrusted twigs and pine plumes to see Dr. Earnest. He was of no help whatever and I shan't go again. He said the shortness of breath and head pains I have had at night are due to my attitude toward my work. He lectured me with a lot of platitudes about "being of some service in the world, and not being a parasite," and accepting life since I couldn't escape it. He spoke of my being "against everything, paddling upstream"—a lot of stuff that I never told him. He has either jumped to conclusions, an unfortunate trait of his, or he has investigated me at the office, inquiring about my attitude and character. He said, "I urge you to see my friend, Dr. Stout." Dr. Stout is a psychiatrist. I sat there meekly angry listening to his line of inspirational Y.M.C.A. and big-brother bunk, then told him, "I am quite satisfied with my attitude toward life." I was seething inside.

Feeling all upset and more depressed than ever, I hastened to Dash's warm little room. As I hurried down the hall I heard Randall's growling laughter rumbling through the door. Dashie invited me in, very cordially and smilingly. He told me cheerily, "Sorry, Jeb, but Randy and I have an engagement." Randall lifted a glove off the bureau and let it drop, over and over, until I left. Walked home deeply wretched. Got out my Whitman and read all of "Calamus." It seems that all my strength and vitality have gone toward loving Dash. I feel as if I'm frozen in time, left behind somewhere while the world goes on, stuck in the summer and fall of 1927, lost in the illuminated roar and mists of Niagara Falls, the surf of Atlantic City, those cozy breakfasts at Allies Inn, our happy rambles and our beautiful nights together. Don't know what I can do about it, though. I love him yet.

*Tuesday, 24 December 1929*

At Allies Inn people were singing Christmas carols. The place was lighted by candles and the pretty Christmas tree. Dash dined with me, Randall having decided to escort his wife and mother to Christmas Eve services at Washington Cathedral. We had a delicious meal. The cute, flirtatious girl at the dessert counter usually jokes with Dashie and teases him, and tonight she came out with her tray and joined us. They made a pretty picture in the dusky court, their faces lit by the candles on the table.

After dinner Dash and I went up to his room. As I watched him loosening his tie, a simple gesture that for some reason never fails to endear him to me, we heard a great clatter and scream and roar of fire engines. From the window we saw smoke billowing beyond the State, War, and Navy Buildings. Dash got on the telephone, and the operator told him the White House was on fire. We were thrilled and shocked and immediately put on coats and hats and rushed to the White House, running precariously over icy walks. All around we heard a roar of fire engines. The Executive Offices in the west wing were afire. Water streamed down the opposite side of the street. Firemen and police people worked everywhere amid clouds of acrid smoke. From the State Department steps we watched flashes of flame burst through the roof. Brilliant flares for the taking of movies were burned all around us. Constantly we heard the sharp reports of flash powders of photographers.

My feet became numb and I began to feel chilled through. Finally the fire seemed under control, so we hurried back to Dash's room, where I toasted myself by his radiator. Dash threw himself down on his bed and said, "To think that it was the White House building on fire! One thinks of the White House as sacred—immune from fires." He was flushed from the cold and the excitement. I gazed at him, and told him, "I need you, need you more than anyone else does. I can't be happy unless I see you frequently." He said, "I want your friendship. But friends shouldn't see each other too much—there should be an element of spontaneity." He shook his head in a slow, insisting way. "Tonight, while we were watching the fire, I felt that you and I were finally *friends.*" I started to say that I could hardly stage a burning of the White House to ensure the appropriate attitude each time we saw each other, but thought better of it, and departed for my cold room.

*Tuesday, 31 December 1929*

Another year gone. Another decade gone. Dash and I settled down in my room for this last evening of the year. No heat whatever, thanks to Wu. The temperature in the room was fifty-nine degrees. What a hell of a joint this is. We kept on our overcoats and were comfortable, fairly. I felt sad to see the end of the year, although it has not been a good year for me as regards Dashie-boy. The high point was my wonderful trip out West.

Dash read *All Quiet on the Western Front,* which had been my Christmas gift from Mama. I mused, watching the clock get closer to the new year. We ate fruitcake and on the brink of midnight lighted cigarettes, having no drinks, and smoked to the success of 1930. Then, hearing the roar outside, I opened the window and jangled my bell out into the night. Felt a surging thrill go through me at the thought that it was the start of a new decade full of limitless possibilities, and I resolved that I would do great things in the thirties. The din died down. I closed the window and faced Dash again. He had sat quietly in his chair all the time.

# 1930

*Thursday, 2 January 1930*

At the office two incidents in the afternoon caused an uproar as well as embarrassment: I said there ought to be a couch in our room, during a discussion of the lack of one in the men's rest room. Mrs. Green said, "I hope it would be for men and women both." After a moment she burst into embarrassed laughter, saying, "Oh, that was terrible—I didn't know what I was saying," and rushed out of the room for a glass of water. I hadn't even noticed any double meaning. Later we were talking about walking. Miss Contadeluci remarked, "I don't walk as much as I used to, when I lived in Maryland." I replied, "You have become effete since moving into the city." Not knowing the word she looked it up in Webster. She was so shocked she sat down hastily, laughing foolishly. The dictionary gave the meaning as being sterile, no longer capable of bearing young. The meaning I had intended was given inconspicuously. Uproarious laughter. I lost control of myself, although laughing silently, and my tears flowed. The Green nearly had a fit and ran out of the room to tell the Utott. As we were leaving the office at 4:30, Miss Contadeluci said teasingly, "In future, you should use words *only* if you know what they mean . . . " .

I found Junior in Dash's room, settled into the chair by the radiator "like a little doll," as Dash once said of him. We both were polite to each other, the first time we have spoken since our quarrel. Dash said to me, "I'm dining with Junie." Junior insisted that I come along but Dash told him it would be all right, that "Jeb and I have an understanding that we should have no standing engagement." I said to Junior, "You don't have to have me along, every time you dine with Dasham." Junior said, "Well, I feel foolish," but finally stopped urging.

Later, Dash stopped by to see me. It was the third night straight. So sweet to have my boy back again, even if not in the old way that I miss and want so much. He visits me because Randall is at Catherine's family home in Charlottesville, but no matter what the reason I have been much pleased. He made himself comfortable in my big chair and read in *All Quiet*. I puttered around and watched him. When he put on his coat to go, he said he had enjoyed the evening. There was no heat, either, except for a few minutes.

*Friday, 3 January 1930*

I heard a slight noise at the door. Opened it, and there fluttered down another of Wu's disagreeable bulletins stuck in the door. This one implies that Dashie is, in Wu's words, "a puerile person to whine" at being reminded of the lateness of the hour. I wrote a sharp note to leave for Wu tomorrow. That old swine!

Dashie arrived, bringing Max, both of them exclaiming about the coldness of the night. Fine chance they would have of getting warm in *this* place. I kept the Victrola going and served cider, now near the dregs, fairly hard and noticeably alcoholic. Dash and Max danced together. I watched, deeply annoyed. I pulled the shade down but said nothing.

*Saturday, 4 January 1930*

At breakfast I remarked lightly that dancing in my room was hardly necessary. Dash became offended. I was sorry I had spoken of it. Went off to the office feeling depressed and angry.

*Tuesday, 7 January 1930*

At breakfast I questioned Dash about his dinner companion last night. He said it was Max. I told him, "I asked you yesterday at breakfast if it was Max and you said, 'no.'" "I did not say, 'no.'" "Did Max specify that I shouldn't be there?" "He didn't say anything about you. He didn't mention your name." I ate my waffles in silence, then remarked, "It was selfish of you, when a mutual friend was dining with you, to send me away to eat by myself." Dash said nothing, scowling at his plate. Finally he said, "People regard us as Siamese twins. Why do you try to force yourself on people?" I replied, "I didn't know I was so obnoxious that people tried to get away from me."

Dash became extremely angry, and said too many upsetting things for me to put down here. It was time for me to leave but I didn't want to go away without disposing of the quarrel. "Do you want to see the paper?" "I have a paper," he snapped, and pushed his empty fig-saucer away so violently that it rattled against another dish. "Why are you getting excited?" I asked pleadingly. I tried to make the remains of my cigarette last a bit longer and we left together. He gave an expressionless nod in reply to my "good-bye." I walked on rapidly toward the office with something within me crying out for deliverance from this intolerable situation, this love that knows no bounds and gets in return so little that it demands.

*Thursday, 9 January 1930*

Found Max drawing. He was not inspiriting company. He has new body-building equipment—a Christmas gift from his aunt. There were several things I wanted to say, but Max seemed interested only in telling about himself. He and his aunt had been having one of their arguments. This one started because she objected when Max hung one of his male nudes—a modest one—in his room. Max said, "She and I have to live separately. Damn the Depression. No one hires artists!" He was rather blue about it. He has had an enormous influence on my life, but we seem to be drifting apart. I think Max has deteriorated in the last year or two. He showed me Bolling Balfour's pornographic pictures from Cuba, at my request.

*Sunday, 12 January 1930*

Sex has been on my mind. I wish there were some better solution to the problem than I have been following for the last three years. Decided to go see if Dash's lights were on. They flashed on just as I looked up and I could see him in the room, the first time I had set eyes on him since Wednesday morning. I waited at the car-stop to see when he was coming out so I could precede him to Allies. Gave up and went alone. As I was finishing my dinner, Dash strode smilingly to my table with his tray. He began telling about a youth who came into the Y with a hard-luck story. He said the fellow was not an ordinary panhandler but was an authentic "case." I went back with Dash to the Y and found the rough-looking chap loitering in the hall. He was not shy about telling Dashie what he wanted. Dash gave him shoes, trousers, underwear, cap, socks, and shirt. I am sure he was just an ordinary bum, but these days it is hard to tell. Anyway, I didn't spoil Dash's pleasure in helping a deserving case by sharing my real opinion.

A peculiar man named Dr. Houndstooth, an astronomer, has moved into the room next to mine. He is quite thin and energetic. Tonight he knocked at my door bearing two hot cups of tea, and invited himself in for ten or fifteen minutes.

*Sunday, 19 January 1930*

Out to the house. In the sitting room I found a Majestic radio, just installed yesterday. So they have succumbed—at least Mama has, for she bought it. I went outside and pulled my niece Daisy around on the sled for a while, then went back in to listen to the radio. A good radio, when you can control it yourself, is not so bad. I may get an Electrola myself some time. Mama urged me to stay for supper. Thinking of Dash I refused, even though I should have liked to stay. I hastened downtown to Dash's but was brought up with dismay to find his transom dark. I have no one to blame for my disappointment but myself. I knew that Randall was back in town.

*Thursday, 30 January 1930*

Deep snow, the heaviest snowfall since the Knickerbocker disaster in 1922. Beautiful driving snowflakes falling through the air and piling high. I love the snow. At lunch time I met Dash at my little cream-colored stone bank, my bank with the carved squirrels on it. His brother is in need of money, having lost considerable in the Wall Street panic. I got a loan of $150 and lent it to Dash to lend to his brother. No streetcar came, so we walked together back to our offices, delighting in the snowstorm.

At night, for the celebration of Dash's thirtieth birthday, Randall, Dash, and

I had dinner at the Tally-Ho Tavern, an old stable. When we came outside the wind ran away with Randall's hat. I watched Dashie chase through the whirling gusts of snow to rescue it, then walked home alone through the piercing wind.

*Thursday, 27 February 1930*

In front of the State Department I saw Isador and Randall clambering over the hard, messy snow. Randall had his hand on Isador's arm to keep from slipping on the ice. When he caught sight of me he raised his eyebrows and said, "If Dashie is not with you, and Dashie is not with me, then where is Dashie?" Isador answered placidly, "He went to the movies tonight with Junie and Muriel Phillipson." Isador knows everything about everybody's business at all times.

They invited me to have dinner with them, and I did. Isador talked incessantly from the moment he tucked his napkin into his lap and picked up the menu—he with his ridiculous gossip and confessions and effeminate gestures. And Randall tried to impress us with his importance. Conceited, posturing fool, telling of his blue blood, his fortune in five figures, his "society" friends, his local prominence as director of the Art Promoters, and the alleged fact that he has been invited to send in his biography for *Who's Who*. I was disgusted and made sarcastic remarks. Finally he dropped his pose and talked in an interesting way. Through most of the meal both of them laughed and joked in their rather loud and boisterous way. I could not join, for that sort of thing is alien to my nature except at rare times.

Isador and Randall depressed me. I left the café dreaming of breaking away from my futile routine and going to sea. To run away to sea—like a fifteen-year-old. The time for that was in 'twenty-two when I was slaving behind the counter in the grocery store. I wanted to break away then and do something reckless, but instead I got caught in the Government and here I am yet—eight years later.

*Sunday, 4 May 1930*

Pouring rain. Spent about twenty minutes trying to call the house by that damned dial system, which went into effect last night. I finally left in disgust and called on a real telephone in a drugstore, but then got no answer. Swam over to the Y and got Dash. We sloshed through the rain to Allies. The D.A.R. convention opened today and Daughters are everywhere. The place was crowded and rain thundered on the glass roof over our heads. The dinner seemed fair but Dash was determined not to like it and grumbled. Tonight Dash was, somehow, curiously uninspiring. If only he would not talk about food so much!

When I got home the thin man from next door, Houndstooth, joined me and looked at my coin collection. Later Max visited, bubbling over with good spirits, sharp commentary, and physical well-being. I felt like an old man. He has been swimming at the Y pool, and exhibited his muscles recently acquired.

> ***"Damned dial system"*** *refers to the advent of the rotary telephone. Jeb was accustomed to picking up the phone, telling an operator the number he wanted, and having her transfer his call.*

### Saturday, 10 May 1930

Max drove us in his aunt's car down to Herzog's Sea Food Café, upstairs in the fish market building. We had a delightful evening. It was the first time Dash had eaten raw oysters on the half shell. He liked them. Max and Dash had shad, and I had deviled crab. The full moon came up high and the pink sunset faded away behind the Lincoln Memorial. Max did sketches in his sketchbook, most of them "obscene." Below, a one-legged black man played a sort of banjo and people threw coins to him. From one of the freight-sloops we heard an accordion. We strolled down on the wharves and idled there by the fishing boats in the dimness. The smell of dead fish only added to the atmosphere. The Potomac stretched off in the gray moon-mist. Dash and Max tried to say from memory that line from Rupert Brooke's that they had heard me quote—"The chilling sweet and rotten, unforgettable, unforgotten river-smell."

### Thursday, 15 May 1930

It seems to be impossible to get friendly with that Contadeluci woman without her becoming insulting. She called me a "weakling," without justification. I didn't speak to her the rest of the day except on business.

Dinner with Dash at Cleves. He planned to spend the evening with Randall and remarked, "Randall demands that you join us." I wanted to be with Dash, so I decided to accept the invitation. We took a streetcar to Georgetown. Dash and Randall danced together until Randall's wife and mother arrived from the movies. Then we had conversation and refreshments—doughnuts and Postum. Randall told an amazing story about Miss Paravan, the deaf lady who is Dash's boss at the State Department. "Abigail Paravan was here, talking to my mother on business about the Art Promoters Club. When I appeared at my door in silk underwear, the poor woman said, 'I cannot resist you. Let me kiss you.' At that, she walked over to me, pulled aside my undershirt, and kissed me on the nipple. Then she asked me to sit in her lap—and I did—until she complained that I was too heavy." Both Randall's mother and his wife vouched for the facts. Catherine said, "The moral of the story, Randy, is that when you are wearing silk underwear, you must *never* appear in front of anyone but me."

*Friday, 16 May 1930*

Miss Paravan strode into the State Department, stood before Dash's desk, and said, "You, Mr. Dasham, have been kind." She then left the building. Late in the afternoon when no one had heard from her they called her apartment, but there was no answer. They then telephoned her sister, who said Miss Paravan was taking "an extended leave of absence." Poor woman!

*Saturday, 24 May 1930*

An unpleasant lunch, with two sluts opposite me fanning away my cigarette smoke and talking about me. Afterward I walked down to the Tidal Basin, which was full of speed boats dashing nonsensically about at terrific speed, with an ear-splitting noise. This was the first time I have seen them in the Basin. I hope it is not a permanently granted privilege. Overhead flew a procession of planes in groups. I counted 126 of them, the most I had ever seen at one time. Their din was nerve-wracking. I walked back longing for peace and repeating to myself the words of Yeats' "Innisfree."

Though feeling no sense of guilt about taking a long time for lunch, I felt afraid of the disapproval, even though unexpressed, of Miss Contadeluci. I deliberately set about to consider her as an insect sort of creature about five inches tall—that is, for psychological purposes. There's no reason why I should allow myself to be tyrannized over by Miss Contadeluci. It's just a feeling on my part— same as with Mama, whose presence had a crushing and subduing effect on me when I was a child, and even when I was a young man.

When I got back to the office ominous black clouds gathered in the west. Miss Contadeluci and I had to close the windows to keep out the chill damp wind. The Goodyear blimp *Vigilant* was struggling in the sky against the wind for hours, unable to land, and we watched it from the windows. On my way home I saw Max sitting on a bench on the windy, damp Ellipse. He told me I had a second-rate intellect, and he had, too. I thought it a crude and unnecessary remark and said I resented it. I told him, "Perhaps you have a second-rate mind but I am first-rate. Besides, anyone who is convinced in youth that he is a second-rater is too lacking in self-confidence ever to amount to anything." It took me some time to get over Max's saying such a thing. The question of the truth or lack of truth of the statement is, of course, entirely beside the point.

*Thursday, 5 June 1930*

The front page of the *News* contained startling and disagreeable information. Tony Baretto, the butler at the Portuguese Embassy with whom Dash had relations, was arrested at three this morning while leaving a Connecticut Avenue gift shop with stolen goods. Two policemen caught him after a chase with gunfire. When his apartment in the McReynolds was searched, the police found silverware that was said to have been stolen from the Portuguese Embassy. Because of my aversion for Tony, it has been years since I have had any social relations with him. However, I feel profoundly sorry for the fellow. He is facing a prison term of *years!* I should go insane if put in prison for *any* length of time. I'm glad I've never been mixed up with Tony, as was my Dashie-boy.

*Saturday, 7 June 1930*

Hans had a harrowing experience, as regards the Tony Baretto scandal. I learned about it at Cleves from Junior, who leaned over his plate and tried, fairly successfully, to tell the story *sotto voce,* so others in the restaurant wouldn't hear him. "On the night Tony carried out his burglary, Hans was staying in Tony's apartment with a Dr. Nelson, a professor at Sweet Briar College. At five in the morning, Hans and Dr. Nelson were awakened and found *five uniformed policemen* surrounding the bed."

I was horrified. Junior said, "What would your *sex life* be like afterward? And Dr. Nelson is a British citizen! The police treated them in an outrageous manner. They were insulted at every turn. They were carried off in a patrol wagon to the precinct station and then taken to the District Building, fingerprinted, and photographed." I said, "Poor Hans!" Junior said, "Mrs. Fowler employed a criminal lawyer to get Hans out, but he was in jail until late afternoon. And Mrs. Fowler thought Hans had been with Tony Baretto! Finally she understood that it was Dr. Nelson who was with Hans in Tony's apartment. Mrs. Fowler helped Dr. Nelson, too, but he wasn't released, I think, until this morning. Hans was a nervous wreck when they let him out. Muriel Phillipson took him down to Shellfield Beach for the weekend."

The story upset me terribly. Such a horrible, humiliating experience to go through. I left Junior and came home and started drinking Virginia Dare port wine tonic. That stuff is around twenty percent alcohol. It's a wonder such a potent alcoholic beverage is allowed to be sold. I became reckless, roamed out into the night, and brought home a young boy I met across from the Army & Navy Club. He left before daylight.

*Sunday, 8 June 1930*

Dashie was appalled when I told him about Hans' experience. He spoke not a word about his own incident with Tony Baretto, saying, "Isador is the original cause of everything—because he first introduced Tony to us." We decided to try to get Junior to come to my room tomorrow night, so we could get details of the story.

### Monday, 9 June 1930

Junior arrived at my room bringing Hans himself. Hans was still in a nervous state, and subdued. He had just learned from Muriel Phillipson that his and Dr. Nelson's names were printed in the late edition of the *News*. It is an outrage that their names should have been published when they had no actual connection with the case. Poor little Hans!

### Wednesday, 18 June 1930

New panic on the stock market and my profits are wiped out. That's the least of my worries, however. In the evening soon after I got to Dash's room, Hans and Junior arrived. Hans is taking the affair much to heart. At my request Dash put on his light-colored shirt and his knickers. He looked fierce in knickers and much younger. We took Hans to dinner at Allies Inn, but he wasn't himself and ate little. We talked mostly of the Tony Baretto case. Junior carried on his usual foolishness, but not objectionably loudly. In the midst of our soup we were joined by Isador. Dash suggested that Isador was to blame for the trouble caused by Tony Baretto, by having introduced Tony to us. Isador vehemently said, "I deny that I am responsible in any way." He pointed out that other persons have accepted Tony and made friends with him during the five years since Isador met him. I began to think that he was right.

Junior tried to persuade Hans to go with him to the meeting of the Art Promoters Club at Muriel Phillipson's. Hans wouldn't go. Junior had to go off without him. Isador suggested that the rest of us go to a speakeasy, "since tonight's sultry weather is just right for beer." We walked over to speakeasy Isador knew of, in the front of a house on L Street. The proprietor was a stoutish fellow with his sleeves rolled up in the heat. The room was furnished like a living room, with the addition of a table in the center. We sat on a big sofa and drank and enjoyed ourselves. The beer sold for 25 cents a bottle, but was worth it. When we left, Hans seemed less pathetic. Isador bought half a pint of alcohol, too, and carried it away with us. We went up to his place, where he served us grapefruit juice with the pure alcohol in it, iced—a delicious drink.

### Sunday, 6 July 1930

To Cleves, where I found Hans trying to find Symonds, a young friend of Isador's. We ordered dinner and soon Symonds joined us. He's a young boy with dark liquid eyes; rather "obvious" type. After dinner we went to the outdoor concert in the Pan American Building gardens and listened sitting on the balustrade of the D.A.R. building, looking at the moon above the Lombardy poplars. The last part of the program was broadcast on short waves to the entire world. When it was over Hans murmured to Symonds, "Shall I walk home with you?" Symonds demurely answered, "Yes." As they walked away I heard Hans raise his voice, for the first time in weeks, to sing that silly song he loves, "Do You Want to Take a Walk?"

### Saturday, 28 July 1930

Hans dined with Dash and me at Danish Rose. Junior, who was having his dinner across the room with Muriel Phillipson, pranced over to our table and suggested that all of us go to Glen Echo in Muriel's car. This we did and had an enjoyable long, cool ride. At Glen Echo we wandered about looking on at the diversions and the throngs. A big crowd there, mostly youngsters. We explored the Midway, deriving considerable amusement out of the distorting mirrors and the blowholes. Muriel is a good sport. She laughed harder than any of us when the air from a blowhole thrust her skirt high around her waist. Dash and Junior rode on the coaster dip, and we all rode on the swinging airplanes—a fearsome thrill of flying above the treetops at such an angle that our bodies were almost parallel with the ground. I was glad when the planes settled again and I could go down to firm ground.

### Monday, 25 August 1930

Tonight is the anniversary of the first sexual experience I ever had—with Randall, ten years ago. It was then that I thought I had finally joined forever with a loving friend and companion. I still cherish the memory of that beautiful moonlit night. No matter what happened afterward, "that night I was happy."

**"That night I was happy."** The phrase is from one of Jeb's favorites among Walt Whitman's "Calamus" poems.

### Wednesday, 17 September 1930

A red-haired fellow in the office, named Cox, was sitting in my visitor's chair by my desk, reading the papers and idly conversing with me. Miss Contadeluci asked Cox to do some work for her. He refused. "You make me tired," she exclaimed angrily, "You sit around, while I have more than I can do." I was glad to see Cox assert his independence. I told him, "Miss Contadeluci is fond of trying to boss people around, so be careful not to get under her thumb."

When I got home I was surprised to find Mrs. Planter, the maid, in my room, holding my copy of *The Well of Loneliness*. She told me, "I just read your book." I said, "Really!" She said, "I think the author might have chosen some other subject to write about." She was afraid the book might put wrong ideas into the heads of young girls. She rattled on for a long time. "A young man became fond of my boy. I could tell by looking at that young man that he was double-sexed." It seems the "double-sexed" young man wrote in his diaries about a woman—the same type as Stephen in the novel—who gathered around her all sorts of "people of that kind"—and so on and so on.

### Friday, 19 September 1930

Isador, suntanned and with a carnation in his buttonhole, arrived in my room and settled down in my rocker to tell me about his vacation in Trinidad, or, as he put it, "my goodwill tour of the Islands." Interesting as always. An extraordinary person is Isador. I never cease to find him an amazing, stimulating, and fascinating character, although I should not want to see him too often. Hans and Junior arrived. Junior tried to behave himself, but made offensive remarks and emitted shrieks in his effeminate manner that I detest. Hans practiced his part in *Penrod* on Isador. I played the Victrola and talked inconsequentially with Junior.

After they had gone, my energetic neighbor Houndstooth came in whistling "You're the Cream in My Coffee," and bearing two cups of coffee. He told me that Mrs. Planter, our erratic maid, had left in a huff. Houndstooth said that Wu asked her why she was leaving. She said it was because Wu, Houndstooth, and I were dope fiends. I was enormously amused and laughed heartily. Sorry to lose such an interesting character, though.

### Thursday, 9 October 1930

I was speechless with amazement when I heard that Thompson, that contemptible swine of a house-manager at the Y.M.C.A., gave Dash three days to move out. He told Dash, "You have people stay overnight without registering them." Dash said, "I demand that you name one." This Thompson refused to do. Of course Thompson's real reason is personal dislike. The high-handed insolence of it! Thompson showed Dash a printed card that said according to the law in Washington, D.C., roomers could be asked to vacate within three days with no reason given. Poor Dashie. His dear room that he is so fond of, and the views, and the showers—how can he replace them elsewhere?

### Friday, 10 October 1930

Miss Contadeluci left a note on my desk saying that "Mr. Dasham of the State Department" had telephoned. I called him back from a booth. The dear boy had been to see the Y.M.C.A. manager, Field, in the presence of Thompson, but got no satisfaction. The two Y Christians stuck together in their innuendoes, evasions, and bluff. Dashie said he told Field and Thompson, "If evicting me from my room is an example of Christian spirit, then I'm not very proud of being a Christian."

### Saturday, 11 October 1930

After work I hurried over to the Christian Y and found Dash, Randall, and Hans discussing the situation. Dash exhibited a priceless letter from the Y.M.C.A., explaining that Dash had never taken part in the activities of the Y and seemed out of sympathy with its "character-building program." Dash said, "I wouldn't want to stay here, anyway, after learning the true nature of those men." I told him that under the circumstances it was not a disgrace, but something to be proud of. Hans and Randall agreed. I walked home thinking about this country that could breed such swine as Thompson and Field. Thought of Paris with infinite longing. Decided to try to write a story. Struggled for two hours, paced the floor, racked my brains, glanced at clippings, all to no avail. I finally gave up, reluctantly, and full of bitter thoughts. I have ideas, imagination, the ability to write well, and yet I simply *can not* write.

### Thursday, 6 November 1930

Dash's new bed has been delivered to his new room, and he doesn't like it. He has rented the top floor of a house belonging to people named Harrison. The room is larger than his room at the Y, and has a new-looking bathroom. A well-mannered brown dog named Foxie wanders upstairs and into Dash's room at will. The dog makes a pleasant diversion. Dash has brought in desk, chair, landscape prints, and curtains, all of which Muriel Phillipson donated, so the new room is already more habitable.

### Tuesday, 25 November 1930

Stopped at United for "Ovaltine," the new hot milk drink, and then came home and put on my new suit. I like it, except that it is a little too tight fitting. It is a sort of pepper-and-salt, black-and-white effect, and sporty looking. I wore it to Dash's. He liked it, too. We dined at Allies Inn with Hans, who irritated me. He likes for people to wait on him, and Dash does too many things for him. Hans never gets his own water at a cafeteria. Always Dash or I get the water for the three of us, but tonight I went to the fountain and drew two glasses of water and gave Dash one. Dash went out and got another for Hans.

Now after midnight. My neighbor Houndstooth brought me in a cup of coffee, humming "Here Comes the Bride" and keeping time with his feet as he marched in. A jolly soul.

### Wednesday, 26 November 1930

At the office everyone was resentful because we did not get off early, even though Thanksgiving is tomorrow. Cox and I had to take leave to go to the concert at Constitution Hall. We walked up together in the cold wind, Cox looking very handsome.

We saw Paderewski himself drive up in an automobile and get out with a woman. He was striking in appearance, with purplish-brown overcoat that seemed not any too new, and a hat perched atop his bushy hair. Cox and I went inside among the throng, checked our coats and hats and packages of shelled black walnuts purchased from Miss Contadeluci, and found our seats. The auditorium was filling rapidly and eventually almost every seat was taken. Dash arrived, very handsome. He looks so young for his age. I introduced him to Cox, and sat between them and enjoyed having them on either side of me. Paderewski's recital was superb, and was greeted with prolonged applause after each rendition. But sitting between Dash and Cox was distracting. I enjoyed their presence greatly but after all, music can best be appreciated when one is alone.

### Thursday, 27 November 1930

Out to the house for Thanksgiving. Quite cold; invigorating weather. After a delicious turkey dinner Dad built an open fire in the sitting room. We sat about and listened to the Pennsylvania-Cornell football game over the radio. It was like being at the game itself, almost, and I got a thrill from the cheering and the excited account of the game.

Took a streetcar downtown and hastened to Dash's. He had visitors—Hans, Junior, and Muriel Phillipson. Hans put on Muriel's fur coat and Dash told him he looked like Admiral Byrd. Later Muriel drove us out to her beautiful home on Connecticut Avenue. We sat in the drawing room, an impressive place decorated with marble and mid-Victorian furniture. Muriel's wraith-like niece, Felicity, joined us. The rest of the Phillipson family remained in the sitting room. Junior played a number of lively tunes on the piano, then Muriel took us up to her bedroom. She has recently had it done over in rose and white. We drank homemade wine, delicious elderberry with milk in it. Five of us lay side by side on the great Turkish couch, made over from a large bed, while Junior played classical compositions on Muriel's organ. Muriel lay beside me and leaned heavily against me.

The drinks had made me feel sleepy and contented. We listened to the organ music and were drowsy and quiet. I felt happy. I felt as if I never wanted to stir.

*Wednesday, 10 December 1930*

At breakfast Hans was gloomy and said little. Eventually he told us the whole story, how Dr. Nelson, his professor friend of the Tony Baretto scandal, has suddenly thrown him over in favor of Isador. After telling his troubles he seemed more cheerful.

To work, surrounded by a beautiful fog through which I could see nothing. The sun was a gleaming dish suspended in gray vapor. Junior overtook me, bobbing out of the mist—a strange apparition. "Good news, Jeb. My office has been moved into your building and to your own floor." What a malicious trick of fate to play! The last person that I want to have near me. Junior is such an obvious type and so damned talkative and unfeeling. Oh, well . . . I shall have to make the best of matters and as much as possible forget him.

Tonight I sat in my big chair and read the complete account, in *Murder for Profit,* of the gruesome murders of thirty or forty boys and young men by the "Ogre of Hanover," a homosexual who killed his victims in an erotic frenzy. Afterward I felt a strong revulsion from the entire subject and longed toward idyllic peace—flowing waters and cows grazing and a country cottage. Now almost one o'clock in the morning. Houndstooth visited me to show me two of his scrapbooks. I am glad to have Houndstooth next door. The chink of light under his door when I pass gives me a sense of companionship.

# 1931

*Monday, 9 February 1931*

Had a conflict with that damned bitch, the Divine Contadeluci. Acting as if she were in charge of all the editorial work. I was so furious that I could scarcely control my voice. The Green bolted in to see Dr. Kraznovski about the situation. Dr. Kraznovski called me in and I told him that Miss Contadeluci had taken over Winegardner's big desk and was trying to give the impression that she was over me. Dr. Kraznovski said, "She knows her place, even if she is trying to give another impression." Working for the Government is a dog's life, not nearly so soft as is thought.

Hans had said he would join Dash and me at Allies. He never appeared, being utterly undependable at all times. In a way I was glad. He is a dear friend but his sex obsession gets on my nerves. Dash spoke little and I tired of trying to humor him. Neither of us spoke as we walked up toward the Avenue. At the corner he stopped without a word. I said good-night and was plunged into dejection again—thinking of the companionship that I am missing because of my morbidly shy nature. I trudged home in the rain. Houndstooth visited me for his usual chat. He told me the heat had been turned on for a short while. I showed Houndstooth my current letter to Wu, which starts, "I want heat, not hot air. I am not a fool . . . " After Houndstooth left, I sat on the bed to take off my shoes and the bed broke down. I feel as if I never want to see the office again, except Cox, dear boy.

*Friday, 20 February 1931*

Junior is back from his Florida trip, extremely sunburned. He brought Dash, Hans, and me each a little pelican made of whole shells, standing on coral, and brought Isador a live alligator about a foot long. Isador screamed when he saw what it was. Junior had two marijuana cigarettes and allowed us to smoke them to get the effects. We took turns at puffing at them, so I had only about half of a cigarette. Even so, it had an exhilarating effect, much like wine. But walking home I got into that horrible state of mind that Max used to call my "Curse," in which I imagine everyone is staring at me. And the more I feel that way, naturally the more of a hang-dog lugubrious expression I have and the more people do notice me. I was grateful to reach the haven of my room.

I put on the green and yellow slippers Isador gave me, and my blue, black, orange, and yellow blazer, unbuttoned my vest and shirt collar, ensconced myself in the leather chair with my Indian pillow under my head and my feet on the straight chair, and settled in for a cozy evening of reading. I got out diaries and read bits in 1923 and 1924 and was horrified at my amazing frankness regarding the life I was leading. Thank God—or rather thank Dash and circumstances— that sort of thing is buried in the dead past.

*Wednesday, 18 March 1931*

My five gallons of Vine-Glo was delivered—a keg with a jug and tubes on top. It stands by my bookcases, suggesting a bootlegger's establishment, and must not be touched for sixty days. Hurrah! Now at last I may have a solution to the woes of damned prohibition. Vine-Glo is a California wine-preparation which turns to wine after two months, and yet is legal. I ordered it at the Service Pharmacy, where I have been buying my wine tonic, and selected "burgundy," among the six "flavors" available. The company's representative will bottle the wine when it is ready. It ought to be ripe about May 20. Oh, boy!

Dash said he would visit me tonight. I lingered at the window until I saw the well-beloved figure in the brown overcoat appear across the street. He waved and I hastened down and let him in. Later Hans arrived and lay on my bed and did most of the talking, of course. He will be playing the White Queen in *Alice in Wonderland* at Wardman Park, disguised, and acting the part under the name "Lydia Featheringay." He told of the strange telegram he received from Mrs. Fowler on Saturday. It read, "Do not drink anything absolutely a dream." It seems that Mrs. Fowler had had a dream of hearing Hans crying for her from the depths of the water lilies at Kenilworth, and of hastening to him, and finding him in a serious condition from something he had been given to drink. She was so deeply impressed that before eight in the morning she sent him the telegram. "But," said Hans, "it was not so unreasonable. She has had strange things happen. She once found Muriel Phillipson unconscious from poison in the women's room of the Mayflower Hotel, and she hadn't even known Muriel was at the Mayflower . . . "

*Thursday, 21 May 1931*

Four years ago today Lindbergh landed in Paris after his record-breaking flight, and a few minutes later Dash landed at Norfolk after his mule-boat trip to Spain and Italy. Glorious adventure!

Got up this morning in time to receive the Vine-Glo men. It took them forty-five minutes to prepare and bottle, in twenty-five bottles, the five gallons of burgundy. I stayed and watched, sampling the wine on an empty stomach, and was slightly wobbly when I left for the office. All during the day I watched slate-black clouds piling up in the sky. The storm held off, though, until I got home. I played the Victrola and relaxed in the big armchair with cigarettes and my new Vine-Glo burgundy, and gazed out the window at the wild beauty of the storm. The gingko and poplar trees thrashed their branches in ecstasy as the wind and rain possessed them. I felt exhilaration of body and spirit.

Finally, I rambled off through the rain to see Isador. We took a streetcar to visit his grandmother—poor little soul. Mrs. Pearson is feeble now. But she remembered me, although I haven't seen her in two or three years. When we went back to Isador's apartment I was still under the liberating influence of my glorious wine and was able to hold up my half of a delightful conversation. Isador asked me to spend the night with him. I refused. He urged, "Jeb, I swear it—no one will ever know." Ho! Ho!

*Tuesday, 26 May 1931*

Dash and I carried two bottles of the Vine-Glo burgundy into the yard, and laid them in the shadow of a bush for Dash to take home after we had dinner. When we returned we saw a policeman chatting with two women. When Dash and I turned in at my house, the policeman flashed his light into the yard. We watched through the front door. The policeman unlatched the gate, entered the yard, and began searching around. Dash returned with me to my room. I didn't want him to get pulled in for transporting liquor. After a time we tiptoed downstairs striking matches for light. He moved toward the gate and looked about, then returned and put the bottles under his coat and slipped away.

### Saturday, 13 June 1931

Had a drinking party with my constant companion, Jeb Alexander. Wine, music, and tobacco! What blessings they are. Got to feeling fine. I rode downtown to the barber shop and waited for the Adonis-like youth with the chair nearest the door. While he was giving me a haircut and shampoo, I asked him up to have wine with me. He refused, saying he didn't know what time he would get off.

Strolled down to the reflecting pool. There, by chance, I found Dashie seated on a bench on the north walk. It was cool and breezy there in the shade. On the other side of the pool, lying on the grass close together, were two dark-haired youths whom Dash said had been there when he first sat down. Finally the pair got up and we recognized the one in the green sweater as Isador. We were much amused. He looked sheepish when he spoke to us as they passed nearby.

### Sunday, 14 June 1931

To the house. After dinner Mama expressed interest in going out to the water lily farm, so we took a drive to Kenilworth. Many people out there, wandering about and looking at the aquatic gardens. Hans came out of Mrs. Fowler's house, wearing suspenders. I introduced him to Mama, Dad, Eunice, Henry, and Daisy. Mama told him that he must come by the house and visit sometime. Dad bought four fantail goldfish from Hans, then I showed the family around the pools. When we got back to the house we went into the back yard and watched Daisy put the fantails into the pond with the other fish.

### Monday, 15 June 1931

Drank the last of my burgundy, with appropriate sentiment, for now it is all gone until the next batch matures. I lay back in my big chair and listened to records, and gazed at summer lightning above the swaying green branches of the gingko and the poplars. I was feeling good when I went down to Dash's. As I approached his building I saw three policemen, so I walked as straight as possible and thought no one would guess that I had been drinking. But an old black man selling papers said, "Get something to eat and you'll feel better." I told him I was feeling fine already.

Dash was not home. Having nothing else in mind, I walked all the way to the Library of Congress and poked around, examining Maritime Registers to learn the fate of Dash's mule-boat ship, *Hydaspes*. I found that she arrived at Genoa on April 1 of this year to be broken up. Poor old ship—she's dead and gone now. She was a symbol of romance to me—the ship in which Dash made his adventurous voyage to Spain and Italy. When I came out, the western sky was alive with heat lightning. I sat on the steps on the terrace of the Capitol, watching the sky, thinking about Dasham, trying in memories to recapture the spirit of those moments of true contentment beside him. There came to mind a line from the play version of *Camille*. That was once Randall's favorite play and he used to quote it frequently: "No more we shall roam in the gay twilight . . . "

### Thursday, 18 June 1931

When I got to Isador's I heard from the hall a great deal of laughter, and guessed that some of the Muriel Phillipson crowd would be there. Nicky Bowman opened the door. He is a pudgy fellow with the soft accent of the native Washingtonian and an odd charm, but I never have been able to feel at ease with him. Soon Hans arrived, to my surprise. Hans and Isador are scarcely speaking because of Nicky. In fact Nicky looked exceedingly winsome tonight, with rose-petal complexion and wistful blue eyes.

There were seven of us altogether. We ambled over to Seventeenth and had dinner, seated on the balcony at three tables made into one long one. Isador sat at one end, with Nicky at his left and I at his right. An hilarious meal. Afterward Isador asked me to go with him to the hospital to see Randall. I said, "I hadn't known the Snake of Georgetown was in the hospital. He bit himself, did he?" Isador said, "Try to have compassion, Jeb. Randall is suffering from arthritis, and is in a great deal of pain. He has both legs in casts, and his left arm, also."

When we got to the hospital Randall looked pitiful, trussed up in casts and trying to make light of his situation. He thinks the cause was too much bootlegger's alcohol. He expects to be hospitalized another ten days, and doesn't expect to be able to drink again before Christmas. Isador was sweet to him, plumping up his pillows and telling in a sly, outrageous manner the obscene stories that Randall enjoys.

### Monday, 29 June 1931

Had a good time finishing up the Virginia Dare sherry tonic. Felt wonderfully free and easy and poised. Would to God I could be like that always! I joined Dash at Cleves. My exuberance annoyed him, unfortunately, and he left when he finished his meal. I suddenly decided to go see Randall in the hospital. Took a carton of Luckies and rode out in a taxi. His attractive wife Catherine was visiting him when I got there. While she helped him change his lounging robe, she looked over his bulky casts and cheerily remarked, "Yes, once we get Randy home, he's going to be a homebody for a long time . . . "

Catherine left and I had a talk with Randall. He says that every night he gets so discouraged that he cries. He asked, "Do you ever cry, Jeb?" I evaded answering. I left the hospital feeling despondent, but shook it off, knowing that no good can come of brooding.

### Saturday, 12 September 1931

With Dash to see the South Sea picture, *Tabu*. It was marvelously poignant and I reveled in it. Simple, primitive, happy people far away from this machine civilization that destroys one's soul. One of the finest I have ever seen. Walked home afterward feeling cheerful. Houndstooth knocked, so I served him a glass of wine. He danced a hornpipe to the tune of the music I was playing.

### Thursday, 1 October 1931

Settled in my big chair and turned on the music and smoked the marijuana cigarette that I bought from Junior. I felt dreamy and dazed, carefree and happy. Dash knocked at my door to get me for dinner. I laughed uncontrollably and even in the line at Cleves I could not control myself, but became almost hysterical in my laughter over the slightest thing. Dash hissed, "You are disgracing yourself." I felt that I was, but could do nothing about it.

### Tuesday, 20 October 1931

Hans called me at the office. When I answered the phone he said, "Jeb, this is Jesus Christ," and I heard a giggle from the next room, showing one of them— the Contadeluci or the Green—was listening in. Hans told me he has decided not to renew his permit to stay in the United States. In my opinion he will fare worse among the fascists in Germany than he has fared here, but the closing of the aquatic gardens each fall turns him fallow, and he hasn't gotten an acting job for so long that poverty has made him desperate. Mrs. Fowler is paying his steamship ticket and will accompany him, as a temporary visitor in Germany.

After work I got a *bon voyage* gift for Hans—a pair of pajamas. Walked with my present through the chilly evening to Dash's room. Found Hans wrapping the American records he is taking to his brother and sister in Germany—negro spirituals such as "Swing Low, Sweet Chariot," and "Way Up in de Middle of de Air"; also such songs as "St. James Infirmary Blues," "Smoke Gets in Your Eyes," and "The Last Round-up." It seemed odd to think of those American songs going to people in Germany as a representation of our culture.

We took Hans to a farewell dinner at Danish Rose. Dash presented him with a blue Brownie camera, box type, and showed him how to use it. I presented the pajamas. Hans kissed each of us on the cheek, then hurried away to a going-away party being given for Mrs. Fowler.

*Wednesday, 21 October 1931*

Dash, Hans, and I had a farewell breakfast. They walked with me to the White House, where I shook Hans' hand warmly and told him good-bye. He seemed to be rather upset over it. I hastened on toward the office thinking I might never see him again.

To Dash's room after dinner. Hans was there. We accompanied him to the streetcar stop and I told him good-bye a third time. As he swung his long legs onto the streetcar he said, "Yet, I might see you once more, after the going-away party given by Muriel." He waved and called, "Wait up for me!" We returned to Dash's room. Eventually I got sleepy and started home. Dash ran after me to say that Hans had just called. Hans arrived, and we helped him carry packages down to Mrs. Fowler's roadster. Mrs. Fowler sat snuggling in furs, looking cross and sleepy. We wished her a good voyage, and told dear Hans good-bye for the fourth time.

*Friday, 23 October 1931*

Walked under damp skies to visit Dash. When I knocked, his landlord Harrison answered and said, "Your man hasn't been in . . ." I wondered if he meant anything more than he said. Walked down to the McReynolds drugstore and had raspberry ice. When I came outside I found Isador talking with his sweet friend Nicky Bowman. They invited me for a ride in Nicky's car, an open-top foreign machine meant for two persons—but the three of us crowded in. It was delightful to see the moon and the lights on the trees as we rushed along with the breeze in our hair. We crossed Chain Bridge and rode into Fairfax County. In low places the air was deliciously cool. Isador and Nicky talked about something I had not known—that Nicky tried to commit suicide last spring. He had become a close friend of a wealthy manufacturer, and the wife of the manufacturer sued for divorce on account of Nicky.

*Sunday, 1 November 1931*

To the house. Henry has become a complete businessman, accepting the sordid philosophy of material success and sneering at the real things of life—truth, art and beauty, peace and freedom. He and Eunice and Daisy left soon after the meal was over. Mama served cherry wine, two glasses apiece, for Dad, me, and herself. She showed me her wine closet in the cellar, her great secret.

At night I went to see Isador. As I approached the doorway a bareheaded, nice appearing youth asked me for a cigarette. He said he had gone up to visit "Paul Pearson," but that "Paul" was not in. I questioned him and he said he met Isador yesterday and spent last night there. He came up to my place, where we had a nice time with the Virginia Dare sherry tonic. The boy and I walked back to see Isador, who, when he opened the door and discovered us together, shrieked and leered. Isador put on masks and cavorted about, amusing us considerably. He is a unique and amazing character and I enjoy him. He received two other visitors and five telephone calls during the hour I was there. Walked home feeling wonderfully at ease for some reason.

When I got home I found that Wu had put a bed in the hall across from my door. An ashen-faced man was sleeping there. The man's suitcase was tucked under his bed and his hat sat on top of his neatly folded coat on the floor.

*Friday, 13 November 1931*

Walked to the wharves after lunch. The river was beautiful in the misty light. Oh, ho! I should throw up this paltry job and go off to the South Seas. But travel where I might, I could never escape from myself. With this curse upon me I should be unhappy anywhere. When I got home, the man who has the bed in the hall said, "I suppose you're going to play your records." I told him, "I might." He said, "Don't play jazz—play something old. And don't play anything American. America's bankrupt." I didn't know what to reply. I went into my room, and, after looking through many records, didn't play anything. Houndstooth dropped in. He says the man in the hall rents the bed from Wu for $10 a month, has a wife in Tennessee, and is out of a job and trying to earn money up here as a salesman.

*Monday, 7 December 1931*

A disagreeable wind laden with dust blew most of the day. Hundreds of "hunger marchers" swarmed over the Washington streets, in town to march on the White House to protest unemployment across the nation. By nightfall the weather was quite cold. I drank port tonic to strengthen myself for the visit to Randall. Dash, Isador, and I rode out to Georgetown in a cab. Randall was in good spirits, free of his casts and using one of his mother's canes to walk. Isador gave character sketches, including his usual imitation of Whistler's mother. Catherine Hare and old Mrs. Hare-Worth had gone to a lecture on health and returned about ten-thirty, taking off their coats and hats with a hum of conversation. I often wonder what would happen if those two women found out about Randall's private life. When they joined us we had fruitcake with a delicious orange cream sauce of Isador's creation. Cooking is Isador's latest craze.

*Friday, 25 December 1931*

Sipped Vine-Glo while wrapping Christmas presents. Left for the house. Gave and received presents. Had a good turkey dinner. Afterward the family went for a drive through the cold countryside. When we got back to the District, I invited them up to my place for wine. Mama had one glass, the rest had two each. Daisy ate an orange. As soon as I started playing my new double-faced records of Stephen Foster's songs, Dr. Houndstooth knocked. I didn't enjoy Houndstooth's part of the visit. He stayed too long, singing to the tune of "Camptown Races," and displaying card tricks. I know Mama and Henry both were bored with him. Dad and Eunice seemed to enjoy him—but Dad and Eunice are always so polite that one can hardly tell what they are thinking.

Late at night the man who sleeps in the hall gave Houndstooth and me each a piece of fruitcake. He told us that his wife in Tennessee mailed it to him for his Christmas gift.

# 1932

*Wednesday, 13 January 1932*

Unhappy about Dash and my hopelessly sex-starved life. Came home to a cold room, obviously unheated all day. I banged violently on the radiator. Immediately I heard Houndstooth trot down to complain to Wu. Presently the radiator began gurgling and heating up. I invited Houndstooth to have some wine. He drank a little too much.

Later I went to see Isador. I usually flee to Isador for comfort when Dash has deserted me, although I never discuss Dash with Isador. He was putting on his coat and hat when I got there, preparing to go to the Y.M.C.A to hear Sherwood Anderson speak. I decided I ought to accompany him, and was glad I did, even though Anderson's lecture announced his conversion to a belief in the machine—the machine that he has fought for years. He was a short solid man in a brown suit; a shock of graying hair over his forehead; a mild, kindly face; the face of a dreamer. His lecture was interesting but then he read a long poem of his own on a machine, a train that took him from Chicago to Miami. In it was a line, "Are you ready to give up individuality?" To accept the machine age—and Anderson expressed his acceptance of it—for me, never! I shall hold to my individuality as strongly as I dare. Isador afterward had my copy of *Winesburg, Ohio* autographed by Anderson, then walked home with me. Later I invited Houndstooth in for a glass, but sometimes he bores me.

### Friday, 22 January 1932

My Vine-Glo port and sauterne were brought here today but Wu wouldn't let them deliver it. It will be delivered tomorrow, but I was furious at that old bastard. Opened one of my precious three remaining bottles of sauterne. When I was ready to bring in Houndstooth for his usual convivial visit, I concealed the Vine-Glo and got out the Virginia Dare port tonic and served him that. Played some of Houndstooth's favorite records for him—Lander's "I Love a Lassie," and "On the Road to Mandalay."

After he left I decided to go to see the film version of *Dr. Jekyll and Mr. Hyde*. A beautiful and horrible picture—Fredric March was superb in the double rôle. I found that I was identifying myself with Jekyll and Hyde in a disturbing way, and walked homeward struggling for poise and not finding it. Always the tyranny of the human face—the mocking smile, the leering eye, the scornful laugh, the contemptuous word. Fight, fight, fight—be strong and proud—leap the mountain and walk among the clouds and tear the stars from their sockets.

### Saturday, 23 January 1932

On my way to see Dash's new office in the State Department building, I joined a crowd watching a raid on a gambling establishment. Two patrol cars full of prisoners drove away. Then up to Dash's cozy nook on the fifth floor, with windows overlooking the back yard of the White House. My office view cannot compare with his. Dash and I, thinking the Senate was still in session, got on a streetcar to go to the Capitol. We wanted to see what we could learn about that damned Hoover's proposed pay cuts for Government employees. Seeing no light on the cupola of the dome, we got off the streetcar and went to a movie. I vigorously hissed the appearance of Hoover in a news reel. Dash was so annoyed that he moved to another seat on the pretext of getting nearer the center.

### Thursday, 16 February 1932

After lunch I hurried over to the Monument to look at the army dirigible

R-71, which had landed on the lawn there for movies to be taken. The rudder had been damaged in landing. Quite a throng collected to view the great glittering silvery airship. Among the crowd I saw Dash, Randall, and Isador, the three having walked together over from the State Department. They were strolling around the big ship and animatedly discussing her. I made an absurd slip of the tongue, greeting Dashie as "Mr. Hare." Imagine my not being able to think of Dashie's name! When I returned to the office I became afflicted with that curious dejection that so often engulfs me after I have left Dash.

*Friday, 17 February 1932*

At night I went to see a fascinating, horrible picture called *Freaks*. When I went outdoors again I felt deeply unhappy. Randall seems to have got Dash under his thumb to the extent that he is attempting to destroy Dash's friendship with me. In my room I played music, becoming sentimentally dejected and weeping. May as well be truthful, even though I don't put myself in a very heroic light. Have a headache now—from wine and tears, I suppose.

> **Freaks** *(1932; also released as* Nature's Mistakes *and* Forbidden Love). *With the production of* Freaks, Metro-Goldwyn-Mayer *was trying to out-shock audiences who had responded to the film* Frankenstein. *Apparently almost by accident, MGM produced a bizarre, flawed morality play about freaks in a circus that became a deeply disturbing cult classic, and a textbook for producers of modern baroque films.*

*Tuesday, 8 March 1932*

Alone to Keith's. When the vaudeville show began, my evening therefroth was spoiled by the slimy ham called Harry Rose. Merely because I showed that I was bored by his antics he began to make remarks at me, standing in front of me on the stage. He repeatedly came back with such remarks as "I'm afraid you're not enjoying the show." I was so enraged that I trembled all over. When I rested my face in my hand and shut my eyes, he got a stage gun and fired it in front of me, making jeering remarks to the accompaniment of laughter from the audience. I longed for the physical strength and courage to step upon the piano to the stage and knock him down. The rest of the performance was a nightmare, but I stuck it out. I was still nervous when I left. There is nothing more contemptible that an actor can do than to pick on members of the audience, who have no recourse. I have spent the evening writing a letter to the manager of the theatre, referring to Harry Rose as a "slimy swine" and a "ham actor without sufficient wit, talent, or intelligence to amuse the audience," and mentioning his crude antics that were inexcusably insulting. All futile. The letter accomplishes nothing except to release my feelings. I have got all upset again while writing this.

*Sunday, 19 June 1932*

This evening in my memory is now a riotous kaleidoscope. Dash, Isador, Nicky, Junior, and I drove in Junior's car over to a big party in Alexandria. The liquor flowed—and it was real liquor, too, brought in from Canada. Our host was a Harvard student clad in a white linen suit. The house was lovely. In back a flagstone patio led to a lawn that sloped into darkness toward shadowy woods. Rows of colored lanterns were strung from tree to tree. The effect was delightful. I was already feeling fairly tight from Virginia Dare tonic, and to avoid losing the intoxication I had worked on at home, I took the needless precaution of immediately drinking two whiskeys, straight.

I was outrageously drunk, and joined in with reckless gusto in the singing and dancing. Sweet Nicky approached me wearing a crazy cardboard sombrero, and handed me a Chinese cap with a pigtail. I wore that thing cocked at a crazy angle on the side of my head with the pigtail in front over my shoulder. I danced with Dashie. That shows how drunk I was. It is the first time in my life that I have danced in public, that is, anywhere other than a private gathering. Dashie was in an ebullient mood, having drunk several martinis, and we swayed and dipped. When the band played the music of "Always," I sang the words against his cheek. "I'll be loving you, with a love that's true—always . . . "

Junior entertained with improvisations, dancing and prancing and putting on improvised costumes. He was in top form and I never have seen him funnier. There was some hot loving going on. Saw Harvard White Linen in a passionate embrace with Nicky. Later I saw him beneath the trees with Isador. I sat under the lanterns drinking Scotch and soda, and joined in the singing. When they played Hans' old favorite, "The One Girl," I missed dear Hansie. I got hiccoughs, as is so often the case when I drink too much. Most of the time I had a grin on my face, and I was swaying to the music, hiccoughing, with that silly hat cocked on my head. I must have been a sight.

I don't know what time the party broke up or whether we stayed to the end. I do remember Junior hovering over me in a rather kindly fashion. "It's time, Jeb—try to use your legs when you stand up." And I remember Casanova of Harvard, the well-bred host, extricating himself from his latest conquest to assist me into Junior's car. His white linen suit was quite disheveled.

*Monday, 28 August 1932*

Fierce tropical heat. Dashie and I and Max had dinner at Herzog's, overlooking the harbor. The sun sank gloriously over Washington. The yellow moon rose among the masts and shrouds of the schooners at the wharf. Nicky Bowman drove down to the wharves, sounding his horn. The other two shouted to him to come up. Finally he did come up and sit with us. Although I am fond of Nicky, tonight I was resentful of his "horning in" on our engagement, because he, Max, and Dash dined together two nights ago, and I was excluded, and then the three of them went together to the movies last night. I felt disgusted with Max, too—his rude assertion, once more made, that I am "swell-headed and have a superiority complex." Nicky went and got his car, which is only supposed to hold two, but after some discussion we all got in, Dash sitting on my lap, and drove back to the Y.

Tonight Houndstooth told me that Wu has put out the man who has been sleeping in the hall for months. The man was unable to pay his rent in installments. Wu removed the cot, leaving the man's effects on the floor. The poor man did not know what had happened until he returned tonight. He packed up and left, Houndstooth told me.

### Wednesday, 28 September 1932

Received a startling letter from Lansing Tower. He has tendered his resignation from Berkeley so that he can go to Europe. He married about a year ago. His wife, named Maria, is from Spain. He said he had been saving for years for the purpose of going abroad. Lansing knows what he wants to do and just goes ahead and does it. He told me to look for the first issue of *Man!*, a new anarchist paper published in San Francisco, on which he has worked. He said one of the worst things for a writer is reading and criticizing the manuscripts of others—and I realize that in my own case. Never mind, I'll show them yet what I can do!

### Saturday, 31 December 1932

The old year is gone. I was puttering around with no plans, when to my utter delight Dash arrived. Soon after, here came Max, pink-looking and wearing a tuxedo, with a bottle of rye, three bottles of White Rock, and two lemons. Dashie went out and got ice and we settled down to music, drinks, and conversation.

As midnight approached, Max grabbed my bell and rang it vigorously, but we heard no noise outside. Later we heard whistles, but nothing like the usual din. I rang the bell as loudly as I could out the window, Dash rang the oriental chimes, and Max screeched. Then we continued on with drinks, smokes, and music into 1933. When they left around two o'clock, Max started sliding down the last part of the banisters. I looked over the railing from the third floor and shook a finger as Dash glanced up. He smiled his beautiful smile. Then I turned back to my room and began to straighten up. So many glasses, lemons, bottles, and ashtrays.


# 1933

*Wednesday, 1 March 1933*

Junior caught up with me on the way to the office. Every morning, the closer I get to the building, the more I watch out for him, but sometimes he trots up from behind. He told of a party Muriel Phillipson gave last night. It seems everyone was drinking and the guests ended up in the basement. Muriel went down and found men and women in evening dress swinging by their hands on the overhead pipes and singing at the tops of their voices, "The Man on the Flying Trapeze." She wanted to introduce Isador, who arrived late, to a certain woman older than he. Searching for the woman, she found her embracing Isador, to whom she had not yet been introduced. "We know each other now," Isador said.

Junior also chatted worriedly about the restrictions on withdrawals adopted today by the banks. When I got to my desk I started thinking over what he had said. I became so panicky about the possibility of my money being tied up in a "bank holiday" that at lunch I rushed up in a taxi and withdrew $380 from my savings. Walked back to the office past the reviewing stands all along the Avenue, flags and decorations everywhere, in readiness for the great event Saturday. By happy chance I met Dash. We returned to our offices together, clambering in and out of the skeleton of the big inauguration stand erected in front of the White House.

*Saturday, 4 March 1933*

Crowds and excitement, waving flags and cheers, martial music and marching men and women. Isador, Junior, and I went together to the parade, and shared the furor and clamor and spectacular splendor of our greatest Inauguration in many a long year. At Fifteenth and the Avenue we had a glimpse of Hoover and Roosevelt in an open car. Having seen them off, we took a streetcar for the Capitol. We could see President Roosevelt take the oath of office that in one minute made him one of the most powerful rulers on earth. Although he delivered his address in a firm clear voice, Junior, Isador, and hundreds and hundreds of other people were talking, struggling, and pushing so much that I missed most of the speech. We made our way through the crowds, stopping to see what we could of the parade. Scores of persons were standing on boxes, baskets,

stepladders, propped planks, and anything else that would raise their heads above
the crowds. Many women were standing with their backs toward the street
watching the parade in vanity mirrors. Junior purchased a small periscope for
similar use. We each took home as souvenirs some sprays of cedar and greenbriar
from the President's reviewing stand.

*Monday, 6 March 1933*

At the office there was much discussion of Roosevelt's swift action in the
banking crisis. Every bank in the United States was closed today, but we seemed
to get along. My bank had a sign, "Legal Holiday," by the door. I have enough
cash in my pockets to last till the banks open Friday. There are so many things to
think about these days. These are interesting times.

Received a card from Lansing Tower in Spain. He said that he crossed in the
*De Grasse,* a rough trip, and went to Madrid, Toledo, and Cordoba, hastening
south in search of warm weather. He has rented a furnished house and expects to
stay until June, then go to England. The lucky devil. He said he hopes I'll book
passage for a trip next summer, so we can get together in England. I like the idea
and have begun to plan for it.

I walked up to see Dash. Found him in bed with mumps, apparently a bad
case. He had some fever. From vague, maybe feverish, references in Dash's conversation, I gathered that Randall had deserted him. I said nothing, but after all,
I knew that Randall would. Stayed all evening. Dash had received a letter from
Hans and I read it out loud. With Germany poised on the brink of civil war, and
fights in the streets against Hitler's fanatical followers, Hans wrote, "I sing
American songs to the cows. While I milk them they like to hear 'Moo-o-o-d
Indigo.'" Late in the evening I went out and got Dash some groceries. It hurts
me for Dashie to be sick in bed, but I left feeling guiltily pleased about Randall's
desertion of him.

*Friday, 7 April 1933*

A big day, and I don't mean beer alone. Last night I heard a great din of
automobile horns, whistles, gunshots, cheers, as Washington celebrated the ad-
vent of legal beer. Then this afternoon Winegardner called in everyone separately to ask whether we had dependents and any outside income. He said he wanted
to have the facts ready if they were needed, and needlessly mentioned that there
were thirteen million unemployed in this country. I told him I had only a few
dollars in dividends outside my salary. I became nervous and upset. Miss
Contadeluci said I was "white as a sheet" when I got back and told her he wanted to see her. Damn Roosevelt, anyway. All my enthusiastic admiration for him

has turned to bitterness. Roosevelt is ruthless and unjust in his treatment of Government employees.

### Wednesday, 3 May 1933

The crackbrained Green's desk was put next to mine. Winegardner told us that we would have to be doubled up and have to do overtime work. He said we must accept the situation "cheerfully." Hell! Long-legged old bastard. It seems a cruel fate to be positioned shoulder-to-shoulder with the Green. Today she ate almonds from a bowl on her desk. Once when she darted out of the room, Miss Contadeluci murmured, "She has a mouth like a buttonhole and chews as if she had only two teeth."

Out to freedom and into the cool wind. Stopped by the Earle "drug store" (three fourths of the shelves are lined now with bottles of beer) and drank a bottle of Tip Top. Beer gives me a mellow exhilaration, soothes me and makes me placid and dreamy. A noble institution is beer.

### Sunday, 11 June 1933

To the house. After dinner we sat in the backyard watching cardinals, catbirds, robins, and sparrows. Eunice brought an ashtray from the den and asked me for a cigarette, and smoked in front of Dad and Mama.

When I left, I went down to the Metropolitan and saw *The Story of Temple Drake,* a prettified version of Faulkner's horrible novel, *Sanctuary.* Coming out of the theatre I saw Dashie and Isador leaving ahead of me. We chatted until Isador sallied off on one of his engagements, waving good-bye effeminately. Dash asked if he might walk with me to my room. I was delighted. We had a wonderful time here. Music, wine, and conversation. Outside my window the gingko tree was threshing its branches in the night wind and spilling the petals of its glorious mass of wisteria blossoms. Never before have they made such a magnificent display, all the way to the top of the tree, higher than this house. We looked over my scrapbook of our trip to Europe in 1928. I felt as if I wanted to go on and on, talking with Dash and listening to the marvelous music of Gershwin. After he left I got into that unhappy state that often follows his visits, and brooded about sex, my failure to achieve a solution to that problem, and about my failure to accomplish anything in the way of writing. Now I *must* get to bed. I shall seek solace in the dusty gray poppies of my dreams.

### Monday, 12 June 1933

Strolled through the warm night to Dash's house. I waited outside and was looking in the other direction and didn't see him until he was almost upon me.

He was walking rapidly, smiling at me and wearing a white sleeveless sweater, white ducks; no coat. We spent the evening conversing, reading the *Star* and *Times*. It was almost like old times, except for the sexual part of our relationship—which is never now mentioned. As I prepared to leave, he drawled, "Visit me tomorrow?"—but I declined. These last weeks have been almost too good to be true, and I must be careful not to upset anything. I don't want to wear out my welcome.

### Tuesday, 4 July 1933

Dash and I rode out to Georgetown to go canoeing. The river was high and muddy. Many others were canoeing, though, so we went ahead. Paddled up river, hoping to get to Chain Bridge. It was a slow process against the strong current. We gave up in sight of the bridge and started drifting downstream, taking it easy. I read aloud from Whitman's poems in the *Little Blue Book* edition. Everything was beautiful—blue sky and scattered clouds, green trees and grass on the shore, the brown Potomac sweeping toward the sea, the many boys and girls, most of the boys stripped to the waist, the warm sun on our bare skin (we had stripped to the waist, too, when we started back), and the breeze rustling the trees on shore and turning our canoe from its intended course.

### Sunday, 16 July 1933

Dash had been exercising and answered the door looking sweetly tousled and damp. He says he is not prospering in his gymnastic and dancing classes. He's alone in the house, Mrs. Hamilton being in the West and Mr. Hamilton having left for New York "to find some work," as he said in his note. Mr. Hamilton is afraid of losing the house to the mortgage lenders.

We read the Sunday papers. Dash played with Foxie, the sweet-mannered dog, hiding bits of chocolate and letting Foxie find them. He told me about his family home in Natchez and their financial troubles. In these hard times Dash is the only family member with a job. They have decided to deed the home to Dash, get a $1500 loan from the Federal Home Loan Bureau to pay the bank, and let Dash pay off the loan at the rate of $20 a month.

### Thursday, 20 July 1933 (Baltimore & Ohio train en route to New York)

Dash sat in my big chair, reading *Vanity Fair* while I packed for my vacation. I worked steadily, and at last told my room good-bye. Dashie accompanied me in the taxi to the station. We had a last chat at the gate. Then a hearty handclasp and I was on my way to the wharves of New York and the ship that would take me to England, where I expect to meet up with Lansing Tower. Far down the track I saw Dash's little white-clad figure still watching. He waved once more.

*Friday, 21 July 1933 (SS Manhattan, en route to Plymouth)*

A blustery day with a high sea sprinkled with white combers. The ill-bred couple from the cabin adjoining mine have been assigned deck chairs next to me. The wife sat wrapped in a blanket, frowning at the sea. She said, "I feel like I'd slept on a pretzel all night." The husband responded, "You was talking all night but you didn't say nothing. I've slept better than this in jail." He leaned across her and tried to start up a conversation with me. "The three quickest methods of communication—telegraph, telephone, tell a woman . . . Nobody loves a fat man, but how a fat man can love . . . I send my clothes to the laundry and they send 'em back, say they don't do up tents . . . what I saved on tourist class I spent on having my clothes pressed. I'll see you in the streets of Paris. I'll have nothing but a fan on." Later the wife's conversation drifted by me. "She has the same exposure as Margaret. She was love sick." I read, watched the sea, and wrote letters to Dad, Isador, and Dash.

*Thursday, 10 August 1933 (London)*

Left the hotel and strolled around, making my way leisurely over to Piccadilly. The sight of a swarm of American sailors made me homesick. When I got my mail at American Express, I found two disconcerting letters from Lansing Tower. The first, mailed as soon as he received my letter from the ship, told me to go down to Rye, to the place he and his wife were renting there. The other, mailed yesterday, said they were leaving for Scotland, where the poet Conrad Aiken and Aiken's wife would join up with them in Edinburgh. They were to stay in Edinburgh three or four days, take a bus tour, and return to London, and then go down together to Rye. He urged me to take the first possible train up to Scotland to join their party.

I sat in a pub reading Lansing's letters again and again and trying to make up my mind whether or not to go to Edinburgh. I haven't any more decision than a jackrabbit. Finally I did decide that I would go up to Edinburgh to join the Towers and the Aikens. Returned to the hotel and told them to wake me at seven.

**Conrad Aiken** *(1889–1974) was a poet and novelist, born in Savannah, Georgia. His life was haunted by the murder of his mother by his father and his father's subsequent suicide. He lived for a time in England and won a Pulitzer Prize in 1930 for his Selected Poems.*

*Friday, 11 August 1933 (London)*

The maid knocked at seven. I tossed in bed and turned over in my mind the various phases of the proposed trip to Scotland. I'd like to see Lansing, and meet Conrad Aiken, but finally I decided not to go. It was almost eleven when I got downstairs. At that hour I was ashamed to ask for breakfast. Wandered along Oxford Street, thinking about going up to Edinburgh. I imagined myself talking and drinking with Lansing and Conrad Aiken—I, the one man among three who in youth had proclaimed that he was going to be a literary artist, the only one who had neglected his talent, procrastinated, done nothing. Then, too, Conrad Aiken and Lansing are accompanied by their wives. I should never have fit in.

Went to the hotel bar and had draught ale and talked, rather sentimentally, with the pleasant barmaid. Fairly tight, I went by subway to the Marble Arch Station and continued drinking at a nearby pub—Duke of Something, I think. Met up with a Welshman so eager to get to the U.S.A. that I was disconcerted. I tried to make him take a more reasonable view of things. I promised to meet him at the Marlborough Bar on Sunday night, but knew that I shouldn't want to meet him again. I decided not even to linger in London and go down to Rye when Lansing and his wife and the Aikens returned from Scotland. That had been my initial idea, as a sort of compromise. Instead I packed my bags, rode to Piccadilly, left my forwarding address at American Express, got $20 worth of Belgian money, and purchased a ticket to Brussels.

*Saturday, 12 August 1933 (Brussels, Belgium)*

Across the aisle sat a youth, whom I judged to be English, since he wore immaculate English checked coat and gray flannels, and read the *Daily Telegraph.* He looked at me in a friendly way as if he wanted to talk. Finally I borrowed his *Telegraph* and that opened the way to conversation. We conversed through the lovely green fields of Kent, placid in the afternoon sunshine, to the white cliffs of Dover and then on the rough, windy crossing of the Channel. His name is Nigel Smythe.

*Monday, 14 August 1933 (Brussels, Belgium)*

Nigel and I dawdled along in our dressing and shaving and didn't get out until noon. After the mild weather of England, Brussels seems deliciously warm; Nigel made no bones about calling it "very hawt." Spent the evening in this brilliantly lighted, densely populated town drinking and conversing with my charming companion.

*Sunday, 20 August 1933 (Brussels, Belgium)*

I was awakened by Nigel kissing me good-bye. As he leaned across me I smelled on his breath the grainy dark scent of Belgian smoking tobacco. Felt a languorous sorrow. I shall probably never see Nigel again.

*Saturday, 2 September 1933 (SS* Ile de France, *en route to New York)*

Alongside the ship the wind tore off wave tops in clouds of spray. As I left my stateroom and started up to lunch, my roommate came down to his berth with his tall girl. They locked the door immediately and no doubt had a good fuck as they have had every day so far. I played shuffleboard with the cheerful, freckled schoolteacher from Idaho. Won both games. Treated her to a martini cocktail. After dinner I wandered up to first class and looked in on the dancing. The jazz music was wonderfully gay and lively. I bought the drummer two beers and had two myself. Now for a turn about the deck and a look into the impenetrable ocean before going to bed. How I hate to end the voyage and my vacation. What a perfect life is that of a passenger on shipboard. Farewell to the sea and the wind, rain, and driven spray—farewell with wild regret.

*Thursday, 7 September 1933*

Washington looked small and rather provincial. Wu seemed drunk when he greeted me. Took a taxi to the office. Found it impossible to adjust my mind to that damned work, so visited people and talked about my trip. Dash arrived in the evening, I having called him in the afternoon. He was delighted with the marmalade in the decorated pottery jar, and the tartan tie. To my regret, Houndstooth in my absence moved up to Lanier Street, disgustingly pronounced "*Lan*-yuh Street," by most people in Washington.

*Monday, 16 October 1933*

A letter from Lansing. He wants to know what happened to me in Edin-burgh and Rye, why didn't I show up? He said he and his wife and the Aikens had a wonderful trip. By God, I've got to settle down and write before I get to be a doddering old imbecile. I never dreamed things would come to this. I am inter-ested in Lansing and his work because I like him so much, but far more I am interested in myself. It's a challenge whenever someone writes a book and Lan-sing is the greatest challenge because he is someone I have known.

Well, Lansing has got ahead of me in writing. I'm going to make a strong effort to work out an idea for a novel and soon, too. In addition, I must write Lansing, offering an apology or explanation for not joining him in Edinburgh or Rye. I don't want to lose touch with him, especially not for a reason so unfound-

ed as that accursed awkwardness I felt in London. I keep telling myself that
because tomorrow is my birthday, it begins a new year for me. I will try to make
it a better year, try to reach closer toward the heart's desire.

*Tuesday, 5 December 1933*
   Today is the historic day of the Repeal of the Prohibition Amendment. With
my present hangover, I have no intention to celebrate. My head ached all day
from the cocktails I drank last night at Junior's party. Junior was slightly less
boisterous than usual. I woke this morning lying on top of the bed, wearing only
my pajama tunic. I was chilled through and through. It came back to me that
Dash and Nicky had been here and were helping me undress, but I had insisted
on lying down to relieve my hiccoughs. There they had left me, and there I had
stayed.
   Finally dressed and left the house, still feeling shaky. Strolled downtown.
Stopped for a shoeshine and was surprised to find Max. I sat next to him and
asked him how his aunt was. He said, "The other day in my absence she took
down a drawing I had made of Bolling Balfour's head from the wall and tore it
into bits. I didn't miss it for a day or two. Then she apologized, saying she ripped
it apart because the eyes in the picture were following her about the room." It
didn't seem to bother Max much. "She's bottled up emotionally, being a Puritan
and having no outlet." He can't move out of his aunt's house, being one of
America's millions of unemployed. He said he went to several office buildings
and offered to paint murals on the walls at day-laborer's wages. All turned him
down. In a depression, art becomes a luxury that few can afford.

*Saturday, 16 December 1933*
   Dash is having a hard time. He has practically supported his brother and sister-in-law and their children, and is supporting his mother. In addition, he has
paid $600 in the last two years on the mortgage on the family home in Natchez.
He also has insurance and must pay the premium this month. I volunteered to
lend him more money. We went up to his room. His landlord Harrison and the
dog Foxie followed us up the stairs. Harrison said, "I must turn over the house to
the mortgage-holders. The wife and I have lost everything. Time for a new start,
eh?"

*Sunday, 31 December 1933*
   No heat in my room on this New Year's eve, although I complained vigor-
ously to Wu. The liar! Finally the radiators began sputtering. A few minutes later
Dash, Max, and Nicky showed up. Max was feeling pacifistically inclined, and

had much to say about Hitler and the prospects of war. Dash also was talkative. At midnight I leaned out the window and rang my bell. The others cheered. And now, here's to 1934. The milkman's horse is clattering past, a wistful sound to usher in the dawn of a new year.

# 1934

*Saturday, 6 January 1934*

I got up at noon to allow the sweeper and the bedmaker to fix up my room. After lunch I set out by bus for Maryland. From the District Line I walked in a drizzling rain to Silver Spring, and found the dispensary where I bought the first legal liquor I have ever purchased in the United States. I got a bottle each of sherry, port, and sauterne, all made in California. Returned by bus with my legal bottles in a big paper sack. Found my door open and Max inside helping Wu move a black leather rocker into my room "for my guests." The rocker is bulky, shabby, and old. Max sat down in it, while Wu and I waited for his judgment. He writhed about, then intoned to Wu's keen displeasure, "You have been clever, Dr. Wu. You have stolen and stuffed King Kong's fist, and have disguised it in my friend's room as a chair."

I walked with Max over to his studio on H Street and I watched him painting political figures on a fourteen-foot-tall mural. While he painted a halo above the head of Huey Long, he talked about his adventures last night with an artist friend of his named Erich. "We got quite tight. Erich tried unsuccessfully to get me to go to a whorehouse. We wound up near your place and stopped to see you, ringing the bell and whistling, but we couldn't get an answer." It seems Erich "goes in for" whorehouses. According to Max, Erich seems especially attracted to black and Filipino girls. Well, each to his taste! When I left Max's studio, I walked through the chill night to Dupont Circle. A well-dressed chap about my age started a conversation and invited me for a ride in his Packard. The car was so big that I thought the fellow must be married, but I was mistaken, and he soon invited me to his room. Each to his taste!

**Huey Long** *(1893–1935) was a Louisiana governor, U. S. Senator, and quintessentially Southern in his "good old boy" methods of manipulating the dreams of poor people in his state. Robert Penn Warren's Pulitzer Prize-winning novel,* All the King's Men, *offers a skilled fictionalized version of Long and his reign.*

*Friday, 26 January 1934*

I heard the familiar chirping in the hall that Dash employs to herald his arrival. Opened the door and found him with Nicky. We settled in, drinking wine and playing the Victrola, Dash selecting the records. They kept on their overcoats, and I put on my faithful gray woollen scarf—my "shawl," as my friends call it—over my striped blazer, and we were fairly comfortable. Nicky and I conversed about books, morals, and sex. Unfortunately, when people talk literature, philosophy, or kindred subjects too assiduously, Dash develops an inferiority complex and is not his best self. Anyway, we had a good time. We finally went out and had something to eat at Child's. A jolly party of intoxicated persons in evening clothes invaded the restaurant. We went on to have beer at Ramon's, which also was full of loud, merry people in evening clothes.

*Wednesday, 28 February 1934*

Watched Max work on his mural. He was drawing a picture of a youth stripped to the waist. I recognized it as a portrait of his former model friend, Jimmie Staunton. "You're right," Max said. "It's a memorial to past love." He said that a couple of years ago Jimmie had a bad case of gonorrhea, and worried so over the possibility of its becoming chronic that he had a serious nervous breakdown. Now Jimmie is a mental patient at St. Elizabeth's Hospital, though considered cured of the gonorrhea.

Washington went wet at midnight, so Max and I set out for Child's. Such a strange feeling, to look over a list of cocktails, highballs, wines, and order what one desired. "Isn't this exciting," Max said to the waitress, a jolly Irish woman. She said they were all excited "back there," meaning the place where drinks are mixed behind the scenes. My drink was surprisingly strong. I had feared they would skimp on the whiskey but they didn't. I had expected to find overflow crowds, but it was only comfortably filled.

# 1935

*Tuesday, 1 January 1935*

Alone in my room. Last night's was the quietest New Year's Eve I have spent in years. There I sat, an invalid, waiting for 1934 to make haste and die. It was a cruel year. I tried so hard to be happy and yet blow after blow rained on my head from a pitiless Fate.

Sat on my cushion at the window looking out at the snow and watching for

Dash. Around eleven, when I had given him up, he whistled outside in the snowy night, "Why Am I Always the Bridesmaid?"—Hans' old favorite tune for signaling. Dash said he had been writing letters and time had slipped up on him. He had not been more than five minutes when I heard a shout and saw Max trudging along with Nicky through the snow. They had already had whiskey and were feeling "rosy," as Max said. I served them almost an entire bottle of port. Could not drink anything myself because of my diet. Dash played records on the Victrola. Nicky talked in a blue streak. He and Dash danced to "La Cucaracha" and "Negra Soy," and he danced with Max to "Frankie and Johnny." At midnight when the whistle blew outside I raised my window and rang my old dinner bell. To hell with old 1934—it's dead and buried. They left around two. Max absently put on the coat of my suit, thinking it was his overcoat and not noticing the difference in length till I told him of it. I opened the window and leaned out to watch them walking up the street. The snow that had been falling had turned to sleet and things were beginning to look glassy.

### Sunday, 6 January 1935

Out to the house on a streetcar, sitting uncomfortably on a side bench, bumped against by standing elderly churchwomen, but resolutely concentrating on my reading. Found when I was getting off that Mama had been on the same car. After dinner I rested, slouched in an easy chair in front of the radio. Mama brought me cake and a cup of coffee—sweet of her. She has grown deeper, more mellow and kindly over the years, I think. Tomorrow I go back to the office and dread the kindly inquiries about my health and the explanations I shall have to give.

### Thursday, 10 January 1935

Max was in Dash's room, showing Dash wash drawings of a nude model which he made tonight at Studio House. I left when Max did. As we walked through the snow, the artist friend of Max's, named Erich, joined us. Erich is German, a blond of the Scandinavian type. He has a strong foreign accent and gesticulates vociferously as he talks. There is something stimulating and Continental about his conversation. He got wrought up over seeing people in the "Bingo" arcade place. He said, "People who could waste their time on such frivolous pursuits might as well be thrown in an incinerator." He said there were at least twenty million such people in this country, and talked in a very intolerant strain about them.

*Tuesday, 29 January 1935*

A horrible day of illness and pain. Dr. Belt said an abscess had broken and I was lucky I was no worse off than I am. He gave me another injection of vaccine. I tottered home in utter misery. Crawled in bed, and there I have remained ever since.

*Wednesday, 30 January 1935*

Dash brought me my lunch. I gave him, for his birthday present, an Irish Sweepstakes ticket. In the evening he returned with a supper of milk, cheese sandwiches, and stewed apples. As he was getting ready to leave, Max and Nicky, accompanied by the vociferous German, Erich Hestle, shouted up from the sidewalk. Dash let them in and they stayed all evening. Max and Erich drew caricatures of each other and of Dashie and Nicky, and of me lying in a grotesque state in my bed. There was much laughter and banter. I was sorry when they left.

*Wednesday, 13 February 1935*

In the afternoon Miss Contadeluci and I received sealed comic valentines. Fearing it was something insulting, I wouldn't open mine until I was in the taxicab on the way to Dr. Belt. Found it merely an innocuous thing about my talking so little. I gazed into the park and was taken with an emotional awareness of its beauty—cold trees, flurries of rain and snow. In Dr. Belt's waiting room I was surprised when Junior Whorley walked in as I was leaving.

So discouraging to feel that I am slipping backwards in health. Never mind—some day I shall be in good health again and sailing across the sea in a ship. Dash brought me supper. He has been so good to me while I have been sick, cheerful, obliging, tireless in doing everything he can to make me comfortable and satisfied. As noble and fine a friend as anyone ever had.

*Tuesday, 21 May 1935*

Another injection of vaccine in my arm. When I got back to the office, I met Junior in the corridor. He told me why *he* had been going to Dr. Belt. I told him nothing.

At night I found Randall visiting Dash. I haven't seen Randall in two years or more. I decided not to stay, but it turned out they were going up to Max's studio, so I walked up with them. Dash posed so Max could make sketches for figures in a new mural. Max's gray kitten, a tiny creature who has been given the name of Jones, frolicked with joyful abandon. Randall annoyed me. When I said something about self-respect, he growled derisively, "Oh, who has self-respect any more?" I replied emphatically, "I do."

*Saturday, 13 July 1935*

Dr. Belt said, "Be patient. One day you will be well." I dragged myself over to Max's studio, which was sweltering hot. I took off my coat and tie and read the newspapers, watching Max work on his mural, and enjoying the antics of Jones, the gray kitten. Max drank rum. We talked about art —and about Dashie. I told Max, "Dash is to me a rock in a stormy ocean. I didn't know what I should do without Dash."

*Thursday, 17 October 1935*

My thirty-sixth birthday— leaves falling and drifting. At lunch I went to the State Department and got Dash. We ate in the garden at Allies Inn under an umbrella. Sparrows hopped about begging for crumbs. When one of them alighted on the table Dash took hold of the handle that held up the umbrella and twirled it, caroling, "Waltz me around again, Willie, round and round and round—" The startled bird flew away. The bright transparent shadows on the table whirled round, too, and gave me a dizzy feeling, as if I were floating in air.

*Monday, 2 December 1935*

Bitterly disappointed to be told by Dr. Belt that my improvement didn't warrant my starting to drink again. I went gloomily to the Albany and played pinball, then plodded bitterly home. Isador arrived to see me — the first time since last summer. He tried to cheer me up, saying he didn't understand why drinking was important. I told him, "Well, it is to me, especially after more than a year's abstention."

We heard the familiar chirping in the hall and found Dash at the door. I had been eagerly waiting to hear about Dash's trip to the Army-Navy game with Pamela. Dash said they spent Saturday night in Philadelphia at the Bellevue-Stratford Hotel. On Sunday, they joined an aviator friend of Pamela's, who flew them to New York in a private plane. They had a wonderful trip through the air, were put down at North Beach, Long Island, and went into New York to see *Jumbo* at the Hippodrome.

I am glad he had a good time, even though he did spend much more than he expected. He left before Isador did. I was glad to see Isador but it would have been better if he had come last night, when I was not having a visit from Dashie and was worrying about Dash.

***Pamela.*** *This entry marks the appearance in Jeb's diary of a "fag hag," a woman drawn to gay men. A very good woman Pamela turns out to be, too. This first mention of Pamela appears after one of Jeb's bouts of not writing for a while in his diary, so the reader is not* *immediately provided with information about who Pamela is. One eventually learns that she works at the Department of State with Dash, Isador, and Randall, and she often has "the boys," as she calls them, over to her home.*

**Jumbo** *was entrepreneur Billy Rose's 1935 circus-musical at New York City's aptly-named Hippodrome. In 1962 Hollywood made a musical called* Jumbo, *starring Doris Day and Jimmy Durante, loosely based on Rose and the colorful extravaganza.*

### Monday, 16 December 1935

Max and Bolling Balfour arrived. Bolling is such an elegant, sophisticated, and suave person that I have never pressed him to come to this dingy, dilapidated, sentimental room of mine. We played records, and Max showed me an article from the *News* about his mural. There was a picture of Max, and another picture of the section of his mural that shows the caricature of Huey Long with a halo. Max was all agog because the Associated Press interviewed him by telephone about the Huey Long caricature. However, he said that Principal Daniels of Tech High has refused to permit him to hold his exhibition of his mural "because of the unfortunate publicity in the *News.*"

We discussed and argued the situation with animation. The invitations had been sent out, including to President and Mrs. Roosevelt. My advice to Max was, "Fight the school authorities to the last ditch and if you still aren't allowed to hold the exhibiton, then give the story to the newspapers and get more publicity than the showing would have given you." He said, "I want the mural to be seen, though." They went out to Pamela's to discuss the situation with her and decide what to do.

### Wednesday, 18 December 1935

Wanted to find out more about the mural controversy, so I went to Max's studio, but he was not in. I thought of various places he might be and imagined gay gatherings of Max, Bolling, Dash, Nicky, perhaps Pamela, and others, with drinks and jollity following the Tech High showing of the mural, and I left out in the cold. Finally I became so anxious for companionship that my loneliness, as Nicky once said of his own, was pathological.

### Thursday, 19 December 1935

Was browsing in the bookcases on the sidewalk in front of Pearlman's, a chill wind blowing, when Max came out. He asked me to help him select a book for Nicky as a Christmas gift. He chose J. T. Farrell's *Studs Lonigan* trilogy. We chatted with Pearlman, then started toward the studio. Max told me about the mural affair. "I removed the halo from the head of that devil Huey Long and paid for extra watchmen, so I was allowed to have my showing. Everything went smoothly, except that none of the prominent persons invited attended. And, by the way, why didn't you show up?" I told him, "I was not invited, and furthermore, I didn't know whether it was to be held or not." He said, "All my other friends attended."

### Sunday, 22 December 1935

Pamela's neighborhood, a pleasant area of detached framed houses and trees, was covered with sparkling, powdery snow. After supper we gathered in the music room in front of a blazing fire, and Pamela played while the rest of us sang. Max spread a blanket in front of the fire, and he and Pamela sat on it. Dash read her the enthusiastic review of Max's mural by Leila Mechlin, the art critic of the *Star*. It was pleasant to be snugly indoors with jolly singing and conversation while the snow fell outside in a world of white. At midnight we began to get ready to go. It had stopped snowing and was clear and cold, with stars shining. We opened up the rumble seat of Nicky's new car, and Pamela and Dashie swept off the snow from the roof. Dash and I rode in the rumble seat, which was just big enough for two.

### Thursday, 31 December 1935

As I was going through my mail, Dashie and Nicky put in a welcome appearance. They were gay, having had several brandies at Dash's. Dash was even a bit befogged, or at least he was after having two glasses of my Spanish sherry. When we went to dinner he "bawled out" the waiter several times. He ordered, among his vegetables, "bees and peats," without noticing the slip. He left early to go to the Wanderbirds' Ball in the Capitol Yacht Club. I watched after his departing figure, thinking, *Good-bye, dear boy. Happy New Year. Don't know what I'd do without you.*

Nicky and I spent a quiet evening in my room—the quietest New Year's Eve I have had in years. I was glad for Nicky's companionship. He has a soothing influence. When midnight came, I felt a thrill, thinking, *This is 1936.* I rang my big bell out the window and when the slight din had died down, I played on the Victrola, as the first record of 1936, "When I Grow Too Old to Dream." And thus old 1935 passes. For me a year of illness, weakness, and pain.

# 1936

*Wednesday, 1 January 1936*

When I got to Max's studio, I was disappointed to be greeted enthusiastically by Pamela. Her presence changed the entire tone of what was to have been a
stag party. I agreed with Max afterward that it would have been pleasanter without her. She told me blithely, "I crashed the party." At the table, bedecked with a
centerpiece of red balloons, were Max, Nicky, Dash, Bolling, Isador, Pamela, and
me. Isador had stomach illness and sat with a green hot water bottle against his
stomach. We called it his "green baby."

The rest of us heartily enjoyed the roast goose, biscuits, quince jelly made by
Pamela, nuts, and fruitcake. Later Erich Hestle, the loquacious Nazi, arrived. He
seemed more subdued than usual, possibly because he had had so much to drink.
Pamela sat in Max's lap a while. Nicky and Pamela danced and fell down, and
again fell into the table. Every time the new "hit" song, "The Music Goes Round
and Round" came on the radio, everybody joined merrily in the chorus. Hours
went by—hours of merriment and mirth, drinking and eating, music, singing,
dancing.

*Monday, 20 January 1936*

To dinner at Candlestick through a cold sleet. Dash, Max, and Nicky came
in, accompanied by Erich, the dictatorial Nazi fanatic. I joined them, moving my
dinner with me. They were jolly, having had cocktails earlier. The Nazi kept
telling them what to do but they more or less ignored him. In the midst of our
meal a small boy entered the restaurant with extra editions of the *Times,* carrying
a large headline, *KING GEORGE IS DEAD.* I told the boy, "I never buy Hearst
papers." He looked crestfallen and I was sorry I had spoken. I felt stirred by the
headline, though. Tomorrow England will get up and go about its business
under a new king.

*Friday, 7 February 1936*

A blizzard all night and all day. The snow is over a foot deep, the heaviest
snowfall since the Knickerbocker disaster in 1922. In the snowstorm I met Dash
taking pictures of Junie Whorley, for Corpus Christi consumption. I chatted
with them, then pushed on through the drifts to Max's studio. The radio was
going, including singing by Lily Pons, which I didn't like. Later the Nazi, Erich
Hestle, arrived. I argued with Erich over the persecution of the Jews in Germany,
which he tried to compare with discrimination against negroes in this country.

Max and Erich played with the cat. I protested because Jones was not feeling well, having been in a fight and injured a leg. We got in a discussion of the possibility of our being in another war. It seemed that we were just about all pacifists with no desire to fight. When I left it was cold and sparkling outdoors. Moon and stars shining. Gangs of negroes on Connecticut Avenue shoveling mountains of snow into trucks to be carted away. I was cheered by the snow.

**Lily Pons** *(1904–1976) was a French-born operatic soprano.*

### Saturday, 21 March 1936

Dr. Belt began the new treatment. It seemed to be several minutes that he kept the needle in my arm. I said to myself, "Be with me, Dash," and imagined Dash to be standing behind me with his warm hand on my shoulder. Then I was able to stand it. Not that the pain itself was bad, but the idea that the needle was thrust into my flesh and was remaining there, depositing medicine in my blood, made me feel rather sick.

At night, Dash and Nicky and I went to the National. The show was the DuBose Heyward-George Gershwin production, *Porgy and Bess*. It was a fine thing which the three of us enjoyed greatly. The National admitted negroes for the first time, since it was a negro production. A year ago blacks made a great howl when they were not permitted to see *Green Pastures*. The cast of this show refused to perform in Washington unless the National gave in, so they admitted negroes without saying anything about it. However, I saw not more than half a dozen, all going to the orchestra.

### Monday, 13 April 1936

The sunshine was welcome after so many dreary days. Set out to see the egg rolling at the White House. I was annoyed by the running and screaming of children, and walked up to the Monument, recalling a September night when Dash and I swung gaily across the dewy lawns under the moon, and he sang love songs and I quoted Shakespeare. At the Tidal Basin I sat on a protected bench in the sunshine. Felt tired and jaded. Two youths, tourists from the North, had me take their picture together with their camera.

Dragged myself off to see Charlie Chaplin in *Modern Times*. Charlie is as good as ever, if not better. When I got out, I was afflicted with despondency. The downtown region at 7:30 is depressing. I was reminded of so many hundreds of similar times in the past when I have been along F Street alone, feeling self-conscious and aimless. Symptoms tonight of another relapse. Squirming and tossing on the bed, now, with my old striped bathrobe over my feet as I write this.

*Saturday, 23 May 1936*

I think last night I had scarcely a consecutive ten minutes from the horrible discomfort and pain that kept me twisting and struggling. It was a sort of aching and itching inside my body, and I was helpless to do anything. I walked the floor and saw the outdoors gradually lighten. Dawn crept upon the world. A night bird endlessly sounded its call, "Cheerup, cheerup," in the garden across the street. I hated that bird and felt that I could gladly strangle it.

Dragged myself off to Dr. Belt. I told him the treatment seemed not to be doing much good. He replied, "Well, I changed the formula of the serum." Crept home and started the enormous task of putting past years of my canceled checks and stubs in order. I became surfeited with the past—years, once so much the here-and-now, treading on one another's heels into oblivion. Rich, full years— where are they now? Oh, Lord, how lonely! How sex-starved!

*Wednesday, 15 July 1936*

Miss Contadeluci and I closed the windows and pulled down the shades. With two fans going and the door shut, we kept the room cool compared to others. It was 89 degrees there, when it was 105 outdoors. A hellish Washington day. I had received an airmail letter from Dash on his trip to New York, and read it again at work. He enclosed a separate note asking for the loan of $10, so I wrote an answer, enclosed a check, and got it off by air mail. The sun was blazing as I trudged across the sidewalk to the mailbox. The tropics would be cooler. I was exhausted when I got back to my office. As I sat with my head in my hands, Mrs. Utott looked in to say that "all who could be spared" were to be excused. It was the first time since the twenties that we have been excused because of the heat. I felt on the verge of bursting into tears.

Crawled to Dr. Belt. Had a cystoscope examination, a painful ordeal, but good came of it. He discovered that I have a cyst in the urinary tract and he is going to remove it next week with an electric needle. Then I might get well.

*Sunday, 19 July 1936*

To the house. Conversation and argument as usual. I rested, languidly sitting in front of the radio, listening to soft music. Dad drowsed in the den and Henry sat and glowered. I learned that Henry has been turned down for insurance because he has albumin in the urine. All of us poor mortals have our troubles. I told Dad of my impending electrical operation for the cyst, and soon after Mama appeared in the parlor door, asserting bitter opposition to any kind of electrical treatment. She said, "I've known of cases where it caused cancers, or death," and strongly urged me not to go through with it. I became upset over the thing, whereas I had been calmly looking forward to it as being rather simple and at the same time important to my health. Began to lose confidence in Dr. Belt. I wish Mama had said nothing about it.

### Tuesday, 21 July 1936

Dr. Belt said, "I've never heard of cancer developing from such an operation. It's X-ray treatment that causes cancer, not this little 'radio needle.'" The operation was a nervous nightmare. Several shocks were painful; most of them I could feel but without pain. Novocain was used. It seemed as if he never would finish. The radio in the waiting room was giving the baseball game and every few minutes it would blare out the tune "They Cut Down the Old Pine Tree"—the theme song of that program. Every time I hear that tune in the future I shall probably think of this day. I left feeling weak and shaken. Called the house and reassured Mama about the operation. She said Dad and Henry had driven down to see me, and when I looked out the window there they were, pulling up in front of the house. They drove me to Allies Inn and sat with me while I ate a good dinner.

### Saturday, 1 August 1936

Dash bathed and shaved and finished packing for his vacation with his mother in Natchez. I lay on his bed listening to comfortable songs on the radio— "My Home on the Range," "Springtime in the Rockies," and others. Dashie told his room good-bye and we left, he carrying his bag with the European stickers on it, and I carrying his little zipper bag, which also went with us in 1928 to Europe. We were in good time at the station. Dash got his ticket, checked his bag, and gave me a strong handclasp. The goodness, sweetness, and steadfastness of his loyal, generous nature shone from his wide, serious, green eyes. That may sound like a rhapsody, but it's God's truth.

I know the awkwardness of waits outside of train windows, with conversation impossible after a person has got on board, so I moved down the platform to the steps leading to the concourse. There I waited, looking at the great green locomotive as it hissed and blew off steam, as if eager to be on its way. Along the platform suddenly came a low hand-truck bearing a casket on which lay wreaths of waxen flowers. I realized with something of a shock that a dead person was accompanying Dash on the train, that some poor soul was being taken back to his native South for eternity. I thought with a quick uplift of the heart, "We who are alive must make the most of it." And I lifted my eyes to a streak of rain-wet sky visible under the shed roof, and thought of the richness and beauty of life. When the train started, I watched for Dash's car. He saw me and stood up waving and smiling, and then was gone—under the Station, under the Plaza, rumbling under the Capitol, to come out beside the placid river and head into the night.

*Sunday, 23 August 1936*

Read disturbing news of the tragedy in Spain and the threat that Europe will be engulfed in war. There is enough horror in what is happening in Spain. It sickens me to think of Europe at war.

Waiting for a car I saw my precious landlord Wu cross the street—belly sticking out, coatless with sleeves rolled up. He ogled a girl and darted into a cheap restaurant. He came out so quickly that he obviously had had only a drink and not a meal. Later I stopped at the Ellipse to watch the game for the sandlot championships. Negroes and reeking whites, loud-mouthed morons, pimples and sweat and dust and heat. Walking home I was delighted to see a storm coming. I got home just in time. It was a beautiful storm—wind in the trees, vivid lightning and booming thunder, glorious breezes of cool damp air sweeping through the room. I put out my lights and watched the storm from my bed.

**Spain.** *Jeb's references to conditions in Spain are to the Spanish Civil War (1936–1939).*

*Sunday, 13 September 1936*

Dash had gone on a hike near Harper's Ferry with the Wanderbirds, and I prepared to wait for him on a bench in the little triangular park where stands the statue of Longfellow. Nicky arrived, also looking for Dash. I enjoyed Nicky's company, his whimsicality, his humor. Once necessity drove me up a garbage-scented dark alley. Dash arrived and told us he had enjoyed his outing greatly. It seems Randall also was on the hike, and Dash learned that Randall's wife, Catherine, has given birth to their second child, another boy.

*Sunday, 11 October 1936*

To the house. Wore my gray herringbone suit and my new suspenders—the first pair of suspenders I ever have worn (and I find them very satisfactory for holding trousers up, more comfortable than a belt on the whole). At dinner Henry made the remark that "America would be better off if somebody would assassinate Roosevelt." I was furious. All during the discussion, which fortunately was toward the end of dinner, I was so wrought up that I became alarmed at my inability to keep calm. After all, Roosevelt is certain to win, so it doesn't matter how his enemies rave. Mama then got furious because Dad and Henry got into a wild argument about chain grocery stores; about Henry's work with the Community Chest; and again about Roosevelt, with their argument, or rather their shouting me down, with assertions that Roosevelt was as much a "dictator" as that tyrant, Mussolini.

Later things quieted down. Mama went upstairs to rest. Henry drove Daisy into to the country for a pony ride. Eunice lounged on the parlor sofa, reading Willa Cather's *Lucy Gayheart.* Dad and I sat in the den smoking Dad's aromatic Cuban cigarettes and reading the newspapers. The only sounds were the radio, tuned almost too low to hear, and the occasional turning of pages.

*Tuesday, 3 November 1936*

Election day. When I got home I played "Happy Days," with my door open, just to let the house know where I stood. Opened a bottle of wine. The first glass was a toast to Dashie, as every first toast of mine always will be. Then a toast to Roosevelt. In my enthusiasm I stood in front of my picture of Roosevelt on the wall, and addressed him aloud. "I'm for you, regardless of what you do to me personally as a Government worker. You're a gentleman, a man of discrimination, of imagination; a man of courage, independence, and intelligence!"

I played "Prairie Moon" on the Victrola. Looking out the window, I suddenly noticed that the beam of light from the Monument grounds, intended to show how the election goes, was pointing north across the White House, indicating that Roosevelt was in the lead. I felt a thrill of joy. Just that second came the words of the song out of the phonograph, "There's a wonderful light in the sky tonight." It seemed so apt. I hastily donned my coat and hurried downtown to join the crowd at the *Star* building, listening to amplifier broadcasts of the election results and watching cartoons, bulletins, and movies on the two screens. All was for Roosevelt! How the crowd cheered! Many happy people, and yet I didn't see any actual drunks. Home about two, hearing somebody's radio on the second floor playing "The Star Spangled Banner." Sweet is victory!

*Friday, 6 November 1936*

I hastened toward the Avenue to watch the President drive along. Junior caught up with me, intent on the same mission. We heard cheering and saw the crowds returning, so we rushed through the White House gates and took part in a demonstration of loyalty such as I never have seen before. A struggling, cheering mob crushed around the portico, chanting, "We want Roosevelt, we want Roosevelt!" The President had to come out three times. There was such a dense crowd that I could see only the top of Mr. Roosevelt's head, and little Junie could not see him at all. The shrubbery was badly trampled. The gates had to be closed because so many people were pouring in. Junior and I didn't get to work for hours.

# 1937

*Wednesday, 20 January 1937*

I awoke from a tremendously vivid dream. It seemed that I was in Dash's place, in a bed with blue-eyed Nicky. I felt baffled and frustrated. A girl stood in the hall in a dressing gown, and I went up to her and tried to force myself upon her to have sexual intercourse. She vaguely resisted and seemed all bound round for protection. The girl said that she must "go back to Mama," and disappeared in an elevator. I said, "It's so dark here," and went running on and on until I felt myself falling down between rafters—in the attic of the State Department. I yelled and felt a firm strong hand pulling me back to safety. I knew it was Dash. At that I woke up. I staggered out of bed, and thought how true the dream was— that I was always in the dark, baffled and frustrated by both men and women, and that my best friend Dash was my savior.

Today was the second inauguration of Franklin Roosevelt. Finally got a taxi. Crept through torrents of rain and traffic. Sloshed up to the Capitol. I could see the oath-taking through my theatre glasses, but could not make out the words that came from the amplifier because of the loud pelting of rain on umbrellas around me.

*Friday, 5 February 1937*

Missed getting my *Life*—so went to ten different places searching for it and they all had "sold out." It was a great disappointment. I have subscribed but it hasn't started coming yet. I set off for Dash's, partly to read his *Life*, and stopped at the National Drug Store to make a try of *Life*. Was lucky enough to find some-one releasing his reserved copy. I got it for myself with joy. Went to Dash's and read *Life*. As I was ready to leave, Max arrived with a gay girl of about forty-five. They had been to the Philadelphia Symphony concert together. She was a viva-cious, amusing creature, and sat on Dash's bed and did practically all the talking. When I got home, Wu, drunk and untidy, came upstairs to see if there was enough heat.

*Monday, 8 February 1937*

Horrible day at the office. The wild-eyed Green got into a state over her ridiculous notion that she ought to be promoted again. I told her frankly that she had been well treated. Miss Contadeluci talked to her emphatically too. The Green galloped out of the room and returned about twenty minutes later and was subdued the rest of the day. The poor creature ought to be a farmer's wife out on the prairie.

After work I ran into Isador, walking on Constitution Avenue with one of his Scottie dogs. We stopped to chat, braced against a fierce evening wind. He paid me for the bet we had made months ago, on whether or not the Duke would marry Mrs. Simpson. Isador and his little dog eventually hastened away. As they hurried down the street, Isador's coat billowed like a sail in the wind. I feel so lonely these days most of the time.

> **The Duke and Mrs. Simpson.** *This love story in its day riveted the world. In 1936 the idolized prince of Wales acceded to the throne as Edward VIII, and announced his desire to marry a mature, twice-divorced American woman, Mrs. Wallis Simpson. Great Britain went into crisis. Edward's abdication was shared with the world in a radio broadcast announcement that included the famous words, "I have found it impossible to . . . discharge my duties as king . . . without the help and support of the woman I love." The crown went to Edward's brother, George VI. Edward took the title of duke of Windsor and with "Wally" Simpson began married life on the Continent, while on the front pages, the shadow of war grimly eclipsed their story.*

### Wednesday, 14 July 1937

More problems with the Green. Have concluded that she is jealous of me because I receive more money than she does. My God—what does she expect. A mere high-school graduate. To hell with her! To hell with the Government! Life begins at 4:30 for me. Left the office and went to the Palace to see the Marx Brothers in *A Day at the Races.* Funny and I enjoyed it a lot. Walked with my coat over my arm and my tie loosened, up to Washington's new P Street Bridge. The neighborhood seemed run-down, so different from what that section used to be. I was accosted by a young bum with a polite, well-modulated voice. Washington is overrun with panhandlers, bums, and hobos. Ran into Dr. Houndstooth. He looked excited and wild-haired, although well dressed. While millions of others have suffered with the Depression, Houndstooth has sailed along. He said he had received an official invitation to the Coronation.

### Thursday, 15 July 1937

Things not so well at the office. I began discussing *Gone with the Wind* with the Green and the Contadeluci. We are all three reading the book. I made the comment that Melanie and Ashley were intended to represent the traditions of the Old South, whereas Scarlett and Rhett were modern characters placed in that setting for the sake of contrast. Miss Contadeluci angrily shouted, "Baloney!" and drowned me out. I was disconcerted at such rudeness and we were cool to each other the rest of the day. To hell with them! I didn't get my work very far along, and didn't even get to tea.

I had intended to go without drinking, but I weakened as I walked past the New Bavarian. Started with a couple of Löenbräus as usual. Music was being made by men in Bavarian costume. A Viennese man, who said he was an employee of the Austrian Embassy, was seated next to me and expressed condemnation of the "sexual perverts" whom Hitler sought to destroy. I said an abrupt goodbye.

*Wednesday, 28 July 1937*

When Dash arrived I suggested we go to the Gay Nineties program, put on by the employees' chorus of my department, so we went down in a taxi. We enjoyed the old-time songs, costumes, and clowning, including Junior at the piano. Afterward Dash and I strolled out into the dim coolness of the Mall. The terraced lights of the Capitol rose in the distance. Dash told me there is a vacancy in his building and said Nicky is interested in the back room, which has a separate entry, and is looking for someone who would take the front rooms and share the bathroom. I told him I would talk to Nicky about it.

After I got home, I looked around my familiar, untidy home. What I'd miss most is my view—my walled garden, my gingko tree, my Lombardy poplars, and the lights of the Hay-Adams House. It gives me a pang to think that my days in this house may be numbered.

*Wednesday, 27 October 1937*

I took "Vincent," my porcelain figure I got in 1928 in Paris, down from his perch. It was the first move in dismantling my room. Washed him with a damp towel. Wrapped him and put him in a suitcase, carrying Buddha tucked into my other arm. It was Buddha's first trip outdoors since I moved from the Y.M.C.A. in 1927.

When I opened the door to my new apartment, I saw that Nicky had painted the floors maroon, a pleasing, rich color. Heard conversation from the bathroom and joined Max, Nicky, and Dash in there. The workmen had finally moved their paraphernalia out. We discussed the fishes on the new wallpaper, the advisability of putting in a door to the steps on the second floor, and other interesting matters.

*Thursday, 28 October 1937*

Dash, Max, and Nicky worked nobly and got my books dusted and packed. I sat and cleaned my kitty-cat collection and didn't seem to get far. The boys left about one in the morning, carrying with them framed pictures and handbags with toby jugs. The room looks utterly dismantled and seems no longer mine. Thus ends an era.

*Saturday, 30 October 1937*

Worked feverishly until 4:30 a.m. Slept till seven; called up the transfer company to see if they could postpone my moving. They could not. Worked like a demon. The moving men appeared when I still had enormous quantities of stuff to pack. The white mover helped me put things in boxes, the two of us frenzied, trying to keep up with the negroes who took out the boxes. My face streamed with sweat. My hands and nails were black with dust. I kept going on nervous energy, at top speed. At last the nerve-wracking business was over. Took a taxi to the new place and found my studio couch had arrived. I liked it even better than I did in the store. Overhead I heard Dash's brisk footsteps, then his door closing. In a moment he bounded down the stairs and stopped in to see me. We played the Victrola, the first record in my new apartment being "Home, Sweet Home," sung by Galli-Curci.

> **Amelita Galli-Curci** *(1889–1963) was a celebrated coloratura soprano. She had an impressively aquiline nose and wore gypsy combs in her hair. Isador sometimes did impersonations of her.*

*Tuesday, 2 November 1937*

Was locking my door on my way out to work as Dash ran down the stairs from his apartment. We walked downtown in the sunshine and had breakfast together, the first time in years. A nice way to start the day. At lunch I went up to Woodward & Lothrop's and purchased a bedspread with a design of ships and seashells, and a laundry bag—green with design of blackberry leaves. In the evening Dash helped me unload books. Nicky painted windowsills. Max labored on the cabinet in the bathroom. Isador knocked on the door, holding his Scotties in his arms to keep them from investigating Nicky's paint cans. Isador says he has gotten a new job in the Protocol Division of the State Department. It ought to suit him much better. He invited us to take a break at his apartment for a "snack," which turned out to be hominy grits, country sausage, hot biscuits, sherry, pineapple juice, salad, and tea. We toured his apartment. He recently acquired a beautiful Chinese rug and a noble old sideboard on which his silver is displayed. On the floor of his bedroom are two dog beds for the Scotties.

Tonight in my own apartment the heat in the radiators is sizzling. I have been so pleased with my new rooms that I have poked around instead of going to bed. Now it is three in the morning. I just heard Dashie and Max pass by in the hall, and could tell Max had had whisky, because he talked in a strained, loud voice. Milkwagon horse klop-klopping in the street below. A few automobiles passing. I am crazy about my new home.

*Sunday, 19 December 1937*

To the house. Dad was ill and in his bed. Dr. Teichmann (Nazi defender) paid him a visit. He thinks Dad should go down to Miami and rest in the warm weather. Mama had a quarrel with Dr. Teichmann over his treatment of Dad and its failure. After Teichmann left, Dad talked in a maudlin strain about dying. To hear him carrying on like that put me into a sort of brisk superiority and a desire to help him. I said, "Snap out of it, Dad!" and before leaving, "Don't give up the ship!" He lay there looking weak and wasted.

When I left, I decided to walk over to the old reservoir. It is to be demolished tomorrow. I turned off through the woods and into a thicket and unexpectedly came upon a youth and a girl in a brilliant red coat engaged in heavy lovemaking. I gazed for a moment, since they were too busy to notice me, and then retreated. But the sight excited me so much that I slipped into the thicket for another look. This time they were so tangled up with each other that I hoped for the best, that is, the most extreme thing they could be doing. I fled before the fellow looked up. He exclaimed, so he may have seen me.

Hurried away what is left of my old "Beauty Field"—that clearing containing an ancient orchard, once filled with flowers and buzzing bees and sun-soaked childhood dreams—now cut in half by a straight street. Strolled on through new neighborhoods. In the window of a florist's, a gorgeous mass of poinsettias. Red flowers have a vividly stimulating effect upon me. Then downtown. Foolishly dined at Candlestick. The desire to urinate hit my bladder hard. I knew there would be no men's room in a place like that. Swallowed my meal whole, and rushed away to the Kosmos. There I found relief. Stayed on, drinking beers. The lonely, precarious existence of a bachelor!

*Saturday, 25 December 1937*

To the house. A nice Christmas there. When I got back to the apartment, Dash pattered downstairs to look at my Christmas presents. We listened to my Bessie Smith album—her songs of about fifteen years ago—"There'll be a Hot

Time in the Old Town Tonight," "Alexander's Ragtime Band," "St. Louis Blues," and others. Heard a tapping at the door and it was Max, with facetious remarks about our making too much noise. I played more records and watched Dash and Max dancing. Felt happy. We had a nice time until Max mentioned his New Year's Eve party. He plans to go in the morning to Pamela's to cook the goose himself, saving the cost of having it cooked. Dash abruptly said, "I can't take leave from work to attend a two o'clock dinner." Max said placatingly, "Pamela and Isador also work at the State Department, and *they* have no difficulty in getting off." Dash remained silent. Max offered to change the hour to five, but Dash wouldn't even agree to that. Sometimes he gets cantankerous, and is difficult to handle.

When Max got ready to leave, I accompanied him into the hall. Dash remained in my armchair wearing his stubborn face. I told Max, "I'll try to persuade him not to spoil things." Returned and remarked to Dashie, "My big table is a mess." He said crossly, "The floor hasn't been swept since you moved in. Your bed needs new linen and the bathroom plumbing needs cleaning." I thought to myself, *Ho hum! I simply am not a housekeeper born,* but quietly asked him if I might borrow his vacuum cleaner. He cheered up, as he always does when he has an opportunity to be useful. By the time he hurried upstairs for the vacuum cleaner he was amenable to allowing Max to give a five o'clock New Year's Eve party, and was even prepared to take leave from work if the party were held at two.

*Friday, 31 December 1937*

I found Nicky at Max's studio, darting about preparing for the party. Max was at Pamela's cooking the goose and other things. Nicky had laid the table out beautifully—a broad board stretched across two card tables, red and white crêpe paper tablecloths, blue glass dishes, silver cutlery and platters, tall red candles. There was a beautiful Christmas tree with only blue electric lights on it. Dash telephoned from downtown and said he would bring the ice. He had already brought out four bottles of champagne at noon.

Nicky kept buzzing around, making ready. Dash appeared and fixed delicious Manhattan cocktails. Soon Pamela, Max, the goose, and the rest of dinner arrived. Pamela as usual was rather destructive, falling over things. She greeted me warmly and thanked me for my Christmas card. When Isador arrived, we seated ourselves at the beautiful table and had the roast goose and other good things, and an amazing variety of drinks—champagne contributed by Pamela; also burgundy, Cointreau, martini, gin, bourbon whiskey, Puerto Rico rum, brandy. Everyone was gay and happy. Dash was sprightly and acted as a sort of assistant host or master of ceremonies. Pamela was wobbly in spite of the coffee that Dash made. She and Nicky got giggly and lay on the couch together and later on the floor in the hall. Then Dash lay on the couch with his head in her lap. Max gave her some passionate loving which she seemed to enjoy.

# 1938

### Thursday, 13 January 1938

I left work early to go to Washington Airport to see Dad off to Miami. Found them already there—Dad, Mama, Henry, Eunice, and Daisy. We sat on couches facing the plate glass window that looked on the landing field. When Dad's plane flew in from New York, it was gray and labeled "The Great Silver Fleet" (belonging to Eastern Airlines). A plane bound for "Knoxville, Nashville, Memphis, Dallas, and Fort Worth" was announced by loudspeaker. Finally the departure of Dad's Miami plane was announced. We walked out with him, Henry and I holding his arms, since Dad still is unsteady on his feet. At the barrier Henry, Eunice, and I told Dad good-bye. Mama walked with him into the plane. He waved from behind the glass and held high the "airsickness" container, smiling. Mama hurried down the steps, and there was a roar of propellers and a gust of dust-laden air that struck us and got into Eunice's eyes and blew off Mama's hat. We watched Dad's plane taxi across the field and into the sky. A few moments before, Dad had been standing on the ground beside us—now he was far up in the air traveling at great speed.

### Tuesday, 25 January 1938

Woke when I heard Dash running down the steps. Hurried to my front window and looked out, but he was out of sight. Had a headache from too much to drink last night. Decided to take the day off from work—it simply must be the last. Depressed and guilty and worried about the office. In the afternoon I heard Dash getting home and looked into the hall, then went up in my pajamas and bathrobe to his apartment. He said he was tired, so I came back downstairs. Browsed through my bookshelves and picked out Lansing Tower's novel. Sat reading *Palm Avenue* in my Morris chair. Nicky got home, and recognizing the novel I was reading, told me, *"You* could write a novel as good as your friend's, if you didn't spend your time drinking beer." I told him good-naturedly, "Don't preach to me." Down below the sound of Julia Cunningham's Victrola throbbed with dance music. Her pupils' feet beat on the floor. From overhead I heard Dash's heavy rapid footsteps, then the whirring *whirrr* of his vacuum cleaner.

Kept on reading passages of *Palm Avenue* and became emotionally disturbed at my failure to accomplish anything in the way of writing. It took an effort to put aside Lansing's book. Got out old diaries, looking for references to Lansing. Found several uncomplimentary ones, I'm afraid. Became engrossed in the diaries. It is strange to relive one's life in that manner. So many complaining, unhappy days, so few contented ones.

*Wednesday, 26 January 1938*

Forgot to set my alarm last night and would have slept for hours if Dash had not knocked and whistled and awakened me. I dressed at top speed and rushed to the office. This *must* be the last time I'm late!

At night Dash and Nicky invited me to go for a walk in the snow. I was glad to accept; then Randall Hare arrived. Dash never mentions Randall, not even when he talks about his work at the State Department. I haven't seen him since 1935—a night when he was an irritating visitor at Max's studio. His thick hair is turning gray and there's a vein that throbs on his temple. Dash and Nicky walked ahead. Randall and I followed, neither of us saying a word. Hundreds of young people coasted on a hill that started beside the Shoreham Hotel. When Dash and Nicky decided to go to a drugstore for something to eat, Randall and I sat almost wordlessly watching the coasting and sledding on the snowy slope. I was glad when we started home.

*Tuesday, 15 February 1938*

Nicky urged me not to go out drinking, but I went anyway. I came home with a soldier with a bristly reddish moustache. Where on earth I met him, I probably never shall know. We finished up my bottle of California wine and I broke both the glasses by lurching against them at the edge of the table. He stayed the night. I passed out completely the moment I got into bed.

*Wednesday, 16 February 1938*

My guest jumped up and said he was due back at Marine Barracks at 6:30. I gave him fifty cents for taxi fare and looked out the window after he left and saw him running along the street. Felt so terrible I couldn't think of going to the office. Blister on my finger and burns on the coat of my new suit. Probably brushed the flame of my cigarette off with my finger. Such unutterable folly! Couldn't find my keys and decided the boy had carried them off, planning to return and rob the apartment at his leisure.

Sat in my striped bathrobe and read *Life* in a wretched daze. Decided to dress, about five, and found the keys where I had laid my trousers last night. Such glorious relief. The poor chap was all right after all. I opened a bottle of sherry to celebrate, and eventually felt so gay and free that I began to dance around slowly by myself. Nicky got home and assured me he would not mind the music, so I kept on.

*Saturday, 5 March 1938*

At Murphy's I bought highball glasses and coasters for my party, to which I invited ten guests. Home feeling rather panicky when I thought of how much I yet had to do. Made the bed up, cleaned the floors with Dash's vacuum cleaner, put clean towels in the bathroom, emptied trash boxes. Nicky helped by scrubbing the marble mantelpiece, to be used as a bar. Was doing final things to the apartment when Pamela arrived in evening dress with a corsage of gladiolus and iris. She had gone to another party earlier. It was the first time I had seen Pamela since Inaugural Day, when I was fearfully drunk and spanked her. I felt foolish when I recalled that occasion, but anyway, I have seen Pamela herself plenty drunk and doing things just as undignified.

The second guest to arrive was Bolling Balfour, a help with the conversation. Dash had promised he would be here early, but he didn't show up till nearly ten o'clock, much to my annoyance at the time. Max appeared early. Isador brought with him a country-countenanced youngster named Tip. At first we sat in chairs near the door. Pamela then decided to sit on the couch so Nicky sat there with her, and things centered around that end of the room.

I served first the quart of bourbon, making the drinks strong, for I like to see people get gay and lose their inhibitions. Pamela laid her legs across Nicky's lap, put her black bolero on him and they played with each other's hair. When Isador and Tip arrived, things were getting gay and I gave them strong drinks to help them catch up. We had dance music on the radio, and I danced with Pamela, whirling her round and round until I marveled at my sense of balance and complete lack of dizziness in spite of the drinks I had had. Dash a couple of times went to Pamela and loudly whispered, "The stretcher-bearers have come for you." This angered me and I accused him of trying to drive Pamela away. He went upstairs to get his coat and hat, telling me, "I'll see her home in a taxi." She insisted she could get home by herself, but he accompanied her anyway. After they left Isador and Tip danced together, and Bolling danced with Max.

Now it is around three. While I have been writing I have been playing records and finishing up several of the drinks which were left almost undisturbed.

The liquor had been so expensive that it seems a shame to waste it. It was a memorable party and I shall have another in a few months or so.

### Sunday, 19 March 1938

Wretched day. Woke up and tried to get my "guests" to leave. They were both bums, but I was too drunk last night when I invited them here to realize it. The taller one became mean and ugly. He demanded more whiskey, asked for money, and began to get more truculent, saying, "Listen, I could beat up the two of you with my eyes closed." The creature had powerful muscles. He insisted on my pouring a pint of my bonded rye into a bottle for him to carry away. Said, "Hey, do you have a clean shirt I could use?" I gave him my old blue striped one. He asked for a tie, too, but didn't repeat his request, so I gave him none. But later I slipped my red striped tie that Henry gave me out of his pocket. The other said, "I'd like a shirt, since he got one," so I gave him one, and an old tie. While he was putting the tie on, his friend wanted to fight him to show who was the stronger.

I began to despair of getting them out of here, and was afraid I should be driven to calling on Dash, Max, and Nicky. Finally I lost my temper and talked loudly and violently to the creatures. I managed to get them to the door after what seemed like a hideous eternity of nervous cajolery and maneuvering. Slammed the lock and bolted it. What on God's green earth persuaded me to get so drunk as to invite those bums into my home?

### Monday, 28 March 1938

Saddened by the desperate situation in Spain, where the Government is fighting with its back to the wall against the fascists and the invading Italians and Germans. These are sad days for civilization, when barbarous tyrants like Hitler, Mussolini, and the Japanese war lords are carrying on bloody wars and ruthless oppression.

Henry dropped in. I was surprised, and glad to see him. He suggested going out for beer. We drove to the Lafayette and talked about family and childhood. He remembers Mother so much better than I do. After we parted, I strolled toward home and fell into conversation with a young fellow. We sat on a bench, talking in the mild pleasant night. It was almost five in the morning when we walked up to my place. He stayed for what remained of the night.

### Sunday, 17 April 1938

To the New Bavarian. They had German music, mostly accordion. "Der Wacht am Rhein" was played. I hissed vigorously without many people seeming to notice. Busloads of D.A.R.s poured in. The Daughters were enthusiastic, demanding, and noisy, as ever when they descend on Washington. The bartender had all he could do. Home in a taxi. Stood reading in Joseph Conrad's *Mirror of the Sea,* which I keep at my bedside. It is just at that time that I feel keenly the desire to be on board a ship at sea. Lapsed into a reverie in which my dream-boy, Vincent Eric Orville, was my companion in a storm in mid-ocean . . . The ship rolls, and spray sweeps across the deck . . .

> **"Der Wacht am Rhein"** *was a German song which appeared toward the end of the nineteenth century. In Hitler's era, the Nazis sang the song with fervor and sentiment to symbolize the invincibility of Germany and the Nazi cause.*

*Saturday, 12 November 1938*

To the Parkside, where I had one beer after another. The orchestra became "hot" and the jitterbugs seemed to be in ecstasy. Got into conversation with an older man from North Carolina who had been drinking there when I arrived. He informed me for no apparent reason that he was queer and I was surprised. We talked on for some time.

# 1939

*Sunday, 1 January 1939*

To the house. Dad and Mama had been earlier to a New Year's eggnog party, and were mellow and talkative, especially Mama. I enjoyed her company. We played a game of rummy that Dad won, and then Eunice took Dad's place and won. Home and mulled over my *Post* until three in the morning. The beginning of a new year. So much trouble in poor old Europe! Stars shining on this wretched world.

*Wednesday, 11 January 1939*

Dash said that last night when Max and his guests showed up at my place, he awoke, and hearing the noise, had the notion that I was being beaten up. He suffered a terrifying moment before he recognized Max's voice. He had mistaken their loud footsteps on the stairs for banging on my door. After all, Max gets so loud when he gets tight. Dash said, "I have not yet got over it." I felt very sorry. Nicky got home. The three of us went up to Dash's apartment and had a good conversation, largely about the Spanish war. Nicky, like me, is strong for the Government forces and against the fascists, although he is nominally a Roman

Catholic. Left Dash's around eleven and felt a desire for beer. Went around to Maynard's. At a front table I saw the old Maynard itself, big and calm as ever. It made no move to speak. I have detested the creature for years, ever since it snatched a glass of beer out of my hand just before closing time. Got tight and walked home following the cracks in the sidewalk, in case anybody was noticing me.

*Wednesday, 12 July 1939*

Walked out of the bar into the sweltering night with Isador, who had appeared for coffee before going to the opening Watergate concert. We stood chatting on the pavement. Dash came along, wearing his seersucker suit and a short-sleeved sport shirt. He told me, "I can tell when you're drunk a block away." I asked, "Why have you taken such an intolerant attitude toward me?" He made no reply.

*Saturday, 29 July 1939*

Hot and damp in Isador's apartment. Isador wore a garment that he said was a Bahaman type, a light blanket with a hole in the middle for the head. It enabled him to carry out successfully his usual poses and theatrical tricks. I sat on a sofa covered with loose dirt from the two dogs lying there. Isador talked at me, showed me autographed books and programs. It is amazing the contacts he makes. I became hot and thirsty and tried to leave before twelve. It took fifteen minutes for Isador to finish the wind-up of his conversation and his questions about my trip abroad next month. Walked down to Martin's over Georgetown's dark, uneven brick pavements. Swallowed two glasses of beer quickly before the pubs let out. Soldiers, shirt-sleeved men, and tough-looking young women were loitering about, many of them unsteady of mind and foot.

*Friday, 18 August 1939*

To the house for my farewell dinner with the family before I leave for my vacation in Europe. Eunice remarked, "Two-thirds of what we're hearing about Germany is propaganda." Henry snorted and said, "You'll land in a concentration camp and not get home for five years." Dad intoned, "When you return, if I am not here—" and Henry interrupted, "Meaning, if you are dead—" and Dad lowered his head and continued, "then, son, I want you to think well of me." I left them with an uneasy, pessimistic feeling.

Home by taxi and dawdled over a letter to Dash. I took my time, knowing the train wouldn't leave till two, but of course time slipped up on me. Nicky stopped in, telling me, "You ought to reconsider your trip. Pamela had reliable information that war is expected on the thirtieth of this month." I answered, "I don't expect war by then. If war is going to break out on the thirtieth, why would Randall take Catherine and the boys to Europe at such a time?" Nicky answered patiently, "Pamela works in the intelligence section. Randall does not. Pamela told me because she's worried about *you.* Anyway, Randall won't have his family once he goes to London. They travel with him only for a farewell vacation." "How well I know," I said bitterly. I haven't forgiven Randall for booking passage on the *Noordam,* the same ship that I'm going over on. He did it on purpose. Dash, Max, and Nicky admit that, though they think it's amusing. I do not. I love being on shipboard and resent having my pleasure spoiled by Randall. Oh, well! Put on my traveling clothes, told my rooms good-bye, and rushed away in a taxi.

*PART FOUR*

# THE SECOND WORLD WAR

*Monday, 21 August 1939 (SS* Noordam*)*

I awoke and looked across at my roommate, a middle-aged Frenchman lying with his striped pajama trousers open and his penis throbbing and erect. Wondered what he was dreaming about. Dressed and went up to look at the sea. The ship rolled and dipped in the great blue swells of the ocean. Randall, Catherine, and the two boys, family bustle and noise, appeared on deck. Randall behaved cordially. We strolled about in the wind, the adults talking on many subjects—Catherine is really very amusing—difficult situations in mixed company, the prudishness of unmarried persons and the commonness of married persons, incidents of unbuttoned trousers in public, and other weighty matters. The boys, named Edwin and Fenton, climbed about and seemed in danger of falling into the sea. Randall remonstrated, but Catherine remained calm. "They'll be all right," she said.

In the evening Randall took Edwin and Fenton to the movie, *Mutiny on the Bounty.* Catherine joined me at the bar. She said, "You looked lonely." As a matter of fact I *had* felt a kind of loneliness while watching Randall taking his two sons into the movie. But of course that was silly—I am merely being frank.

*Thursday, 24 August 1939 (SS* Noordam*)*

The ship rolled in a gray sea under a gray sky. I thought of England and her precarious situation. How I abominate that creature, Swine Hitler. To think that the peace and happiness of the world rest in the hands of one megalomaniacal fanatic.

After dinner almost everybody filed in to see the movie, *Hotel for Women.* I took my diary up to the deck to write. Was prevented by the arrival of Randall, with a whiskey and soda in his hand. He sat on the arm of the next chair and spoke of sending his wife and sons straight back if war breaks out before we land. After hearing how worried he was, I felt more worried myself. I put away my diary in the cabin and went to the lounge with him. We both decided to stay a day or two at a hotel in Rotterdam, at least long enough to find out what is going to happen.

*Friday, 25 August 1939 (SS* Noordam*)*

Sat in my deck chair and wrote postcards with almost identical messages to

Dash, Dad, and Miss Contadeluci. Became fascinated, as ever, by the waves, their peaks dissolving into spray sending a steady drizzle onto the decks. Spent a long time thinking about the depressing probability of war. Up on top deck I watched four Dutch people doing an odd dance, standing in a row. One of the Dutch women, attractive, who wears gray slacks each day, told me, "You must either join us or evaporate." I pleaded "a broken ankle" and was excused.

An "extra" bulletin was put up. In the latest dispatches from Berlin and London, Hitler was said to be "in high spirits." The foul, murdering beast! Randall and Catherine, and an attractive girl, Jane Poe, sat next to me in the lounge. I told Catherine, "The only thing to do is to get drunk." When the topic of Hitler's "high spirits" arose, I said, "I wish Berlin would be bombed, just to give them a taste of what it is like." Jane Poe is an awfully nice girl and I like her. I assured her I'd be willing to marry her. And I am told by Catherine that I proposed to Jane again in the smokeroom. Now good-night. God knows what Europe will bring me.

*Monday, 28 August 1939 (Hotel Central, Rotterdam)*

With Europe teetering on the brink of war, here I sit in a bar in Rotterdam. Randall has gone back to the hotel out of sheer sleepiness. To begin at the beginning…This morning as we were bringing our luggage into the lobby of the Hotel Central, Randall ran into a State Department acquaintance of his, a bearded American named Markowitz, who had just fled with his father from Munich. Markowitz told Randall, "You picked a fine time for a London assignment, but there is nothing to be done about it now." He advised me, "Go as fast as you can to Scandinavia. The war is certain to start in a matter of hours."

Catherine took the children up to their room, and Randall and I went out in the hopes of finding news. On this trip I have begun to realize that Randall is not nearly so "high up" at State as I had been led to believe—maybe not even so high up as Pamela. It is the clothes he wears that makes him look important. It is his independent income.

He is a fast walker, like Dash, and kept a few steps ahead of me. Wish he could amble along slowly, but he is too much the vigorous American. We saw a number of white posters along the way, announcing mobilization of the country on Tuesday. People were showing interest in the notices but seemed to accept the situation quite calmly. At the Tivoli we had gin and bitters and Randall, with his breezy Western manner with strangers, got into a conversation with a Dutchman who spoke English. The Dutchman's companion seemed bored. While the Dutchman's friend was inside for a few minutes the Dutchman told us, "He has been in Rotterdam for eleven years, but he is a German and a Nazi sympathizer."

When the German returned, Randall asked him his name. The German replied merely, "I am Wolfgang." I didn't like him or his manners. He had chewing gum and pulled it far out of his mouth in a string, remarking, "That is the way Americans do." I told him only low-class Americans did that.

The Victrola played music and our Dutch friend amazingly pulled two pipes about eighteen inches long from his pocket and played in tune to the music while we beat time on the bar. Queen Wilhelmina was to speak to the nation by radio. Wolfgang scoffed at her. "She'll only tell us to eat more fruit." He left the bar and sat elsewhere as if determined not to listen. The speech came clearly and the Dutchman translated it for Randall and me—interesting to hear under such circumstances, though she said nothing new or startling. Wolfgang returned and remarked, "Tuesday, the day of mobilization, will be dry in Holland, because in 1914 when the Dutch soldiers were mobilized they were too drunk to do anything." He wanted to rush off at once. However, the Dutchman was exceedingly cordial, urging us to call him up or come see him at his office.

Randall and I went on to a plaza where news was appearing in a running band of lighted letters. Impossible to read the Dutch, though. Nearby, a red-faced old man asked us in English what we thought of Hitler. Randall answered evasively. The old man replied, "Ve hate Hitler. Ve hate him."

*Queen Wilhelmina (1880–1962) came to the throne of the Netherlands in 1890 as a ten-year-old, with her mother as regent. In May of 1940, when the Germans invaded Holland, her unexpected departure for England demoralized the country; with the bombing of Rotterdam soon after, Holland became occupied by Germany.*

### Tuesday, 29 August 1939 (Hotel Central, Rotterdam)

Americans are fleeing like scared rabbits, trying to get home. Some say war will break out tonight. The Dutch government has asked U.S. citizens to leave the country, as they do not want to be embarrassed with the presence of foreigners. The rail connection to Copenhagen through Germany has been suspended. Randall received word through the Consulate that he is to report to London at once. The Consulate was besieged by Americans and others, but the people there were helpful, arranging to get me and Catherine Hare and the children reservations on a steamer for Norway.

### Wednesday, 30 August 1939 (SS Jupiter, Rotterdam to Bergen)

The Hares wanted to take Edwin and Fenton to bathe in the sea at Scheveningen before Randall departs for London. They rented suits and I spread my London paper on the sand and sat a while. Randall's suit had a top but few other men's suits had. Catherine played with the children in the waves, very attractive with her curly hair cut almost as short as theirs. It was a pleasant beach with good surf. When we returned to the promenade, we saw a trench lined with sandbags and manned by soldiers with fixed bayonets. It is difficult to see how one little armed trench could protect Scheveningen.

Back to Rotterdam and to the hotel. Paid the bill and departed by taxi for the dock. We stood on deck and talked. Randall mused, "I find it peculiar to think of you and Catherine traveling together." Finally the bell rang. Randall kissed his wife and children good-bye, shook hands with me, and strode down the gangplank. The ship pulled away.

After supper Catherine sat on deck with me, listening at the radio-operator's door to a depressing news broadcast in English. "All the grim details of getting ready for war," she exclaimed, "as if war were inevitable." Well, here we are, fleeing together to Norway to be out of war. I have my misgivings about the trip and I think Catherine rather regrets it. At least she makes disparaging remarks about the ship. I can manage, though, as long as she doesn't talk too often about Randall.

*Thursday, 31 August 1939 (SS* Jupiter, *Rotterdam to Bergen)*

Little Edwin rushed into the lounge to tell me a German plane was circling above us. I hastened out and saw it circling above our ship. Catherine, in a deck chair with Fenton on her lap, said vehemently, "The sight of that plane makes me so angry!" We talked with a Polish man who was determined to get a picture of the plane, and did. He told us, "Poland is fighting for existence as a nation." He gave us the latest broadcast news. London has evacuated all the children. England has mobilized.

The plane kept circling around us, sometimes disappearing behind low-hanging clouds. We went into the lounge for dinner drinks. The Polish man picked up with the blonde Norwegian girl he was raving about yesterday and brought her to our table. We were joined almost at once by a muscular Spaniard, who turned out to be the Norwegian girl's traveling companion. The girl, named Elise, translated a news broadcast in Norwegian for us, saying Russia had signed an agreement with Germany. The Spaniard and I got into a violent argument because he said he fought for Franco. I did not hesitate to say exactly what I thought about the Spanish War and the assistance rendered Franco by Mussolini and Hitler. The argument became so heated that Catherine and Elise suggested we change the subject. The Spaniard, however, kept on bringing in the subject on every occasion. Drinking makes me more assured, so I was ready for him.

Finally the head steward came up and urged us to come to supper, the gong having sounded some time before.

*Francisco Franco (1892–1975) was a chief of the Spanish State during the Spanish Civil War (1936–1939). He assumed the powers of a dictator after the capture of Madrid (March 28, 1939).*

*Friday, 1 September 1939 (Hotel Bristol, Bergen, Norway)*

This will go down in history as a black day for civilization, a day presaging death and tragedy for millions. At five this morning, according to the radio man, Hitler issued a proclamation that his patience was at an end, and ordered the bombing of Warsaw, Gdynia, and Cracow. The war has begun.

Here on the coast of Norway we sail between rocky islands sleeping peacefully in the sunshine. The mist gathers on the mountains of the mainland. News broadcasts have been coming in. The Polish man translated for us. The Spaniard, José Martinez, joined us and spoke of the bombings of Polish cities as being "amusing." He remarked, "War, occasionally, is good for any nation." When he sauntered away the Pole said bitterly, "The Spanish are a cruel race." The radio reported that the Poles had shot down one German bombing plane—too bad they can't shoot down a thousand! The British Parliament was to meet at six in the evening to declare war, and the French Parliament in the morning. It was reported that Hitler had declared that he would shoot himself unless he could have what he wanted, and that his successors would be Goering and Goebbels in that order, and then a Senate. What a fantastic, hysterical fanatic.

All day we sailed beneath a light sun in blue waters. We passed between hundreds of green islands scattered with wooden houses. In the afternoon we put in at the town of Hampsend. Catherine and I and Edwin and Fenton went ashore for a walk. Strolling up onto a curious cement bridge that overlooked an inner harbor, we came upon the Spaniard, José Martinez, and Elise, the Norwegian girl who is traveling with him. Elise has been worried over her chow dog, having heard that since he is ill he would be quarantined for six months. Yet she took the dog ashore for a stroll at Hampsend without question. After Martinez and the girl had passed by, Catherine murmured, "I'm glad *I* don't have any such complications as having to take a sick dog and a Spaniard into Norway."

In the afternoon, frequent Norwegian news broadcasts on deck. Elise provided vague, puzzling translations. Then, rounding a couple of headlands, we had the city of Bergen laid out before us, pleasing with its terraced appearance of houses rising toward the slopes of the mountains. The mate said good-bye to me in jolly fashion as "Mr. Washington, D.C." Ashore and by taxi to the Bristol

Hotel. I took room 301 and Catherine and the boys took 307 and 309. After Catherine had left off her inevitable laundry at the desk (she and the children must make a complete change of clothes every day), she tried, without success, to telephone Randall in London. Then we sallied forth into the streets. We saw our Spaniard and the chow girl going out of the Norge. Later they came to our café. They had acquired a dog doctor for the chow and Martinez treated the dog to coffee. We all went together to a newspaper office, where there was a good-sized street crowd waiting for war bulletins. Elise translated for us. The Germans are attacking the Polish frontier with considerable success. What we all are wondering is, how can France and Britain help Poland before it is too late?

*Saturday, 2 September 1939 (Bergen, Norway)*

While Catherine and the boys rested in their rooms I set out alone into the street. Saw Elise and José arrive at our hotel. The chow dog was carried into the hotel in a crate—a strange way to quarantine him. At the suggestion of Elise and José I went with them over to the Norge and listened to the orchestra, watched the dancing, and drank dark beer. The waiter appeared and announced that Hitler had taken Danzig and the Corridor. "Now that Hitler has what he wants," he said, "there will be no war." I waxed indignant at such a notion. "Good God —if there is to be no war merely because Hitler has been successful in grabbing what he wants, then what of the honor of Britain and France?" Elise protested, "Surely they will not let him keep what he has taken by sheer brute force." The poor waiter apologized for venting his opinions. Elise murmured, "It is impossible to understand just what is the situation. I can't believe an ignorant waiter knows very much."

*Sunday, 3 September 1939 (Bergen, Norway)*

Before I had even got to my shaving, Catherine and the boys rushed in to announce that England had declared war against Germany. They stayed talking with me while I was shaving. We walked to the Norge to eat, to be shocked at finding it closed and the chairs piled high upon tables. Catherine and I sat on a bench and talked dismally about the war. The trees were green and peaceful and the sun shone upon clear green waters. I felt infinitely distressed at the thought of the millions of young men who will be dead at the end of the war, and of broken families and bereaved mothers, fathers, wives, and children. Finally we strolled back. Overlooking the fjord we saw a German ship below with its foul swastika fluttering in the breeze. I told Catherine, "I feel a great desire to throw a bomb into that ship and blow it up." On the way back to the hotel I cabled to Mama and Dad the following: "Safe Norway. Return October. Inform Dasham."

*Monday, 4 September 1939 (Bergen, Norway)*

Catherine surprised me in my underwear when she knocked, as I thought the light knocking had the sound of Edwin or Fenton. I hastily wrapped my bathrobe around me. Catherine gave me the news, the main thing being that the SS *Athenia* from Glasgow to Montreal had been torpedoed and sunk. She was loaded with American and Canadian passengers, fleeing home. We discussed plans seriously. We are thinking of going by steamer to Oslo. Catherine volunteered that she could lend me money if I ran short, and I playfully joked with her, saying I must stick with her.

In the afternoon she appeared at my door with Elise, José, and a bottle of Scotch. She prepared highballs with water from the faucet, saying, "How I *do* regret the lack of ice." José lay on my bed with his shirt open. He drank his highball and told jokes, many of them dirty. From time to time he let out a roar of laughter.

*Tuesday, 5 September 1939 (Bergen, Norway)*

It began to rain—a dismal prospect. Catherine, the boys, Elise, José, and I stayed at the radio in my room. There was music from England, including my own record of "A Tisket a Tasket," which seemed to take me right home. I also thought of "September in the Rain" as I looked out at the rain on the Bergen pavements. Elise ordered ice, and we had Scotch and water to cheer us up. José drank his while looking through the window with my opera glasses.

The rain poured down outside. Elise talked about wanting to get back to Berlin to get her luggage, which, she said, contained her winter clothes, "including about $2000 worth of furs." I said emphatically, "You cannot go to Berlin under the circumstances." She lifted her eyebrows and said, "But—I leave for Berlin in the morning." Elise seemed to be learning things, having hitherfore traveled as a rich tourist without ever seeing below the surface. After a while she seemed convinced, as I told her, that it was preposterous to go to Germany.

*Wednesday, 6 September 1939 (Bergen, Norway)*

Around noon I heard martial music in the square, and leapt up to see what was happening. A long column of troops passed beneath the windows. Scores of boys ran along beside the marching men, but there were few shouts and no cheering. People ran up from all directions to watch the troops pass. Supplies were carried on two-wheel carts drawn by tan ponies. From my window I saw Catherine and the boys dash out of the hotel to join the crowds.

*Thursday, 7 September 1939 (SS Richard With, Bergen to Molde)*

The steamer is very small. At last we got underway, up the dark coast in the rain. As I retired to my cabin I felt regret at not being able to sleep alone. Catherine asked that I share the larger of the two available cabins with the boys. Oh, well! Edwin and Fenton were awake and tossing and tumbling on their bed. When I set to work on the letter that I have been writing to Dash, they asked me what I was doing. I said, "I'm writing to a friend of your father's." Don't know why I said that to the boys, but I did. Now it is cozy in here with the rain beating on the deck and dashing against our black window shade. It comes in a little. The ship rocks and the lights become a little dimmer. The boys have begun to settle down, and I am being lulled to bed by the rain and the steady soft rush of the sea past us.

*Friday, 8 September 1939 (Molde, Norway)*

Edwin and Fenton were irritable and irritating all morning. When Catherine had several times spoken to them, she turned on me. "These children," she said sharply, "are exhausted for lack of sleep. They have been martyrs to your diary, to listening all night to you lighting cigarettes and to your drinking water." Edwin urged her, "Tell him also about his sniffing noises." She ignored him. I felt resentful. There were two beds, but close together and fastened together. I had no sooner gotten to sleep when Edwin and Fenton woke me to say I was snoring. After that it was my impression that they woke me every ten minutes to tell me I was snoring. I would go to sleep with the feeling that I must try above all to avoid snoring. The boys tried to produce their own snoring noises, and Fenton laughed uncontrollably and wet the bed.

Catherine is a mighty fine woman altogether and one for whom I have great respect, but she is not, after all, easy to get on with day after day at close quarters. I had to rather smack her down. All most unpleasant. God knows there is nothing that I detest more than a shrewish, nagging woman. I endured enough of that in my boyhood until I finally escaped.

*Tuesday, 12 September 1939 (Andalsnes, Norway)*

Today was Fenton's fourth birthday, and at his request Catherine insisted that we go rowing. She got hold of an English-speaking shopkeeper who dickered for her with a fisherman who had a rowboat. Once out into the center of the fjord, the water became choppy and the boat rose and fell sharply, at times making me rather nervous. I never complained about the heaviness of the oars and the work, although when we started back it was a hard pull. Finally we got back to the pier, where our fisherman was waiting.

A perfect day, with brilliant sun in a cloudless sky. Catherine took the boys back to the hotel for lunch. I set out, determined to make the most of the fine weather and the opportunity to be alone. Walked across green fields, delighting in the stimulating air and the magnificent mountains ranged in the distance.

*Thursday, 14 September 1939 (Oslo, Norway)*

Knocked on Catherine's door but she was bathing Edwin and Fenton. Her concern about clothes and baths gets on my nerves. I went alone down to the lobby. At the desk registering was a tall girl wearing a black sombrero. She spun around with a smile, and turned out to be Elise, whom we knew in Bergen. She put her hands on the sombrero rim and said, "Do you recognize me? I am 'Cactus Lil.'" José appeared, dragging in the chow dog, Cheops. José said they had just returned from Berlin. "We were successful—she brought back her winter clothes." Elise told me she purchased a watch and a pearl necklace to get her money out of Germany. She spoke of the kindness of the Germans. She is pro-Nazi, but is an unthinking person, and unobservant, though a warm-hearted person. José is anti-Hitler, even though he was in Franco's army.

Catherine and the boys appeared, ready to go out to eat. Elise's dog Cheops went along and was fed from our table. Elise had said "he is a kind dog," but he attacked a small dog on the sidewalk and was chased by a man with a stick. Elise had to dart through the open window to rescue him. Edwin and Fenton shouted and had to be held back so as not to clamber through the window after Elise. Things settled down eventually.

*Sunday, 17 September 1939 (Oslo, Norway)*

The café was delightfully peaceful, with brilliant geraniums between the tables, the pine trees around, the view of woods and mountains, and a glimpse of the blue fjord in the distance. We talked about the war. Always it hangs heavily over us. I had beer, Catherine coffee, José tea, and Elise and the boys each had an orange bottled drink. The others ate cakes but I didn't. It was serene there at sunset. Elise took a fruit knife and sliced off the icing of her cupcake, and, placing it in her mouth with her fingers, said, "I think the British Empire is doomed. The English can't defeat modern Germany." Catherine made a sound of protest and said, "Those foul Nazis—how I hate them!" José fumed and fretted, and finally tossed a few ten-kroner notes to Elise for their meal and stalked off—a rude thing to do.

*Thursday, 28 September 1939 (SS* Bergensfjord, *Bergen, Norway)*

I was alone on the other side of the ship when I suddenly noticed we were sailing. The band played the Norwegian anthem and then the "Star Spangled Banner." Weeping and waving people walked along the quay trying to stay alongside the ship as long as possible. There is nothing like hearing one's national anthem played in a foreign country. A lump came into my throat as we slid out the sea toward America, and I fought back tears.

*Saturday, 30 September 1939 (SS* Bergensfjord, *somewhere in the Atlantic)*
José and I, wearing raincoats and hats, stayed a long time talking on deck. Our exact location here in the North Atlantic is a secret known only to the captain. José said, "There is one Nazi aboard. It would be better not to say anything against the Nazis, because if you do, you might be taken off if a German ship stopped us." I replied, "I shall say what I damn please about the God-damned, savage régime of Hitler, regardless of who is aboard." To hell with Hitler, and I don't care who knows that I feel that way.

*Sunday, 1 October 1939 (SS* Bergensfjord, *somewhere in the Atlantic)*
Several Norwegian women sat with me in the smokeroom and had a great deal to say about Elise and José, whose romance seems to have started tongues wagging ever since José abandoned Elise for lively "La Cubaña" and her crowd. I don't feel sorry for Elise, though. She sat in front of me and Catherine and the boys at the movies tonight, and after the pictures of Japanese bombings in China I remarked loudly to Catherine, "It is like Hitler's savagery." Catherine answered loudly, "Just as uncivilized." Elise turned around and stared at us, and we stared back. We had said it for her benefit. To hell with Elise—and with the whole God-damned lot of Nazi sympathizers, of whom there seem to be plenty on board.

*Monday, 2 October 1939 (SS* Bergensfjord, *somewhere in the Atlantic)*
The barometer dropped and there was a strong wind blowing. José and I played shuffleboard. The wind kept up a mighty roaring and our game was mostly a matter of lurching about. José asked questions, since this is his first sea voyage and his first gale at sea. He was particularly worried about what to do with his car when we arrived in New York. He wanted me to drive it for him because he was nervous about driving before learning the regulations. I had to tell him I didn't drive.

Stormy petrels flitted low over the water, flying through the breaking tip of high waves that were snapped off by the wind and turned into floating spume and spindrift. A sailor came up and said we could not play because the noise might disturb Kirsten Flagstad. We played anyway. They then roped off the deck around Flagstad's cabin and put up "Silence" signs. We went down to the lounge and joined Catherine and Edwin and Fenton. José danced with "La Cubaña." Catherine murmured, "Well, at least to *her* credit she hates Hitler." Catherine and the children went to bed. I stayed but partook only slightly of the endless discussion of the war, America's neutrality, the position of Russia and Italy, and so on and on.

The ship creaks and groans interminably. The waves make a loud, wild sound. Out here in the mid-Atlantic amid the salt-smelling wastes of waters—how it pleases me. Now the foghorn sounds. Such a mournful, eerie sound. I hope it keeps on, for I love to hear it.

> **Kirsten Flagstad** *(1895–1962) was a Norwegian operatic soprano, best known for her interpretations of Wagnerian roles. In the diaries it is not clear whether Flagstad sailed from Norway because it was common knowledge that the Nazis planned to make Norway another target for conquest, or whether she was sailing aboard the SS* Bergensfjord *for an American operatic tour. In either event, José and Jeb in the uncut diary entries for some reason manage nearly every day to make themselves a noisy presence close to her cabin, despite the remonstrations of the seamen assigned to ensure Flagstad's quiet and peace of mind.*

### Monday, 25 December 1939

To the house for Christmas Day. Dad was ill and sitting in his room. Henry and his family finally arrived, and we sat in Dad's room talking. Daisy tugged about a huge, brindle-colored Great Dane dog that Henry and Eunice gave her for Christmas. Henry was rather sympathetic about the German cause in the war and deliberately started an argument, with Dad and me on the Allied side. I felt so strongly that I felt as if I were going to explode through the back of my neck. When they left it took a big struggle to make the dog descend the stairs.

Otherwise a pleasant Christmas day. Now I am home, lying back in my easy chair with my feet on the leather hassock that Mama gave me for Christmas. The radio, static sputtering, is playing softly "Scatterbrain" from some night owl station. My glass of water, the glass with the Spanish dancers on it in white and green, sits beside me. Magazines, books, and junk litter the cocktail table at my left, the two-desk table at my right, and a chair within reach. This is my nest—this cozy disorderly corner where I have so many things within reach, including the radio and the wastebasket, now overflowing.

Some time—and it mustn't be too far away—I shall discover the key that will unlock what I have in my soul and mind, that I may pour it out on paper and have it given to the world. Am forty years old. I can scarcely believe it. Life is the brief flame of a candle that shakes in the wind and goes out before it has burned to the bottom.

*Sunday, 31 December 1939*

Dash was wearing a new suit, brown tweed and well-fitting, and over it, his handsome dark brown overcoat. We rushed down by bus to Candlestick to have a meal before going to Max's New Year's party. Then by taxi to the studio. Max had his usual magnificent Christmas tree, this year drenched in glittering spun glass. He served a drink made of gin and cherry brandy, and all kinds of delicacies to eat. We talked for hours. Much discussion of the Nazis and Allies, and Russia and Finland.

Dash left early, having been requested by Catherine Hare to escort her to a dinner dance. I went by taxi to Isador's party. Isador had several negroes as attendants, including one to check hats and coats. More than a hundred guests had been at his party at one time or other and there was still a large number. The people were spread out both upstairs and down. I saw Junior, Muriel Phillipson, and Helen Falconer, who was at a sort of bar upstairs. She told me, "I always thought of you as a snob." I don't know why. I met her only once, about ten years ago. I chatted with her and hugged her once.

Among the last of the guests was a dark-haired young chap who was rather far gone. Somehow we left together and he went home with me in a taxi. Don't know what time it was, or what we were hearing on the radio, but the idea of seeing the new year in at midnight escaped my befuddled mind altogether. My guest, in the middle of a glass of wine, got up and wove his way to the bedroom. I found him undressing for bed. He was much drunker than I.

# 1940

*Saturday, 13 January 1940*

I still look with amazement at those magical figures *1940* on the cover of my diary. It doesn't seem possible that we actually are in the year 1940, which once seemed so far in the future, like a year that could never arrive.

A bitter, intolerable wind out of the northwest. By the time I got to Pennsylvania Avenue, I began to feel almost faint from my struggle against the cold and the wind. Walked over to the reflecting pool where hundreds of people, mostly young, were skating—bright colors in the clothing, and bright, pleasing young faces. Victrola records were played through a loud speaker, making a gala atmosphere. There was even a policeman on skates to keep order in the crowd.

Now in my nest. Interference on my radio from the new neon sign downstairs in the Cunningham dance studio window. To my disgust the Cunningham woman kept on going after the time she usually stops on Saturday night. Laughter and applause of her students pounded up faintly through the floor to my room. Dash stopped in for wine. He didn't stay long, though. I went out to the Lafayette Café. It was raining again and misty. The Capitol Dome dissolved into the hazy sky, in spite of the struggling skylights. Dash says that when I got home I couldn't get my door unlocked, so he came down in his bathrobe and opened it for me. I don't remember that. This is really too much. I do remember wandering into Nicky's place to join him and his friend. We danced and had a good time and were quite gay. Afterward I fell asleep in my nest and woke at five in the morning, fully dressed with all the lights on and the radio going, but no sound from it except a buzz of static.

### Tuesday, 5 March 1940

Eunice served a delicious dinner in her beautiful new home on Connecticut Avenue, with roast pork and dressing and other things. Leroy dropped in. Years ago he was a young friend of Henry's; now he is worth more than $100,000. He and Henry discussed law and business. Leroy has fattened and has so much assurance that he was amazing to me. We listened on the radio to "Pot o' Gold" while Eunice was doing the dishes. A man in Bradford, Pennsylvania, failed to answer the telephone so he will get $100 instead of $1800, and the pot next week will be $2800.

When I left I went downtown on the streetcar. Looked out at the cold March night and felt a vague deep dejection, inexplicable and crushing. Thought of the literary endeavors I never get done, my weak succumbing to every indulgence, the disorder that has taken over my apartment. I was glad to see Dash entering our building ahead of me. His cheery smile warmed me.

> *"Pot o' Gold."* This radio quiz show, with hosts Rush Hughes and Ben Gramer, played on NBC starting in 1939. While listeners were being telephoned to be asked prize-winning questions, music played to build tension. When contestants answered their phones, Gramer made famous the phrase, "Stop the music!"

### Thursday, 30 May 1940

Had coffee at People's Drug Store and read the *News*—horrible accounts of the Nazi air attack on British troops retreating from Dunquerque and the Belgian coast. When I got home I invited Dash down for sherry. We chatted while I rushed through my parting for my little seashore vacation. Hastened off through the chill rain.

### Friday, 31 May 1940 (Norfolk, Virginia)

Sultry and hot in Norfolk. I walked to Child's for breakfast and there, oddly enough, encountered my brother Henry, who paid for my breakfast. Dad had several days ago told me that Henry expected to be in Norfolk. Henry leapt up unexpectedly and called Eunice, who planned to take the train down for the weekend. I set off in the brilliant sunshine up the beach. Tumbling breakers and sand dunes and wavy lines of deposited drift. Was amazed to run into Isador, stark naked and bronzed on the lonely beach. He was delighted to see me. He is staying with Bob Estelwater in a cabin on the Seashore State Park.

Back by bus and telephoned Henry, but he was not in. Went out to Old Heidelberg. The place was swarming with slim, handsome sailors in white. From the misty night outside, I heard foghorns, soft whistles, and signals.

### Monday, 10 June 1940

A rainy dawn. When Dash, Nicky, Max and I came out of the bar, Max found that his battery was dead. He had to call the AAA, and we were towed in through silent Washington streets past houses full of sleepers. Then a black, bleak day. The foul gangster Mussolini has entered the war on the Nazis' side, just when France stands with her back to the wall and the barbarians are thundering at the gates of Paris.

### Monday, 17 June 1940

When I got up I turned on the radio for the news. "France has surrendered," were the first words that came. I simply collapsed in my armchair and cried. When I dressed I put on a black tie for the first time since the twenties.

# 1941

### Wednesday, 15 January 1941

Steady rain. I slept through my alarm but Dash woke me as he was leaving. I heard him announce through my closed door, "Get up at once. You've been snoring so loudly that I thought it was someone knocking on my door." Dragged myself out of bed feeling dazed. Opened the bedroom window and snuggled back into my warm bed and slept till midafternoon.

When I finally got dressed I took a walk down to the south bank of the Tidal Basin. There the shoreline is being completely revised in order to fit the now nearly completed Jefferson Memorial. A dredge splashed into the icy water and hauled up great mouthfuls of black mud. I wish I didn't have to work for a living! How many times Max has said I make him think of a bird in a cage! Maybe I am a misfit, but all I want is to enjoy life in my own way. I kept on thinking of James Joyce. He is gone—and Thomas Wolfe is gone—two of the greatest writers of my time. But I am left and why couldn't I yet accomplish something?

In the evening Dash stopped by for a stern moment. "Jeb, you are devoting your life to drinking and carousing, and your office eventually will find they can get on without you . . . " I returned to my armchair feeling unhappy, insecure, and trapped.

### Saturday, 1 November 1941

Paradise lost. Expelled from the Garden of Eden so our apartment building can be torn down and replaced by another—all of us scattered to the winds. Dash and Max were lucky enough to engage the top floor of a building on I Street. Nicky has found a two-room apartment in Georgetown. And here I am sitting among unpacked crates and boxes in my new, silent, lonely apartment on Massachusetts Avenue—and so what?

### Wednesday, 3 December 1941

I walked the long way homeward past the dear old apartment, our erstwhile happy home. Observed the blank, empty windows and was overwhelmed with regret that our establishment there had to be broken up. It used to be that just Dash's footsteps overhead gave me warmth and companionship. Hastened on through the stingingly cold night. After dinner, wanting to see Dash, I telephoned from the drugstore. There was no answer. I walked through the pelting rain to their building. Stared up at the dark windows and longed to be snug in Dash and Max's new place—so cheerful, with the familiar pictures and objects about. I rang their bell, waiting a futile moment for an answer.

Home and puttered around. I love to hear the rain beating on the skylight of my kitchen. Like Thomas Wolfe's mother, "I love the night," and I find it as hard to get to bed as to get up. But once I start going to bed how wonderful it is to sink into the soft sheets under my green Mexican blanket and drift off to slumber and dreams . . .

*Sunday, 7 December 1941*

A momentous day in history. I was at the house looking over old family snapshots, when suddenly the radio announced that the Japanese had bombed Honolulu and the Philippines, and declared war on the United States and Great Britain. The family gathered around the radio, tremendously upset and excited. Dad's reaction seemed to be amazement that Japan should do such a thing. Eunice spoke of the girls whose sweethearts were among the soldiers killed. Henry made cynical remarks, and Dad became furious. Mama was upset and tried to make peace with them. Outside, a little boy went by calling extra papers. Mama and I, both agitated, bought copies.

Later at night, downtown, many extra policemen strode restlessly about in the vicinity of the White House. The two Executive Avenues were closed to ordinary traffic. Lights shone from windows in the White House. Many lights, too, at the State Department. Tomorrow will come President Roosevelt's message to Congress, to be followed undoubtedly by a declaration of war.

> **Bombing of Honolulu and the Philippines.** *This was the historic surprise attack by the Japanese on Pearl Harbor. Approximately 3,500 American sailors, marines, and civilians were killed or wounded. The United States responded by declaring war on Japan and entering the world war.*

*Monday, 8 December 1941*

Along with the Contadeluci, the Green, and a horde of others, I hastened down the hall to Mrs. Thatcher's radio to hear the President's speech. Junior, scurrying past in the opposite direction, invited me to listen over his automobile radio. I was glad to accept. We hastily set out for the parking lot. There in the front seat of Junie's Oldsmobile, I listened to President Roosevelt's momentous address, his declaration of war, while I gazed through the window to a stately magnolia that presided over the yard of an old home on Maryland Avenue. I was deeply stirred, but kept my emotions under control.

Junie and I stayed on in his car to hear the debate in the House of Representatives, and finally the results of the Senate and House votes—82 to 0, and 288 to 1 respectively. The pathetic pacifistic bitch from Montana, Jeanette Rankin, was the only one in Congress to vote against a declaration of war. I told Junior emphatically, "God knows what her reasoning is. Japan has already declared war, so our only alternative is to surrender." Junior snapped, "Probably the idiotic female is in favor of that."

> **Jeanette Rankin** *(1880–1973) was a suffragist, pacifist, and Republican congresswoman from Montana. She had earlier been one of forty-nine members of Congress who*

*opposed entry into World War I; then, as Jeb notes, she was the sole member of Congress to oppose declaration of war against Japan after the bombing of Pearl Harbor.*

*Tuesday, 9 December 1941*

A story circulated around the office that New York was at that minute being bombed. I called up Dash, but he had heard nothing in the State Department about such an attack.

Later, while the Green was getting ready to read proof with me, she said, "You have to give the Japanese credit for doing a smart job of it. You can't expect scruples in war nowadays." I flared up and suggested she should join the Japanese army. Miss Contadeluci chuckled, and the flustered Green said, "Well! We treated Japan badly enough to *make* them attack us." I replied sarcastically, "Yes, our own country is always wrong and the enemy is always right." The Green made no reply, but as she read from the galley proof her voice trembled more and more. Finally she stopped, saying, "That's all I'm going to read," and dashed from the room. What a woman! She is a crackpot and I must not take her seriously.

> **"We treated Japan badly enough . . . "** *Mrs. Green is probably referring to the fact that in March of 1941, without Congressional approval, Roosevelt froze the external money assets of Japan and cut off Japan's oil supply.*

# 1942

*Monday, 16 February 1942*

I weighed 183 pounds this morning. It seems incredible. Must try to cut down on my weight. For years, I weighed around 145 pounds, and then in the last two years I have shot up to 183. It simply is too much. My belly is extended in an unseemly line beyond my chest. I don't like it.

Got off work early to register for conscription, for the second time in my life, the first being back in September of 1918. Took the streetcar in a pouring rain out into Georgetown. Splashed over to Gordon Junior High School. It was the end of my trousers crease below the knees. A schoolteacher registered me—a not overly brilliant woman in her late forties. Out again through the rain to Hammond's Bar. Had a number of beers.

When I left I decided to go by the old apartment. Trudged through the heavy rain past the dark building and saw that Dash's apartment on the top floor was entirely gone. It made me heartsick. Work had started on the destruction of my floor, but the window frames were intact. What a damnable chance that we had to lose that place! Sloshed back to my hermitage, singing aloud in the rain the old tune that my mother used to sing to me:

> Gaily the troubadour came from the war,
> And as he rode along strummed his guitar,
> Singing, "From Palestine, hither I come.
> Lady love, lady love, welcome me home."

I have remembered those lines all my life. It is now 3:40. What an hour to go to bed. I seem to be sliding downhill. Well, the war has done tremendous things to me—I don't mean since Pearl Harbor, I mean since May of 1929. From the radio comes "Parlez-moi de l'amour"—melancholy, haunting echo of France.

### Tuesday, 24 February 1942

When I got up I found an airmail special-delivery letter from Lansing Tower, saying he was arriving for a classified temporary assignment in Washington. He suggested I call a Miss Lewis at Censorship for details of his arrival. To his letter he added a postscript—"Does Hotel Alexander have any space?" I was horrified. My place is so disorderly that I don't welcome visitors. I felt panic-stricken at the thought of having to clean the junk off my living room couch to make a bed for Lansing Tower. When I got to the office I called Miss Lewis at Censorship. She exclaimed, "I didn't know he was expected here. That's exciting!" She went off and found Lieutenant Somebody and returned to the telephone with the news: Lansing is expected in two weeks. The unfortunate part is, I have been realizing how much I need a vacation. Have been thinking of going off just at the time when Lansing is expected. Perhaps I shall get away, anyway.

### Monday, 9 March 1942 (New York City)

The last day of my little vacation in New York City. Walked along dreary Fifty-second to the river front to see the wreck of the beautiful ship *Normandie*. She lay greasy and fire-stained, half under water, a stricken hulk like her motherland, France. As I got there, fire engines came tearing up alongside and traffic was diverted. I saw no smoke and they eventually quieted down. I said good-bye to the once grand and lovely *Normandie* and started back.

Had a hankering for the cozy Park Circle Tavern, which I visited Saturday night, so I went up there. By the time I reached the bar the rain had soaked my scant hair and soon would have been running down my neck. I settled in at the corner of the bar. Watched a girl who was tight and had become tiresome by saying in a strong New York accent, "Good-bye, Mr. Chips—Mr. Potato Chips," to everyone she talked with. Plain, not young, wearing glasses, yet she has sexuality, vivacity, and the ability to attract men. She drew to her side a boyish sailor. Another girl joined them. A number of them left together, including the glasses and the sailor. I left, too, out into the wind and the rain. Stopped in another bar. A soldier and a marine were being harangued by a loud-mouthed, offensive man with a strong accent. His English was so bad that I couldn't figure out what he was driving at. I decided he was a Hitlerite and asked the bartender to throw the Nazi out or have him arrested. The bartender made him lower his voice. He told me the man was born in Colombia.

Out into New York's streets again. Stopped in the Esquire, and looking around, I realized that it was a queer place, although sedate. It seems to be the most popular place along that stretch of Sixth Avenue, for that matter. Had two beers and went on to the Alton, a bar that seemed to be a hangout for Scandinavians. An Icelander was drunk and asleep with his head on the bar. His friends were trying to rouse him when I left. Thus ended another siege of pub-crawling. I enjoy it, but sometimes become lonely.

> **Normandie.** *She was a French luxury liner, in her day the fastest in the world, able to cross the Atlantic in under four days. In February 1942, a workman's torch accidentally set the ship afire in New York harbor. Jeb loved the SS* Normandie *in part because he loved ships and the sea, but also because on more than one of his annual summer trips to Europe he crossed on the beautiful* Normandie.

> **"Good-bye, Mr. Chips."** *The woman whom Jeb called "the glasses" probably was not referring to the novel of that name by James Hilton, but more likely to Metro-Goldwyn-Mayer's highly successful 1939 film, starring Robert Donat as the dignified schoolteacher.*

### Saturday, 11 April 1942

The wacky Green lost a file of correspondence that was supposed to be returned to another division. I lost patience and gave her a thorough bawling out. She searched for hours, tearful and penitent, but never found the file. Idiotic fool! Dash called up to have lunch with me and to borrow money to pay for the bridgework he is having done on his teeth. He never calls me unless he wants to borrow money. We met and lunched at Evergreen. They had some of my favorite foods—onion soup and beet greens. He told me that Max has escaped the draft, being 4-F because of his diabetes.

After lunch we walked in a light drizzle to the Corcoran Gallery. Looked at the Washington Water Color Club exhibition. We learned that Susan B. Chase, whose watercolor of George Washington's headquarters I purchased years ago from Meg Deveraux, was at the desk. She had two paintings in the show. Dash voted for her picture, *Somebody's Garden,* for popular prize.

Raining hard when we parted. I took a streetcar home. Found a drinking party in the apartment on the second floor, and the apartment of the five gals at the rear was also in full blast—an apparent combination of forces. When I got to my own flight, a sailor in white was violently embracing a little gal under the stairway.

### Wednesday, 6 May 1942

After work to People's Drug Store. Had to turn in the used tin tube to get a new tube of shaving cream. Tried to get after-shave lotion but apparently no more for the duration because of the alcoholic content. No matches with my cigarettes and no paper around them until I requested it. They had no Lyons tooth powder. The toilet paper shortage seems to be over, so I got eight rolls.

Then to Crescent. Soldiers and sailors going in and out. I played Viennese waltzes on the machine. Late in the evening, who should sashay in but Dr. Houndstooth, the eccentric old fellow who used to live next to me at Wu's place. I was delighted to see him, even though he has become so oddly animated-looking that I had to struggle to avoid feeling embarrassed about sitting with him. We drank a number of beers. He pointed out four women in a booth as being "women lovers" and "lesbians." I told him, "Do you want to shoot them? They were born that way, and we might as well be tolerant."

### Sunday, 10 May 1942

Isador and I had a quiet evening together in his apartment. He seemed unusually calm and contented, in an excellent mood. He said he would have told me about his marriage had I come out to see him on any one of the occasions when he invited me. He and Rachael, the widow of his long-time naval officer friend Harry (whom I used to know and like very well, and who was lost at sea), were married last week in Alexandria. About a dozen close friends attended the ceremony. Isador and his wife drove down to Williamsburg for a honeymoon. He showed me wedding gifts and served mince pie that he had made—quite good, too.

### Saturday, 23 May 1942

Got my draft questionnaire filled out. It must be in by Monday. I might be thrown into jail if it isn't. Called Dash to arrange for lunch. We had a pleasant meal, except that as usual he finished before I did and was restless as always when waiting for me. Still, I enjoyed being with him. We walked down to the Jefferson

Memorial, now completed except for the statue. It was Dash's first visit there. We sat on the stone coping, talking for such a long time that I became sunburned on my forehead. At the moment when we stood up, the air-raid test alarm sounded. All traffic in Washington halted and there was a stillness over the whole city.

### Sunday, 2 August 1942

I was awakened by a knocking at my door. Jumped out of bed and combed my tousled hair and made myself fairly presentable even in pajamas—the canary-yellow silk pajamas that Dash gave me way back at Christmastime in 1935, with the word "Jeb" embroidered in purple thread over the pocket. Rushed to the door just in time to hear Nicky Bowman's voice below me and the slam of the front door. Ran to the front windows.

Saw dear little Nicky, wearing his white Naval officer's uniform, already too far down the street for me to call. Because he graduated from the Citadel, he was offered an Army commission, but preferred to join the Navy. He got to the corner, hesitated, and turned toward the Capitol. It was probably the last I'll see of him before the war is over, and possibly the last in life, for after he receives training he'll be sent to sea. I felt guilty and sorry not to have gotten to the door in time to invite him in. For the rest of the day my mind was up in the air, winging westward through the clouds with Nicky, toward the Pacific and the grim sea war.

### Saturday, 5 September 1942

Uptown through streets swarming with sailors and soldiers. Went to see *Mrs. Miniver* at the Columbia. The film was wonderful. I agree with the critics that it is among the best ever produced. I had a hard time holding back tears. I strolled away along I Street, noting scattered lights in old 1607, now occupied again after months of vacancy following Wu's death. It was strange to think that the home in which I had lived for ten years was occupied by newcomers, ignorant of me, of Houndstooth, of Wu, of all the past inhabitants.

Through the breezy night to a delightful gathering at Dash and Max's apartment. Isador was there. It was a wonderful evening with old friends exchanging news, telling stories, listening to Max play the piano, drinking highballs. Dash passed around a letter he received from Nicky Bowman. Nicky has been sent to the Navy radio school at the University of Colorado in Boulder. From there he'll be assigned to a ship in the Pacific Sector.

Max told us that Tommy Freskin was rejected by the military, but is giving up his job to become a Red Cross ambulance driver. And Isador said he had heard that Tony Baretto has long been in the Army, stationed in St. Petersburg, Florida, unhappy, assigned much to KP and stable duty.

**Mrs. Miniver** *(1942). Starring Greer Garson and Walter Pidgeon, MGM's touching film was a tribute to the spirit of the British during World War II.*

*Thursday, 17 September 1942*

I had hardly got home when Isador arrived, bringing me back the Havelock Ellis book, *Sexual Inversion,* which I lent Junior way back in 1928. Junior left for Corpus Christi to live, on the first of the month, and Isador salvaged my book for me after fourteen years. I served sherry and we had quite a nice visit and conversation. Isador told me of Junior's vicissitudes. It seemed Junie got terribly drunk the night before he set off for Texas and went to see Catherine Hare and Mrs. Hare-Worth and revealed to the two women scandalous episodes of Randall's past life. To think that Catherine was treated that way! Damn Junie, anyway!

Isador was to sleep above Whyte's bookshop before leaving for his wife's Connecticut farm, since they have rented out the Georgetown house. When he left, I prepared for bed. At midnight came a constant knocking and I found it was Isador. He had been locked out and wanted to sleep on my couch. We talked more, I wrote my diary and did some chores, and neither of us got to bed till around 2:30.

*Saturday, 19 September 1942*

Lunch with Dash at Evergreen. Afterward, we walked down the railroad yard, seeing a couple of troop trains go by, to the Tidal Basin. We went to the shady grove behind the John Paul Jones statue and for once found a vacant bench. We sat for over an hour, talking mostly of the war. Dash said he had inquired about his prospects and had been told he probably would be called in the next thirty days. That means me, too, for I am ahead of him in order. The dogs of war are panting behind us. When I think of being drafted I feel terrified. I would make a no-good soldier; I couldn't take it at all. Surely they would not want me! Dash on the other hand wants to go, and only worries about holding onto his apartment for the duration.

Eventually we walked up Seventeenth and parted at the Avenue. I went on to the Trans-Lux. The color picture, *The Battle of Midway,* affected me quite emotionally and I couldn't help weeping quietly through most of it. The incidental music—"Star Spangled Banner," "America," and "Onward Christian Soldiers" —had a powerful effect.

*Sunday, 25 October 1942*

A night that brought horrible unhappiness. I had gone up to Max and Dash's place for the first time in a month or more. While they were preparing to go out to supper we talked about changes in Washington and other things pertaining to the war. When they went out I stayed alone, seating myself at their dining room table to read the *Times*. It seemed like the old days—the *New York Times* and Dash's place on a Sunday night. But on the table lay State Department documents, the top paper marked "classified." I saw enough of the page to read Hans Vermehren's name. Other pages described other men.

I was reading the material when Dash and Max returned. Max, seeing what I held in my hand, disappeared into his room. Dash hung up his coat, watching me. "That's classified," he said. I asked, "Are Hans and these others incarcerated for the same reason?" Dash said briefly, "Pretty obvious." I went to the window and gazed out into the darkness. Dash said, "Not one on the list is 'valuable' in the State sense. If not for Pamela, nobody would try to locate them at all." When I left, I felt almost as sick-hearted as I can remember.

> ***Homosexuality in Nazi Germany.*** *What happened to Hans is not known. Homosexual practices among men were illegal in Nazi Germany, though lesbianism was not. Under Hitler, thousands of homosexual men were imprisoned in German concentration camps. When the camps were liberated by U. S. troops, individuals who were incarcerated because of German laws, as opposed to individuals who had been placed in concentration camps for political or ethnic reasons, were not freed. A brief, grainy black-and-white piece of film footage from the era, available in a documentary film called* Pink Triangle, *shows a homosexual man, his starved legs dangling, being carried by two U. S. soldiers back into a prison.*

*Friday, 13 November 1942*

In my mail box was the hated and feared notice to report for my physical examination. God knows I am patriotic, but the military life is simply not for me. I got on the bus in a daze. Rode along looking at autumn leaves sweeping across streets in gusts of wind. Then a weary day at the office. The Green was absent after her near-hysterics yesterday. The Contadeluci got away early. Cox showed me letters from the department's directors in Tennessee and Arkansas about the O.W.I. publication, *Negroes and the War.* The letters were pretty strong. The Arkansas director flatly refused to distribute it.

At night, Max and Dash joined me to go to see Thornton Wilder's new play, *The Skin of Our Teeth,* starring Tallulah Bankhead. I was thoroughly cheered up by the weird, utterly mad play. A little circus-like band tooted away in a box between the acts. Tallulah romped through her glorious part, and Montgomery Clift as the young son was particularly good.

> **O.W.I.** *Office of War Information, a U. S. Federal agency (1942–1945) created to disseminate information about World War II. Based on Jeb's text, it would appear that the O.W.I. publication* Negroes *and the* War *dignified the participation of African-Americans in the war effort.*

### Tuesday, 17 November 1942

I was due at Emergency Hospital at seven, but Dash had told me to get there at 6:30, to avoid waiting in line. Actually I got there at 6:45. The physical exam was futile and foolish. They admitted that all would be graded 1-A and the final decision would be left to the examiners at Fort Myer. Had a farce of a blood test. I feared it in advance, but it wasn't so bad actually. The worst moment was seeing the big bowl of bloody water, presumably disinfectant, in which instruments were dipped. Finally was examined stark naked in a cursory way and then all was over. It was a nervous ordeal. Still an interesting experience seeing the men, young and middle-aged, rich and poor, weak and strong, black, white and yellow, brought together by the inexorable dragnet of "Selective" Service.

> **Selective Service.** *Under the Selective Training and Service Act of 1940 over sixteen million men in the U.S. were registered on October 16, 1940 (the day before Jeb's forty-first birthday) for the draft. Men were subsequently classified according to eligibility to be drafted—for example, a classification of 1-A meant the individual was fit to serve in the armed forces; a classification of 4-F (such as Max received because he had diabetes) meant the individual was physically, mentally, or morally unfit. "Morally unfit" included being homosexual, but in fact innumerable gay men and women served in the armed forces during World War II.*

### Saturday, 5 December 1942

Glory be! This afternoon the War Department announced that no more men aged thirty-eight or over would be inducted. It is such a wonderful relief. Even though I was almost sure I should be rejected, still there was the horrible ordeal of going through being examined physically and otherwise.

Out after work onto Independence Avenue and recited my Saturday night incantation. It means a lot to me in shaking off the mantle of officialdom: "'Tis always Saturday night, *la trêve de Dieu.*" The quotation is from Stevenson and relates to Edinburgh, "the lamp-lit city," in his college years. I have felt that way so often that the experience has come to be a weekly ritual. Walked across the always-thrilling vista of the Mall between the Capitol and the Washington Monument. The Monument was beautiful with the afterglow behind it, the tints of amber and ash and old rose, the soft lights around the base, and two rounded elm trees in silhouette flanking the obelisk, making it more than ever like a phallic symbol.

**"La trêve de Dieu.** " *The truce of God.*


# 1943


*Saturday, 17 April 1943*

Had the alarm clock in its little tin bucket, resting astride a tin plate. Still I slept right through the din. Got to office after three. The Contadeluci was querulous, saying that she hadn't been able to do her work because of having to do mine. I didn't answer, which I have found to be the best system. Wish to God we could have our old thirty-nine-hour week back and the Government could keep its God-damned overtime pay. And I know "there's a war on." The fact is, we in the Government are guinea pigs—examples to bully private industry into accepting the forty-eight-hour week. Oh, to hell with the office.

Today I wore my beautiful new suit which I got from Woodward & Lothrop after a week for alterations. It is a Harris tweed, hand-sewn, pale brown with bits of blue and gray and whitish mixed in and shaggy loose hairs on the surface—just the sort of rough material that appeals to me. While I was going to supper, rain began to sprinkle down, but anyway, the suit is waterproof.

I strolled up to Crescent. Dash came sauntering along, intending to join me inside. He expressed admiration for my new suit, which, after all, is not commonplace. We were able to get seats at the bar. In trotted the old, unlamented rubber and pornography seller of the old days of Lafayette Square. Dash didn't have any idea who he was. Houndstooth showed up looking none the worse for wear, though he was knocked down last night by a marine. Dash asked him about the incident. Houndstooth said the marine took him for a "fairy," and hit him and knocked him off his bar stool. "You heard me falling," he said to me. "Yes," I said, "I looked around just in time to see you hit the floor."

Dash has taken to calling Houndstooth "Lord Beaverbrook," which seems to delight Houndstooth, though for that matter Houndstooth is delighted by almost anything. After a while Dash and I set out for coffee. Because of the war it is difficult to find coffee at night nowadays. We got it finally at the White Tower.

*Wednesday, 4 August 1943*

The hottest day in weeks; the humidity terrific. I wore a blue sport shirt with no coat. Busy at office. Cox took away the manuscript I still had to mark for the printer. He has no conception of the work I do—damned red-headed bastard. Then the Green was moved to a room down the hall. It became wildly upset, and dashed off saying it wanted leave to go to Colorado. Poor creature—she actually is in the way of losing her mind.

At lunch time they wouldn't let me buy butter for my potatoes. The supercilious waitress said, "This is wartime, and butter is sold only with bread." I know it is wartime!

Later at Crescent, Houndstooth joined me and started talking a blue streak. He told a stupid alleged joke about Churchill's needing an operation for hemorrhoids but they were afraid to operate because they might cut off Roosevelt's nose. I refuse to laugh at that sort of *Chicago Tribune* filth. We talked about money as usual. Then Houndstooth launched into a discussion of homosexual people. He said, "I know a man when I see one." I suppose I should feel pleased that for all these years he has put me in that class. But his conversation betrayed such prejudice that I was disgusted and wished that he would talk of something else.

*Sunday, 17 October 1943*

When I got to the house Mama greeted me with warm wishes for my birthday. Daisy and I smoked cigarettes together in the parlor. She is nearly as pretty as I remember Eunice being at that age, with the same delicately chiseled features. She told me she had tried to get into the Army Ferry Service as a flyer, but couldn't get in till June, so she plans to return to her studies at the University of South Carolina. Unpleasantness began at dinner when I disagreed with Henry's brazen dicta of disapproval about the draft. He began sneering at me for my civilian status. I snapped, "Go to hell!" and Henry replied in the same vein. He had by then finished wolfing down his dinner in his usual hoggish manner, and jumped up, stating coolly, "You are *free,* you are *unencumbered,* and *you are a slacker. "* I had become so wrought-up that my hand shook when I drank my coffee. He returned to the table for my birthday cake and ice cream, but I avoided talking to him.

Later I tried to relax and read the *Post.* Eunice and her husband and Daisy left. Eunice called out, "Good-bye, everybody!" Daisy called out, "Happy birthday, Uncle Jeb!" Henry pompously preceded his family down the walk to his Chrysler.

*Thursday, 28 October 1943*

Today is the twenty-fifth anniversary of the first time I ever saw Dash. I still remember that foggy afternoon on the athletic field at Washington & Lee. All day I had hoped that somehow I would run into him, but I hesitated to call him just for that sentimental reason. Months go by without our seeing each other.

Stepped outside after work and was surprised to find how cold it was. Wind creaked the tin pennants on the automobile lot with a doleful sound. I stopped at the Greek delicatessen. The old racketeer behind the counter didn't ask for my ration points. I gave them to him anyway. Home with my raincoat buttoned tightly about me. Yellow leaves plastered on the wet pavements. Dark wind in my face, and rain. I sang as I walked along—making up songs about "Heigh ho, the wind and the rain," and about Washington. I was thinking myself alone when a vigorous Wave, walking rapidly and suddenly, overtook me and threw me into confusion.

> **Ration points.** *Food rationing and rationing of some other goods took place in the U.S.A. during World War II. Items requiring ration points included gas, tires, shoes, sugar, coffee, and canned meats.*

> **Wave.** *A Wave was a member of the women's branch of the Navy (Women Appointed for Voluntary Emergency Service, or WAVES).*

*Tuesday, 7 December 1943*

The second anniversary of the "day of infamy." Delighted today to find in my mail a Christmas card from Nicky Bowman, from aboard an "attack transport" in the Pacific. Don't know what an "attack transport" is but it sounds like a dangerous situation for Nicky.

Temperatures stayed below freezing all day. I tried at two chain drugstores to get Camels and Lucky Strikes. Neither drugstore had Camels at all, as they are being monopolized by the Army, and they had no Luckies in cartons. As I hurried home, feeling the cold penetrate through me, I saw Dash striding into the Greek delicatessen. Followed him and gave him Nicky's letter that had been addressed in care of me. Walked shiveringly with him to his apartment to learn what Nicky had to say, but it was only a Christmas card with no message except Nicky's signature. I was disappointed to miss Max, who had gone to bed.

Quiet now, except for the hum of the refrigerator. Sometimes I feel lonely to an extent that the average person might find inconceivable. All that is something I never tell anyone. There is no one I can tell, not even Dash, who for that matter is no longer close to me as he was in past years. Oh, well, I must not whine.

*"Day of infamy."* *The "day" was December 7, 1941, when the Japanese bombed Pearl Harbor. The reference was from President Roosevelt's War Message, as read to Congress by his proxy General Watson. The exact words were, "a date which will live in infamy . . ."*

# 1944

*Monday, 6 March 1944*

Stayed after work reading my *Post,* which I hadn't had a chance to do more than look at—except for Milton Caniff's "Terry and the Pirates." That comic strip has such a fascination for me that I can never put off reading it. Usually I start reading it by the time my streetcar gets to Constitution Avenue, and finish it just before the car pulls into the tunnel at Fourteenth and C.

Strolled uptown. Noticed the budding branches of the elm trees along the street. War or no war, spring is coming to Washington. On to the Trans-Lux, where the main picture was the searingly vivid Technicolor film of the marine attack on Tarawa. Hideous fighting, dead bodies of Japanese, and most overpowering of all—bodies of our own marines in gray-green uniforms floating at the edge of the beach, bloated and stiff and some half naked, all dead and gone forever. My eyes were filled with bitter tears.

I headed for the Crescent. Ordered a beer and on the jukebox played "Down in the Valley." Listening to that haunting tune as I looked over the men gave me a feeling of sadness, and at the same time a lofty kind of exhilaration. Lots of servicemen. Some had beards—"combat kids." Near me was a marine, sad-faced, alongside a young blond sailor in whom he appeared to take an absorbing interest. A foreign-seeming chap was acting friendly with the toothy waitress. Many men were regulars. The scene, with its undertones, seemed to become crystalized while those lonesome strains of "Down in the Valley" were playing.

Felt the slap of a newspaper on my shoulder and turned around to see Isador, with a wide grin on his face. He took the seat beside me, absently drinking just one beer, falling into a noisy fit of talking. Joe, the bartender, retrieved a lady's black hat and veil that had been left in a booth, and pranced around and "camped" for a while, arousing roars of laughter—especially from Isador. I laughed too, but as a rule I dislike intensely female impersonations and feel acutely uncomfortable when I have to witness them. To our right sat the "Sailor Slug" (my private designation for him)—a pale sailor, quite uninteresting, who occasionally makes remarks and then retreats into his shell. Of course a slug has no shell, however.

I went back to the men's room and there was a boy in uniform with two artificial legs who had "passed out" sitting on the seat. Isador was behind me. Like the always Good Samaritan that he is, Isador helped to look out for the chap, who finally was got back to his booth. A common slut dressed in brilliant green sat in the place evacuated by the Slug. I was disgusted by her arguments. The "Green Hornet," as I decided to call her, raved that "England wanted to take over Ireland again," and so on. Isador was trying to give her facts, but she shouted him down. "And who's running our elections?" she yelled, and replied to her own question, "England!" There are thousands of that type, but why in hell do I have to encounter them? Winston Churchill has made it plain that the restrictions are to last only for the duration of the invasion emergency. The invasion! That ghastly business that looms closer and closer. It can't be more than a matter of a few weeks.

When Isador and I parted, I hastened home in the chill night air, wondering about the sad-faced marine and the sailor boy with his cap hanging onto the back of his bushy blond hair.

*"Terry and the Pirates."* In the intricate adventures of this comic strip, created by cartoonist Milton Caniff, the central character Terry Lee started off in 1934 as a young, blond kid, and went on to become a virile hero fighting against the Japanese as a World War II air force pilot.

*Invasion.* References made to "the invasion" in several 1944 entries of the diary were to the highly classified date for D-Day, June 6, 1944, when Allied troops landed in Normandy and fanned out over Northern France under the command of U.S. General Dwight D. Eisenhower.

### Thursday, 16 March 1944

Late in the afternoon Dash telephoned me and told me that Nicky Bowman was missing in action in New Guinea. Miss Contadeluci left the room when she realized I was receiving bad news. I put my head in my hands and cried. I remember when Nicky was a winsome boy who broke hearts—and mended them, too —and how far our thoughts were, then, from any idea that he would be lost in this hideous, horrible war. The more I have thought about the thing, the more sick with horror and overwhelmed with sadness I have become. Dear little Nicky —so often last thing at night have I thought of him when I've gone out on my back porch to enjoy a last cigarette—thought of him serving his country, those thousands of miles away.

I was too miserable to stay at work. Not wanting even the contact of strangers on a streetcar, I hurried away on foot. Thought how Nicky used to urge me to use my talents and write. After all, I believe Nicky was one of the finest persons I ever have known. Day after day we read about boys and men who have been lost, but when it is someone that we have known over the years, the tragic horror of the war is really felt.

**New Guinea.** *During February–April 1944, U.S. naval forces commanded by Admirals Halsey and Nimitz engaged in sea battles off the coast of New Guinea, preparing the way for General Douglas MacArthur's push to the Philippines.*

### Sunday, 2 April 1944

The cherry blossoms around the new Jefferson Memorial are blooming. Lots of people down there. All was bright and lazy. For a while one could forget the war. Strolled up to Crescent and found it crowded, so I had to sit "out of my neighborhood," as Dash says. Eventually I got down to the front end of the bar, and had beers and pea soup and a Swiss cheese sandwich—a combination I have found to be a solid basis for beer drinking. Dash arrived, but only for one beer. Sadly, we talked about Nicky Bowman.

Better get to bed now—almost two in the morning. Listening to WABC—right now a lovely piano rendition of Tchaikovsky's beautiful, lonely "Trinka en Traineaux"—one of my records that I got back in the twenties when I was young and probably less happy even than I am now.

### Monday, 17 April 1944

As so often is the case these days, no draft beer was being served at Crescent. They had only a weak, lousy bottle beer made at Cumberland, Maryland. The place was noisy. I felt a finger run down my back and, turning around, discovered Dash. We talked about how wearisome are our devilish wartime hours at work. But as Dash pointed out, the invasion is coming up soon.

### Friday, 5 May 1944

Took my *News* to lunch with me. In Ernie Pyle's beautifully written column there was one passage that appealed to me powerfully: "Men at home at the end of the day in the poor, narrow, beautiful security of their own walls . . . " That seemed to describe me when I return to this disorderly haven of refuge and shut out the callous world.

At night I got to Crescent moments after Dash, but slightly ahead of the blackout. We sat in a tiresome semi-darkness. In spite of several requests, the bartender wouldn't have the transom opened and had trouble with some marines. He sent for the MP's and SP's, who arrived in force. Dash and I talked with a pretty curly-haired sailor, polite and gentle. The boy made complimentary remarks about my being a gentleman, and so on. At last the blackout ended. The curly-haired sailor walked out without finishing his beer, saying he wanted fresh air. I patted him on the back and wished him good luck. Dash said, "You have an infinite capacity for being bored." I replied that I was not bored, I had found the boy an interesting character study.

I have stayed up wretchedly late. Cats have been yowling in the back alley but now all is quiet except the nocturnal hissing of the ice plant.

**MP's and SP's.** *Military Police and Naval Shore Patrol.*

**Ernie Pyle** *(1900–1945) was a highly respected American war correspondent during World War II.*

### Sunday, 28 May 1944

I was awakened by the screams and yells of the Chinese children on the pavement below. One maddening little boy kept on bleating like a goat. The Government girls upstairs opened their windows and pleadingly called down and persuaded the children to leave. I drifted off to sleep again.

Up after noon, and dressed. Took a car for the Union Station, where I lingered observing teeming hundreds of soldiers and sailors milling about and hastening away and waiting. I averted my eyes for good-byes, which make me sad. Strolled toward the Capitol. Hundreds of servicemen sleeping on the lawns. One handsome soldier, lying on his back with a girl leaning across his chest, had a conspicuous erection showing under his clothing. He didn't seem to realize it or else didn't care who saw.

**Government girls.** *In Washington the phrase was often shortened to "G-girls," a lump-name for thousands of entry-level women in innumerable agency offices.*

### Saturday, 3 June 1944

Another sultry day. We kept the windows open to get the breeze. Miss Contadeluci and I both left promptly. Outside, the sun was bathed in orange mist and could be looked at. To Palace Laundry to ask about my missing sheets and towels, and reluctantly accepted someone else's nameless package, which contained approximately the same thing—a couple of sheets, pillowcases, and towels. The woman assured me that they were sterilized and that I would do better to accept them than to wait for months to get repaid for the loss. Took them

home. Spent a while at the back windows. On the roof next door, a broad-shoul-
dered young man was enjoying the last rays of a sunbath, face down and almost
nude.

Got away to Crescent and was disgusted to see a sign saying, "Two beers to a
customer." I asked Joe whether it meant two beers for each person, two beers an
hour, or two beers each time one came in. He replied seriously, "It means two
beers every three hours." I gave up. Anyway, the old fool is going to apply the rule
only to strangers. I am a privileged character there, and expect to pay no attention to the rule.

### Monday, 5 June 1944

Radio stations were still going around 2:30 in the morning when I got home.
Wondering if this could be the night of the invasion, I hurried to my chair to
hear the news. It was being announced that German stations have reported that
the Allies have landed on the Continent. The Blue Network announced that
because of "the importance of tonight's invasion operations," they will stay on
the air. So this is it. I intend to stay up and listen all night. To hell with the office!

Now 3:30, and it has been announced from Eisenhower's headquarters that
naval powers have begun landing operations in Northern France. So this really is
D-Day. Over there, our men have invaded France for better or for worse, and I
can do nothing. God help them!

### Tuesday, 6 June 1944

Arrived at the office in mid-afternoon. Mrs. Thatcher's radio was blaring out
King George's speech, with the door of her room open. Usually she shuts doors
and transoms whenever she turns on her radio, being a timid person. Everyone
seemed to be interested in the invasion but taking it rather in stride. I walked out
before 5:30, like hundreds of others. There was a weird light in the sky.
Washington's wet streets reflected the light. I thought of the boys overseas fighting and dying, and thought of poor dear Nicky Bowman. When I got to
Crescent, the place was terrifically noisy—the jukebox screeching at top power
for the benefit of horse-laughing marines. In spite of the "Two beers to a customer" sign, the beers flowed free and easy to anyone who wanted them.

### Sunday, 11 June 1944

Intended to arrive at the house on time, but I got to fixing up my white shoes
and getting out my Palm Beach suit for its first wear of the year. Got off late,
went by taxi, and found the family had a pool on the time of my arrival. Henry
won $1.00.

We sat on the porch and talked about the invasion. Rocking in a rocking chair gave me a peaceful feeling. I gazed at the breeze-stirred trees and enjoyed myself. Daisy drove away with a young air force pilot. Later, after Eunice and Henry went home, Dad lectured me about being intolerant of Henry. He reminded me that Henry had done his share of fighting as an aviator in World War I. I told him emphatically, "Everything for Henry now is sheer materialism. I cannot put up with his unpatriotic, seditious conversation and don't intend to listen to it." Dad begged me to come out to the house more often, saying that he and Mama would soon pass away and I'd then have no house to go to, just to make me feel miserable and guilty. I did feel miserable and guilty. Walked away in the night filled with inexpressible sadness.

### Friday, 16 June 1944

Out to Isador's place in Georgetown. His wife is away for a week in Connecticut. No answer to my knocks, so I waited on the bench outside the door. Isador finally arrived breathlessly. We set out for dinner and as we walked through Georgetown he pointed out home after home and told me its history or who was living there, or had lived there. Isador knows Georgetown thoroughly. We strolled across the bridge to the Hot Shoppe in Rosslyn. The Potomac looked still and beautiful and the woods dreamlike in their hazy green. A storm was blowing up, and after we got to the Hot Shoppe it poured rain. The food was good but expensive.

Spent the rest of the evening in a wing chair in Isador's living room. Rain cascaded noisily off the roof. We drank scuppernong wine—pleasant-flavored and not too sweet. Isador showed me innumerable books, mostly pertaining to his favorite subject, the writers and artists of the late nineteenth century. The rain poured. I stayed on. Isador kept showing me things and handing me things to look at. I began to want to get away. It was not till about one in the morning that the rain slackened and I could dash away past the sleeping houses of old Georgetown.

### Thursday, 17 August 1944

The Mall was filled with driving rain that rendered the Capitol invisible. When I arrived at Crescent, someone had turned on the music machine and the din of those swing noises was maddening. It seems incredible that anyone could pay cold cash to listen to such a blare of noises.

I was joined in conversation with a young, handsome marine. He wore no insignia to indicate where he had been, remarking, "The problem of laundry is enough without sewing on those little stripes from Guadalcanal." Late in the evening old Houndstooth marched in, full of high spirits, and joined the marine and me. He told a joke about Winston Churchill's visit at the White House. "Late at night President Roosevelt comes along the corridor and sees Churchill sneaking out of Eleanor's room. He shakes his forefinger at Churchill and says, 'Winnie, I don't want any more of that!' Churchill replies, 'I don't blame you, Frank. I don't want any more of it either.'" We discussed the war news, which continues encouraging, with the exception of the horrible robot bombs that keep taking their terrific toll of lives and buildings. Our troops are about thirty miles from Paris. It thrills me to think of Paris on the verge of liberation. Tomorrow, the 18th, is the day I picked in October 1943, for the end of the German part of the war. I was too optimistic. Still, the date Miss Contadeluci picked went by months ago.

*Friday, 1 September 1944*

Wound up the last manuscript and walked out of the office feeling a sense of accomplishment. Interesting to see the servicemen, many with girls, pouring along the rain-washed streets. Handsome lads—more power to 'em. And one wishes—

To Crescent and sat down with my *News*. Relaxed with draft beer. Reports tonight are that our tank columns have reached the German border and others have crossed into Belgium. Glory be! It was exactly five years ago that Archdevil Hitler began this hideous war. How vividly do I remember the morning—stepping out on deck on the steamer that brought Catherine Hare and me from Rotterdam. We saw, gleaming in the sunshine of Norway, the Hotel Victoria and the white wooden buildings along the waterfront of Stavanger. The radio officer, in his precise foreign English, told us that Hitler had invaded Poland. The war had started. But the beasts can't last much longer, now.

*Friday, 8 September 1944*

To go up to Dash and Max's party I changed from my rain-wrinkled gray suit into my white suit, with a bow tie, and felt distinguished-looking in my harmlessly vain way. Got there just as Isador and Bill Courtland arrived. I hadn't seen Bill since that summer night in 1929 when he visited my room. He liked "Pagan Love Song"; I liked "Carolina Moon." We got along, though. Now Bill is a worn-looking man. He went through the adventures of being torpedoed on the *Zam-Zam* in 1941. Then he was a German prisoner, and finally was transferred by exchange back to the United States. He is lame from an injury while a prisoner and walks with a stick.

Isador played on the Victrola the lilting strains of "Lili Marlene." Dash and

Max served bourbon highballs, potato chips, pretzels, and stuffed olives. Before we left, Isador gave me a package. When I opened it at home I found it was volume of Rainer Maria Rilke's poem, *Das Marienleben,* a gift in honor of our twenty years of friendship. Faithful Isador!

### Tuesday, 27 September 1944

As I walked out in the sunshine, the dancing shadows of the sycamore leaves on the sidewalk gave me a thrill of joy. A certain slanting, shapely sycamore tree on C Street is one of my favorite trees. I always look up its trunk that inclines strongly toward the south and have an uplifting feeling, as if I were leaping its length into the green foliage. Recently I have taken to touching its trunk as I pass—a love pat. Walked up Pennsylvania Avenue in front of the White House. That stretch of walk was reopened to the public about a month ago. A lieutenant squatted unabashed on the walk to feed a troop of pigeons and squirrels. He grinned at a couple of pretty women who were passing by and who seemed to be amused.

Continued onward filled with gnawing hunger—the craving for love and affection. Just a love-starved old bachelor. I think of myself always as a young man and I dress the same as I have done for the last twenty years. But that's a good thing, I believe. No use being old before my time.

Tonight I browsed in a number of my books. Began to read about birds. My imagination has been quite captured. If only it could be captured in a way that could bring me to settle down to the toil of composition, to try and accomplish something while there is time! There still is time. I shall be forty-five next month, but presumably a number of years remain to me. And now here I am in my pajamas, ready to go to bed. Shall have to put on the green Mexican blanket tonight.

### Saturday, 30 September 1944

I walked outside and rounded the building in the sunlit drizzle—just enough moisture to feel on my forehead and to enjoy, but not enough to wet the pavements. Chanted as usual from Stevenson's essay the line, "'Tis always Saturday night—*la trêve de Dieu,*" as I walked uptown with hands in trouser pockets and my raincoat fluttering behind me. Everything was bathed in a misty glow. As I approached Pennsylvania Avenue, I saw hundreds of starlings in the air. At Crescent I got a seat at the bar. A decent-looking young marine sat next to me and rubbed elbow and knee against mine. I ignored him.

# 1945

*Sunday, 25 March 1945*

The din of those horrid screaming Chinese pests out in front kept me tossing fitfully. I felt like beating out the brains of the one that bleats like a goat, pretending to imitate the sound of an "ack-ack" gun. Read the *Post* and then decided that I must get out to enjoy the sunshine. Walked downtown, facing returning crowds from the cherry blossoms, largely servicemen. Strolled along the river's brim watching sailors in heat kissing and hugging girls as they lay upon the lawns.

Tonight I have been daydreaming about Vincent, my ideal comrade of years ago. He has become in my imaginings my distant cousin from Virginia. I am at ease with Vincent, clever and not tongue-tied. The dream became so real that I actually saw him sitting in the arm chair in his naval officer's uniform. His presence soothes me and makes me feel happy. Dash arrives and I introduce them and the three of us have a delightful evening together. Dreams, dreams!

*Monday, 9 April 1945*

Mrs. Green returned to the office after more than two weeks of work on her mouth. The dentist gave her plates but they must have been misfits. Today she had only front teeth and talked like an old, toothless woman. The Contadeluci was having a lull in her work and was a veritable fussbudget. She cleaned out the files for hours and said something about doing two people's work, but when I asked her which two people she referred to, the subject was changed.

Late in the afternoon, to my astonishment Catherine Hare strolled into the office. She placed her handbag on my desk and looked around the room. "To think that after our European adventures together," she told me in the presence of the Contadeluci and the toothless, open-mouthed Green, "now we never see each other!" I didn't know what to do with her under the circumstances. I took her upstairs for tea. She chattered about her two boys and their lessons, and told me that last summer she had been in Los Angeles and had run into José and Elise in a nightclub there. Good old José and Elise!

I didn't ask her about Randall, dreading what she might say as a result of those imbecilic, drunken revelations from Junie Whorley about Randall's past. But Catherine volunteered, "Randy is still in London. We've separated—have you heard?" I said, "No." She switched the conversation to Baudelaire, who is her latest interest, and gradually we began to talk of the twentieth and eighteenth centuries in comparison with each other. When we parted at the elevator she warmly said good-bye and said she would call me so we could have dinner together some time.

Spent much of the evening thinking of Randall and Catherine. Played Burl Ives records while manicuring my nails. Became melancholy. So much unhappiness in the world! Had Mother only lived I'd have been a different man. Now I'm ready for sleep. I have been wandering off in daydreams, so that writing in my diary has stretched out considerably. I keep on thinking I ought to write poetry—write it until I learn to do it well. When I was eighteen I felt that my destiny was writing—that I was going to be a great author. And now here I am, forty-five, my hair thin, my waist thickened, standing at my bureau in my green and floral pajamas, ready to go to bed. Rainwater is dripping from the roofs and the nighthawk is crying as it flies about in the darkness.

### Thursday, 12 April 1945

A day of grief for the world. At the White House hundreds of people stood on the north sidewalk or in Franklin Park—silent, grief-stricken figures. The death of President Roosevelt is a hard blow. Cars left the gate and flashlight pictures were made. To think of this terrible tragedy, just in time to turn victory into ashes.

### Saturday, 14 April 1945

We were notified that we were to be excused to attend the memorial for President Roosevelt. I had planned to go view the procession regardless. I have felt a personal sense of loss. Up to Twelfth and Constitution Avenue. The most silent crowd I have ever known lined the Avenue. Many negroes were present. A girl behind me was sobbing audibly. That made it all the more difficult for me to hold back tears. I succeeded, through a stern effort. I thrust my left hand into my trouser pocket and clutched my wadded handkerchief. With my right hand I pressed a match cover. Even so, I had to struggle to keep the tears back. It was sad to see those young men of all the different services, many of whom remembered no other President, marching in the funeral procession of their Commander-in-Chief.

The caisson, bearing the flag-draped coffin, appeared, and there was Franklin D. Roosevelt returning for his last trip to Washington—a dead body inside a casket instead of an animated man waving to the crowds. A great man had died before he could take the triumph of victory. In the elm trees overhead birds sang, oblivious of the mourning throngs. Lucky birds in the leafy treetops, not knowing humankind's heartache.

*Wednesday, 2 May 1945*

To Trans-Lux and there saw the unutterably horrible and gruesome pictures of the German concentration camps. Heaps of starved bodies. Gaunt survivors. All that we have been reading about in the newspapers. Tears ran down my cheeks, especially when I let myself realize that Hans must have been among those who had experienced such suffering.

*Wednesday, 8 August 1945*

Did straightening up of the most obvious places that would reflect upon me when Isador arrived. He got here and we drank sherry while darkness gradually settled around us. It was terribly hot. We both had our shirts open. We talked of friends and acquaintances, mostly of Harry, Rachael's first husband, and his literary tastes and interests. A flash came on the radio that a second atomic bomb attack had been made on Nagasaki. Isador said, "Poor Japanese!" I felt the same way. I feel pity—a feeling I never had toward the Germans. We opened another bottle. Isador became louder and more vehement than I have ever known him. He was unsteady on his feet when he left.

*Tuesday, 14 August 1945*

An evening I shall remember as long as I shall live. I have seen a celebration—! But to get back to the beginning: I ran into Dash looking at prints in the window of Loudermilk's, and while we stood talking we became aware of clamoring automobile horns. Dash thought it must be a wedding procession. Then paper streamers cascaded down from the windows of the Press Club Building. Suddenly it dawned on both of us that the great news had come! The war was over!

People ran in the direction of the White House and Dash and I rushed off in that direction, too. Hundreds, shouting and screaming for President Truman, dashed from Lafayette Square. I was so overjoyed that I suppose I was almost hysterical. My face worked and I had to struggle to keep tears of joy from flowing. I became so hot and wet that I wanted to escape but people kept on pressing in from all directions. President Truman appeared, and walked toward the fence with his wife and a number of men. People yelled hysterically. Truman was wearing a "powder blue" suit. After waving in response to thunderous cheers, he seemed to be talking through a loudspeaker. Neither Dash nor I could hear a word, though we heard people all around saying, "Sshh!" After Truman returned to the White House, the crowd milled around in spite of MP's with drawn bayonets. Finally we managed to get out of the crush. On Pennsylvania Avenue, people by the thousands rushed eagerly downtown. We pressed on, pushing into the wildest, most unrestrained celebration either of us had ever seen, or ever hopes to see.

Hordes of servicemen carried bottles of whiskey and drank from them openly, uninterrupted by police. Pretty girls were seized and kissed, usually by force, by sailors and soldiers. The sailors seemed more aggressive than the soldiers and marines in that respect. Through the roaring throngs we made our way to where the Madrillon orchestra, out on the fire escape, was playing joyous music. People in the street were dancing. More bottle swinging, more staggering, drunken servicemen—bless 'em—and more grabbing and kissing of girls. Some girls protested and then gave in and seemed to enjoy it. A tiny minority fought off their attackers as if seriously opposed to the operation. Endlessly bits of paper and streamers fluttered down, transported in the breeze and settling over crowds that were mad with joy. Traffic was shut off. An SP jeep tooted through the crowd and carried away a red-headed sailor who had passed out. Boys and girls sat along the curbs kissing and drinking and carrying on oblivious of all. On through the throngs. We saw a sailor in passionate embrace with a girl, their bodies pressed together. They started walking off, he with an obvious strong erection.

Dash had to get home. I watched him struggle to board a packed, noisy street car, then I hastened away to the White House, where a crowd had gathered to sing in the bright lights around a lamp post. A Jewish soldier climbed high up on the lamp post and called out the songs to be sung. We sang lustily and sentimentally—"The Star Spangled Banner," "My Country 'Tis of Thee," "Roll Out the Barrel," "Home on the Range," "Halls of Montezuma," "Caissons Go Rolling Along," "God Bless America," and "Dixie." When the Jewish soldier requested "Marching Through Georgia," drawing a big "boo" from me, he corrected himself and led us in "Battle Hymn of the Republic."

I reluctantly pulled myself away from all those alluring people, and started home. Could still hear honking horns of celebrating motorists and shouts and screeches of pedestrians. Thank God, thank God, the war is over. The war, the hideous, horrible, unhuman war, is over at last.

### Monday, 15 October 1945

Catherine Hare stopped in to my office to borrow the Modern Library edition of Baudelaire's *Poems in Prose*. She sat in my chair and leaned across my desktop and said, "I'm so interested in poetry these days that I hate to think of anything else." She lingered, talking with Miss Contadeluci. When she left Miss Contadeluci said, "That is what I call a *beautiful* woman." I agreed that Catherine was handsome, and well-preserved, too, for a woman in her forties.

At night to Crescent. Read my *New Yorker* and found a poem written by

Lansing Tower about "John and May and Bob and May," a reference to youth and dances at a boy's college. I thought back on the old days and saw them through Lansing's eyes. I read the poem over and over and realized again how my nature has brought my energies into a hundred meaningless directions without concentrating them on poetry or something else where I might have achieved at least—say a foothill. I am so sad about myself tonight.

*Monday, 5 November 1945*

As I was preparing to leave work, when Miss Contadeluci and Mrs. Green fortunately had left for the day, Catherine walked in with some old books she had discovered at an antique store in Virginia. She asked me to look them over. I did, and this started a discussion of my "work." I admitted, "I hate my work, but I don't want to be quoted." I called my work "drudgery." She seemed surprised by my attitude, and suggested that we go to dinner by the waterfront and have a good talk. I demurred that I had other plans.

She said, "Why is it that you are so reserved, Jeb, and unwilling to get really acquainted? Are you afraid of people? Afraid you'll get hurt?" I could hardly come out flatfootedly and say, *Yes, I'm afraid of people, afraid I'll be hurt.* The psychology of it is much more complex than that. I don't understand it myself— why I should have refused her offer of having dinner together, even though we might have had a delightful time. She said, "I want to know you better, but I'm baffled as to how to go about it." By that time I was feeling exceedingly distressed and self-conscious. She asked, "Why can't you change your plans? Don't you ever change plans?"

She simply wouldn't drop the matter. She told me, "You know that I have no one with whom I can discuss literature and such things. Don't you care about other people's disappointments?" I told her she seemed to be trying to make me feel like a cad. I felt sorry for her, for God knows I know what it means to lack stimulating companionship of the kind that one longs for. I said that one couldn't be sensitive in this life; one must learn to develop a thick skin. I quoted Thomas Wolfe's remark, "You're born alone, you live alone, you die alone." In desperation I said frankly that she was persistent, and that she appeared to be intent on "beating me down"—that is, overcoming my opposition. Suddenly she flushed and said, "I'm truly sorry. I hadn't realized what a nuisance I was making of myself." She seemed genuinely hurt and got up and started out.

I felt utterly, thoroughly miserable. I walked on out without stopping to finish my *Post* or anything else. Why must people be like that? God knows if I asked someone to go to dinner and was refused, I'd accept that answer without trying for a whole hour to persuade him otherwise. All Catherine achieved by her stubborn persistence was to get herself hurt and to make me feel mean and unkind. I don't know when I've felt so unhappy. Afterward, walking uptown in the cool darkness, I was partly angry with myself and partly angry with Catherine. In the first place, I refuse too often when people want to be friends—I am wary, and also keen for my solitude and freedom—my solitude and freedom to be lonely and unhappy, in fact, is what it amounts to. Why am I like that? Yet Catherine's behavior was inexcusable, too. She should have dropped the matter when she saw that I didn't want to go and had made a sort of excuse.

While I ate my dinner I couldn't get the incident out of mind. Of course, Catherine had brought those books in late, just before I left my office, as an opening. Maybe it's all feminine wiles and I took it too seriously. Still thinking about the incident, I went to Crescent. Don't know when beer has affected me so slightly. It was as if I were drinking water. I swatted a cockroach with a beer pad and upset my glass—it gives the impression of being intoxicated, and I was not.

Finally I started home. As I crossed the street I noticed a soldier standing on the opposite corner. A heavy-set woman in her thirties stood about fifteen feet from him. When she started to go up the street the soldier suddenly started running after her. She began running, too, and when he caught up with her, I heard her forcibly tell him, "Leave me alone!" Abruptly she darted toward me and asked me to see her home. She said, "This soldier thinks I'm a whore. I had a couple of drinks with him and he won't let me go. Oh, I can't get mixed up in this . . . "

I agreed to walk with her. The soldier stood at the curb, apparently undecided, then followed. She was hurrying so fast and was so exceedingly agitated that I could scarcely keep up. I tried to soothe her, telling her to keep calm, that everything was all right. Fortunately the soldier didn't go any further. The poor woman kept rushing along, though, and I had a hard time keeping pace with her. At the corner to her street I asked if she was all right, but she still asked me to go on. At the entrance to her building she thanked me profusely. I turned back, walking slowly down to my own place, full of bitter thoughts. What a life this is, anyway.

*Tuesday, 13 November 1945*

The Contadeluci has been jumped to Professional 3, so that she now gets more than I do for the first time. It was a blow, making me realize anew how others are passing me by. At once I resented working on her damned proof. But after all, I wasn't doing it for her personally but for the office.

At lunch I walked out under the bare sycamores, observing the last wavering, peaked chrysanthemums. Walked to the bridge over the Tidal Basin. There by chance I encountered Catherine Hare, who had been to visit the Jefferson

Memorial. She seemed unnaturally shy and different from her old self. Above us, an airplane circling in the pale sky was blaring and yelling out pleas for buying Victory bonds. It was a Navy propaganda plane that had been used against the Japanese to give them our story. It is a public nuisance. Even the seagulls, soaring free and beautiful above the water, were driven away.

Catherine said, "Would you like to go with me to see Mr. Stone's show of watercolors at the Whyte?" I refused, saying I had already seen Max's exhibition and did not want to go again. She asked, "What did you think of Mr. Stone's new work?" After a pause I told her, "I think he has improved." I didn't know what else to talk about with Catherine. I have been wanting to make up with her ever since that unhappy day when she urged me to go to dinner with her. It occurred to me to offer her as a gift the Modern Library *Poems and Prose of Baudelaire* that I had lent her. She said, "Oh! I'll buy it from you instead." I insisted on giving the book to her. Finally she accepted. I felt much better—relieved, in a way. We said good-bye and she started on to go look at Max's paintings.

Since she is enthusiastic about Baudelaire, it was a happy circumstance that I was able to give her the book. After all, I have another copy. I bought a copy for myself in 1920, but the copy I lent Catherine is a duplicate presented to me by Randall about 1927. For years I intended to give it to someone but never encountered anyone sufficiently interested in Baudelaire.

*Friday, 21 December 1945*
The office party started off with "gifts"—cheap gimcracks—being handed out by Cox. Finally mine came up but it was just a harmless sailboat. Afterward I began to almost enjoy the damned party. I must have drunk six glasses of punch, hoping that someone would have spiked it at the last minute, but no one did. I ate candy and popcorn, too. Went back to my room feeling as if I were a part of things. Maybe I ought to mix in more.

When I got away I walked up to Dash's. Found Max and Pamela fixing highballs in the kitchen. I hadn't seen Pamela in years. She looked older, naturally, now gray and wearing glasses. I was astonished to find Junior Whorley there, drinking a Cuba Libre. He is visiting in Washington for a couple of weeks, and since I last saw him has put on an amazing number of pounds. He announced, "If I keep gaining weight, I'll be an absolute monster." Very true. Isador arrived, accompanied by his wife Rachael. They had already had Fish House Punch at the Manhattan Club and were noisy and ebullient. Isador gets more cherubic every year.

I learned with regret that Muriel Phillipson had died. I was amazed to hear that she was seventy-two. I had no idea she was so old. Dash served delicious bits of food of one sort or another. Junie fell asleep on the couch—"passed out," in other words. When I left, he was still snoring there.

*Saturday, 22 December 1945*

Got away before seven for Allies Inn. Dash came in and joined me and invited me up. We had a pleasant evening of conversation. Dash showed me his recent acquisitions of small prints, botanical and otherwise, and said that Junie Whorley was beaten up by two marines and had to be sent to Emergency Hospital. As Dash heard it, his hotel room was "a shambles."

*Tuesday, 25 December 1945*

Christmas Day. The wind has been blowing so strongly that my roll of paper towels was blown out of the bathroom window and partly unrolled on the sidewalk. I opened the packages I received from Dad and Mama in Florida. Dad sent a gaudy-colored tie in the current fashion. Mama sent a nice wallet made in England. I decided not to go out, largely because so many restaurants were closed. My Christmas dinner consisted of a can of boneless chicken with crackers, olives, and V-8. About midnight I stood on the back porch gazing with quiet joy on the magnificent sky—a pageant of torn, fantastic clouds sailing rapidly across the half moon.

*Monday, 31 December 1945*

New Year's Eve. Away from office about six. It was raining and I was wearing the handsome butterfly tie that Dad sent me from Florida, and I also didn't relish the rain in my hair, such as it still is. Therefore I went down to the subway and rode uptown. I detest that underground station and its pushing crowds. It wasn't a solitary New Year's Eve, fortunately. First, to my pleasant surprise, I ran into Dash at Allies Inn. We ate dinner together and I walked with him up to his place. Max was there and they served me two glasses of delicious sherry. As usual, they were going to Pamela's New Year's party, and I left with them when they departed for the party. Then walked in the rain down to Crescent and got a seat at the bar. Houndstooth blustered in, bundled against the rain. We talked and had a good time. So many boys in the bar tonight, back from the war. Without saying anything to Houndstooth I drank a silent toast to the memory of dear Hans, who has simply disappeared, and to sweet Nicky, who will never come back because he is a skeleton at the bottom of the Pacific. It hurts me to think about them. When the clock behind the bar struck midnight I banged a salt shak-

er against my glass to make a noise, and together old Houndstooth and I sang
"Auld Lang Syne."

> Should auld acquaintance be forgot,
> And never brought to mind?
> Should auld acquaintance be forgot,
> And days of auld lang syne?

. . . *I woke from a vivid and disturbing dream: Dash and I, travelling by train in the far north, came to a scenic lake, with beautiful snows around it. Here everyone was supposed to transfer to rowboats for greater enjoyment of the scenery. When I got to the boat, Dash and other people were sitting in water almost to their knees. I was worried about ruining my camera in the water and getting my clothes wet, but I prepared to descend into the boat. Then I thought to myself, "Why should I get in just because everyone else has done so, like a lot of sheep?"*

*And I decided not to get in. Another train, going in the opposite direction, went sweeping along the far banks of the other end of the lake and its whistles gave a long, lonely wail that echoed across the waters of the lake. Then I woke, never knowing what became of Dash and the rest . . .*

*—Saturday, 5 December 1959*